# SAVAGE GRACE

# SAVAGE GRACE

Natalie Robins & Steven M. L. Aronson

William Morrow and Company, Inc.
*New York*

Library of Congress Cataloging in Publication Data

Robins, Natalie S.
Savage grace.

1. Baekeland, Antony. 2. Crimes and criminals—
United States—Biography. 3. Murder—United States—
Case studies. I. Aronson, Steven M. L. II. Title.
HV6248.B18R6 1985 364.1'523'0924 [B] 85-7117
ISBN 0-688-04373-9

Printed in the United States of America

First Edition

1 2 3 4 5 6 7 8 9 10

BOOK DESIGN BY RICHARD ORIOLO

For Christopher, Rachel, Noah—
"My strength and song."

N.R.


For Katharine Johnson & Jesse Kornbluth,
Deborah Young & Charles Maclean—
in fond friendship.

S.M.L.A

# CONTENTS

PART IV: RIKERS ISLAND

They were *the* perfect happy-American family: the one one hears about, and sees so often in the ad photos in the *New Yorker* and in all the commercial magazines, but which one so rarely meets in life. Certainly there was absolutely nothing to indicate there might be deeper darker strains to their lives they might be hiding.

James Jones, *The Merry Month of May*, 1971


I sometimes think that there is a malign force loose in the universe that is the social equivalent of cancer, and it's plastic. It infiltrates everything. It's metastasis. It gets into every single pore. . . .

Norman Mailer, *Harvard Magazine*, 1983

# SAVAGE
# GRACE

# PART I
# LONDON

# 1

# THE
# CRIME OF CRIMES

Friday, November 17, 1972, dawned hazy and cloudy, but by four o'clock the sun was shining with unaccustomed benevolence for London. The leaves in Cadogan Square had turned and were dropping in the gardens. All her life—and she was only fifty when she died, a little later that afternoon—Barbara Baekeland was partial to fall colors. Even in summer, when everyone would be wearing white, she persisted in dressing like an autumn leaf. The rust-colored skirts and bronze shoes she favored suited her beauty—the bonfire of red hair, the milkmaid skin. A friend had once said of her that she had the quality of intelligent flamboyance.

Whether in Boston, where she was born to a family of modest means called Daly; or Hollywood, where once upon a time she was given a screen test; or New York and Paris, where she created salons for herself; or such resorts as Long Island's East Hampton, Ansedonia on Italy's Argentario, and Cadaqués on Spain's Costa Brava, where she was forever taking houses in season and out; or, finally, in London, where she had acquired a penthouse duplex in Chelsea, Barbara Baekeland could be counted on to turn heads.

"London ends by giving one absolutely everything one asks," Henry James wrote in his preface to *The Golden Bowl;* the city was, in his opinion, "the most possible form of life."

"London with its six-times-breathed-over air seems such a dream," Barbara Baekeland wrote to a friend in New York that November Friday. "Had *Le Tout* London here last night. My *oeuvre* has had a great success—everybody loved what I've done to the flat."

The very first thing one saw on entering the apartment was the portrait of a beautiful boy. The subject was Barbara Baekeland's son, Antony, who had sat for the drawing one summer in Ansedonia, years before. Tony was twenty-six now, and something of a painter himself.

He also liked to write. In Paris, the novelist James Jones had taken an interest in his work, and now he was being encouraged by the poet Robert Graves. Graves was a neighbor on the island of Mallorca, from which Tony had come back to London with his mother in September.

The Baekelands had always had the freedom to travel at will. Tony's great-grandfather, Leo Hendrik Baekeland, had invented the first totally successful plastic, Bakelite—"the material of a thousand uses." Tony's father, Brooks Baekeland, liked to say, "Thanks to my grandfather, I have what James Clavell has called 'fuck-you money.' Therefore I need not please or seek to please—astonish, astound, dazzle, or be approved of by—anyone."

Brooks Baekeland had movie-star good looks. He also possessed what many of his peers considered to be one of the finest minds of his generation. A brilliant amateur land analyst, in the early 1960s he had conceived, planned, and executed a parachute jump into the Vilcabamba mountain fastness of Peru in search of a lost Inca city. He never found the city but his exploits filled most of an issue of *National Geographic*. Somebody had once described him as an intellectual Errol Flynn.

Tony's father was now living in France—with, everyone said, Tony's girlfriend.

At one o'clock on Friday, November 17—"Fridays are always suspect, don't you think?" she had once said—Barbara Baekeland called out goodbye to Tony, leaned down to stroke her Siamese cat, Worcester, affectionately called Mr. Wuss, and set out to keep a lunch date she had made at her party the night before with an old friend from Spain; Missy Harnden was also now living in London, in a rented house on nearby Chapel Street.

Barbara Baekeland arrived in a particularly extravagant mood and launched at once into a postmortem of her party. Missy Harnden's seventeen-year-old son Michael, whom everyone had always called Mishka, cooked the lunch—filet mignon wrapped in bacon, green beans, and a tossed salad—which he served with a Spanish red wine. They ate in the big kitchen-dining room, whose walls were covered with the organic black, blue, and green abstract paintings of Arshile Gorky, to whom the house's owner had once been married.

"Barbara's theme that day was Tony," Mishka Harnden recalls. "Her theme was persistently Tony—how marvelous he was, how talented. Everything was always absolutely rosy and happy—'Tony *adores* London, Tony's *mad* about the flat.'"

At three-thirty, Barbara Baekeland got up to leave, thanking the Harndens for the "marvelous lunch" and mentioning that Tony was cooking dinner for her that evening.

At approximately seven o'clock the telephone rang in the house on Chapel Street. Missy Harnden answered. It was the Chelsea Police Station inquiring as to the time of Barbara Baekeland's arrival and departure that afternoon. They would not say why they wanted this information; all they would say was that something had happened. But a few seconds later Missy Harnden heard herself being asked: "How well did you know the deceased?" She was too shocked to answer, and handed the phone to Mishka, who had just come into the room.

At the end of the conversation the police requested that they both come down to the station to answer a few additional questions. Missy Harnden could not bring herself to go, so Mishka went alone. "It was very clean, very sterile," he remembers. "A quite natty English police station."

Once there, he would find out what had happened.

## DETECTIVE SUPERINTENDENT KENNETH BRETT, RETIRED*

I was called to the address of Antony Baekeland and his mother, but cannot remember how the call was made—by the ambulance service or other agency. On arrival I was told that a maid, believed to be Spanish, had run from the house because of a quarrel between Antony Baekeland and his mother. The flat was not disordered. I saw in the kitchen the body of Mrs. Baekeland. She was dressed in normal

* Brief biographical notes can be found on pages 479–489.

clothing—I seem to remember it was a dress. She was on her back. Very little blood was seen. There was a knife on an adjoining worktop or draining board. This was a kitchen knife and showed signs of blood.

There was a small wound visible in the victim's clothing in the region of the heart. I recollect that death was caused by a severed main artery. A doctor certified she was dead, and arrangements were made for the body to be removed to a mortuary after examination by a forensic officer. The only other sign of violence—which was discovered at the postmortem—was a bruise above the right ear, but this did not have any real significance as it could have been caused by the victim's fall to the ground.

Antony Baekeland was, on my arrival, in a bedroom, sitting on the bed, using the telephone to phone, I believe, a Chinese restaurant to order a meal. I cannot remember the exact conversation I had with him, but Antony Baekeland was intimating that he was not responsible for the crime. I have a vague recollection that he may have mentioned that his grandmother was responsible. He was completely unconcerned.

You know, he considered himself an artist, and we did find a rather large painting, said to have been done by him. It was the weirdest thing imaginable—we just couldn't make out what it was.

I seem to remember that his father was not called immediately as we had to discover his whereabouts. Mr. Baekeland came either the next day or even later—from France.

Antony Baekeland was taken to the Chelsea Police Station. He was interviewed, and much of what he said was incoherent, rambling. I cannot remember what his statement contained, except the opening sentence was so unusual that it has stuck in my mind. He said it all started when he was aged either three or five and he fell off his pogo stick.

## PAMELA TURNER

I was the service tenant at 81 Cadogan Square, but I was not on the premises when he stabbed her. When I got home I saw the ambulance outside and I wondered what was going on. Then the ambulance men came down from the top floor and asked me if I knew Tony and I said I did. I used to pass the time of day with him or have a chat, although his mother was always very protective of him. And they said would I talk to him on the telephone while they got the police. And I rang him from my phone and had a long conversation with him and he told me how he had been out for lunch with his grandmother. Well, I knew *she* was in New York. He was quite calm, quite lucid, and chatted to me—he was always polite and nice, I never thought of him as a violent person—and in the meantime the ambulance men on their phone in the ambulance got the police. Tony had called for the ambulance himself. And then the police came and that was that.

Tony told me his grandmother had stabbed Barbara. I loved Barbara's mother, Mrs. Daly. I remember her as a dear little old lady quite happily going up all those six flights of stairs! She used to come here and take over, like the head of the family.

Whenever Barbara rang me from the States, she'd say, "Hello, this is Barbara of MGM." She told me that she worked in public relations for MGM, but I don't know whether she really did or not. She would ring occasionally, mainly to tell me she was coming to England and would I get milk, etc., in for her. I also looked after all her plants, merely because I am extremely fond of house plants, and in fact I still have a weeping fig of hers.

She was a very beautiful, flamboyant woman. I particularly remember a black gown she wore, a very low-necked black gown. She wore it with a huge diamond crucifix dangling from a chain. She was magnificent, and she went out a lot. I suppose the most terrible memory I have is of the plain wooden box being brought down the stairs by the policemen, and opening the main doors for them to pass through. I understand that the next day was her wedding anniversary.

The night of the stabbing, I got concerned about the cat—you know, Mr. Wuss. There was a policeman guarding the flat and I asked him if he had seen a cat. He told me, "There's no cat." But I knew Mr. Wuss had to be somewhere, so I went in and looked under the bed, and there he was! After the stabbing, Mr. Baekeland came to see about the belongings. I found him very businesslike and hard. He put all the contents of the flat into auction with Sotheby's. And I asked him, I said, "Well, what should we do about the cat?" And he said, "Oh, destroy it." Well, I gulped, and I asked if *I* could take the cat if I could find a home for it. And Mr. Wuss is still alive. When last I heard, he was leading a good life. Of course, Barbara was very wrong to bring him into the country as she did, ignoring quarantine rules.

ELIZABETH WEICKER FONDARAS
Poor Barbara. The last time I saw her was at an art opening in New
York and she had a look of old furs and feathers—like a Jean Rhys
character.


## Letter from Barbara Baekeland to Sam Green, May 4, 1970

Read Jean Rhys's *Good Morning, Midnight*, which profoundly
depressed me. She is so much of my skin that I am alarmed—
like suddenly seeing oneself in a harsh unlovely light—all those
many flaws and her despair honed by that extraordinary sen-
sibility—I hope I am saved—


DR. W. LINDSAY JACOBS
I saw Antony Baekeland for the first time on October 30, 1972—
eighteen days before the crime—and afterwards I told his mother,
"Your son is going to kill you." She replied, "He's been murdering
me since he was born—whether for him or his father, I don't know.
I'm used to murder." "This isn't a metaphor," I told her. "This isn't
an analyst's game. I think you're at grave risk." And she said, "*I
don't.*"


DAVID MEAD
When I heard Tony had killed his mother, I felt like I'd been *at* the
murder. The year before, out in East Hampton, Barbara all of a
sudden raised her voice at me—you know, just over nothing—and
Tony came flying in. He was absolutely furious, I couldn't believe
how mad he was. And then instantly it was between the two of *them*,
and I no longer mattered. And they started getting madder and madder at each other, and it got uglier and uglier, and finally the knife
point came. He got a knife. I managed to wrestle it out of his hand,
but you know what I'm saying—this was the dress rehearsal.


## From a Psychiatric Report on Antony Baekeland Ordered by the British Courts, January 5, 1973

He is a well-built, physically healthy young man with an occasional marked stammer. He appeared normally anxious and

depressed for a man in his situation but denied feeling depressed or ever having contemplated suicide. He gave his account with some natural confusion about times and places. On the day of the offence he had a conversation on the telephone in which he heard some reference to his having fallen down a lift shaft; and later began to wonder if this had occurred. After a minor argument with his mother she started to write a letter. He could not read it but knew the meaning and this produced a degree of rage which he had never experienced before. She did not say or do anything to resist his assaults.

## ROSEMARY RODD BALDWIN

Barbara wrote to me in Turkey just before he killed her and said, "Rosie, you have such a wonderful influence over Tony, a sort of Nini influence." Nini, of course, is Barbara's mother, Tony's grandmother. She said, "Will you come to London and live in the flat with him for the winter?" I got the letter on the Wednesday and I was making up my mind. On Thursday one of my daughters, Mandy, who'd had dinner with them the night before, sent me a telegram saying, "Mummy, be careful. Things are very difficult in Cadogan Square." And on Friday he killed her. So.

And I'll tell you the other thing. He had a little Pekingese he adored that got lost in the mountains somewhere in Italy when he was a child. He was a child for a long time with us, you see. And this dog got lost and they were desperate, and finally they found it. And after it died, years later, he kept its collar, like Jinty, my eldest daughter, did with *her* favorite dog. And Barbara took this collar and threw it out of the window into Cadogan Square, and that was what *I* understood was the thing that was the end.

## Letter from Antony Baekeland to Cornelia Baekeland Hallowell, December 30, 1972

Dear Grandmother,
I just got your letter. I will try to explain as best I can what happened. You know I loved and still love and adore my mother more than anyone in the world. During the time preceding what happened a lot of rather strange things were happening. I think my mind was slightly wacky and I was very much under my

mother's powerful influence. I felt as though she were controlling my mind. Anyway that afternoon my mother was out and I
had a strange telephone call from a friend of ours who lives in
Wales. She told me that I had fallen down an elevator shaft. I
thought this rather strange and yet it had a profound effect on
me. She asked me if she could come around for a drink that
evening. I told her yes, that we would be glad to see her.
Mummy came back a little later and told me that she was annoyed that I had asked her to come so early. I can't remember
exactly what started the fight but it began in her bedroom. Then
she went into the dining room where the maid was ironing and
began to write something on a piece of paper. I can't remember
what it was she wrote but it infuriated me and I tore it out of her
hand and tore it up. Then she ran into the bedroom where I hit
her, then she ran into the kitchen. I ran after her and stabbed
her with the kitchen knife that was lying on the table. As I ran to
call the ambulance I saw the maid just leaving the flat. The
ambulance took hours to come and by the time it came my
mother was dead. It was horrible—I held her hand and she
would not look or speak to me. Then she died. The ambulance
men arrived and I was taken away in a dreadful state. For several
days I didn't know where I was. Past memories kept flooding
into my mind and I felt that I was reenacting parts of my former
life.

Nevertheless I feel better now and even feel that a great
weight has been removed from my shoulders. An odd thing is
that she told me that I would kill her this summer several times.
I thought this the most unlikely thing in the world.

I wish I could remember what it was she wrote on that piece
of paper.

Love,
Tony

HELEN ROLO

I remember the knives, I do remember the knives. I rented that apartment from Barbara Baekeland for a couple of weeks in 1972. It was
within a few months of when she was killed. I didn't even know her
particularly well. I thought she was attractive and charming and that
she lived a very happy kind of life—I mean, to have an apartment in

New York and a house in Spain and also an apartment in London. A happy-from-the-outside-looking-in life, that is—because I remember when I called to discuss the details of renting the place she suddenly had to hang up. She said, "I'll call you back—I'm having a problem with my son."

It was a rather grisly apartment. You had to walk and walk and walk to get up there, you just went up vertically at a ninety-degree angle, up and up and up, at *least* four flights. I knew it wasn't an elevator apartment but I certainly hadn't expected to walk up *that* far. And when you finally *got* to the landing and opened the door, having walked all that way—opened the door to the apartment *gasping*—you really had to have a strong heart!—and a strong hand to carry your luggage—you walked in and collapsed when you saw that there was another bunch of steps to go up—it was a *duplex*!

And it was spooky because in the foyer, straight on in front of you, was a portrait of her son with a light on it. I don't know how old he was in the picture. He was fairly young, I'd say a teenager. I'd never met him, I'd never even seen him. But there was his portrait to greet me at the top of the steps inside the apartment.

Directly to the left of the foyer was a doorway to the kitchen. I remember there were pretty cut-crystal glasses—sort of little scotch-and-water glasses. And later of course, I remembered those knives. I had *used* those knives—long ones, short ones.

To the right of the foyer was a bedroom. It was the only bedroom that I can think of. It was the only room that seemed a little bit cozy. There was another room off the foyer and that was a room that I never even walked into except twice, I think. Once I walked in and said, Oh, I never want to go in there again, and then I think I went in there again to see whether I didn't want to go there again. I kept the door shut. That was the spookiest room of all. I assumed it was the dining room because there was a dining table. I don't know why but there was a lot of small tight grillwork around— it reminded me of what you might see in Morocco, but without the sun. It was ice-cold in there. There was a small cot, somewhere on the side. Maybe that's where the son slept. It was a *hard* room, that's the only way I can describe it.

Oh, and the color of it—oh, a horrible horrible . . . I'm looking at a bottle of Montclair mineral water with a dark blue top, a *mean* blue, and the whole room was a mean sinister blue, very gloomy and dark.

The living room was the whole top floor of the house. You put the light on and the first thing you saw was a decapitated bull's head with horns. There were a couple of Louis Quinze chairs of sorts, and a couple of floppy leather beanbags. The carpeting was brown, the room gave the impression of a lot of brown. And then there was a bench, a park bench, one of those old metal or steel benches from the seventeenth century—with a cold seat if you sat down on it. I'm beginning to visualize things that I'm sure weren't there, like a street lamp. I don't know, that just came into my mind. Because of the park bench, I guess. It might have *been* there, too.

It was a room without much natural light. The windows were slightly below waist-level, I guess because it was the top of the building. And not such a nice view of the gardens, either.

In a funny way it was a rather glamorous room. I gave a small cocktail party there, as I recall. I hardly ever used it—it wasn't a room you wanted to sit in.

But most of all I remember the knives. I wouldn't have remembered them particularly, except after I heard they'd been used for purposes other than those they were usually used for, I did remember. There was nothing unusual about any of the knives. I remember a bread knife—a long bread knife, with a wooden handle. There weren't that many knives. It was a very minimally outfitted kitchen, so certain things you remember, I guess.

They were knives I was *handling*, for Christ's sake! I used to cut lemon peel for martinis with them. The idea that I had used the knife or even touched the knife that had killed somebody made me sick. I've never even killed a little insect. I can't even do that very well. It was a terrifying awful feeling to think that I'd touched a *weapon*.

## Miwa Svinka-Zielinski
A son killing a mother is Greek tragedy but this is much worse—much much worse. I think that *she* killed *him*.

## Samuel Parkman Shaw
That's a real question—who killed who. It was a real dance, a minuet.

# 2

---

# IN CUSTODY

Around five p.m. on Friday, November 17, Tony Baekeland was escorted unhandcuffed from 81 Cadogan Square by two police officers; it is not the custom in London to use handcuffs unless a person is violent when arrested.

He sat silent and self-absorbed as the unmarked car made its way through the narrow streets of Chelsea, one of London's most fashionable and historic districts. Richard III and Sir Thomas More once lived there, as did the writers Thomas Carlyle, George Eliot, and Oscar Wilde and the painters Turner, Sargent, and Whistler. Bounded on one side by the Thames, Chelsea is bordered on another by the smart shops of Sloane Street with which Barbara Baekeland had felt strong kinship, and by the boutiques, restaurants, and discotheques of the bohemian King's Road that had so fascinated her son.

Tony Baekeland walked through a side entrance into the modern-style Chelsea Police Station. He was told that he was being detained pending his first appearance in lower court on Monday morning, November 20. He was then taken to his cell. It contained, in addition to a toilet, a bench bed with a regulation foam mattress and a couple of blankets. "In view of the charge," a Scotland Yard official recollects, "he was watched closely to make sure he'd not harm himself."

The next day the London papers headlined the matricide. "The life of the wealthy American woman who had a villa in Spain and apartments in Paris and New York ended as she died screaming from the blows of a knife attacker in her penthouse near Buckingham Palace," the *Evening News* reported. "The 50-year-old—she looked much younger, said neighbours—was in the American film business," the story erroneously went on, "and her work as a film executive took her all over the world on locations of films about romance, adventure and murder." It was true that Barbara Baekeland had her flickering moment in Hollywood, making a screen test with Dana Andrews, but that had been a long time before; and she had indeed been at the center of a world of romance and adventure all her life, only never in the capacity of a film executive.

In New York, the *Daily News* bannered: "MOM IS SLAIN: NAB YANK SON." The *New York Times* headlined: "BRITISH CHARGE AMERICAN, 26, WITH SLAYING OF MOTHER."

In Barbara Baekeland's hometown, the *Boston Sunday Herald* quoted her Cadogan Square neighbors: "'They appeared to be wealthy globetrotters. They were both witty and charming. She was very attractive and looked about 30. She had a wardrobe full of expensive furs. . . . Ambulance men said the flat was in a mess and it was difficult to recognize her.'"

By now, reports of the murder were being circulated in all the many places the Baekelands had lived, and friends were rallying to console Barbara Baekeland's seventy-eight-year-old widowed mother, Nina Fraser Daly, in New York.

## NINA DALY

Oh, Barbara was beautiful, I thought. She was noted as a beauty, you know. She had lovely hair. *I* used to have naturally curly hair when I was little, but no more. I'll be ninety in two days, the 27th of May. That's old, you know. Barbara's hair was an orangy red, and mine was just red but it wasn't that sharp red you see on redheads that stares you right in the face. And Tony was another little redhead.

Barbara was a natural beauty. She was so natural herself. And she loved people. Oh yes. She was so sweet and kind and loving. She was a wonderful daughter. I miss her so. I used to see her every day. She was a great companion. We were very close, very close.

She worshiped him. And he loved *her*. He loved her more than he loved anybody. His mummy. He loved me next, and then he loved his father next, after me. He loved his father but they weren't as close as Barbara and Tony or Tony and I. His father wasn't one of those fathers that goes gaga all the time, but he was good to him and gave him what he wanted and everything that he needed—a bicycle and things like that.

I worshiped Tony. He was a dear. He was always trying to do something for you. I lived nearby. I used to walk down the street with him. The happiness he gave me! We'd have lovely walks together, through the park. He loved nature. He could take the name of every bird that ever flew. He used to draw birds all the time.

She took him everywhere. Everywhere she went she took him. She never tried to get rid of him. I was always ready to take him. We both loved him the same. She was a good mother. She just had the one child. I wish she had had more children.

She was a good wife, too. I love her husband. Brooks. He was awfully kind to me. Just like a brother. He's six-four, and so good-looking. The grandfather invented the plastics, you know.

Barbara did all these paintings. Everything in the apartment here she did. She painted so well, and she painted quite a lot, too.

That's Cape Cod up there. We went there as children in my family. Always went to Cape Cod. There was a big thunderstorm coming up, and I walked over to where she was, and she said, "I'm painting that now, Mother." And I said, "Oh, yes, I see, dear." So I always loved that picture. There was a great big cloud just like that in the sky that day, you'd think it was coming down and sitting on top of your head.

She was left-handed, you know. She couldn't do anything with her right hand. She just started being left-handed and I didn't change her. I'd rather she be right-handed. I think it's so natural. I can't do anything with my left hand. It seems so awkward to see a lefty. I'd see Barbara turning the paper and writing with that left hand. I was afraid Tony was going to be, but he wasn't. We didn't try to change him, but he turned out to be a righty. Oh, Barbara worshiped him.

MICHAEL ALEXANDER
He told me that there was a bit of a struggle or something and that he got the knife into her—one single thing. He happened to do it in the wrong place, that's all—the heart. And then, he told me, he had sort of a problem about what the hell was he going to do about it, and *this* shocked me—he said he thought about putting it out of his mind!

Of course, his granny was always encouraging him to think it wasn't his fault. She didn't believe he could possibly have done such a thing. Because he was such a gentle boy, you know. Her blue-eyed boy.

## ELIZABETH ARCHER BAEKELAND

Nini was just devastated. I used to go and see her after Barbara's death—until she became too difficult. She kept going on about Sylvie, how all this never would have happened if Brooks hadn't run off with "that bitch, that bitch, that damn bitch." On and on—about how first "that bitch" took Tony away and then she took Brooks.

## BROOKS BAEKELAND

After years of resisting, and after wearing out four lawyers, starting with Louis Nizer, Barbara had finally agreed to give me my freedom. When Sylvie and I received the telephone call in the house I had built in Brittany telling us that Barbara was dead, we thought she had committed suicide, for it was November 18, 1972, our thirtieth wedding anniversary. "I give you your freedom and my life"—that would have been typically Barbara.

## SYLVIE BAEKELAND SKIRA

When this happened, Brooks's cousin, Baekeland Roll, and his wife were staying with us. I always took the telephones because Brooks was too grand-ducal to ever answer the telephone, so I answered and it was the police in London who said, "We believe that Mrs. Baekeland has been killed." I came back to Brooks with this news and we, neither of us, believed it really. Brooks said, "She's again found a way to get at me." And then they called again, and it was true. This time they said, "We believe her son is involved." And I put down the telephone. I was frightened. I was so frightened I remember very well I fell into a sweat—you know, I smelled like a bad animal—it was something so abominable, and I rushed upstairs to the cousins.

It was a horrible thing for me, but for Brooks . . . he suffered the way you could not imagine. Brooks went out *hollering* in the garden. He was desperate. He was horrified that Barbara had died. That the boy had done it was something else.

We left Brittany and we went together to London. Brooks didn't have the heart to go and identify her, so it was Baekie Roll who did. Brooks never saw her body, but what his cousin saw was that Barbara had a black eye, and he told Brooks, and I think that hurt Brooks more than anything—that she would have had a black eye on top of everything. We stayed in a hotel that wouldn't be too conspicuous, because of the press and so on—Blake's Hotel, where it turned out anyway there were a lot of rock-and-roll stars staying at the same time. And Brooks kept seeing lawyers and police and so on because of the inquest. And afterwards, he had her cremated. She had been three weeks in the morgue.

Meanwhile Brooks had been given everything that was in her apartment by the police. Every piece of her mail he made *me* read, because he said it would hurt him too much to read it. And then there were the cassettes! Barbara had made a whole series of cassettes of a novel she was writing. The police said they were very damaging documents for the Baekeland family and he should take them. Can you imagine writing about going to bed with your son!

In Brittany we didn't have a cassette machine in the house, we had a record player, but we had a cassette machine in the car. Brooks played them in the car. For hours and hours! Yes. Until I broke down in front of him and he got earphones so he could listen to them without me having to listen.

### Gloria Jones

Jim and I were horrified. It was the worst thing we ever heard. We were in Paris and we went to London and tried to help. I called Scotland Yard and I said, "I think I'd like to talk to you." So these two marvelous policemen came, and we were staying at a wonderful hotel, not Claridge's, the other good one, the really good one—the Connaught. And there was a bar there—you know, all stocked—and they said, "We don't drink as a rule but, you know, all right," so we gave them a couple of drinks and they were thrilled with us and we all sat around and I said, "I think you ought to know that she probably aggravated Tony. Can I give some money for cigarettes for him? I want to help him, you know. Can you get him a lawyer?" They wouldn't let me see him. It was only the day after or two days after. They said they were doing everything.

I asked if I could bury her, you know, because I felt that Brooks wouldn't do anything about that. They said I couldn't. Brooks did have her cremated later. I think her mother has the ashes.

### Barbara Curteis

Jim Jones wrote a novel about the Baekelands, you know—*The Merry Month of May*. But he wrote it in 1970, before the denouement.

### FRANCINE DU PLESSIX GRAY
Ethel de Croisset telephoned us that Tony had killed Barbara, and I felt shock and horror. And then a few days later I bumped into Peter Matthiessen at the Styrons' and he said to me—we said to each other—almost simultaneously we said—"Are you ever going to use it? Are you ever going to use it?" Use it in a book, you know. And we both said no. Peter said, "*I* can't do it, I don't think *you* can do it. I'd keep away from it." You know, there's only one title for the Baekeland story and it's already been used—*An American Tragedy*.

Cleve and I met them at a party in New York in the middle fifties and we made this passionate kind of instant friendship with this very flamboyant girl with red hair and a huge smile and all those very prominent big teeth. I always remember the mouth—my mother would say, "She's very pretty but she has too much gum." And here was this handsome millionaire that she was married to, Brooks Baekeland. And the first impression we got was that they were the ideal couple.

In the summer of 1960 we shared a house with them in Italy. Tony was just about to turn fourteen, and he was ideally beautiful— you know, glistening and angelic and with beautiful manners and a sweet smile. When we were a newly married couple in New York trying to have children, Cleve and I used to say to each other, "Wouldn't it be wonderful if our child looked like that!"

### ROSE STYRON
We had a house in Ansedonia during the summer of 1960 and the Baekelands were neighbors. We had mutual friends, Gloria and Jim Jones, who had told us they were there, but they looked *us* up, I think. Well, they were very good-looking, very sociable, fairly snobbish—I would say Barbara particularly liked the grand Italian life.

I liked Tony. I really liked him a lot. He was a very lonely but self-sufficient boy, and I liked his gentleness with animals. I remember going up to his room a couple of times and he had all sorts of snakes and animals. I liked the fact that he seemed to want to hide from whatever else was going on in the family and keep to himself. The two or three times we were over there I just found myself gravitating to him. I guess I probably knew him better than I knew Brooks or Barbara, who I didn't have much connection with.

I remember Gloria talking to me a lot about Barbara. She was always telling me what the latest chapter was in the Baekeland saga. And one detail after another was so fantastic.

## GLORIA JONES

After Barbara died, Muriel Murphy, this really great friend of all of ours, sent me one of Barbara's Chanel dresses. Barbara really knew how to dress, you know—she always had the real Chanel. I guess Muriel had gotten the dress from Mrs. Daly. I was in Haiti, staying at the Oloffson Hotel, and Muriel asked Bill Styron, who was on his way there, to deliver this package to me. I opened it and put the dress on and it was bloodstreaked all down the back. It was the kind of dress you *would* wear to be stabbed in. Later I asked Muriel, "Why did you send this dress to me?" And she said she hadn't noticed the bloodstains. I was so freaked that I buried the dress, I actually dug a hole in the ground out in the back of the hotel. That dress is buried in voodoo country, in Haiti behind the Oloffson Hotel.

## WILLIAM STYRON

I didn't know exactly what was in the damn package. I knew it was some kind of garment, but I didn't have any idea that it had any bloodstains, nor was I present when Gloria opened it. But I'm sure Gloria is accurate.

I remember in Ansedonia that summer there was a lot of partying, a lot of going out on boats, and Brooks had one of those Mercedes sports cars, and there were a lot of drives in the Mercedes sports car with Tony around. And Tony was an absolute young Adonis—if you can be an Adonis at that age. I mean, he was a beautiful kid, he was just charming, and I had no inkling certainly at that time of anything potentially weird. I do think possibly I sensed a "Mother's darling boy" relationship—not a terribly uncommon relationship with an only child. But I thought he was terrific. Bright. A little withdrawn, maybe. But he was just a figment to me, because I never really got to know him outside of this vision of this beautiful lad—great swimmer and that sort of thing. And a serious young man.

I had the sense of a small little family, a couple and their lonely boy, who were sort of misplaced out of some Scott Fitzgerald novel. Barbara and Brooks seemed a bit like Daisy and Tom Buchanan but in a different era and somewhat fish out of water for that reason.

I remember exactly where I was when I learned about the murder. I'm in the room right now, up here in Roxbury, Connecticut, where I was that Sunday, whatever date it was. And I was just leafing through the Sunday *Times*, as we all do, and there was a column of print that said something like "Young man stabs mother in London" and of course the names were right there, and it just shocked the hell

out of me. Had I known more about them, their connection, I probably would have been less astounded. But I knew nothing of any
stirrings or rumblings psychologically.

God, it's a fascinating story, and the horror of that kid is classic
Greek. I do think that the terrible quality of the whole story has got
some resonance about our period in some curious way. It has some
very large metaphorical meaning.

## Brendan Gill

I was trying to remember when it was I first met Barbara and her
husband and it was a night when Rose and Bill Styron were there and
I think it was at Tom and Sarah Hunter Kelly's house in New York,
on Seventy-first Street. I remember talking with Brooks about the fact
that he had jumped into the Peruvian jungle. He was a true adven-
turer, the opposite of an adventuress. I was fascinated by his account,
also because of my interest in his grandfather and Bakelite—that's
just my kind of thing: inventions, making good in America. Brooks
seemed tall and heroic because—well, it would be like Lindbergh.
My definition of a hero is a man who tests himself by a series of
ordeals, each more difficult than the last; he's not competing in the
world at all, he's competing only against himself. And that's what it
seemed to me Brooks was doing—testing himself.

Barbara was a very good-looking girl. I also liked her spirit. She
was of an affirmative disposition. She always made you feel good, so
that made her a wonderful hostess, of course. I think one of the
reasons a great partygiver like Ben Sonnenberg liked her so much is
that he liked women who were sunny, who were never down, who
didn't need to be brought *up* to something, and he probably also
admired her because he always admired women who were adventuresses—I mean, women who had succeeded—and she evidently
had been one of those.

## Pico Harnden

I was living around Europe at the time and I used to call my mother
and my younger brother, Mishka, in London every two or three days
to see how they were doing, and one day my mother said, "It's finally
happened." And I said, "What happened?" And she said, "Barbara
has been killed by Tony." And I—I started laughing. Because everybody knew it was only a matter of time before it happened and finally
it did happen and, well, you know, it was so absurd it was almost
funny. But my mother was a very religious person and she got very

angry because I was laughing, but *she* was laughing, too, because even my mother, who was the least cynical person you could find, knew how the story was going to end. There was no other ending to the story.

### ETHEL WOODWARD DE CROISSET

You know, there was a charming woman, Missy Harnden, a Russian—her husband was an architect who had built me a house in Spain—and after Barbara died she came to see me. She had been to this cocktail party on Cadogan Square the night before Barbara was assassinated. There was this crowd of people there and the boy was evidently looking in some strange bright-eyed way into space, and Missy thought, "I must warn Barbara." She had this feeling, you see. And then she had not done it, and now she felt terribly badly. She was a very—could one say puritanical?—Russian. You know how Russians are when they're really good people—they're so straight. She was somebody that was so straight and so good, you know, and she felt she'd failed Barbara.

### ELIZABETH WEICKER FONDARAS

I called Saul Steinberg when I heard—just to talk about Barbara to someone. It's so much easier in a small town when something like this happens. People gather in the street and you can rush out and talk about these things. In New York you can't do that. Saul spoke of Barbara's *whiteness*, her white skin, her Irish skin, white lovely skin, red hair—her fresh marvelous look.

### JASPER JOHNS

She was beautiful.

### ANDY WARHOL

Oh yeah, I remember her. But after I heard how she got killed I just wanted to forget her.

### ROBERT BEVERLY HALE

I was simply having a cup of coffee in Chock Full o' Nuts and there it was in the evening *Post*. It was a great shock. I can't tell you how attractive Brooks and Barbara were and how they attracted people. I never met anybody more charming than that couple when they were organized and underway. Way back, of course.

36                                          SAVAGE GRACE

## WILLIAM THAYER
I was over in London painting Ambassador Annenberg when it happened and I saw it in the headlines and realized, My *God*, that's Tony Baekeland! I even thought of going and doing something, then I thought, Well, it's none of my business really—I mean, *she'd* been killed and there was nothing I could do, and *he'd* been hauled off to jail. He was a damn good artist, too—awfully good.

## MICHEL NEGROPONTE
I bumped into him in the elevator about a year before—my parents lived in their building in New York—and he invited me up to their penthouse for a drink. He I guess at that point had just come back from Paris and was going to some art school in New York. I remember I just talked to him for about an hour in his room—he had this tiny little room. And I remember being astounded by his paintings, which were so incredibly bizarre. Some of them I think were even portraits of his mother—decapitated and with serpents sort of wrapped around her neck. And those were paintings that he had done *recently*. I think two or maybe even three were actually hanging in the living room. And then a few months after that I was going up in the elevator and I saw the headline in, you know, the *Daily News* or whatever it was—"Wealthy mom slain by . . ."—and, I don't know why, it just flashed—I had this strange feeling that it was the Baekelands. And then I looked down the page and it was, in fact. There was something about maybe just being in that elevator where I had run into Tony, especially because I couldn't forget those paintings. It seemed to me that the entire series of events that happened afterwards were really kind of mapped out *in* them.

## AMBROSE GORDON
I read it here in the Austin, Texas, newspaper, where the name Baekeland was all garbled, but the ages and details checked out enough so that I was pretty sure it must be them, and then sometime later it was confirmed when Brooks wrote me about it. The newspaper account said they looked—that *she* looked extraordinarily young and that they looked more like—that they didn't look like mother and son so much as like . . . the newspaper certainly couldn't have used the word "lovers," but it at least planted that suggestion in my head.

## RICHARD HARE
It was a Sunday morning, I was in East Hampton, and I usually get up at seven, seven-thirty, and walk to the village to get my *Times*.

And when I got back home I opened it up to read with my breakfast and I hadn't turned more than two pages when I saw this article datelined London. *Well.* I said to my wife, "Anne, you won't believe what I've just read in the paper!" Then the telephone rang and it was Liz Fondaras. She said, "Richard, have you read the *New York Times?*" I said, "Have I! I was just going to dial *you.*" And of course we commiserated with each other. And five seconds after we hung up Barbara Hale called. I was just about to call *her.* She said, "Richard, can you believe it?" I said, "I can believe it. How about *you?*" She said, "Well, *I* certainly can believe it. It was bound to happen any minute!" Well anyhow, we *all* lived through *that.*

## WILL DAVIS
What month was she killed? November? My own child had just been born and I can remember saying to my wife, "I can't shake this Baekeland thing." I mean, it was like something out of the *Oresteia.* The closest thing I ever experienced to it is the first time I saw morgue activity—autopsies and stuff. I was fine during them but when I got outside I couldn't get the formaldehyde out of my nostrils, I couldn't eat red meat for weeks.

Then, way after she was murdered, Brooks sent me this photograph of her in the mail. God, I'd kill that man if I saw him again, I'd absolutely take a brick and kill him in the street! It was a color photograph, and he had written on the back, "From Barbara the lion-hearted." Because that was what I used to call her—a lioness. Women never mind being called either lions or tigers. They don't want to be called armadillos or camels, but lions and tigers are fine.

## BROOKS BAEKELAND
Barbara was a fine animal but quite untamable. Her two leading—and I think great—characteristics were pride and courage, both highly exaggerated and therefore dangerous. She was a born fighter and died in battle.

## FRANCESCA DRAPER LINKE
I dreamt that I saw Barbara—she was in this incredible penthouse apartment somewhere and we were talking and it was like she was the one that was alive and Tony was the one that had been killed. It was very strange because it was almost like in the act of what had happened she had been released—she was happy, she was happier in this dream than I'd ever seen her in life.

RICHARD HARE
The memorial service in New York was at St. Vincent Ferrer, I
think—on Sixty-sixth and Lexington. And *we* weren't invited. Anne
and I weren't even told where it was, so we didn't go, unfortunately.
It wasn't in the paper, it was all done by telephone and that was it.

PHYLLIS HARRIMAN MASON
As I went in, I saw Daphne Hellman with a black hat on. It was such
an awful service. Everybody was looking around to see who was there
and hobnobbing. I was, too. There was also some kind of service in
London.

## Letter from Brooks Baekeland to James and Gloria Jones, November 24, 1972

There will be a mass given by Barbara's friends who knew her
well and remember *what was lovable and brave in her*, at St.
Mary's, Cadogan Gardens, at 6:30 p.m. on November 30.
      She would have been happy to know you had been there, too.
I know that. I write for her—not for myself.

## From the Last Will and Testament of Barbara Baekeland, April 21, 1972

I, BARBARA DALY BAEKELAND, of the City, County, and
State of New York, give all of my property, real and personal, of
every kind and wherever situated, to my trustee, hereinafter
named, to invest and reinvest it and pay the net income there-
from to or for the benefit of my son, ANTONY, during his life.

## Codicil to the Last Will and Testament of Barbara Baekeland, April 25, 1972

1. I give to my mother, NINA FRASER DALY, if she survives
me, my Coromandel Screen.
2. I give to my mother-in-law, CORNELIA HALLOWELL, if
she survives me, my yellow Eighteenth Century Clock.

3. Both of the articles referred to above are presently located in my apartment at 130 East 75th Street, New York City.


## Tom Dillow

I helped Nini clear out the apartment, and she gave me Barbara's *Larousse Gastronomique*, the wonderful thirties edition—you know, the great big one with the color prints of the best kitchens of the time, those wonderful huge kitchens in France. We even cleared off the stuff from the terrace, the trees and all that. I was there for two or three days helping Nini go through all the stuff—Barbara's wild-animal rugs, those leopard toss pillows, the Audubon lithos, that eighteenth-century Mexican crucifix she had, the Louis Seize breakfast table . . . Then I called up Vito Giallo, the antiques dealer up the street, to come on over.


## Sylvie Baekeland Skira

Brooks hasn't got a cushion from that apartment. Nothing. He made a point of not touching anything and letting Nini have it all because, you know, her first words when Barbara died had been, "Send me Barbara's jewels from London so that Sylvie doesn't wear them!" She thinks, poor little woman, that I'm terrible, that I was the wrecker of this fabulous trinity—God, mother, and son. It's normal—she can't think otherwise. Her daughter was her dream. *I* think Nini is very well-loved and very sweet. "Send Barbara's jewels so that Sylvie doesn't wear them!" You can imagine how I would have worn her jewels!


## Nina Daly

All Barbara's things were expensive. She had all her clothes made, she hardly ever bought them. I guess most of them were made in Paris. She had a nice, a lovely dressmaker there. I had some things made in Paris, too, you know. People used to ask me where I got my suits and I'd say, "Well, I guess most of them were made in Paris." Tony liked clothes. Barbara bought him his clothes, but he had things made, too.

Barbara's clothes were all good-quality. And that's the thing that I care about, the quality of the material. The ones that I have, they're all good material. They last a long time. They last forever. They never really wear out.

Poor Grace Kelly. I feel terrible about her. I think it was a terrible shame what happened to her and her daughter—you know, the little one. She went berserk, you know, sort of. But you never know. You have to accept it and take it. Make the best of it. The best you can. You can't sit and weep over it. That doesn't get you anywhere. You never know what it all will be until it is yesterday.

# 3

---

# AWAITING TRIAL

On Monday morning, November 20, 1972, Tony Baekeland appeared in lower court. There he was formally charged with the murder of his mother and remanded to Brixton Prison.

He was transported in a police van to a district so different from the London he knew that it might have been another country. The squalor of Brixton is alleviated only by a colorful market where anything can be purchased from exotic fruits and vegetables to such old cockney delicacies as jellied eels.

The van, turning down a narrow, two-lane road lined with soot-stained brick buildings, proceeded through an open gate. Ahead was a second gate, controlled from within Brixton Prison and opening onto a barbed-wire courtyard patrolled by guard dogs.

Tony Baekeland had traveled a great deal in his life, and over some grim frontiers, but never over one as forbidding as this. The four-story Victorian-style buildings that loomed in front of him looked like a cross between a factory and a low-income housing project.

The cell he was assigned had been built for single occupancy, but due to overcrowded conditions he would have to share it with two other inmates.

### Letter from Antony Baekeland to James and Gloria Jones, Undated

115709 Baekeland                                    Her Majesty's Prison
                                                    Brixton
                                                    Jebb Ave.
                                                    London

Dear Jim and Gloria—
I am in prison at Brixton in London. You must by now have heard what happened. I feel much better for the rest I am having here and I feel a lot clearer in the nog. I've had a lot of visits from my London friends and this has cheered me up a great deal. I thought of you both a great deal all summer. I would like very much to hear from you—letters cheer one up as you can imagine. So much has happened in the last few years that I am having a little trouble sorting it all out. I have a great deal on my mind and need someone to talk to.

                                                    Yours with love,
                                                    Tony

### TOBY ROSS

I went to visit him in Brixton just a couple of days after he killed his mother. What happened was my friend Catherine Guinness wanted to go and she didn't want to go alone, and we were both sort of friends of his from Spain, from Cadaqués, so we decided we'd go together, and it was very strange. I mean, he didn't seem to know he'd killed his mother. He asked Catherine how his mother was. He said something like "How is my mother? Is she well?" And Catherine and I just both went into instant shock. I figured out later that maybe he was aware of the fact that he'd stabbed her but he just wasn't sure whether he'd killed her or not.

Neither Catherine nor I knew really what to say to him. We were only there for about fifteen or twenty minutes, the legal limit. There was a meeting room that you came into, with little booths. It's not like that anymore—I know, because I was put in Brixton a year later myself—for having a passport that was out-of-date. The English are kind of funny, you know. I said to them, "Listen, I have dual nationality. I have two passports. I came in on my American one and it expired while I was here, but I have an English one." And they said, "Sort it out with the judge," and they threw me in Brixton for two days. The charge was "illegal immigrant."

When I was in there myself, the visiting room was entirely different from the way it was when I was there visiting Tony—you could actually sit at a little table and have physical contact with the person you were speaking to, you could touch them and you could kiss them hello. But when I sawwTony, there were two little booths with plate-glass windows and a little telephone you picked up and spoke through—just like in that old film *Birdman of Alcatraz*.

### CATHERINE GUINNESS
I went to visit him because I felt sorry for him—he was a friend of mine and I liked him. I just sort of sat and we chatted about this and that in a booth and he was sweet as usual. He said he wanted a copy of Dante's *Inferno*, so I sent it to him. You see, when I knew him, I just felt he was one of the gentlest people I'd ever met. I met him in Cadaqués one Easter. I remember going for a walk with him and my father, and he was sort of talking about the soul and how he was trying to find out about his innermost depths—he felt his soul was sort of like an onion and you had to peel all the layers. You know that theory—there are various layers and you can get down if you really try, by sort of meditating and thinking.

### KAREN RADKAI
Look at the photographs of him! Look at him, what he looks like. I took him along on a picnic. Oh, he made drawings! He was as companionable, as gentle as a lamb. These must have been done about 1966. I made them in Cadaqués.

I'll tell you something—my first impressions are always absolutely right. I mean, I very rarely fail. The first time I looked at Cadaqués, I said, "This reminds me of *Camino Real*"—you know, the Tennessee Williams play. There was an absolute aura of decadence about it, a kind of strange decadence, remote almost. There were some extraordinary characters walking around, I can tell you. They lived out Surrealism almost, do you know? I mean, Cadaqués had nothing whatever to do with anything else I've seen on the Mediterranean.

It had enormous beauty, really extraordinary beauty. Cap de Creus, this marvelous mountain, these huge gray rocks, the sea that glistened—I've never seen the sea glisten that way. But it was a Nordic sea—strange, you know. It wasn't that Mediterranean glistening, it was a dark sea. But there were big rocks, and mountains, and wonderful wonderful rows of fishermen's houses going up and up, and a wonderful golden church with a wonderful light coming through.

I really do take photographically what I feel, not what I intellectualize—do you know what I mean? What I see and what I feel, and this is what I felt.

## MISHKA HARNDEN

Do you know John and Dennis, the Meyer twins? They were friends of Tony's from Cadaqués—sort of flower children. They used to pose for Dalí a lot. And they were actors, sort of, too. Do you remember *Women in Love*, the Ken Russell film? There's a pair of twins in it that look very Indian—well, that's them. Anyway, they had this wild idea to take Tony out of Brixton and up to this farm they had in Wales or Scotland and just have him get far from the madding crowd—that kind of thing.

## PHYLLIS HARRIMAN MASON

I wrote to Tony in Brixton to say I was very saddened by his news—I made it very ambiguous. He wrote back and said he felt so much better now than he had before.

I spent that last summer with the two of them in Mallorca, June to September, and in spite of everything that went on, I had a nice summer. Robert Graves came to the house several times, and one night we went to dinner at his house. Afterwards Barbara and Tony had a big argument—Tony said Graves wasn't a great poet and Barbara said he was. But she also said, "The more I see of him, the more he gets to look like an old woman."

## Letter from Barbara Baekeland to Elizabeth Weicker Fondaras, June 29, 1972

> Miramar
> Valldemosa
> Mallorca

. . . Averell Harriman's niece, Phyllis Mason, is staying with us. Last week Robert Graves came to lunch and saw Tony's poems. He wrote him a marvelous letter.

We are settling into this beautiful place. The house was designed by the Archduke Luis Salvador and is unique and distinguished if not very comfortable. Little by little I hope to make it more so, but we live here, at present, in an old-fashioned way. If there ever were a place where one could find peace and tranquillity, this is it.

### ALASTAIR REID
That summer I watched in horrified fascination and that summer was tearing the tops off everything.

There's this enormous great semicircle of mountains where Barbara and Tony were living in Mallorca that's like an amphitheater. It's as though it invites the people who are there for the summer—or compels them—to give themselves up to the demands of the landscape and act in a certain manner. It's really the perfect setting for Mediterranean ritual drama.

In fact, the whole landscape of Mallorca has always reminded me of Greek tragedy, and that's what I said to Phyllis Mason, when I went down to swim with her, and it was then, when we were sitting after swimming, that she said that something terrible was really happening. I wrote her after Tony killed Barbara. She was the only person I did communicate with, because of that.

### PHYLLIS HARRIMAN MASON
You'll laugh when I tell you this but after she died I went to a psychic to try to make contact with her, and during one session some woman actually materialized—some apparition—and she had on a flimsy sort of see-through gown, very décolleté and provocative, and I said, "That's Barbara!"

### ETHEL WOODWARD DE CROISSET
Barbara had a violent Irish streak in her. She wanted everyone to do what she wanted. I mean, she was a redheaded dominating person. She wanted to move everyone about. When I thought about it, it seemed to me that what happened was the most ordinary termination of this wild life.

Tony wrote to me a lot from Brixton—letters which were so terribly sane. You know, people who are nervously upset or mentally upset can write with such clear writing, a very clear steady hand, and say such logical things.

## Letter from Antony Baekeland to Gloria Jones, Undated

115709                                          H.M. Prison
                                               Brixton

Dear Gloria—
Thank you for your lovely letter. I am feeling a lot better now. It
is very sweet of you to write. I also got a letter from Ethel which
was very cheering. How exciting about Jim's new novel. Please
give my best to Mrs. Chambers. Life here is very quiet. I get a
lot of reading done and am getting my head together!

                                        Yours as ever with love,
                                        Tony

P.S. Very happy to hear about Kate's marriage. I remember her
very well and send her my best. T.

## From a Psychiatric Report on Antony Baekeland Ordered by the British Courts, January 5, 1973

On admission to prison Baekeland had been extremely disturbed
for a time and when asked to write an account of the offence
wrote and drew several pages of frankly psychotic content. However he improved fairly rapidly, and when I saw him he was
quite cooperative and composed and said he felt much better
than for many months.

When he was twenty-one or twenty-two his parents separated.
Antony had since been living with his mother in Mallorca and
England, and his father lives in Brittany with a woman of thirty-
five whom Antony once regarded as his own girlfriend.

### SYLVIE BAEKELAND SKIRA

Brooks and I were married on January 24, 1973—two months after
Barbara died. But by then I had been living with him for five years
and I had had it—yes. Because I was very conventional in those days
and I was very humiliated to be living with someone whose wife I was
not. I thought that during those years certainly a divorce could have
been obtained, and it had not been obtained—for whatever intricate
reasons there were between them. And the charm had gone, and I
was ready to leave Brooks. Perhaps this is why he finally did something—he could feel that I had had it.

I married him because my heart really went out to him when she died, because I saw how he was suffering. You can't leave someone in that state. Everybody will tell you how, you know, I was trying to get all the Baekeland money. This is grotesque. When she died it was the most horrible moment of *my* life, it really was, because I understood that certain events will not allow you to live, even to exist. After I married Brooks I saw that instead of having a husband, I had a widower on my hands.

### ADDIE HERDER
I ran into Brooks—it must have been early in February 1973. I came into this little brasserie on the Île Saint-Louis, and it was crowded as usual, there was no place to sit down. And there was Brooks, sitting at a table with a woman, and I didn't want to sit with him. But I was shepherding a black painter by the name of Beauford Delaney, a very good painter—a friend of Georgia O'Keeffe and Henry Miller and Jimmy Baldwin—who was having an opening later that day. Beauford was old so he sat down at Brooks's table. So then *I* had to! Brooks greeted me with all sorts of affection and said he wanted me to meet his wife, you know—which really upset me, because it was too *soon* somehow. Then he said to me, "That terrible boy—he killed that wonderful woman." And he went on in the same paragraph to tell this new wife how much he admired my work, my collages. Well, he had two pieces of mine, which *Barbara* had bought, many years ago. And after this he wrote inviting me to come visit them where they were living, somewhere in Brittany, and he described the house and how wonderful it was and he listed the people who were going to be there. This was, you know, just after his wife had died!

### GLORIA JONES
Jim and I were getting ready to go to the opening of Beauford Delaney's art show and the doorbell rang and Brooks just walked in and we were very cold to him. He said that Tony had killed the woman he loved. He absolutely said that, quote unquote. We were stunned. I said, "Please don't talk to me," you know, and he left.

### SYLVIE BAEKELAND SKIRA
I was *there*. What happened is Brooks and I lived in the same part of Paris as the Joneses—the Île Saint-Louis—and we were taking a walk on the *quais* and Gloria was at her window, on the quai d'Orléans. She stared at Brooks, who stared back at her, and she closed her

window. Nobody rang her bell. Brooks was not silly enough to go ring her bell. You see, everybody would like to have made a *grande geste*.

## ROSEMARY RODD BALDWIN

When Barbara was killed, I borrowed everything you can imagine to get back to England. I was living in Turkey, and I got back as soon as I could. My daughter Mandy took me down to the prison. I'd never been to *that* one. Well, after all, I had married a man who was in jail in Turkey, so I knew about prisons, but that's another story altogether. So I went to see Tony and there he was. Suddenly he looked up and for a moment there was a flash of this old Tony from Ansedonia—of happy days.

Let me tell you, a more normal boy you never saw. Once we went sailing with my daughter Jinty, the one he loved so much, and my son-in-law, Hugo Money-Coutts, sailing from Porto Santo Stefano in a small boat called a Fifer, and on a small boat you really see people how they are. Tony had his guitar with him, and we stopped in the middle of the sea—in the middle of the Mediterranean near Tarranto—and he played all night and everybody was so happy. Tony behaved like an absolute angel, an absolute normal absolute angel.

Brixton was the first prison I'd ever been in where you have to talk to somebody behind glass, and we were given fifteen minutes and I found it terribly difficult to talk for fifteen minutes and I was getting desperate, and suddenly I said, "Tony, has your father been over to see you?" And he said, "Yes. Yes he has." Which wasn't true. And he brought a comb out of his pocket and he was bending the teeth of the comb, and I realized it had been a mistake to ask him that. So then I burst into tears. And he looked at me and I said, "Well, never mind, Tony, it'll soon be over. You'll see—you'll be out and you'll come and stay with me in Turkey."

## RICHARD HARE

Nini said please write to the poor boy, his father won't go and see him, blah blah blah. This was before Brooks did go finally, I think. Anyhow, Anne felt sorry for him and wrote him a letter, a very careful letter. After all, we'd had some wonderful times at Barbara's. She had had a lot of exposure on two continents, you know, and she knew everyone attractive and interesting. Dalí came frequently with his puma cub or his pet tiger or baby leopard or whatever it was—he was apparently a friend from Cadaqués. And I remember meeting somebody called the Thane of Cawdor there, which was sort of amusing. He really *was* the Thane of Cawdor—as in Macbeth.

## Letter from Anne Hare to Antony Baekeland, Undated

New York

Dear Tony,

This is an awfully difficult letter to write, and I do hope that you will understand if I do not express myself with much finesse. I loved your mother very much, but that feeling did not stop with her, it very definitely included *you*. I'm sure you are going through agonies of remorse so I won't dwell on that, only the positive things.

Richard and I want to keep in touch with you. That is the primary purpose of writing. Even with all the ugliness, we remember a marvelous, talented, sensitive, and understanding friend: You!

Richard, and hopefully me, will be in London in February. We would like to see *you*, if *you* would like to see *us*. You have many friends, dear Tony, who would like to help if it is possible. Could we be put on your lawyer's list of "Concerned Friends"? So that we know your whereabouts.

We want *another* Tony Baekeland drawing to hang near the beautiful one you gave us last Xmas!

With love,
Anne

## Letter from Antony Baekeland to Richard and Anne Hare, January 17, 1973

Brixton

Dear Anne and Richard—

What a wonderfully consoling letter. For a while I didn't know whether I was coming or going but now I am feeling a lot better and people are taking good care of me. I feel more myself. I have a lot of reading to do and so I keep myself occupied in this and in writing letters. I would love to keep in touch with you and would very much like to see you both in February. I shall never forget all the kindness you showed us last winter. I have had a number of visits from friends and this has kept me very happy.

> With love to you both,
> Tony

## ELIZABETH ARCHER BAEKELAND

I was on the high seas when he killed Barbara, sailing from New York to Cherbourg on the *France*. And when I got to Paris everybody had seen it in the papers and told me the good news—you know how people are. And within a few days I flew over to London and saw Tony. I was staying at the Carlton Towers and I remember I went down to the lobby and told the doorman to get me a taxi. He said, "Where are you going, madam?"—you know, they're all dressed in uniform there—and I said Brixton Prison, and he said to the cab driver, without batting an eyelash, "Brixton Prison."

So I went and I waited with everybody else waiting to see the prisoners. And then they called my name out and said booth number seven or whatever. I hadn't seen Tony in I guess ten years. He said immediately, "Oh thank you for coming, Aunt Liz." He was absolutely charming. I was sort of afraid to mention what had happened. I don't think we did mention it. It was all small talk—you know, "How have you been? What have you been doing? Have you been writing any poetry? Have you been doing any paintings?" And *he* was talking, too. Fifteen minutes I was with him. Then right after that he wrote me a letter and said, "Thank you for visiting me. I love you, Aunt Liz. You remind me of Mummy." And I thought, Wow! I'm next on the list! Sam Shaw, my lawyer, said, "Don't go to see him again, don't do anything, and *don't* answer the letter."

## MIWA SVINKA-ZIELINSKI

I saw him in Brixton that January. He knew that he had killed his mother and I talked to him about that and he said, "I dream about her often. She comes to me in my dreams and says that she is not at all angry."

I met Tony and Barbara both in 1970 in East Hampton. When I

met him I didn't know that he was the son of Barbara. He looked very *sympathique* and I asked him whether he wrote poetry, because I said he looked just like a poet to me. He had some kind of a way about him, sort of something lyrical. So he was very pleased, and that's why he started to be very friendly with me. He told me that he was also a painter. Then he gave me a fish, a painting of his. I have it somewhere. I like this fish very much—it has very good color.

## SAM GREEN

Barbara was always telling me—I mean, over and over again—how artistic Tony was. Well, he did have lots of esoteric façade, let's say. I met her on a cruise of the Greek Islands in 1969—Emily Staempfli, a mutual friend, had chartered this big yacht—and Barbara and I became, shall I say, best friends overnight. And right after the cruise I went to stay with her in Mallorca—which is when I met Tony. And right after that, I went to stay with my friend Cecil Beaton in England, at his country house. Cecil was dying to meet Barbara because I had such good stories to tell. They never did meet, but, based on what he had heard about Barbara and Tony from me, he wrote a novella that telescoped them into the future—he had the son kill the mother at the end!

## Letter from Sam Green to Antony Baekeland, April 6, 1973

Fire Island, New York

Dear Tony,

It is difficult to write to someone who has a great deal of time on their hands, as you do, because there can be so many interpretations of what is said, if the words and phrases are dwelt upon for too long a time. It will be easier if you simply give this one a once-over (which is the spirit in which it is being written) and then discard it.

So you're in prison, awaiting trial. Yet another adventure for you—but this one is taking so long. You must be bored rigid. Since you are the one with all the time on your hands, how about a letter from you describing what it is like to be in prison? Do you have any friends among the inmates? Do they allow books to be sent to you? How about visitors—are you allowed any in the way of friends (not just lawyers)? If so I shall try to

stop in and see you when I come to England. Which shouldn't
be too far away in time.

In comparison with your confinement I have been even more
compulsive in my activeness. I spent December and January in
India and Ceylon and can hardly wait to return to the former.

I have a little house on the beach here to which *no one*
comes. It is a cold gray windy rainy day, and I'm looking out
over the water just *so* happy to be here and not at some chic
Sunday brunch in N.Y.

Now, keep your spirits up and make an effort to write me—
not so much your plans—because we don't know what will happen with your trial—but how things are. That would be interesting to me. I hope that Mr. Wuss is being looked after.

Love,
Sam

## Letter from Antony Baekeland to Sam Green, April 15, 1973

Brixton

Dear Sam—
Your letter just came and I am very happy to hear from you at
last—more happy than I can tell. I shall try to answer your
questions. Yes, I am allowed visits and books. Mr. Wuss is in
the country with friends or family of the Turners, who took care
of the flat on Cadogan Square. I had a sweet note from Mrs.
Turner that he is being well taken care of. I wish you would take
him as I cannot have him here. The trip to the Far East sounds
very exciting. I had a similar reaction to it. Yes it is *very* boring
here but I try to be good and not to fret. I am quite lucky—I just
had a visit yesterday from two close English friends. I had a visit
recently from Muriel Murphy, and Emily Staempfli has sent me
books three times. She is so sweet to think of me here. I haven't
heard from my father in a dog's age although I have written
many times. Your house on the beach sounds very romantic and
beautiful. You ask me what it is like to be in prison—just
*exactly* as one would imagine. It has become routine to me but
at first it took a good while to get used to being shut up. Sam—I
want to tell you something very important. Do you remember

all the bad luck we had in Mallorca? Well I think it all came from me and I think I was jinxed. For me it was an exquisite torture to be in such a beautiful spot and among such kind people as the family that looked after Mummy and me—Maria and Sebastian—and to be unable to enjoy the beauty or reach out to them. I do so wish we could all be together again. I spend most of my time fighting evil in myself—I have a bloody mind, Sam, and I don't know what to do about it but I fight it with everything I've got. Sam, another thing is that I have so much in my heart that to let it all out at once would surely kill me. Those last days in Cadogan Square were terrible. I can't tell you exactly what happened but I completely lost my head. I miss Mummy very much. I hope my trial comes up soon. I want very much to go back to Mallorca. Perhaps you will come to visit me if I go there. I hope not to get a big sentence.

Love,
Tony

# 4

# THE TRIAL

On the morning of June 6, 1973, Tony Baekeland was driven from Brixton Prison to Central Criminal Court, known to the general public as the Old Bailey—there finally to stand trial for the murder of his mother.

Built on the site of the notorious Newgate Prison and skirted on its east side by "Deadman's Walk," an open passage along which condemned men once took their final steps to keep their appointment with the hangman, the Old Bailey is virtually synonymous with English judicial history and drama. It is here that the infamous "Dr. Crippen" was sentenced to death for the murder of his wife. And it is here that Oscar Wilde sat in the dock and heard the judge sentence him to two years' hard labor, intoning: "That you Wilde have been the centre of a circle of extensive corruption of the most hideous kind among young men, it is . . . impossible to doubt." And it was here on this June morning that Tony Baekeland became a statistic: one of the 4,509 persons tried at the Old Bailey during the year 1973.

The trial of *Regina* v. *Antony Baekeland* officially opened the moment the High Court judge, who traditionally presides only at the most serious cases such as murder and offenses under the Official Secrets Act, was escorted into the courtroom by an alderman and a sheriff of the City of London, both in violet robes. The judge's robe was red—indeed, he is known as the "Red Judge"—and adorned with slate-colored silk trimmings. Over the robe he wore a black stole fastened with a wide, black belt; over the stole, slung across his right shoulder, he wore a scarlet band. His neckwear consisted of a starched wing collar and two plain white bands hanging down in front. On his head was the English judicial headdress—a wig, abbreviated from the reign of Charles II to one with a single vertical curl at the back and two short rows hanging down behind. In his hands he carried white gloves and a folded square of black silk known as the "Black Cap"—a relic from the days when it was placed on his wig as he passed the death sentence.

Since the trial of Tony Baekeland was being held during the summer months, according to ancient custom, sweet-smelling English garden flowers had been strewn on the bench and the ledge of the dock.

Three sharp knocks on the door of the judge's dais signaled the black-robed usher to open the court with the proclamation: "All persons who have anything to do before My Lords the Queen's Justices at the Central Criminal Court draw near and give your attendance. God Save the Queen."

The counsel representing the Crown wore a long silk gown, long-cuffed black tailcoat, and a waistcoat with flaps to the pockets. Representing the defendant was the barrister-writer John Mortimer, who would later create the character of the portly liberal barrister "Rumpole of the Bailey" for television; he was garbed in the traditional Tudor gown.

To the left of the barristers sat the wigged and gowned clerks of the court, whose function it was to swear in juries, take prisoners' pleas, and record verdicts.

As the trial was getting under way, Tony Baekeland, who had been sitting impassively in the accused's enclosure at the center of the courtroom, exclaimed, to no one in particular, "I would rather have buggered a prosecutor than killed a peacock in paradise!"

### NEIL HARTLEY
I had been out of town working on a film and when I got back to London, at a dinner party John Mortimer, who was a friend of mine and my partner Tony Richardson's and who was always involved in these bizarre cases, said, "I'm representing this interesting case—this

boy who killed his mother." And suddenly I was told that the papers had been full of it.

Barbara Baekeland had bought the apartment on Cadogan Square from me and a friend of mine, Tom Robertsen, and that was really my only association with her. I went back two or three times to parties there. She was pleasant enough. Just before she was killed, we talked—I think the *day* before—and she said she was having a party that night and she wanted me to come.

I must say I didn't like the way she had done up the place. I mean, I preferred it the way *I* had had it. I'd bought it from an Italian antiques dealer on the King's Road—he had done it up for himself and lived in it for a number of years, and he'd done a beautiful job, but *she* . . . I mean, it had a very deep stairwell from the floor below up to a kind of studio room which was the living room, and the stairs had a lovely banister, been there for a *long* time, and she took it all out. I don't know how people escaped without killing themselves going up and down those stairs! Things like that I thought were odd, but, you know, women have their own taste.

After her death I was contacted by her husband to see if I was interested in buying the apartment back, which I thought was a real creepy idea. He showed up in London while the son was being held in prison.


**BROOKS BAEKELAND**
Barbara's murder by her own son was a kind of grotesque, inartistic accident. She should not have died the way she did. It was not so much her kind of death as his kind of . . . She had a kind of greatness—no, a real greatness—of heart, and her murder was illustrative not of her but of that *crapule*, her son. That she had partly made him into a *crapule* is also true. But he was also my son, and I had fought against that in him all his life and failed. I would give anything to have been able to help him. I never could.

Even as a small child he was aberrant. And then as he was entering puberty it became clear—finally—that he was not only homosexual but a practicing one. That was a terrible shock to his mother, who fought against it with him, ferociously. She may even have died in one of their fights over this. She simply could never accept it, try though she did—gallantly, desperately, despairingly—in their last disorganized years together.

SAM GREEN

Barbara just thought Tony was the Messiah and the greatest child that ever was. Nobody was good enough for Tony. She would rent castles in Italy or Spain or wherever and invite important nobility— shall we say specifically the daughters of important nobility. Later on she would invite older girls, hoping that the inevitable would happen. What I mean is she would set Tony up. She tried it time after time and it just didn't work. Finally she got a little more desperate and aggressive about it and when Tony himself finally invited a girl to Cadaqués for a holiday—she was from Paris and a few years older than he was—Barbara practically instructed her to seduce him. Now this is the part of the story that really intrigued Cecil Beaton. In that novella he wrote, he gave Barbara the name "Emily," Tony the name "Jonathan," and "Dolores," I guess, represented Sylvie. Thank God it never got published! Cecil was a photographer basically, but when he wrote he always settled for the most superficial frame around the picture. He revealed incredible tawdriness in his prose. But I hasten to his defense: He never displayed it elsewhere!

## From an Untitled Novella Believed to Be by Cecil Beaton, Unpublished

> Emily continued to feed her son with young ladies. One day she got hold of a girl who was pretty much of a tart. I guess she wasn't, of course, a whore picked up from the street, but she was a well-known, loose young woman around Paris named Dolores. Emily invited this Dolores down to the house in Portofino which she and her husband had rented, thinking that she'd make things easy for Jonathan. Well, playing a role that most mothers don't—I mean it was very odd for her to produce a tart in order that her son should be initiated into the rites of love— Emily had a well-deserved disaster dumped on her. The result is Emily is left alone—with the son who is also alone.
>
> This all happened in Portofino, which, as you know, is quite a tight community, and the arrival of a tart was remarked upon by all those gossips. So you can imagine the excitement when Dolores, who was asked as a set-up for Jonathan's entertainment and satisfaction, succeeded in seducing his father.

## Barbara Curteis

When Tony was twenty-one or twenty-two he said to me, "You know, I'm still a virgin." And a couple of months later he met Sylvie. She was one of the groupies in Cadaqués—French, hippyish. And Tony said to me—this is so sad and moving in light of what happened later—he said, "Sex between men and women—people talk about it and make such a big hooha about it and they say it's so complicated and everything, but when you meet the right girl everything just falls into place." Sylvie was his first girlfriend, you see. He brought her to meet Barbara and Brooks in Paris—brought her home like a kitten bringing its first killed mouse, and laid it at their feet.

That Christmas they rented Emily Staempfli's house in Cadaqués—Barbara, Brooks, Barbara's mother, Mrs. Daly, and Tony and Sylvie. An *in principle* happy Christmas: Mammy, Pappy, Granny, the Only Child, and the Only Child's Girlfriend.

But Sylvie took another look at Brooks and said, you know, "There's more money in it for me if I go with the father than if I go with the son."

## Sylvie Baekeland Skira

I think that that's a good story. People say I caught the Baekelands. The Baekelands do their own catching, very easily—believe me.

You know, I'm not in the least prudish, and if I had had an affair with the son and then with the father, I would say so. It wouldn't bother me in the least to say so.

I met the son first—in Cadaqués, in the summer of '67. He was six years younger than I was. He had that pretty complexion of his mother's. He didn't have that sort of mad face that he had afterwards, of which I only saw photographs. He was soft-spoken, very bright, very gentle. Affectionate. I don't mean toward me, but toward his dog—he had the most charming relationship with the little dog, who he called Digby. "Mr. Digby, will you be good?" Very sweet.

I was going through my first divorce, and Tony and I became great friends. *Not* the way people say—that there was a love affair. It's so absurd—because Tony was a homosexual from the day he was born, I think. But a lot of homosexual men like women—as a companion, to talk to and so forth. We were like brother and sister in a way. Of course, later, when I went away with his father, he resented me terribly.

## From a Psychiatric Report on Antony Baekeland Ordered by the British Courts, January 5, 1973

He attached special importance to certain emotions and incidents, emphasizing especially that he was devoted to both parents and that they continued devoted to one another, that their separation had disturbed his peace of mind. He wept when describing this.

ELIZABETH ARCHER BAEKELAND
Before they separated, Barbara told Brooks, "You know, I could get Tony over his homosexuality if I just took him to bed," and Brooks said, "Don't you dare do that, Barbara!" Fred, my ex-husband, Brooks's brother, told me that Brooks told *him* that—now this is brothers!

ELEANOR WARD
It comes back to me now—the very clear clear clear tone—that she did tell me that she slept with him, because I lived on the next street and I remember leaving her apartment on Seventy-fifth and walking down Lexington and walking back to Seventy-fourth in a state of shock, you know—that anyone could do that to their son.

WILLIE MORRIS
I always heard that the mother and the son had slept together. That's what everyone told me. I had no way of knowing whether it was true but it was certainly the talk of the East Hampton set.

TOM DILLOW
Barbara told me that it happened in that house they had in Mallorca, this archduke's palace, but then, a lot of stuff happened in that house. I mean, it was a real spooky place—huge, no electricity, that kind of stuff. She didn't give me any details. Oh no. Not Barbara. Barbara was a lady.

SYLVIE BAEKELAND SKIRA
I can believe that she would do *anything*—including that. I can't believe that *he* would, that's all. There might be something in a woman where she wants to save her child to a point that is beyond

credibility, but then the child remains a boy, a homosexual boy, and I can't imagine that he would have found this in any way physically possible.

## ALAN HARRINGTON
I was quoted in *Newsweek* magazine about something, I can't remember what, therapeutic techniques, I think, and Barbara called me up and said she wanted desperately to talk to me, and she told me that she had slept with Tony. I said to her I didn't think it was such a bad thing, to remove guilt, but now that I think of it, there wasn't any expressed.

## BARBARA HALE
Sons and lovers—nobody knows the difference anymore.

## IRVING SABO
Barbara Baekeland was in a writing class I took at the New School in New York in the early seventies with Anatole Broyard. Well, I can only say, she was a presence. She only came a few times when I was there, and I went to dinner with her a couple of times after class. The first time, we went to Bradley's, on University Place—there were about ten of us—and she just thought it was all so marvelous. We all went Dutch on those occasions, and she just thought this was great. And a week or two later, she read some of her writing in class, her ongoing novel, which dealt with a mother-son incest, as I recall. Well, it was vivid. She was, I think, a good writer. And after that class, some of us were going uptown on the East Side and she invited four or five of us who were in my car to stop up for a drink.

*That* was a memorable occasion. She had a collection of antiques the likes of which you don't get from any ordinary dealer. She had a lacquered Japanese highboy which was an extraordinary piece—it's very vivid to me because I've designed furniture in my time. It was top museum quality. And everything in the apartment was on that scale, it just reeked of great wealth. She offered some bourbon and I like good bourbon, and I asked for some ice and she said, "Oh, you won't need ice for this. This was made for me, it's a private batch." Well, there *are* distilleries that make special blends for special customers. It's like having a private railroad car these days. Anyway, it was extraordinary bourbon, real sipping stuff. No ice needed.

The living room was full of photographs of a very beautiful young man, I would say in his early twenties. She had taken, I believe, a lot of the photographs. What struck me was the way the camera just dwelled on the beauty of this young man. Now this may be hindsight, but they were not the sort of pictures a mother would normally take of a son. After I saw those photographs, I felt that her novel was autobiographical.

### ETHEL WOODWARD DE CROISSET

I thought the story of sleeping with Tony was perfectly touching, because I think that was a dream of hers, you know—that somebody could make him whole. I think subconsciously she thought that the reason she had lost Brooks was because her son was a homosexual, you see.

### BROOKS BAEKELAND

The incest thing. I don't know. If they had not been taking drugs, I would say, unhesitatingly, *no*. I would say it was a *boutade*—a caprice—that came out of Barbara's taste for the outrageous. *Pour épater les bourgeois*—you know? But I know nothing about the drugged state. So who knows? I know he loved his mother.

He loved his mother more than he loved me, but he loved me, too. And he respected me. I was, in a way, his alter ego. He held to me as an exhausted man does to a rock—barnacled and harsh though I was. But I really did love his mother, you see, and I could never forgive him for killing her.

## From a Psychiatric Report on Antony Baekeland Ordered by the British Courts, January 5, 1973

> His great improvement in prison may be due to relief from the great strain of his relationship with his mother. He requires further medical treatment but the prognosis for his leading an ineffectual but socially acceptable life under medical supervision is probably better than for some time. This treatment could well be provided in the U.S.A.
>
> There appear to be two possibilities—to ask the court to make a deportation order and give a short sentence of imprisonment. He is not really medically unsuitable for imprisonment. But I think it would be better to make a Section 65 hospital order to

Broadmoor Special Hospital. He would be very soon ready for discharge and his transfer to medical care in the U.S.A. could be arranged fairly simply. In either case he would be likely to spend about a year in England and better in Broadmoor than prison.

JOHN MORTIMER
What I tried to do at the trial was get the judge to send him straight back to America. The boy was very nice. I mean, I found him very gentle and calm and nice. But off he went.

## Letter from Antony Baekeland to Sam Green, June 8, 1973

Dear Sam,
I finally had a trial two days ago and was found guilty of manslaughter under diminished responsibility and am being sent to Broadmoor until I am well. Are you planning any trips? The one to India sounded fascinating. When I get out I hope to get a house in Mallorca.

Love,
Tony

## Letter from Dr. E. L. Udwin to Cornelia Baekeland Hallowell, June 19, 1973

Broadmoor Special Hospital
Crowthorne, Berks.
. . . Your grandson, Antony Baekeland, will, of course, require very lengthy treatment—this is only to be expected. He gets what medication his treatment requires. He is, of course, on no habit-forming drugs. He has not to associate with people any worse than himself.

## From "Dreams and Realities," a Lecture Delivered at the Johns Hopkins University by Leo Hendrik Baekeland, October 23, 1931

Dr. Charles H. Mayo in a recent address stated: "Every other hospital bed in the United States is now occupied by the mentally afflicted, insane, idiotic, feeble-minded, and senile. In addition, there is an enormous number of people almost fit for the asylum."

What is the outlook for the next generations? Is it not time to put less pride in the increasing number of our populations, and to look more into the matter of quality? It is quite right that we should try to restrain the immigration of undesirables. But shall we continue forever to encourage the promiscuous breeding of the unfit, degenerates, criminals, and the insane, while keeping on ignoring the biological facts of heredity? If so, more unemployables, more hospitals, lunatic asylums, poorhouses, and prisons.

In the past, raw Nature left to act by herself seemed more merciful than our present civilization. By exercising her rigors, she improved the race through the elimination of the unfit and by favoring the intelligent, the strong, and the healthy.

The Bible tells us that the fall of Adam and Eve started after they had eaten the fruit of the tree of Knowledge. Whatever that may mean, I believe that ignorance—ignorance of scientific facts—is the real "original sin," the sin that has been and still is today the principal cause of our sorrows and of the martyrdom of man.

# PART II

# BROADMOOR

# 1

# THE MATERIAL OF A THOUSAND USES

On June 6, 1973, Tony Baekeland was transferred from the city of London to the small, picturesque village of Crowthorne in the Berkshire countryside. The narrow lanes were ablaze with wildflowers and lush with ferns, the village gardens an iridescent display of irises, peonies, and petunias. The large wooden sign reading "BROADMOOR SPECIAL HOSPITAL—NO THROUGH ROAD" struck an inharmonious note.

"The excellent road invited us to speed on and yet the sensation of loveliness was so predominant that we preferred to stop frequently to better enjoy the charmingly reposeful landscape," Tony Baekeland's great-grandfather had written of this same countryside sixty-six years earlier, in a privately printed volume.

Tony Baekeland would not have the same opportunity to linger that his celebrated ancestor had had. He was driven up a winding road past a cluster of white cottages to the place where he would be detained indefinitely, "at her Majesty's pleasure."

The red-brick Victorian institution called Broadmoor Special Hospital was built in 1863 as Broadmoor Criminal Lunatic Asylum. It is surrounded by a wall of uneven height that weaves snakelike through open fields. With its pink-blossomed trees that line the road in front of the main buildings and its rows of daffodils hugging the walls, Broadmoor looks like a friendly New England college campus. But its blue-uniformed nurses look more like guards and in fact belong to the Prison Officers Association; and all staff members are required to sign the Official Secrets Act. Patients' mail is routinely censored, and occasionally even books are withheld on the grounds that they are "bad influences."

"At Broadmoor, security is the first consideration," a staff member says. "We are always concerned with the escape and welfare of our patients, since we're dealing with very violent and dangerous persons here."

Of the approximately 750 patients at Broadmoor, many have committed "heinous, headline crimes"; more than a quarter have committed homicide or attempted murder. There are also patients who have committed no crime but who are mentally ill. There are over ninety attempted suicides a year, and it has been estimated that at any given time Broadmoor houses between 200 and 250 psychopaths. Indeed, it has been described as "the asylum of last resort."

A Dent of London clock sits above the impressive entrance gate through which Tony Baekeland was led that June 6 into a small courtyard. From there he was taken down a passageway to a door where he heard what would become a familiar sound to him: the jangle of the large metal keys carried by every Broadmoor attendant. The door was unlocked for him, then locked again.

Tony Baekeland was now in the main body of the hospital, which consisted of eight residential "blocks." In 1969, in an attempt to abolish prison terminology, the blocks were renamed "houses," Block A becoming Kent House; Block B, Cornwall House; Block C, Dorset House; and the other blocks becoming Essex, York, Somerset, Lancaster, and Norfolk.

## From *A Family Motor Tour Through Europe,* Leo Hendrik Baekeland, Horseless Age Press, New York, 1907

The farther we went away from London the better became the roads. We were driving through a lovely, rolling country, with a smooth highway and green fields. Now and then we met a cheerful-looking cottage, its stony façade made lovelier by some creeping tea roses. Carpetlike lawns, tastefully laid-out gardens, with very old trees, and everything cared for to perfection—all this gave us a strong impression of pretty, rural England.

The main part of the house under the hospitable roof of which we were going to stay had been built in Shakespeare's time, in the quaint architecture of that day, and the modern additions had been made in tolerable conformity with the original style.

The *ensemble*, with the surrounding gardens and lawns, made a delightful specimen of an English country house.

The liberal supply of rain which makes the British climate so humid is also the main reason why, in that country, it is possible to produce such well-kept lawns, better than are to be found anywhere else, and which look more like immense green carpets.

There, the lawn extended to a sort of terrace, with a green stairway, and reached out toward a very tastefully arranged rose garden. Stately trees, several of them many centuries old, were artistically grouped all over; giant yew trees next to imposing cedars of the Lebanon; exotic-looking araucarias in proximity to glossy-leaved hollies, the latter with trunks almost a foot in diameter. A shady pathway lined by treelike rhododendrons led toward an old church. Everything was harmony and every detail gave evidence of centuries of good care and good taste. Yes, this is undoubtedly the secret of these striking effects of English landscape gardening, which seem so hard to imitate successfully.

The place just described is merely a representative of hundreds of others, some larger, some smaller, but in all of them the landscape gardening has been the result of a slow and well-studied process, extending through many generations and carried out by a succession of owners, the children being able to follow the improvements which their fathers planned.

## Dr. Thomas Maguire

Inside the walls the fact is you'll find it's lovely green, with flower beds that the patients take care of, and rather nice trees and all that sort of thing. The hospital has forty acres of land, tennis courts, a swimming pool, and football grounds, as well as gardens. It's not like a prison where the inmates always see the walls. When you're inside you can hardly see the walls, because they drop down in places.

They're somewhat higher in the areas where the patients are likely to try to make an escape.

Tony was very, very ill in the beginning—he had to be dressed and he had to be taken to the bathroom.

He idealized his mother, you know. He was very sorry and showed great remorse. He often said, "Oh, how a few moments of frenzy changed my life!" The fact is it wouldn't have changed his life, because his illness was just part of a whole picture. There was a deep sickness in the family, and a lack of discipline that too much money will often create.

He was fond of his father. He wrote him bad-tempered letters occasionally but then, within the week, he might turn around and write him an affectionate one. That's the way his illness was.

He had ideas of grandeur about who he was. He thought he was a great painter. He wasn't, but he wasn't bad. He told me that his great-grandfather was included in some encyclopedia.

## From *Science* Magazine, November 1984

The toast of society as well as industry, Leo Hendrik Baekeland appeared on the cover of *Time* magazine in September 1924.

## From *Time* Magazine, May 20, 1940

### FATHER OF PLASTICS

This week Philadelphia's Franklin Institute presents one of its coveted gold medals to a man who is much less known to the public than are the changes his work has wrought in the many common things people use, from toothbrush handles, telephones and false gums, to airplane bodies. Even more than most scientists, the man is publicity-shy. He is Leo Hendrik Baekeland, inventor of Bakelite, "Father of Plastics."

Born in Flemish Belgium 76 years ago, young Leo became an ardent photographer. . . . He entered the University of Ghent as its youngest student, graduated in 1882 *summa cum laude*, promptly became an assistant professor of chemistry. . . . He emigrated to the U.S. and went to work for a photographic supply manufacturer. Then he started his own consulting practice, invented a quick-action photographic printing paper called Velox, organized Nepera Chemical Co. to manufacture it. George Eastman of Eastman Kodak bought him out.

Legend has it that Eastman paid Baekeland $1,000,000, several times the minimum sum on which the young inventor had set his mind. At all events, he found himself, at 35, rich enough to do what he pleased. He converted a stable in his backyard into a laboratory. He found that phenol (carbolic acid) and formaldehyde interacted to make a non-melting, non-dissolving solid like nothing in nature. This was Bakelite, foundation stone of the synthetic plastic industry. After forming General Bakelite Co. (later Bakelite Corp.) to exploit his discovery, Baekeland methodically listed 43 industries in which he thought it would be useful. Today it would be hard to find 43 in which it is not used.

## From the *Bakelite Review,* a Periodical Digest of Bakelite Achievements Interesting to All Progressive Manufacturers and Merchants, Volume 7, Number 3 (Silver Anniversary Number, 1910–1935)

Millions of uses. . . . radios, clocks, bottle caps, baseball caps, phonograph records, lamps, fountain pens, pencils, washing machine parts, shaving brush handles, toilet seats, costume jewelry, artificial limbs, coffins, pipes, cigarette holders, saddles, overcoat and suit buttons, subway strap hangers, control devices for submarines, battleships and destroyers, automobile parts and gear wheels.

## From *The Story of Bakelite,* John Kimberly Mumford, Robert L. Stillson Publishing Co., New York, 1924

Wherever wheels whirr, wherever women preen themselves in the glitter of electric lights, wherever a ship plows the sea or an airplane floats in the blue—wherever people are living, in the Twentieth Century sense of the word, there Bakelite will be found rendering its enduring service.

From *Fortune* Magazine, April 4, 1983

THE HALL OF FAME FOR U.S. BUSINESS LEADERSHIP

The Business Hall of Fame's "Roster of Past Laureates"—leaders whose achievements have endured—includes Andrew Carnegie, Pierre Samuel Du Pont, Thomas Alva Edison, Henry Ford, Benjamin Franklin, Edwin Herbert Land, Cyrus Hall McCormick, Andrew William Mellon, John Pierpont Morgan, John Davison Rockefeller, David Sarnoff, Alfred Pritchard Sloan, Jr., Cornelius Vanderbilt, George Washington, Thomas John Watson Jr., Eli Whitney . . .

Elected this year to the Business Hall of Fame: Leo Hendrik Baekeland (1863–1944).

## From *Selected Writings,* Leo Hendrik Baekeland, Bakelite Corporation, New York, 1944

How did I happen to strike such an interesting subject as that of the synthetic resins? I can readily answer that I did not strike it haphazardly; I looked for just such a subject for a number of years until I found it among the many lines of research which I undertook in my laboratory. And, between 1905 and 1909, I obtained an insoluble, infusible substance which we call oxybenzylmethyleneglycolanhydride now known as BAKELITE.

## From the Private Diaries of Leo Hendrik Baekeland, March 8, 1909

After my lecture the boys were singing once in a while the B-A-K-E-L-I-T-E song which goes

> "B-A-K-E-L-I-T-E
> Stands for Bakelite
> Ten times better than graphite
> And what's the name
> Every photographer of the country knows
> Velox—Velox!"

When I went to the station I was escorted by the whole bunch—
about thirty—marching like soldiers and singing the Bakelite
song.

STEPHANE GROUEFF
In the atomic bomb, one of the most important problems, and probably the most difficult to solve—I think it's still one of the two or three
biggest atomic bomb production secrets in the world, which any foreign spy would have given anything to have—involved Bakelite.
When I was working on my book *The Manhattan Project* in the middle sixties, I had a sort of gentleman's agreement with the Atomic
Energy Commission that I would show them my manuscript because
I wasn't a scientist and the idea was that they would just correct all
the spelling and so forth but that I would keep my total freedom.
They sent me a brochure called "U.S. Atomic Energy Act" or something like that, and every paragraph began, "Anybody who knowingly
or unknowingly has or divulges or even discusses," and ended, "is
punishable by death or twenty years in prison." It was really a very
scary thing.

So I sent them my finished manuscript and then they called me
in, and one of the things they were particularly sensitive about was
anything having to do with Bakelite. They suggested that they would
be most unhappy if I published this information, that it wouldn't be
in the national interest and things like that.

So I took certain things about Bakelite out of the manuscript and
handed those pages over to the Atomic Energy Commission, and
they sealed this file in my presence and put all their stamps on it—
which I signed and they signed—and then they locked it up.

BROOKS BAEKELAND
Had my grandfather known what would evolve from plastics, he
would undoubtedly have withheld his invention—just as I think Einstein might have paused before publishing the 1905 paper on rela-
tivity. Leo Hendrik Baekeland epitomized hope for the human race.
He created himself and he saw no reason why the future could not be
created, too.

## Letter from Leo Hendrik Baekeland to a Friend, January 14, 1934

If I had to live my life over again I would not devote it to develop new industrial processes: I would try to add my humble efforts to use Science to the betterment of the human race.

I despair of the helter-skelter methods of our vaunted homo sapiens, misguided by his ignorance and his politicians. If we continue our ways, there is every possibility that the human race may follow the road of former living races of animals whose fossils proclaim that they were not fit to continue. Religion, laws and morals is not enough. We need more. Science can help us.

### BROOKS BAEKELAND
Had it only been possible for me to have been his son and not his grandson, we two could have taken the world by storm—yes, for we would have pursued the original dreams—dielectrics, textiles, resins, bonding powders for super-strong abrasives and aerodynamic components, molded hulls for boats and . . . but the list is endless. We would not have been able to foresee then the plastic-polluted world that has become such a monstrous joke, the blue plastic bucket and the plastic cups littering the insulted country roadsides—a world whose very destruction, by burning, only pollutes it more. LHB never dreamed of that. He would have recoiled.

## Letter from Antony Baekeland to Miwa Svinka-Zielinski, October 4, 1973

Broadmoor

Dear Miwa—

I am sending you these dreams which I have had during the past few days at Broadmoor:

1. Einstein hides a stop sign from police.
2. I come back to my best friend [Jake Cooper], and we travel the world together. I see a fox eat a squirrel.
3. My grandmother Nina Daly embraces me during a party given by a fellow here and myself. I cut up gobbets of meat.
4. I can fly and go all over the place.
5. I dream I am a successful writer and poet.

I will continue to send you my dreams. There is so little to tell you *except* my dreams. I write them out in the middle of the night—there is no light so sometimes in the morning I have trouble deciphering them.

Love,
Tony

## From "Dreams and Realities," a Lecture Delivered at the Johns Hopkins University by Leo Hendrik Baekeland, October 23, 1931

Youth has many advantages, such as daring, speed of action, and quickness of perception. Intelligence is inborn, and develops by practice and opportunity, knowledge comes quickly to the intelligent; but experience lingers, and is only acquired slowly through life and mistakes.

### CÉLINE ROLL KARRAKER

Grandpapa taught us always to question everything. And he also taught us to recognize the fact that what is true today is not true tomorrow—in science as well as in other things. He loved children, especially as he grew older. He certainly made everything great fun for all of *us*. He would sometimes give out Bakelite things, like pencil cases, and very beautiful Bakelite jewelry that looked like amber. I can remember the gorgeous iridescent colors.

## From English *House & Garden,* October 1981

*Bakelite in the museum.* Everyday objects such as radios and amplifiers, cigarette boxes and soap dishes all look as if they are made in precious tortoise shell, amber, marble, leather and sometimes even in gold. Yet they are all made of Bakelite, that forerunner of plastic which from the twenties to the fifties was all the rage on both sides of the Atlantic.

At the Boymans van Beuningen museum in Rotterdam an industrial product is once again the centre of attention. . . . Three main trends in its use can be identified: the Art Deco style (where it is usually made use of as imitation) in radios and clocks after the Great Paris Exhibition in 1925; in functionalism in objects coming from Germany and the Lowlands and in the "aerodynamic" style of America in the forties and in postwar Europe. In short, a fashion and the symbol of an era.

## From the *Guardian*, June 16, 1983

Apart from the plastic tie-press that spits out your creased cravat as if it were a serpent on heat, the nicest thing about Patrick Cook's Bakelite Museum in London is that he does not take it terribly seriously.

"There is a humorous quality about so much of the Bakelite," he says, fingering a 1950s radio that opens up to reveal a portable vanity case with lights and mirror. "So much of it is a parody. The market in it is very strange. Sometimes I take stalls in the markets and sell things at rock-bottom prices to undercut those dealers who are trying to force the prices up.

"Some of the early Phillips radios go for thousands of pounds, if you can get them. They have almost all been collected out of England into Holland," he shook his head in disbelief. "The prices are very strange. When the Victoria and Albert Museum was setting up their Bakelite show, I let them have some of my early radios for about £30 each—a bargain. . . ."

He began hiring out some of his prize pieces to film and TV period shows like *Pennies from Heaven*, and his Bakelite Museum Society has a TV game called "Spot the Bakelite." They have a Bakelite picnic every other year, lectures, and evenings to swap items and marvel at the invention of Dr. Leo Baekeland.

## From the *New York Times*, "Antiques View," Rita Reif, June 3, 1984

Bakelite. The name summons up a whole mystique of early plastics for Art Deco collectors, producing images of Cubist-styled 1930's jewelry, mock tortoise-shell compacts, ersatz ivory combs, butterscotch-toned desk accessories and what may well be the most glamorous plastics creations of the period—streamlined-styled radios.

There was then, and there is once again, magic in what we call Bakelite radios. When they were new almost a half-century ago, these radios brought into the homes of millions the adventures of Jack Armstrong, the problems of Helen Trent, the jokes of Jack Benny and the nightly news. Now, with nostalgia running high for such vintage wares, the public will have an opportunity to view the most comprehensive display ever mounted of these passports to the past in "The American Radio Show—Bakelite Radios of the 1930's and 1940's," an exhibition opening Wednesday. . . .

## From the Private Diaries of Leo Hendrik Baekeland, October 13, 1909

How few people will realize how much detail had to be gone into before Bakelite was a commercial success!

## From *A Biographical Profile of Leo Hendrik Baekeland,* Carl Kaufmann, Unpublished

Leo Hendrik Baekeland apprenticed in a shoe repair shop, with his father, who was illiterate. His mother also was from a poor family, but she had been a maid and had seen life of families on the other side of the poverty line. She had no interest in having her son grow into a world as impoverished and closed as her own (there was one other child in the family, Rachel, who remained in Belgium all her life) and she looked upon education as his passport.

## From "Dreams and Realities," a Lecture Delivered at the Johns Hopkins University by Leo Hendrik Baekeland, October 23, 1931

My most important discovery at the university was that my senior professor of chemistry had a very attractive daughter. Hence, the usual succession of events.

BROOKS BAEKELAND
Céline Swarts and Leo Hendrik Baekeland were the founders of a
foundered family.

## From *A Biographical Profile of Leo Hendrik Baekeland,* Carl Kaufmann, Unpublished

His personal life had been far from happy since his arrival in the
U.S. Céline had returned to Belgium, at his insistence, for the
birth of their first child. (Jenny, born in 1890, died at the age of
five.) Leo assumed that, because of his modest circumstances,
his wife would be better situated if with her family. However,
after the baby was born, he made no move to bring his wife and
child to America.

Céline begged him to send money for her passage, writing
that her funds were also exhausted, and adding the bitter note
that her own father refused to come to her aid. Leo's letters of
response are not extant, but it is clear from Céline's letters that
he delayed repeatedly, arguing that he could not support a wife
and daughter even if he could raise their passage to New York.
Eventually they were reunited—family records do not specify
when but it appears to have been about 1892—but not before
Céline had been deeply hurt by what she regarded as Leo's lack of
affection. The separation left a wound that never quite closed.
Though Céline remained a dutiful wife, and assisted her husband
in keeping laboratory notes and financial accounts, she built much
of her life around interests of her own, and was frequently separated
from her husband for periods of several months.

## Letter from Céline Baekeland to Leo Hendrik Baekeland, Undated

Dearie—
. . . Every time I am alone, I go back to my own self. It always
takes some time and always takes much sorrow the first week. I
miss you, I miss you dreadfully, then comes the power to crush
that feeling, and unhappily I call forth every reason why I am a
fool, why I should not feel badly, how hard and unkind you are,
etc.—how this is wrong, and I know it, it brings me in a worse

agony yet, and by and by the old Céline pops out, and I long again for you, not for the heartless you, but for everything which is good in you—that is why when we meet we both are good and kind and loving. Now this time I have been more alone than ever, and you might not believe me, but I would not give up my Summer for yours—I have been alone and at perfect peace most of the time.

I have called in you all the good element there is—and I know that when you come back you will be a better man—I certainly am a better woman—and we both ought to have the thought to live the next years in peace and for the best of our children—think of people of our standard and intellect making each other unhappy for no reason whatever! Think of the beautiful life we could have if we both made up our minds to be happy and good to each other—if our lives had for an aim to be as kind to each other as possible. Our unhappiness is in *one* thought, let us tear that thought off and replace it by one of love and of peace.

Yours,
Céline

### *The Creation of the Woman,* a Sanskrit Fable Found in Typewritten Form Among Leo Hendrik Baekeland's Miscellaneous Papers

In the beginning when Twashtri came to the creation of woman, he found that he had exhausted his materials in the making of man and that no solid elements were left. In this dilemma, after profound meditation, he did as follows: He took the rotundity of the moon and the curves of the creepers, and the clinging of tendrils and the trembling of grass, and the slenderness of the reed and the bloom of flowers, and the lightness of leaves and the tapering of the elephant's trunk, and the glances of deer and the blustering of rows of bees, and the joyous gayety of sunbeams and the weeping of clouds, and the fickleness of the winds and the timidity of the hare, and the vanity of the peacock and the softness of the parrot's bosom and the hardness of adamant and the sweetness of honey, and the

cruelty of the tiger and the warm glow of the fire, and the cold-
ness of snow and the chattering of jays, and the cooing of the
kokila, and the hypocrisy of the crane, and the fidelity of the
chakrawska, and compounding all these together he made a
woman and gave her to man.

But after one week, man came to him and said: "Lord, this
creature that You have given me makes my life miserable. She
chatters incessantly and teases me beyond endurance, never
leaving me alone; and she requires incessant attention, and takes
all my time up, and cries about nothing and is always idle, and
so I have come to give her back as I cannot live with her." So
Twashtri said: "Very well," and He took her back. Then after
another week man came to Him and said: "Lord, I find that my
life is very lonely since I gave You back that creature. I remember how she used to dance and sing to me and look at me
out of the corner of her eye, and play with me and cling to me,
and her laughter was music and she was beautiful to look at and
soft to touch, so give her back to me."

So Twashtri said: "Very well," and gave her back. Then after
only three days man came back to Him again and said: "Lord, I
know not how it is, but after all I have come to the conclusion
that she is more of a trouble than a pleasure to me so please take
her back again." But Twashtri said: "Out on you! Be off! I will
have no more of this; you must manage how you can." The
man said: "I cannot live with her." And Twashtri said: "Neither
can you live without her." And He turned His back on man and
went on with His work. Then man said: "What is to be done?
For I cannot live either with her or without her."

## BROOKS BAEKELAND
My grandfather insisted on his own freedom. Most of the year he was
away, somewhere in the world. Yet he adored and admired his wife.
He never used the word "woman" without the prefixal adjective
"silly" in front of it: "sillywoman"—one word. His wife was his one
exception to "sillywoman."

## CÉLINE ROLL KARRAKER
My grandmother started something in Yonkers—Prospect House. It
was a settlement-house-type place for children whose parents were

working in the factories there. As Grandmother said, "The children come after school to be bathed, fed, and to have their talents encouraged." Grandmother always believed in a good meal and a bath!

She was a vegetarian, and a theosophist for many many years, and she brought to this country Indian gurus. And Grandpapa hated all of that. He was a real atheist—he didn't like anything that had to do with anything religious, he didn't like that at all. And then the funny thing was that Grandmother finally went to India and when she came back she stopped being a vegetarian, she quit theosophy, she would have nothing to do with gurus anymore—she was horrified by what she had seen in India. She thought, "If that's the way it is there, if that's what their religion has done for them . . ."

### DR. FREDERICK BAEKELAND

I had a lot of contact with my grandmother over the years, as everyone in the family did. She was a very matriarchal person, rather controlling in some ways but extremely generous also. She was an extraordinary person. She started to paint rather late, at the age of fifty. She was sort of an Impressionist. She studied with Hobart Nichols—which was quite a good thing—and she had a couple of shows.

As a young woman she almost became a concert pianist, but she could never play the piano when Grandpapa was home because he didn't want to be disturbed. He often worked in the house, this sort of old-fashioned house along the Hudson River. It had a tower and that's where his study was and he would sort of secrete himself up there. My contacts with him were extremely limited—I personally spent maybe three times with my grandfather when I was a child. Once he took me into his lab, which was on the property, and electroplated some pennies with mercury for me, and another time he took me up to his study and gave me a scarab. I had it for years and later lost it.

### BROOKS BAEKELAND

I once asked my Aunt Nina, my father's sister, what it had been like, really, growing up at Snug Rock, my grandparents' house in Yonkers. Such a question to my father would not have been thinkable. Her reply startled me: "Shhhh! The Doctor is working."

## CÉLINE ROLL KARRAKER

My grandmother often played the piano for us on Sunday, after lunch, and Grandpapa would just go someplace else. Later I read somewhere that as a young man he used to go to concerts when he was visiting different places. This surprised me because I always felt he was so anti-music. Yet he did go to concerts by himself—you know, alone. I think there was real rivalry between my grandparents.

## BROOKS BAEKELAND

One of my grandmother's teachers was Edward McDowell, a famous concert pianist. He wanted her to "go public"—how vulgar that phrase sounds, even now—that is, give public recitals, be a professional. This was nixed by my grandfather and always grudged against him by my grandmother.

She loved playing the unplayable pieces of Liszt, but her heart was with Debussy, Fauré, Ravel, and Chopin. When I had grown up enough to read poetry and understand women—and understood the passionately unslaked nature of my grandmother as it was revealed to me at her Steinway grand—there was a phrase that always used to come into my mind, particularly when she was playing one of Chopin's celestial nocturnes: "A savage place! as holy and enchanted as e'er beneath a waning moon was haunted by woman wailing for her demon-lover!"

When my grandmother sat with her head bowed—not in benediction—before her piano and then started to play, I often felt tears come to my eyes, especially when she was very old and her playing was full of faults. As a child I made her play and play and play, and repeat and repeat, and play again and again. In my ears the sounds she made were like those of gold coins falling into a chest to a miser.

But my grandfather could not stand her music—that "noise"—and her theosophy, suffragettism, the Prospect House with Harry Hopkins, later an FDR *eminence grise*, and suchlike "nonsense." Nor, she had more than once hinted to me, the fact that her French was better than his and that she sometimes disagreed with him. His German was of course better, and this was part of a Teutonic-Latin tension between them. He had married far above himself socially in marrying her—and never quite forgave her that. We know practically nothing about his own family because he was ashamed of them. His father was an alcoholic who ended up—sometimes—repairing shoes, and he from the age of twelve was, according to my grandmother, the main support for his whole family. That he was a genius there is no doubt—and that he had the most tremendous motivations. That he had adored his mother, though he would never speak of her—or of any of his family—that is not generally known. He simply obliterated the past. There had been no past. Time had started with him. Baekeland time, that is. That is the Zeus of those turn-of-the-century photos, the stern, tall man with the beard. Zeus.

It was an amused old Pan that I knew as a boy. I imply no sexuality, only humor, *joie de vivre*, a love of wine and endless—his own—talk. The man who not only would not suffer fools gladly but not at all. The man who stopped people from kissing, giving them a vivid description of the Niagaras of filth in the forms of bacteria and viruses that they were transferring to each other's foolish mouths. The man who lectured "sillywomen" about the constituents of their lipsticks and creams and the sucker's prices they foolishly paid for them—all this with the highest and most godly good humor.

### CÉLINE ROLL KARRAKER

Grandpapa would take us up to his lab and he'd put various chemicals together and make colors or sweeteners. It was very exciting to go up there. And the smells! I can smell them to this day.

The house is gone now. It burned. But it hasn't burned in my memory. It was idyllic to be there. A wonderful haven for all of the children.

There was an incredible bathroom. It was huge. And from the middle of the wall up was a relief of cattails and ferns and birds and it was all colors and was absolutely beautiful. And there was a stained-glass window as well. And in the corner was a square sunken bathtub. And we kids would go in there and make up a batch of soapy suds. We'd go from one part of the bathroom which was all tile and zoom across the floor into the tub, splashing. Grandmother used to say this was Grandpapa's bathtub and we were not to do that.

### From *I Knew a Phoenix: Sketches for an Autobiography*, May Sarton, W. W. Norton, New York, 1959

How imaginative it was of the Baekelands—for the Belgian inventor and his wife were our hosts—to insist that Mother and I come to them first, and be cherished and spoiled a little before the serious business of our new life was attempted. Their house, rustic stone and brown shingles, with its turrets and verandas, its stained-glass windows, its large portecochere in front, and all surrounded by expanses of clipped lawn, seemed to me very grand. It had, for instance, a polar bear rug in the drawing room. What luxury to compare with that of sitting on a polar bear's head! It also had a square glass aquarium, in which lived a small, wicked alligator who devoured raw meat and looked at me with indifferent, beady eyes. The real glory was the master bathroom with its huge bathtub. A bathtub? Rather, a tiled swimming pool, six feet square and sunk two feet into the floor. Around it lay huge sponges from Florida, and shells with rosy mouths that sang of a faraway ocean. In this bathtub, one could be a seal or a mermaid with no trouble. . . .

I never did feel Dr. Baekeland as a person I knew; rather he seemed to be some frightening masculine force—a god who must be placated, a piece of weather. I realize now that, with his fierce, shy eyes and black mustache, he looked something like Rudyard Kipling; and I realize now, too late, that, though I was frightened of him, he took me into his heart and really loved me in the admiring way of a grandfather with a first grandchild, for he used to come in after I was asleep and look down at me tenderly, and he was amazed that I could play so happily alone. But then, I fear, all I wanted was to run off and be free to go to [the chauffeur's] house where I felt more at home. On my way there I passed the garage, and above it, I had been told, was the laboratory, a very secret and important place where Dr. Baekeland retired to work like a sorcerer, and no one was ever allowed to go. There he was busy concocting queer things in trays, rather like today's ice-cube trays, but the cubes were of a hard yellow translucent material, no good as toys, though he gave me some one day—no good for anything as far as I could see. The name of this invention was Bakelite, still in an experimental stage, and not yet the fabulous djinni it would become. . . .

[Dr. Baekeland's wife] was known to everyone as Bonbon, a name so appropriate that it must have been used by St. Peter at the gate of Heaven, for kindness flowed from her in every sort and size of package, tangible and intangible. Her presence was a present. A small, round woman with bright, dark eyes under a

mass of fuzzy gray hair, she wore for as long as I can remember
the same round beaver hat and long beaver scarf over a suit she
had recopied exactly every year. She could not have worn the
beaver hat in summer, yet I see her so clearly in this hat and no
other that she must be painted in it here. She came from an
intellectual bourgeois family in Ghent, very much like my father's, but now she had moved into a different world, she had
not changed. It was only that riches became her so well, as if
she had always been intended to be a fairy godmother; she had
the rare gift of transforming money into joy, her own joy and
everyone else's, so there was no bitterness in it. Some of this I
came to know later, but from the beginning she had my un-
wavering devotion because I sensed in her a dimension like
saintliness, like poetry, which set her apart. Concrete evidence
of this was the fact that because of her feeling for animals she
would eat no meat. I loved animals, too, and even made re-
solves to follow her example, but then when everyone else at
table except Bonbon accepted the breast of chicken or young
lamb, apparently without a qualm, I forgot my resolve.
. . . Bonbon did not blame us cruder beings, nor make us feel
guilty; that was her triumph. When she and I sat shelling new
peas from the garden on the back veranda . . . I felt a wonderful sense of security and something like being at home, at least
for a little while. I could talk to her, I found. . . . I loved her
Belgian accent, the way she said "Meerses" instead of "Mrs.,"
an accent that gave character to everything she said. She was
very American in her lavishness, but she was also still so Belgian
and so unsophisticated that she was, as I see it now, the perfect
bridge from my Belgium to my America.

New York with Bonbon was Fifth Avenue, the Flatiron Building, Woolworth's (at that time still *the* skyscraper), and she had
the newcomer's pride and delight in the city, as if, almost, it had
been her own creation. . . . And New York was the Plaza Hotel
where we had tea among the palms, and ate little many-colored
iced cakes, while, at Bonbon's request, the orchestra played a
soulful rendition of the "Song of the Volga Boatman," and were
rewarded with a crisp ten-dollar bill taken over to them on a
silver plate. Perhaps I loved her so much because her taste remained the taste of a child, and her love of life, her excitement
(as years later when she waved her hand at all of Yonkers glitter-

ing with electric lights and said proudly, "Every one of those light bulbs has Bakelite in it") was as innocent as a child's.

## Céline Roll Karraker

My grandmother told me she cried for five years in French when she came here to live, and she went back to Belgium whenever she could. My grandfather did exactly the opposite. She never lost her accent. He lost his as fast as he could and named his son George Washington Baekeland.

When he sold Velox to Eastman Kodak, he bought Snug Rock for my grandmother, but he resented the socializing that went on in it. He didn't want any part of that.

## From the Private Diaries of Leo Hendrik Baekeland, April 27, 1907

The complications of our unnecessarily complicated living irritate me. If I could do without inconveniencing my wife I certainly would go and live somewhere where we could dispense with servants and lead a simpler and more natural life. But my wife cannot live without some so-called "Society," a stupid conventionalism and the cause of all our unwarranted conventional and complicated living. What do we want such a large house for, and why all these servants? Why all that complicated trash of unnecessary furniture? All this complication becomes more and more irksome to me. Trash—vulgar—idiotic— trash.

## Céline Roll Karraker

Grandpapa was a great proponent of the simple life—physically. Lived it himself. In fact, my grandmother said—and you know, she believed in reincarnation—that he was a monk in his former life! After he retired he lived down in Florida, in a very simple house.

## Brooks Baekeland

The Anchorage in Coconut Grove had belonged to William Jennings Bryan, "the Great Commoner," and my grandfather used to crow with delight in telling the Victorian elite who dined with him that

"that great bag of wind did not have a single book in his house except a Bible!"

The plantation-style house was deliciously cool—made of blocks of pure-white coral and terra-cotta roofs. Its windows in winter were always open, as were its doors, and its greatest charm was a central patio, hung with orchids. It had a fountain jetting high in its center. There was an aquamarine swimming pool at the front of the house, where one "bathed," not "swam." But what I remember now, when I close my eyes, is the perfume of the flowering trees and that so-characteristic soft interminable clack-clack-clack of coconut palm fronds, day and night—it never stopped—and the windjammer-creakings of the great bamboo groves from Sumatra, towering to one hundred and fifty feet, down near the anchorage itself, which had been made for my grandfather's yacht, the *Ion.* By day the wind blew in over the sea, and by night it blew out again.

Our nearest neighbors were, through a narrow jungle to the north, the Mathiesons of Olin Mathieson Chemical—lovely people—who owned the uninhabited offshore island which was then a coconut plantation which faced us and them about a mile away and was later made famous, or infamous, by Nixon and his pal Rebozo; and, to the south, the Thomas Fortune Ryans, who built a rococo Italian palace, in bad taste. The Anchorage was a simple, lovely place. As was Coconut Grove itself. There was no tourism then, there was no fear and there was no disgust.

### CÉLINE ROLL KARRAKER

Grandpapa lived in that house in a very very simple way. He lived there alone for six months of the year. My grandmother joined him for a couple of months in the winter.

He ate everything out of a can—without heating it! He used to say to us, "Children, this is the best way of all," and he'd open a can of Campbell's split-pea soup and put a little seawater in it and stir it up, and then he'd eat it. Then he'd open up a can of sardines and eat that. And then there was the first instant coffee at that time, called George Washington, and he'd put that in hot water and drink it.

He had no servants, except outdoor people. He adored botany. He was a close friend of the great botanist David Fairchild. He and my grandfather planted the place with all kinds of wonderful plants. We children could pull fruit right off the trees!

## PATRICIA GREENE

Barbara and Brooks, before they moved to that penthouse on Seventy-fifth Street, lived two houses down from us on Seventy-first Street, and little Tony was a little younger than one of our sons and a little older than the other—an enchanting child, very elflike—and he used to come around and play in a very imaginative way. He was very very fond of natural history, and actually, one of the nicest stories about Barbara, who was a beautiful woman—a mischievous look in her eye!—was that when Tony was a baby, I think it was probably during World War Two, she was down in Florida with him and some great naturalist was there and said to her, "Oh that lovely little child. Don't give him any toys to play with, let him play with nature," so she did. And instead of playing with building blocks and trucks and things, he grew up playing with rocks and sticks and mosses and frogs and crickets.

## BROOKS BAEKELAND

David Fairchild. "The aged angel," I used to call him. He always allowed me to come up to his laboratory at the Kampong, his house in Coconut Grove, and interrupt him. I used to walk there all by myself—he lived about two miles away. For me he was a kindly, playful, learned, imaginative human being with a kind of beauty in him that suggested something holy, not Christly but Pythagorean. He was also of course a famous host to all the world's great; everyone in the world came to his house.

He used to like to see how much information I could hold in my head. His own theory, which I was offered at the dining-room table at The Anchorage, was that one could remember fifty-five thousand different species but not more. I remember the Nobelist Dr. Muller was having dinner with us that night. When I was a little boy, I thought that "doctor" simply meant someone who was a man and who had white hair, since all the men I met who had white hair were Doctor something or other—when I was a little boy. When LHB and David Fairchild were together, the talk was all of enzymes. How far ahead of their times those two giants were!

## CÉLINE ROLL KARRAKER

Grandpapa never wore real shoes. He always wore sneakers, white sneakers. He just thought they were sensible and cheap. So he was an individualist and a character. I have a picture of him and Mark Twain all in white, because that was what Mark Twain wore, too.

Grandpapa was always in white, everywhere, no matter what time of year it was. He used to go to the Chemists' Club and the University Club in those white sneakers.

In Florida Grandpapa wore white ducks and a white shirt with his white sneakers. And when he got hot, he'd walk right into the swimming pool—with all his clothes on! And then walk out of the pool, saying, "This is the way to keep cool. The evaporation keeps you cool."

And this physically very simple kind of life was carried even to the house in Yonkers. We'd all be at Snug Rock for a lovely traditional Sunday dinner and he would have his instant coffee and his Campbell's soup and his can of sardines served to him on a Bakelite tray, right at the table with everybody else.

### ELIZABETH ARCHER BAEKELAND

A couple of summers ago I went to Block Island to see Brooks. His cousin Céline Karraker had told me he was spending the summer there, and I just arrived. I was afraid he'd flee if I told him I was coming—he's strange that way. I went to the house he was renting and walked right in. I had heard he was having an affair with some woman from New York who had divorced her husband for him, so I asked him about that right away. And he said, "She was such a good cook we used to have to spend two hours every day shopping and then two hours preparing the food and then we'd eat for another hour and then, because I don't want to be a male chauvinist pig, *I'd* wash the dishes and there'd be ten dishes and five pans, and I just got so sick of the whole thing I finally threw her out." I said, "Who cooks for you now?" And he said, "Simple—Sunday I have a pound of hamburger, Monday I have a pound of potatoes, Tuesday I have a pound of spinach, and so on. So I have *one* dish, *one* pot, *one* pan."

### BROOKS BAEKELAND

I am a man of very simple tastes. My mother calls me a monk. Some of my peculiar habits now—unhabits, in fact—make me think of my grandfather as I knew him in my boyhood. LHB kept only one "business" suit. I haven't even got one. Three years ago I discovered that I had fifteen shirts—I threw away ten of them; that I had ten handkerchiefs—I threw away eight of them; eight pair of shorts—I threw away five of them; umpteen trousers—I kept two; umpteen-plus sweaters—I kept three . . . and so on.

I said LHB kept only one business suit. But there's the story my grandmother used to tell about how she finally tricked him into buying a new dark blue suit. This story involves a neighbor of theirs in Yonkers, the famous lawyer Samuel Untermeyer, who lived on a very pretentious estate to the north. LHB held him in scorn as a lawyer—as he did all lawyers, calling them jackals and hyenas. The Untermeyer estate was full of copies of Greek statues and picturesque Greek ruins and Greco-Roman terracing. It was ridiculed by LHB.

Well, one day in Yonkers my grandmother saw a shop that sold men's clothes. She went in and made a deal with the owner, after she had selected and bought an expensive blue serge suit of LHB's size for—let us say—one hundred and twenty-five dollars. The deal was that the owner was to show it in the window for twenty-five dollars but not to "sell" it to anyone but LHB, who, of course, he knew of— people today have no idea how famous LHB once was. Then at dinner that night my grandmother told my grandfather that she had seen a beautiful suit of imported English serge selling for twenty-five dollars. "Oh, no, Céline—maybe one hundred and twenty-five but not twenty-five. There you have made a mistake."

"No mistake, dearie—twenty-five," she insisted.

And so they argued. They even made a bet.

The next night LHB arrived home crowing with delight. When he could stop laughing, he explained how he had just "done in" that old Shylock Sam Untermeyer. LHB had gotten off the train from New York and gone directly to the shop, where he had seen the suit, seen that my grandmother had been right, and bought it. On the way home to Snug Rock, he had fallen in with Sam Untermeyer, shown him the suit, and sold it to him for seventy-five dollars!

I remember how my grandfather used to come to wake me up before sunrise in those early Florida years, give me a boiled egg and a hybridized grapefruit taken off one of his own trees—and then lead me out in the still-sleeping dewy dawn to see the rabbits and land crabs. Coconut Grove was still very wild in those days; the roads were all of crushed white coral.

Imagine an old man in loose, white, unpressed, probably mildewed cottons, a long shirt over them, and one of those still-worn white-cotton, crushable sailing caps, and a mousy-haired boy, his small, grubby hand in the baseball-mitt-sized big one of LHB, both of them talking continuously, neither listening to the other, and heading for a sail in the dinghy to Mathieson Island.

On the way the small boy learned all about outriggers, centerboards, sideboards, Medusas, man-o'-war birds, the main sorts of ocean waves—surficial and bottom-resonant—the prediction of weather from cloud formations, the various ways to treat snake bite, and—"But, Grandpapa, we have forgotten to bring our lunch!"— answered by Pan's chuckle: "The best lunch you will ever have awaits you. The sea gives it to us."

In the bottom of the tiny boat was a machete, and it was with this that LHB showed me how to open coconuts and husk them and then pierce two of their three eyes to get the delicious milk. We ate coconut meat, crabs, tropical oysters, sour oranges, and the orange hearts of sea urchins.

He never stopped talking, telling me the Latin names of the plants—many of which he had introduced from his travels all over the world—and the insects and birds and mammals, saying it was just as easy to learn a name that was the same anywhere as one that changed from language to language and country to country—which is, of course, why Tony knew as a small child the Latin names of so many things, for I continued with him LHB's practice. From the time Tony started talking, which was early, I decided to give him the Latin names, when I knew them, for plants and animals. By the time he was ten he could read, understand, and remember the contents of texts like Buchsbaum's *Animals Without Backbones*. That was the beginning of a lifelong intellectual bond between Tony and me. And it was not just intellectual and bookish but field-explorative.

### ELIZABETH BLOW

If you saw Tony with Brooks, I don't think you would connect the fact by looks that they were related. He had Barbara's brown eyes and her red hair. He was just a marvelous-looking little boy. And at four years old he was already constantly prowling around and investigating insects and birds—he had a natural instinct for creatures of this earth. He knew all about them and he could be very instructive. I'll never forget the marvelous remark he made to me one afternoon. He said, "B-Betty"—he stammered, you know—"did you know that b-b-butterflies have . . ." I can't remember for the *life* of me what it was, it was some special thing that butterflies have—and it was something that I didn't know. I quoted it for years because it always amused me so. It was that slight stutter, the combination of the "B-Betty" and the "b-b-butterflies" and the actually hard information which he proffered to me.

## From a Psychiatric Report on Antony Baekeland Ordered by the British Courts, January 5, 1973

I examined Antony Baekeland on January 3, 1973, and read the depositions and reports from five psychiatrists who have seen him at different periods. The history based on these reports is that Baekeland is an American subject, an only child brought up with his parents in New York till about eleven. His father is "a brilliant wealthy man who has never actually done any productive work though he made one expedition to South America and wrote an article about it," and "charming but capable of no warmth to support his son." The mother (the victim) was "an hysterical, narcissistic, and impulsive woman, quite incapable of giving a child the minimum of maternal security." She was a great beauty and an accomplished artist. He suffered "marked deprivation of love from both parents, and was exposed to excessive intellectual stimulation beyond his capacity to absorb."

### BROOKS BAEKELAND
Psychiatrists—who are professionally amoral—never understood my reluctance to enthuse about their abracadabra. They were interested in their tricks, and in drugs to numb rage, while in Tony I clearly saw the play of Good and Evil. That was a question not only about him but about a whole generation.

## From "Dreams and Realities," a lecture Delivered at the Johns Hopkins University by Leo Hendrik Baekeland, October 23, 1931

A large part of the tragedy of the human race is caused by the fact that it is well-nigh impossible to transmit fully to others our reactions about the mistakes we committed in our younger years. So we see each succeeding generation ever ready to commit the same blunders over again, and suffer by it.

### BROOKS BAEKELAND
I remember the hold of my grandfather's large, soft hand, and the rich flow of humor and information that never stopped pouring out

of him during our walks those educative, garrulous, affectionate mornings, while the house and the village still slept and only we two were awake and aware of it.

On our returns, with the sun up and the house awake, he would disappear—where, a small boy did not know. It was to study, I now know. I later discovered that whenever he stood—he always seemed to be standing—leafing through some large tome, he was not leafing. He was reading every single word. He had remained a European and an intellectual.

## From the Private Diaries of Leo Hendrik Baekeland, April 20, 1907

In the evening read "On the Danger of Overspecialization" at Anvil Club. Had a lively discussion afterwards on such subjects as morals, religion, ancient literature. I introduced my conception of morality based on reason and the conception of the big universal Ego and universal consciousness as opposed to the little Ego as conceived by the average man. The higher love as opposed to the little or partial (particularist?) love which dwarfs our conception of equity and justice and develops selfishness and fear and makes us question immortality because we commit ourselves too much as individuals and not enough as part of the big Ego. The latter conception sweeps away all thoughts of mortality and makes us a little ingredient of that sublime and universal Ego.

BROOKS BAEKELAND
From his most profound beliefs my grandfather despised publicity, money, fashion, sensation, exploitation, and all the people whose lives were dedicated to such. He was an idealist, a feudal-socialist, a radical theorist, an antimaterialist millionaire. All this was in the same curious spirit as his benefactions during the Depression, such as I got a hint of once when I was with him at the Chemists' Club. He had gone somewhere—to pee? to buttonhole a colleague?—and a sandy-haired, middle-aged man came up to me and asked me who I was. When I told him, he said, "No one will ever know how many of us your grandfather brought through the Depression or what would have happened to us without him." He said this to me very emo-

tionally. I had never heard of this. I asked my grandmother later. She had never known, either. And this was the man in sneakers and one suit who was known as a miser!

He was a benefactor by impulse: utterly without cynicism, without regard to self. Victorians—especially Victorians of his class, the academics—believed in Man and Family. They never doubted Life's purposes.

My real education began at the example and from the words of my Belgian grandparents, who were not unsusceptible to Honor but tended to deride it in its social, self-lauding, self-loving forms—the forms *we* all in fact love so much. Because we love ourselves?

My grandfather, in particular, held all that mutual backslapping in ridicule—despite his own multiple honors, at the reception of each of which he always let the side down by saying it was all due to "luck" and his "marvelous wife." How could he say: "due to my genius and your ridiculous system of self-congratulation"?

The academic class in Europe that my Baekeland grandparents came from put very high value on nonmaterialistic achievements. It despised show. It despised the accumulation of money and power. In the nineteenth century the European university world considered itself—and was considered—an aristocracy. In its heart it put itself above royalty, and did so without any hesitation whatever! It was guilty of an almost monastic pride, and its scientific members put Truth, *the* Truth, above Man—or any man.

So, from those two immigrants—totally out of phase with a society given over *entirely* to show, power, and gain, all of which they soon had, too, almost automatically, due to "luck" and LHB's "marvelous wife," of course—I learned everything, early.

Their only son, my father—George Washington Baekeland—was entirely the opposite. As was my first, ambitious, beautiful, backgroundless wife, Barbara.

SYLVIE BAEKELAND SKIRA
Brooks admired the way his grandfather and grandmother had led sort of separate lives—but in harmony, because they had similar values. Perhaps this was something he missed, because certainly he couldn't have done that with Barbara, ever.

## Letter from Leo Hendrik Baekeland to Professor Camiel De Bruyne, University of Ghent, Belgium, August 27, 1931

Dear Friend De Bruyne:

My wife, who is at present with our whole family in the Adirondacks, feels as if she were in the "Seventh Heaven"! One of the sketches which she painted last year during a short visit to Bruges has been selected as a front cover for the latest number of the *Literary Digest*, one of our best known publications—I am mailing you a copy.

It is a great honor for an amateur; an honor even much sought after by professional artists; because there is always an abundant choice amongst the many offered sketches. I should mention that when her painting was selected, none in the Literary Digest organization knew who Céline Baekeland was. I have reason to doubt whether even today they know it—and she got paid for it, too!

The reason why I write you on this occasion is that when I saw the issue with the sketch, it evoked times long gone by, when you and I walked over that same little bridge, when we were both at the beginning of our career, colleagues at the same Normal School. Could I have imagined then that some time I was to raise a family here, and that I was to have this thrill in seeing the picture of that same bridge published here, painted by the daughter of my former professor, who was to become my wife, as well as mother and grandmother of a new clan in America . . .

Cordially yours,
L. H. Baekeland

## From the "Very Truly Yours" Column, Helen Muir, *Miami Herald*, January 18, 1940

Céline Baekeland is well-known as a painter and Dr. Baekeland, whom Miami claims as one of its distinguished citizens, is very proud of her accomplishments. "She rarely sells a painting; she likes to give them away. But she is naturally proud of the prizes

she has received," he declares, from the terrace of "The Anchorage," his bayfront home in Coconut Grove. In his study is a
painting his wife did for him of a scene in Sleepy Hollow Cemetery in Westchester County, New York. He chuckles as he explains it is his future burial place.

## BROOKS BAEKELAND

LHB died in 1944. He had been greatly gaga for several years—senile
dementia, taking sometimes violent forms as the oxygen and glycogen
were gradually starved from that massive brain. In his middle or late
seventies he no longer always liked it when I asked him specific questions. He would reply testily, "It is not polite to ask me such questions as the name of some exotic hybrid now. Old men's memories
fail." Or he would upbraid me for standing in front of him with my
legs apart—done, though he did not realize it, to shorten my six feet
four to a more agreeable height, he being just under six feet—by
saying, "You don't have to emphasize your height like that!" His
temper worsened, and I think his loneliness—of which state I was
already a precocious sufferer myself—was almost intolerable for the
simple reason that not even delivery boys and Pullman Car porters
would listen to him anymore. Shall I talk of loneliness? Of the loneliness of *that* kind of greatness? In the end he became a pathetic, a
tragic figure, and had to be sent away from home to be "taken care
of." He was violent long before he died, of the final massive cerebral
hemorrhage.

During World War Two, when he was very old and already quite
dotty and I was a trainee Aircraftsman Second Class— nothing
lower!—I called Snug Rock to ask my grandmother if I could come
and crouch there for my forty-eight-hour leave. My grandfather answered and said that my grandmother was in Florida but that I must
come anyway, he needed my help. It was an order: I was to come at
the swiftest.

Now, I loved my grandmother more than anyone I had ever loved
but this time my motive for wanting to come to Yonkers involved a
girl with a divine body, long red hair, green eyes, a taste for Richard
Strauss, and whose father was a football coach. So I said, "Yes,
Grandpapa." I knew Dick the chauffeur's number, called him, and
had him pick me up at the station.

My grandfather immediately made me privy to his problem. In
fact, he had two problems. The first he did not know but I recog-

nized immediately—he had gone over the edge since I had last seen him—and I wondered: "Who is taking care of him? This is dangerous." The second problem was the following: He had just arrived from Florida, he had four heavy suitcases with him, and they were all locked and he had no key.

What he had done is lock the first case, put the key in the second, lock the second, put the key in the third, lock the third—and so on. You see, in that way, you did not have *four* bulky keys in your pocket but only *one*. But he had lost that one! He was in despair.

I was not his grandson for nothing. "Are there any other keys in the house?" I asked him.

"I don't know," he said.

So we went looking, and of course we finally found a huge ball of keys all snarled together, for every good old house has one—keys that no one knows the origin or the function of anymore but that no one dares throw away.

Do not forget that he was talking the whole time, perhaps telling me how he had just escaped with his life from the head-hunting Dayaks in the Sunda Straits in 1913 or about the famous oral exam that he and some colleagues had trained one of their dear but, alas, nitwit friends to pass, and how the friend, asked to explain the polarization of light—a question they had not trained him for, deeming it too abstract for his limited brains—had cleared his throat and said, "Messieurs, in order to explain to you how light is polarized, I must first describe to you the principle of the suction pump"—a question they *had* trained him for. And with that bunch of keys, as I was saying, I began to try, Edison-like, the six thousand possibilities. Of course, I soon got all the suitcases open, to my grandfather's *fervent* joy.

And what was in those four suitcases? Books, papers, diaries, notebooks, checkbooks, manuscripts. He had forgotten to pack *clothes!*

Now, to me this was not just a sign of senility, but an indication of his lifelong priorities. And you may imagine what a great woman it took to wife a man like that and keep her good humor.

I was overwhelmed with pity and so I started unpacking for him, hoping to find at least a pair of pajamas and a toothbrush somewhere in all that incunabula. Nothing. Not a handkerchief.

What I found that startled me was literally dozens of pocket checkbooks from different banks all over America. Ten would not have attracted my attention. There must have been fifty or more, maybe a hundred. As I remember, one suitcase was full of nothing else.

"What are *these*, Grandpapa?"

He chuckled. "Banks," he explained, "are insolvent."

When he saw my puzzled expression, he went on. "They lend money they have not got—that is, they give credit without backing. In fact, they are all bankrupt."

I was still looking puzzled.

"The backing is the depositors' money, but the loans they make are many times, often ten times that. It's a fraud. As long as the depositors don't know and as long as the debtors pay their debts, the banks make money—other people's money, of course—and the banks are called 'solvent.' It should not be allowed. It is highly dangerous. In fact, there is not a solvent bank in the United States."

Poor old man, I was thinking.

"So," he went on, "I play the numbers." He giggled. "I spread the risk. I keep money in banks all over the United States instead of in just one or two where a run of a few days during a panic could wipe me out."

Senile. I offered him the loan of my pajamas. "Healthier," he said, "to sleep naked." He always had. Goodnight. He had some reading to do. *I* had a long, cool, green-eyed girl to see, but of course it would not have done to tell him. He was, as I said, one of the last great Victorians.

But the memory I treasure is this. When I got back, at three a.m. to Snug Rock, afoot—it was not far—I found the house hermetically sealed. I had forgotten my dear grandfather's growing paranoia. I tried every door, every window, every crack—it might have been Castle Bodiam. I was humiliated to think I could not scheme *some* way into that ancestral home. My mind set to working. I would not admit defeat; it was not theoretically possible—whatever I, Brooks Baekeland, wanted, I, Brooks Baekeland, could and would discover a way to get. It was an almost Mosaic law.

But in fact, there was no way short of storming that would let me in. So, just as the first birds were all singing grand opera, making promises too grand to keep, I lay me down on a wicker sofa on the porch facing the Hudson River and the majestic Palisades on the other side—it was a warm July night—and, with a perfectly bad— that is, good—conscience, I fell asleep.

The next thing I knew, the door from the dining room opened and there was Grandpapa looking at me.

"I'm sorry," I said, as I got up and brushed back my hair. "I got back late and didn't want to disturb you."

I had not a clue as to how he might react to this development. What he did was to give me a discourse on the climbing vine called wisteria, genus Wisteria, named after Charles Wistar, an American anatomist who had died in 1818, and which had been developed into I forget how many hybrids by the Dutchman Claus something-or-other into however many varieties, of which this one on our porch was . . . "Would you like to take a bath?" he finally asked. "We will be served breakfast in half an hour." "Thank you, sir," I said.

That was the last time I saw my grandfather alive.

I do not mean that it was on the porch at Snug Rock that I last saw him alive. I was with him all that day and the next, alone—mostly in his laboratory, where he talked to me about his student years and gave me a sample of a "synthetic" beer he had made—it was not bad—or in his wine cellar, where he gave me samples of the very strong Sauternes he also made. He spoke to me about my grandmother as the very model of virtue, as someone we—the grandchildren—should forever appreciate and honor. I was deeply touched by this, since they had never been able to live together for more than a few days at a time, so that we had only seen them together at Christmas or Easter.

He talked to me also of China and Japan—of Taisho, Emperor Hirohito's father, who had honored him for creating the first Western industry in Japan—the Japanese Bakelite Corporation. And about Theodore Roosevelt and his beautiful daughter, Alice. And about Harding and Coolidge. But mostly about TR, who he said was the greatest man America had produced after Washington and Jefferson.

His love of and his reverence for America—what it symbolized more than what it was—was the classic immigrant's, which was why he had named his son after George Washington. "A nigger name," my father growled, and never used the "Washington." I always felt I was not his son. My genes told me that I was my grandmother's.

My grandmother was all to me: teacher, protector, guide—indeed, what any true mother is to any son. There are several basic sorts of women, and their mixtures: mother-woman, sister-woman, child-woman, mistress-woman, wife-woman. My grandmother was mother-woman.

Our minds, hers and mine, were in tune. So were our spirits, in both of which was the same Gallic naughtiness and humor. She loved wit and gaiety, those French virtues, and she herself had them in full measure.

She was attracted to me not only as a mother but as any woman is to an electric young man. We were like lovers. We met always as man and woman. That was our power. It enabled us to see instantly to the heart of things together. I was for my grandmother the surrogate for the missing, vanished, voyaging, discoursing Leo Hendrik Baekeland. I was the young Leo she had loved. He, Odysseus, was gone. I was Telemachus. Even as a young man I was aware of the sexual danger of that transference.

And we became even closer upon her coming death—I mean more aware of what we meant to each other, before a series of hammerlike strokes silenced her forever—not, oh not, quite. When she said to me one day, out of one of our long silences together, "Thank you for existing," she said to me all that *I* felt, too—and all that I mean when I speak about family and what I call "inheritance," not necessarily money but that duty and that deep sentiment we should all feel, upwards and downwards in our continuities. I do deeply believe in inheritance, which in my mind goes mystically *both* ways.

We Baekelands are a powerful race. Did you know that the name is famous in Belgium less even than for the great LHB than for the family of robbers who were all captured together and hanged during the Spanish Occupation—a father and his four sons? Whenever I go to Belgium and my name is seen on my passport, those lovely fools, if it is after their lunch and they are feeling cheery, stagger back and make wild gestures of self-defense, crying, "Les Baekelands! Les Baekelands!" That great robber family is a national myth. There is violence in my genetic past. I am not sure that anyone else in our family knows about this infamous descent. My beloved grandmother told me. She told me everything.

She died in 1957. The contents of Snug Rock were legally—by her will—up for grabs, starting on a certain date. Everything in the house was tagged—furniture, paintings, rugs, anything of "value."

I had always had a Prince Hal–Falstaff relationship with my grandmother's servants—gardeners, chauffeurs, caretakers, cooks, chambermaids, etc. I was living then on Seventy-first Street, in a house my grandmother had bought and allowed me to live in while I was doing graduate work at Columbia, and when I wished to wash my extremely fast Mercedes-Benz, I would motor up to Snug Rock and visit a bit with the chauffeur and his sister or with the gardener and his wife, who plied me with pasta and *vino rosso* and terrible jokes and that marvelous kind of Italian love that adopts all children—they still treated me like a child. My jokes were worse than theirs.

It was a hot summer day. The gardener gave me a key. I wandered through the rooms, remembering. Both my grandparents were dead. Snug Rock had been left to their daughter. There is a housing development there now, I am told.

I took my time. I spent many long minutes in each room and passage, remembering and trying to learn *something*, wanting—always—to know who I was and why. Why, I kept feeling, have you left me alone? I finally understood that that was not my question. The real question was: What was to become of this whole world now that the marvelous, strong, innocent idealism of the Victorians was gone? I thought of Rome, of the Gracchi—the sundering. And of course I wandered through the empty greenhouses, the dusty laboratory, and down through the grape arbors and vineyards, and—pensively—all through the now ruined gardens.

And, back in the house, I finally climbed up to the tower.

What was my amazement! All the great portraits—engravings a meter high by half a meter wide, matted and framed in their gilded wood—of the illuminati of Heidelberg, Tübingen, Bonn, Göttingen, Leiden, Berlin, Louvain—indeed, of all the great universities of Belgium, France, and Sweden—all in formal court dress with their sashes and orders—all of whom had been my grandfather's teachers. They were all still there rising along the walls of the mounting stairway. Not a one of them had been tagged!

Let me interrupt myself for a moment. You will see what I am getting at in a minute. In 1945, just after the war in Europe ended, I used to commandeer a sergeant driver and a corporal and a big car and explore Swabia rather than sit on the air base at Stuttgart and twiddle my thumbs—play poker, screw the local German girls. I discovered the German atomic energy laboratories underground, the ME-262 factories, also underground, and Hechingen, where the Crown Prince of Germany was imprisoned by the French. I went up into Hechingen over French protest and made the acquaintance of the lonely Kaiser's son. We became close friends. He was a total innocent and could have been David Windsor's twin brother. He lived there alone with his French mistress, and I managed, at his urgent request, to frustrate his wife, who wished to join him there—I had connections in SHAPE. I supplied him with cigarettes, and, as he sat in his bedroom in the rumpled disorder of his silk nightclothes and sheets, he supplied me with the inside story of Hitler's Third Reich.

It is a long story, but all I want of it now is this: He took me around the castle and showed me his ancestors' portraits—and hearts, all in their golden goblets in niches protected by small glass doors— and a family tree going back to 815, I think—an ancient and redoubtable royal family, of which he made graceful fun. He had nothing of pomposity, and all he seemed to be interested in was news of his English cousins and the latest in sports—horses, of course—over there. I came to see him many times. In later years we corresponded.

Now, what I want you to understand is that the rising tier of the intellectual great of Europe that mounted up and up into the tower at Snug Rock, and then went all around the walls of the great tower room, was an aristocracy as truly mighty—and conscious of it—as the Hohenzollerns. Not hereditary, but no less awesome. *These* were my grandfather's real ancestors. And mine. And of this modern world.

And up in the tower nothing had been disturbed, for there was nothing up there of "value." There was only the cooing of pigeons.

# 2

## THE GRAND DUKEDOM

On his arrival at Broadmoor on June 6, 1973, Tony Baekeland, according to hospital procedure, was given a number—6787—a bath, and a preliminary medical checkup. No medication of any kind was administered so that his psychiatric condition could surface and be observed. He was brought a cup of tea and some bread and jam, and placed in solitary confinement.

On his second day he was moved to the special admissions ward, where he would remain for the next two months. In early fall he was transferred to Cornwall House, a three-story building that resembled a tenement more than the ducal residence its name suggested. There he was assigned to a second-floor ward, which consisted of dormitories, single rooms referred to by the patients as "cells," and a large dayroom where patients could read, play music and games, listen to the radio, or watch television. Occasionally there was a movie. During the Queen's Jubilee Week, James Bond films were shown; another time there was a screening of *The Exorcist*, at which several patients were observed "laughing away with great relish" in the middle of one particularly grotesque scene while other, more heavily tranquilized patients simply sat by themselves and stared into space.

There was an area off the dayroom of Cornwall House in which meals were served, and also a small kitchen that patients could use at authorized times. All cutlery was counted both before and after meals; if anything was missing, the patients were searched.

They were provided only a locker and an iron bed. For anything beyond these bare necessities they had to depend on the generosity of relatives or friends. In Tony Baekeland's case, his grandfather, George Baekeland, had left him a trust fund, one half of the principal of which would come to him in three years, when he turned thirty, the other half when he turned thirty-five.

Tony Baekeland shared the dormitory with as many as sixty men at one time. The beds were packed tightly together, with sometimes only inches between them. High up on the dormitory walls were blue lights that were never turned off, so that it never got completely dark.

Patients were locked in the dormitories at night, and bathrooms were off-limits. If anybody needed to use the toilet, he had to resort to the chamberpot under his bed, in full view of everybody. "They were plastic, since a pot of any other kind might be turned into an offensive weapon," a staff member explains. Often there wasn't even toilet paper.

"We are wheeling and shining with the *crème de la crème* of European high life," Barbara Baekeland had written to Sam Green three years before. "The Marquis and Marquise de Surian arrive next week—and the Earl of Shaftesbury is just across the way here. Hope to climb on skis up to the Hospice de St. Bernard with him next week. Adelaide d'Eudeville's cousin, the Comte de Vogue, is here and it is peaceful and restful. Flew around in a private plane yesterday—took the controls, made a right turn and almost zeroed in—no, not quite true. But had a good look at the countryside."

A good look at the countryside was one of the few things at Broadmoor that Tony Baekeland could enjoy, and it would be filtered not only through barred windows but through the tranquilizers with which he was often heavily sedated. Sometimes when he stood by the window too long, he would be reprimanded by a nurse.

"I asked him, 'Tony, what do you get as medication?'" says Miwa Svinka-Zielinski. "He wrote me four different names. He said he got one kind in the morning, another kind in the afternoon, and another in the evening, and once a week he got this and that. I showed this list to a psychiatrist friend of mine in New York and he said they were all strong tranquilizers. The worst thing was he was not getting any treatment—he saw a psychiatrist only once a month."

For the roughly 750 patients at Broadmoor, there were only four psychiatrists, working one day a week each. "With the best will and the best scheduling in the world, I could only manage to see each patient for two hours every three months," a former Broadmoor consultant explains.

But Dr. Maguire says, "Tony Baekeland consumed a great deal of my care. He told me I was the only one who would listen to him."

## Letter from Antony Baekeland to Miwa Svinka-Zielinski, November 12, 1973

Broadmoor

Dear Miwa—

Thank you for your letter after such a long silence. I am getting on all right here. I shall try to give you the dream associations you asked for concerning the dreams I sent you in my last letter.

1. Einstein hides a stop sign from the police: I associate this dream with secret, occult, or hidden things.

2. I come back to my best friend [Jake Cooper], and we travel the world together; I see a fox eat a squirrel: I associate this with the library of our house on Seventy-first Street where I was brought up.

3. My grandmother Nina Daly embraces me during a party given by a fellow here and myself; during the party I cut up gobbets of meat: I associate this with the swans on Georgica Pond in East Hampton where as you know we rented a house for several years.

4. I dream that I can fly and go all over the place: this dream of flight I associate with freedom. I have always wanted to be able to fly.

5. That I am a successful writer and poet: I associate this with a manor house that my mother and father rented one summer in France. It had a beautiful garden and a large *potager* where I used to hunt for insects.

I shall keep jotting down my dreams and will send them to you.

Miwa, in my thoughts I am much too brutal to myself—I wish I could have gentler feelings toward myself. Also, I don't understand why but I feel a murderous hatred toward my fellow men—I feel that they are holding me down. I don't always feel this way, just sometimes. I can't understand the reason for this feeling as I have always been treated with the greatest kindness.

Love,
Tony

## Notes from a Psychiatric Consultation on Antony Baekeland, New York, March 12, 1971

Patient's family a strange and difficult one. Patient's father a rigid moody person who is always right about any subject that comes up and brooks no discussion. Cutting and critical in his relationship to everyone and more particularly to patient. He eventually separated from his wife, patient's mother, and established a relationship with the girlfriend of patient, with whom he is now living.

Patient's mother is a very beautiful talented woman, extremely seductive in her relationships with men, and with patient. She finds reasons to have him live with her and alternates between extreme seductiveness and a strange sort of provocativeness which drives patient to distraction. She speaks of suicide frequently to patient.

Patient shows clear-cut indications of a thought disorder. Has had delusions, some paranoid ideation. Although the entire picture is modified by drug use, particularly marijuana, the essential diagnosis is paranoid schizophrenia. Psychiatric hospitalization and psychotherapy recommended, but patient's father is unwilling to pay for this.

## Official Visitors File, Broadmoor Special Hospital, December 9, 1973

VISITOR'S NAME: Mr. Brooks Baekeland
RELATIONSHIP TO PATIENT: Father
SUMMARY: Tall, spare, handsome American now almost Europeanized. He still broods over his awful family tragedy and speaks of tapes to which his now-dead wife had committed her

confused, psychotic thoughts. Not prepared to accept son outside hospital. Was relieved to hear that there was no immediate
prospect of discharge. Will write in advance for an appointment
next time!

### SYLVIE BAEKELAND SKIRA

Brooks and Tony were different in a million ways but they were alike
in the sense that for both of them there were no rules anywhere.
They had the sense of "we are beyond rules, outside laws." Yet Tony
was brought up permissively while Brooks had been very strictly
brought up. Later, of course, Brooks transgressed. He was the
Baekeland son who rebelled, breaking a pattern and going off in different ways—oh yes.

### BROOKS BAEKELAND

I was always free. I was always successful in everything I wished to
do. But I despised success. I despised money and show. I laughed—a
grave offense to those who cannot laugh! I thumbed my nose at my
father and at the sheepism of Man. Subconsciously he knew that I
derided all that he did not dare not to be. I was not only a black
sheep but far, far worse—I was a laughing black sheep who made
him doubt his money-god.

My first wife was one of *them*. And Barbara's poor son got his
values from her—most of them—but he was torn in a war in his own
soul.

### SYLVIE BAEKELAND SKIRA

Brooks's father was dead when I met Brooks, but echoes of him were
with us all the time. I think that Brooks is very much like his father,
though he always compared him to Louis XVI—that is, a man in a
very prominent position who wanted his privacy and would rather
play in the toolshed.

There was opposition there. Perhaps Brooks's father didn't respect
Brooks enough—I don't know. They were two men chasing each
other. But isn't it the classic story of the great captain of industry like
Brooks's grandfather who founds a big thing and leaves so much
money it dilapidates the lives of those who inherit it?

### From the Private Diaries of Leo Hendrik Baekeland, March 24, 1908

> Would like to have my son George's picture as he sits in a big chair, doing his arithmetic, his fine crop of hair slantingly covering half of his broad forehead.

### From the Private Diaries of Leo Hendrik Baekeland, July 16, 1908

> George behaved very brutally toward his sister Nina, beating her when she came up hill with parts of his tents. Reprimands, tears, and punishment.

### CÉLINE ROLL KARRAKER

My mother, Nina Baekeland Roll, who died several years ago, never liked either of her parents—she was a very rebellious sort of child, I guess. I think her brother got all the attention. You know, in a European family the son is the preferred one.

### From the Private Diaries of Leo Hendrik Baekeland, January 28, 1910

> My wife has swollen eyes from crying yesterday evening all on account of silly discussion relative George.

### From the Private Diaries of Leo Hendrik Baekeland, January 30, 1910

> George and Nina went to a party and came back shortly before midnight. George was the only boy who had no tuxedo suit. I like it better this way than if he was the only one who *had* a tuxedo suit.

## BROOKS BAEKELAND

When I was in my teens, LHB would invite me to lunch in New York at the Century or the University Club. Impressed by my dapper father on the importance of correct dress for every occasion, I would appear at these amazing convocations in a proper dark suit—all shined and polished and tongue-tied—and LHB, with a Packard specially built for him so he could wear a top hat in it and get in and out almost without bending, would arrive in his one and only suit for town and the inevitable sneakers. He would poke fun at my sartorial splendor and lecture me on the delusion of "appearances." I was not old enough to guess, then, at the deep and divisive philosophical chasm that separated him—the exuberant, joyful immigrant and self-made man—from the Grand Duke, as we children called our father.

LHB talked to everyone and anyone who would listen or could teach, and had no prejudices. No—he hated fools. His son, Geoffrey Gorer's typical second-generation American, became an elegant and a bigot, and was—I mean it seriously—ashamed of his famous father. He was ashamed of LHB's barefooted beachcombing, ashamed of the *Ion*, because it was not a proper yacht but a sort of Bahama-going houseboat with a couple of "niggers" aboard—a disorderly laboratory that could put up a sail of sorts and where LHB could cook his "disgusting" meals, jump in the "ding" and go hobbling about bare-assed over the beaches of the thousands of unnamed keys, with a small magnifying glass, a notebook, a penknife, and a lemon—no doubt talking to himself. Who in hell else *was* there to talk to? I ask the same question myself!

You see, there was a tension in this family that extended over three generations, and that was reenacted between my first wife, Barbara, and my son, Tony, and myself—a tension between two fundamentally different views of life. I do not care, for instance, what other people think of me, and that was a source of the bitterest philosophical difference between myself and Barbara Baekeland, who lived and fought for what the French call *la parade*—appearances, what other people think, etc.

My father also cared too much about what others thought of him. He had not inherited *his* papa's burning-glass mind. That was not his fault. But he had no sense of humor, and without that a person is better off dead. Oh, he liked jokes and retold them. That is not a sense of humor.

## From the Private Diaries of Leo Hendrik Baekeland, December 11, 1909

George is undoubtedly an earnest serious boy but I am afraid that he is going to turn into a fault-finding criticizing belittling man. Sooner have him less serious, less steady, and somewhat more enthusiastic than to see him grow up into one of those men who always find fault with others.

### ELIZABETH ARCHER BAEKELAND

George Baekeland was completely intolerant of everything. I remember when I met Sterling Hayden and he heard that my name was Baekeland, he said, "Any relation to George Baekeland?" I said, "He was my father-in-law." He said he had crewed on George Baekeland's yacht one summer. This was when Sterling was a young man, before he was a star. "George Baekeland," he said. "Right-wing bastard."

### CÉLINE ROLL KARRAKER

We kids were terrified of Uncle George, but he also taught us to be super sailors, marvelous people in the water and in the woods. He was very demanding—you had to do everything exactly right. And it was frightening, because if you did it wrong you really got it. But we stuck with it, because he knew and he taught us and it was wonderful to learn from him.

He used to take us to the Adirondacks in the wintertime when nobody else in the family would and put up with all these kids. He taught us to iceboat, and later we built our own iceboat and sailed it in the lake.

Uncle George apparently once put a canoe in the Hudson River at Yonkers with his brother-in-law, my father, George Roll, and they decided to go to the headwaters of the river, just paddle as far as they could. And they ended up right near what became our family camp in the Adirondacks.

Grandmother bought the camp in 1923, but I read somewhere that Grandpapa had sent her and Uncle George and my mother off to the Adirondacks as early as 1907, 1908—to the Adirondack League Club for a holiday. So they knew that region quite early.

Grandmother named the camp Utowana Lodge. Later it was called just Baekeland Camp. She loved the place. Even after she'd had many strokes she continued to come up.

## BROOKS BAEKELAND

Until her strokes, my grandmother had always run our camp in the Adirondacks, served by a motley of people, some of whom did not even speak English—a Polish chef, for instance, who wore a chef's hat. But the last and most massive of her strokes left her partially paralyzed and speechless.

It was her doctor's opinion that, along with her speech function, her higher thought functions had also been destroyed. Gradually, as it was deemed that her death was imminent, her daughter and her grandchildren fell into the habit of talking around her, in ways that they would never have dreamed of doing had they thought she could understand—going even so far, I once remember, as to speculate upon her will and her fortune. To tell the truth, I also believed that she was unable to understand. Almost. But in a sort of private romantic tribute to her somewhere spirit, even if it resided no longer behind those lifeless eyes, I would sit for an hour or two at a time when I went to see her, which was as often as my busy life allowed, and talk to her as if she understood, or read to her—I had always read to her while she had her breakfast on a tray when we were at The Anchorage. Believe me, it was a difficult charade—to talk easily, convincingly, and naturally to a person with a clawlike hand and drooling, twisted mouth, a face unrecognizable, a grotesque Swiss woodcarver's mask; to talk, without ever receiving the smallest sign of understanding, as though to the once so civilized, gifted, humorous woman that she was, and then to kiss that cold, necrotic face again in parting, with a promise each time to come back soon.

The poor bored nurses, who treated her as they would a two-month-old baby, used to rejoice on seeing me, for it gave them time off—often most of the day if I could stay that long. They soon gave up trying to get me to talk to *them*, which they craved, for they had long run out of anything to say to each other. I do not know what they thought of my charade but I can guess.

My father paid regular visits, too, but they were to see that his mother was being properly cared for. Her state embarrassed him. Frankly, no one could wish—for her sake—that she would live on, but there was nothing that anyone could, or would, do to abbreviate her shame. I say her shame, for that was what we all felt: how she would hate it if she knew.

One day, after she had been in this condition already for several years, and I was up there studying my graduate physics and mathematics after our usual "talking" and "reading" session, I saw her eyes seeming to look at an open magazine. I said to her: "On this page there is the word 'state' in large letters. Can you point to it?" She slowly extended the hand over which she still had partial control and with her index finger indicated the word. I tried others. Slowly and painfully she identified them all correctly. In a few minutes, using a large and heavy cardboard, I had constructed an alphabet matrix with large letters. I put it in front of her and, taking a pad and pencil, asked her to dictate to me. Slowly she wrote: "Thank you, dear Brooks. Thank you for existing." She had said these same words to me once many years before.

I then asked her if she wanted to dictate a letter to me.

"A telegram," she wrote.

I took it down. It was to David Fairchild's wife, Marian. "My son Brooks"—she didn't say "grandson"—"has given me back my speech. Greetings from Céline Baekeland."

From that moment on, that imperious old lady began to take over some control of her own life again. Her nurses no longer treated her like a driveling baby and her family no longer spoke in front of her as if she no longer existed. She lived on for quite a few more years.

## CÉLINE ROLL KARRAKER

For a few summers grandmother hired a little plane to get up to the Adirondacks—her doctor, who would come along, was terrified of flying in such a little plane but *she* thought it was great sport. She always thought everything was an adventure. The plane would land in the lake right up by the dock and she'd be lifted out. We built this boardwalk for her wheelchair, and she'd be in her wheelchair and fish.

Later on in the family there were some incidents up in the Adirondacks that were very odd and violent. Tony was a disturbed person, I think, very young. His cousins always felt that he was odd. The kids all played together, you know, and they were in the woods once and something caught fire. We had a fire.

The kids and Tony grew apart. They were uncomfortable with him. And you know, for years we didn't see him because Brooks and Barbara went to live in Europe.

Barbara and I were great, dear friends. She was just a delightful, warm-spirited person. And absolutely fearless. A very exciting person! We spent a lot of time at the camp together, especially during the war when Brooks was away.

### SYLVIE BAEKELAND SKIRA
Barbara, I'm told, hated camp. Because there was no glamour. She thought it was all very boring. All that sand in your shoes, and canoeing and so on. It had no dash. This was the "old world" that she had wanted to marry into, but this was the part that she *didn't* want.

### NINA DALY
The Baekeland family had a place up in the Adirondacks. A big place. Members of the family still own it, and every summer usually they go to camp. One family is there, another will come. It's a lovely place to be. You get up there in the hot summer and it's a joy, it's always so cool up there. You always sleep with blankets over you.

### ELIZABETH ARCHER BAEKELAND
Each member of the family had his own cabin, a wonderful old log cabin—Bonbon, the old lady, had had them built so they fit right into the woods—and each cabin had three or four bedrooms. Fred, when I was married to him, used his father's cabin.

### DR. FREDERICK BAEKELAND
Over the long haul, except from sort of a novelistic point of view, the life-as-fiction point of view, the only person in my opinion in this family of any real fame is my grandfather. Not that there haven't been other people, some of whom have been hardworking and achieved a certain amount and so on, but—and I'm including myself—they're rather insignificant.

My father? Oh, my father went to Cornell for two years, then he went off to the Air Force in the First World War, then he graduated from the Colorado School of Mines. Then he worked as a petroleum geologist in Spain, I think in the Spanish war effort, and after that in Africa. And after that he went into the family business. No one in the family besides my father was ever asked to go into the business. You had to be asked.

## From the Private Diaries of Leo Hendrik Baekeland, February 8, 1908

Céline found out that they wanted to make our son George president of his class but he refused and afterwards when asked why by his mother said he was satisfied with the thought that they had asked him.

## Letter from Leo Hendrik Baekeland to George Baekeland, May 5, 1928

Coconut Grove, Florida

Dear George,

I have read carefully your long and excellent letter of May 2. Your whole point of view is perfectly correct and appreciated by me. It is your duty as a father to look ahead to the future and to discount possible events.

But you undoubtedly know that the main reason why I did not urge the directors of Bakelite Corporation to increase your salary or bonus is that I desired to set an example to the others of our staff and not give them an opportunity of thinking that you might be favored as the son of the president.

I am intensely pleased to learn that outsiders have discovered your talents and are now making you offers of a partnership which would put your present income entirely in the shade. In fact, I wonder whether I am not doing you an injustice— whether I am not doing harm to your career by proposing you a more favorable arrangement with Bakelite than the present one, so as to secure the continuation of your services with me—but I believe in the future of Bakelite even if at present you may have better opportunities elsewhere. Furthermore I am getting old and I cannot miss your assistance in my work and responsibilities. If I had to do so I would sooner retire entirely even if this be to the detriment of the fortunes of the whole family.

During the several years you have been working with me I have had abundant opportunity for observing you and the value of your services, your knowledge, assiduity, versatility, and the tact and good judgment you have displayed in matters of importance. In continuing your help in the development of this enter-

prise you will help the interests of the whole Baekeland family as
no one else can.

I believe I have told or written you formerly that I have been
so well satisfied with your services that I am planning on putting
my holdings of Bakelite stock in a trusteeship which would continue after my death and make you the directing and administrative head of these holdings; this Bakelite stock, to be
administered by you for the benefit of your mother or any other
beneficiaries she or I may designate. But all this may involve
delays, as it requires some lawyers' work, also perhaps some
changes in my will or other complications.

So as to make a practical start and so as to make you feel that
any benefit I or our family receive through your excellent cooperation, I now make you formally the following offer which you
can accept or reject after I shall have met you in New York,
which will occur in a few days:

In addition to any salaries, bonus or other compensation you
are receiving from Bakelite Corporation or its subsidiaries as director, officer or other employment, I shall pay you: 1/ One half
i.e. fifty percent of any fees or compensation collected for my
services from Bakelite Corporation after proper deductions have
been made for my income taxes, and other expenses or disburse-
ments made by me in relation thereto. 2/ This agreement shall
run from year to year by mutual consent.

Please be ready to discuss these matters as soon as I arrive in
New York. I can meet you at the University Club where we
shall be able to discuss these matters without being disturbed. If
then you agree, you should signify your acceptance by letter.

Affectionately,
L. H. Baekeland

## Letter from George Baekeland to Leo Hendrik Baekeland, May 16, 1928

New York

My dear Dad:
Although I replied to your letter of May 5th at our recent talk
together at the University Club, nevertheless, for good order's

sake I should like to confirm that reply by saying again that I am
decided to remain with our company out of consideration for
the family ties and all they involve and on account of the generous and promising arrangement which you proposed in your
letter.

I am happy that the whole matter has been so amicably settled
and that it resulted in no misunderstanding. It has caused me a
great deal of concern for fear that you might attribute to it
motives which have not existed, or that you might think me
disloyal or foolhardy.

The outcome has resulted in a decidedly more intimate interest in my work here and an added bond of devotion.

Affectionately,<br>George

## From the Private Diaries of Leo Hendrik Baekeland, March 18, 1908

In fact, the whole history of the development of Bakelite in its
different phases has been the history of looking at matters from
my own standpoint.

### BROOKS BAEKELAND

In the Bakelite Corporation, the Roll descendants—my Aunt Nina
and her four children—held common stock, and the Baekeland descendants—my father and his three children—held, but in considerably less amount, preferred stock, all this in trusts mostly. The Roll
children would inherit automatically at twenty-one but the Baekeland
children would not inherit automatically but at the discretion of my
father and only on his death. Great trust was put in "George's judgment," that he would do the right thing. This extra liberty of action
had been his reward for having given up his career as an exploring
petroleum engineer to enter and become the vice-president of the
Bakelite Corporation, as LHB began to feel himself getting old. And
though my grandfather could hardly have had many illusions about
the suitability of what he was doing—for any fool could have seen
that my father had no business talent—it was in the old European
tradition of family.

I doubt that LHB really considered any other alternative. He knew that time was running out for him. He wanted to retire and to prepare the way—and it *had* to be his son. For him, Bakelite—and all of its ramifications both backwards and forwards in time—was a family business, to stay in the family and be of the family. It is as banal as "Emil Duval et Fils" written over the entrance to a small electrolytic zinc plating establishment in Auteuil.

My father did everything he could all his life to disassociate himself from that, from "Duval et Fils." And thus, as soon as LHB began to become senile—it took twelve years, and in those years Zeus gradually became Pan—and could no longer oversee the Bakelite Corporation, my father sold the whole thing. Disastrously, as it turned out, for the whole family but particularly for his own children. He destroyed the Baekeland fortune. He destroyed the Baekeland family.

He then began to lead that life of a country squire—expensive cars, expensive tailors, elegant yachts, shooting in Scotland, playing bridge with the Duke and Duchess of Windsor in Nassau, and all the rest—that showed him not the son of an American immigrant but an English duke without a title.

That day I climbed up to the tower of Snug Rock, I brought back a lot of early photographs of my grandfather, my grandmother, my father as a boy, and his little sister Nina.

Well, one day he came to visit Barbara and me in New York—he had occasional generous impulses; there was a waiting-to-love man buried there under all that neurotic scar tissue. Barbara was out. I was on the fourth floor—as far as I could get away from my social wife's life—studying, no doubt, when I heard the doorbell ring.

I went down. It was my father. The Grand Duke. A rare and fluttery event. What to do with him? A glass of port? One always had to entertain him—like royalty. He had no conversation. One ended up chattering, feeling a perfect fool. That is perhaps the principal reason royalty has been almost universally suppressed: it is utterly useless and makes intelligent people feel stupid.

And then I had an inspiration—nothing else had worked. I took him up to my study to show him the wonderful photos I had brought back from Snug Rock. I was also hybridizing orchids up there, under all sorts of artificially simulated climatic conditions. The orchids did not interest him in the least, not even the fact that I had some growing in conditions approximating fourteen thousand feet in Peru and Chile and, in a glass case right next to them, some growing at sea level in Sumatra—different pressures, sunrise and sunset times, temperatures, humidities, and seasons. I began to take out all those photos showing him as a small boy on the knee of Zeus, etc.

And he would not, he could not, it almost seemed as though he *dared* not, look at a single photo of his father!

That was when I first grew up, so to speak, insofar as understanding my lifelong problem with Father was concerned. After that day I no longer feared him. I pitied him. I understood his tragedy and it horrified me.

He was first and always the beloved apple of his mother's eye. My grandmother was so besotted she told my mother when she married my father that "George is a combination of Leonardo da Vinci and Jesus Christ." I concluded that he was protected early from Zeus and that he was not intimate with his father, that eccentric tyrant figure, whose lava outpourings of speech and learning and whose intolerance of folly must have made him a dreadful person in the house, an awesome parent. A man who could not stand noise, save it issued from his own mouth. Zeus, the terrible.

Judging from the fact that my father always hated and distrusted "intellectuals" and read with the slowness and concentrated effort of a peasant, and from the fact that the interests and style he soon developed were totally opposite to his father's—that is, all things physical and sporting—and that he spent enormous sums of money all his life on things elegant and beautiful, and became what I call a high-class redneck, to the right of Right—from all this, I take it that he had made, and perhaps with his mother's connivance, a classic revolt against his father.

But—and this is what interests me—my father apparently never actually defied my grandfather. In fact, he obeyed to the point of wrecking his own happiness. You might interpret his obedience to what he feared and loathed as showing a lack of courage, but I think there was a still stronger influence that made defiance unthinkable. Despite his efforts to separate himself from everything that had a foreign accent, so to speak, to be a real—but tip-top-class—American, or even better yet, a noble Englishman, Snug Rock was a thoroughgoing piece of bourgeois Europe, and in Europe, Victorian Europe, filial obedience was total. The only alternative was to "run away to sea"—leave home forever. With his mother's devoted protection, that would never have been necessary. All he had to do was to see as little of his father as possible, and that was easy, for LHB was always working or away.

And then, in the few years before he joined what was then I think the Signal Corps and went to Italy as an aviator, he met and fell in love with the most beautiful girl in the Hudson River Valley—my mother, Cornelia Fitch Middlebrook, a thirteenth-generation American, descended from founding fathers and from governors of New York State, etc., etc. They were engaged shortly before he went off to war. He was the happiest man in the world.

He was unlucky in being sent to Italy. The great Italian immigration to America had already begun, and to him, Italians were fellows in undershirts and paper-bag hats who dug ditches or labored in his parents' gardens and greenhouses. He was sent to Foggia, where he flew Caproni bombers and where his commanding officer was Fiorello La Guardia, later mayor of New York, a small, talkative, emotional man whom he despised. I remember, as a boy, hearing him brag how he would shoulder "wops" off the sidewalks in Italy. Of the Renaissance, of ancient Rome, of Italian science, music, philosophy, mathematics, he knew nothing. "What did Italians ever do?" he would say, in later years. I would tell him. "Oh, artists!" he would say with contempt. I would then cite for him Italian figures in America who were distinguished scientists, politicians, bankers, industrialists, and even—best of all—multimillionaires. He would stare at me in disbelief, offended by such disgusting paradoxes. He felt the same about the Jews—or any immigrant people. When I was doing graduate work in physics he asked me once, in a lowered voice: "Einstein is a fake, isn't he?" And these were all *idées reçus*, not gotten from his parents but from twentieth-century America as it was then.

My father hoped he was a total conformist. In fact, he was not only a right-wing radical but a misanthrope, who never had any friends, except those who could flatter him. Flattery was the only road to him, but his cruelty closed that road for me. He ended up sincerely preferring dogs to people.

But he was not quite the two-dimensional figure that I was then still persuaded he was. No one is. He was a man born out of his place, out of his time, and a man with superb—unused, curdling—gifts. He was, for instance, gifted with his hands—he loved cabinetwork—and he had a love of speed, was as quick and coordinated as a cat. He could be fun and even witty when he was happy, and he loved jokes—when they were on others. He was a man who on a camping trip would nail some friend's shoes to the floor by his bed, his friend presumably drunk and deaf to the hammering, but would

be red-faced mad if someone had done that to him. He was a wonderful practical joker and gave me some bad examples in that line,
but he was never one to see himself in a funny light. I thought, even
as a small child, that that was weird—mad, somehow. I could not
understand it. I am not sure I do now.

He also had—but alas, it was superficial—dash, or what the
French call *panache*. It was show. He was always, metaphorically
speaking, standing at a mirror. He was totally conscious of his own
style. But finally, his arrogance and his misanthropy were ego-saving
rationalizations for a deep shyness and sense of his social incapacities.
I know this because I am his son and have inherited many of the
same disabilities.

My father roared out in the dark to keep the demons away. It was
easy being such a rich and protected man. As my grandmother used
to say, "One of the uses of money is that it allows us not to live with
the consequences of our mistakes." He even fooled himself. I do not
think he ever suspected that he had lived his whole life through at
bay. Think of this. It is sad. After all, we do not have much time
here, and to spend it *all* with our backs against the wall . . . But I
suppose a large part of humanity does, and that is even sadder.

After my father and mother were married they went out to Golden,
Colorado, then a village, where he entered the Colorado School of
Mines. He had decided to be a geologist—geologists lived out of
doors, hammered rocks, prospected for gold, built bridges over rushing torrents in darkest Africa and other romantic parts of the world. It
was my father who gave me my romantic interest in faraway places—
the Arctic, Africa, South America, the sounding seas—ships, adventure, the noble savage, etc.

In Golden, my mother bore him two children—first my sister and
then, fifteen months later, myself. Upon graduation, with the aid of
my grandfather, he was signed on to go down to Tunisia and Algeria
and prospect for oil.

Engineering was the romantic thing in those days. It was the engineers, in their open-necked shirts, riding britches, boots, and pipe in
hand or mouth, who were pushing civilization out into the "native"
parts of the world. It was the tail end of Cecil Rhodes's world, the do-
gooding-but-oh-so-much-money-making world of the British Em-
pire. It was "a man's life." My father had made a choice that I could
have certainly made myself—one part of me would have, for I have
always had both sides in me, the active and the intellectual, and they
have often been in conflict.

Eventually my grandparents decided that my father was to return at "a very good salary" and become vice-president of the Bakelite Corporation in New York, then headquarters for the German, English, American, and Japanese branches, and that "the young people" were to live in Yonkers, not far from Snug Rock, while my father made "a splendid career" in Bakelite. In the summers my mother and her two small children would move up to the Adirondacks.

My father ought to have pursued his open-air, adventurous, super-masculine life. But the promise of that "very good salary" and that "splendid career" and—what?—shame?—hope?— made him take a decision that embittered and diminished him for the rest of his life. In every blow that he beat his two young children there was the rage and bitterness of a man who hated himself—and so hated the world.

After his "very good salary" and other perks became so fabulous in the roaring twenties that he could move away from Yonkers, he bought a place surrounded by woods in Scarsdale where he built a swimming pool—a novelty in those days—and, on the same property, another house for himself, the Doggery, where he lived with his dogs and mounted heads, coming to "our" house only for meals. He did not stay with his wife after dinner but, always in dinner jacket, worked in his shop, making, for instance, sailing boats. He was an insomniac all his life, and, crazy with frustrated sexuality, would swim at night for hours up and down his pool to exhaust himself sufficiently to sleep.

We two—and later, three—children took it quite for granted that on our property there should be two separate establishments, one for my father and one for us and our mother. We always dreaded the black-cloud returns of "George" from his office on Park Avenue. Once, I saw with amazement a rat, not a squirrel, jump from the big sycamore near my bedroom window to the roof of the house. I could not wait to tell my father, for I had not known that rats could climb trees. I imagined it might please that man I so feared and who, even then, I had to entertain and—I did not know it yet—be superior to. Not easy at five or six. Calling me a liar and saying he would teach me a lesson, he beat me with the back of a hairbrush. He could never keep his temper and knew no other recourses than the Gestapo ones—beatings, threats, reprisals. And we were all so weak, in our own ways—such sinful creatures, so culpably misguided, so unable to do right in my father's eyes, so wanting to please, so terrified of doing wrong.

On the other hand, and sadly for my father, I was a person born with an inordinate and growing pride, and I began to stiffen and resist as time passed. As my darling Sylvie has pointed out to me, a child that knows it is loved will accept any punishment from the person who loves him, even when it is unjust, but no child will accept even just punishment from a person who dislikes him. And my father detested his children.

### GEOFFREY PARSONS
They were three of the brightest children I've ever known. Little Cornelia—the family called her Dickie—was the most marvelous child. Very beautiful, and full of creative imagination—a real original. She was wounded permanently by her father. She was a brilliant girl and he cut off her education with boarding school, saying that she was not worth educating. Her response to this was the usual one—she married the first eligible man who asked her in order to get free of family. She's been married three times, I think. Without that father, there's no saying what her life might have been.

As for Fred, the younger boy, he always wanted to be a composer, but George told him in no uncertain terms that music was an avocation, not a vocation, and threatened to cut him off without a penny if he pursued a musical career. So Fred became a doctor, choosing psychiatry as his specialty. I believe he has written numerous scholarly papers. He's also an accomplished art historian.

Brooks was seven years older than Fred and about a year and a half younger than Dickie, and he was always the most brilliant of the children. He had a quick eye and a vivid curiosity. He could have been anything he chose to be. Instead, he's spent his entire life running—from or after something.

### BROOKS BAEKELAND
I was a hunter, I smelled a kill far—oh, far indeed, perhaps one life would not be enough. I was running fast always on fresh snow.

Each of my father's children had to make his own kind of defense. I chose—I had no choice—a sulking, black defiance. My whole spirit was in opposition to my father, though way down in him there was a sweetness that some, even my mother, recognized was there. There is a child in everyone; it is the child we love. It was the child in Barbara that I had always loved. I love my mother, too, as I love children. She was and is the quintessence of the feminine—loyal, sentimental, fragile, beautiful.

## GEOFFREY PARSONS

Brooks's mother is much too beautiful for her own and everybody else's good. Her whole life has been theater, with her own charming self always at stage center. She's just as smart as vinegar laced with a good mustard but it's all buried beneath a foot of the best goose down. The only relation that anyone—man, woman, child, even her own children—can have with her is a flirtatious one, in my opinion. As you can imagine, she's always had a score of admirers—including, I must confess, myself.

## ELIZABETH ARCHER BAEKELAND

A lot of pressure to marry money had been put on Brooks's mother by her family, who'd lost all their money. Poor Cornelia, you know— she was really sacrificed. She was a very sensitive romantic creature and there was just never any rapport between her and George Baekeland.

How she left him is a fascinating story. She wanted to get away one winter and her friends were all going down to some club in Florida, and George didn't want her to stay at this particular club. He said, "You can go only if you stay at *my* club." So she went to his club— alone—and one night there was a fancy-dress ball and she was coming down the stairs and she suddenly caught the eye of this man. He just looked up at her—you know, across a crowded room. Pong! Just like that—love. He went over and asked her to dance.

His name was Penn Hallowell, N. Penrose Hallowell, and he was from Boston and he was married at the time. Now, Cornelia is a very honorable person—I have tremendous love and admiration for her. I think she's the kind of person who probably, once she met Penn Hallowell, couldn't bear to stay with George Baekeland and just said to him, "Look, I'm in love with somebody else, let me go." I mean, she wouldn't make any bones about it. So anyway, he let her go, but on one condition—she had to give up custody of her children. Fred was only seven at the time, Brooks was fourteen, and Dickie was almost sixteen.

George gave her only five thousand dollars a year to live on. And Penn Hallowell didn't support her, because that was against his principles. He would bring her gifts—he would bring her very *nice* gifts—but he never gave any money. So she was strapped in those years.

The children were all away at boarding school, and on vacations they were with Cornelia as much as with George, even though he had the custody. The only problem the boys ever had with her was getting to *see* her. They always had to make a date two weeks in advance or something, she had so many admirers. She was a good mother, though—so charming and so gracious, and so beautiful!

For years after she left George, Penn Hallowell did not marry Cornelia, because, as I said, he already was married. Everybody knew about them but *they* didn't know that *anybody* knew and they were always so careful. And when they finally "came out"—after twenty years, which was when his wife died—everybody said, "Oh, finally Penn Hallowell has married his lovely mistress." He was eighty then and she was sixty-five. He died five years later and she was absolutely distraught. They were lovers right up to the end of their lives.

### SYLVIE BAEKELAND SKIRA

He was her man, yes. Brooks told me that she kept his room just the way it was before he died. His little slippers. His little bathrobe, exactly where it was, and so on. I have never been in Brooks's mother's apartment in New York. I've never been to camp. I was never invited. Brooks never took me. This is why I keep saying, the story is there but I am not in it, I have been a bit player.

You know, she always spoke of her husband as Buck—that was her nickname for him. That's where she was rather touching and sweet. To marry Penn Hallowell was—I don't know—the dream of her life.

### ELIZABETH ARCHER BAEKELAND

George Baekeland married again about two years after the divorce from Cornelia. His new wife came from out West—good American stock, though I heard her father sold watches and inexpensive jewelry. She was absolutely beautiful. And very musical—she played the piano. She's about eighty now, I guess.

I remember Dickie saying about her, "She's *lovely* to *look* at, de-*light*ful to *know*"—you know. So the children gave their stepmother a hard time but they liked her. Of course, they *adored* their mother.

Brooks wrote a story about his mother called "The Shrike." I don't think it was ever published but we all read it. A shrike is a bird that kills its prey with its beak, and the story was based on the fact that five men were supposed to have committed suicide over Cornelia. There was *one*, definitely. And all this upset the kids terribly.

## SYLVIE BAEKELAND SKIRA

Brooks's mother was a great beauty. That's one of the reasons she and
Barbara got along so well—Brooks says because of that great beauty
club that you have in America. Also, Barbara was, I think, very
clever with her mother-in-law—she tried to please her very much
and did.

Brooks's mother is a very difficult person. She came to visit us in
Brittany. Brooks had said to me in advance that she was a prima
donna. All these Baekelands have egos that are tremendous and
there's not much room for anybody else.

Brooks has a great *coquetterie* of mentioning his age all the time,
which can be a sort of vanity if you look very handsome and yet you
say, "I'm as old as Methuselah," so that then the other person has to
say, "My goodness, you're handsome!" So whenever Brooks would
say how old he was, his mother would say, "Stop annoying us with
your age. *Do* stop talking about your age *all* the time!" She disliked
me right away, very much. Because I had replaced Barbara. And
because I didn't pay court to her at all. She told me, "Sylvie, why
don't you put some makeup on? A woman always looks better with
her face made up."

## NINA DALY

Mrs. Hallowell was devoted to Barbara and Barbara was devoted to
her. She's a beautiful woman, you know. A blonde. Blue eyes. Nice
figure. She was Tony's other grandmother.

## SYLVIE BAEKELAND SKIRA

Mrs. Hallowell wrote to Tony right after he killed Barbara. She was
horrified, of course. I can't say that she wasn't horrified from the
heart—I don't know—but she was certainly horrified by the scandal.
She's, I think, in a way an old-fashioned person—no, not old-fashioned, conventional—and she really doesn't think this is a very nice
story. She never liked anything Tony did that wasn't proper behavior.
I mean, she didn't think it was very attractive for her grandson to
come to lunch at the Ritz or some decent tea place dressed like a
hippie, let's say.

## ELIZABETH ARCHER BAEKELAND

I think the drama of it got Cornelia more than anything. I mean, to
write and say, "Tony, why and how did you kill your mother?"

shocked me a bit. Fred was shocked, too—everybody was shocked. She wanted me to read Tony's reply. I just couldn't, though I must admit it was hard to resist.

## BROOKS BAEKELAND

My poor Barbara. She was in so many ways a marvelous person. And—though the world knew it not—impossible. I always felt that I was not a great enough man for her. What she needed was a Henry VIII. But of course she finally had him—in her son, and he chopped off her head. So to speak.

To tell you truly, I think there is only one true kind of love, and that is the love of a mother for a child—utterly brave, loyal, forgiving, generous, and without a jot of self-love in it. That said, I believe that insofar as we really love one another—when we do, and it is rare—it is in this way.

I must now tell you of the last time I saw my poor father. I think it was in 1964 or 1965. I knew he had not many years—or even months—to live, and I went up to Connecticut to see him. I do not suppose that I had spent a total of more than twenty-five hours with him in the previous twenty years.

His wife had left us alone together. He was confused—not just in the philosophic sense, but medically. He was far gone in senile dementia. To entertain him I had brought some slides of the expedition in Peru that I had made with Peter Gimbel the year before. I showed them to him in the living room. He understood nothing, or little. And then, seeing that I was not succeeding in entertaining him, I said that I would now be going back to New York, would someone drive me to the station.

He offered to come with me. His young gardener drove; my father could no longer drive a car. It was while we were driving to the station that I realized—and I am sure *he* realized—that we would never see each other again. As we stood together on the railroad platform, on an impulse I took him strongly in my arms and kissed him, hard, *à l'européen*. I was forty-three. He was seventy. We had not kissed—we had hardly shaken hands—a dozen times in all my life. Both of us were suddenly crying and speechless. Both of us, now that it was too late, asking the other for forgiveness, me for having so disappointed him, he for having been such a lousy parent, and God knows what else—everything, all the *malheur du siècle*, all that we might have done, should have done, did not do, all the beauty lost, all the love not loved.

## From the *New York Times,* February 1, 1966

### GEORGE BAEKELAND OF BAKELITE; SON OF PLASTICS MAKER IS DEAD

Special to the *New York Times*
FAIRFIELD, Conn., Jan. 31

George Baekeland, former vice president and director of the Bakelite Corporation and a sportsman, died today. He was 70 years old. . . .

He hunted big game and shot grouse on the Scottish moors. A crack trap and skeet shot, he wrote *Gunner's Guide,* published by Macmillan in 1948.

Mr. Baekeland was also a yachtsman and fisherman and had ridden in point-to-point races. He painted water-colors and made etchings, too.

Surviving are his widow; two sons; a daughter; a sister; and four grandchildren.

## From the Last Will and Testament of George Baekeland, October 31, 1958

I, GEORGE BAEKELAND, of the Town of Fairfield, County of Fairfield, and State of Connecticut, do hereby . . . give, devise, and bequeath absolutely to my wife, if she survives me, all my real property wherever situated.

### BROOKS BAEKELAND

When my father died and his will was read, I immediately understood what it meant and what had happened. He had disinherited me by an indirect means. He had left to his wife *outright*—rather than in a marital trust that would have given her the income for life, with the corpus going to later generations—most of the money he himself had made on the sale of the Bakelite Corporation to Union Carbide. This, despite how at the dinner table he always used to inveigh against women, saying—according to his lifelong doctrine of misogyny—"Don't ever leave money outright to a woman but always in trust." So now any future inheritance from my father was left hanging. It is thanks to the generosity of my grandparents only that I am self-supporting.

### Sylvie Baekeland Skira

Brooks said that the antagonism between his father and mother had been so great that that was why his father had cut off the children. He also said that his father had sold out the business without even consulting his children.

## From the Last Will and Testament of George Baekeland, October 31, 1958

> I hereby nominate, designate, and appoint HENRY GAS-SAWAY DAVIS to succeed me, upon my death, as Trustee under said trust agreements, each made the 29th day of December 1933, between L. H. Baekeland, as Grantor, and Céline Baekeland and L. H. Baekeland, as Trustees.

### Elizabeth Archer Baekeland

It was Henry Gassaway Davis, a friend of George Baekeland's who had been disinherited by his own father and was very bitter about it, who persuaded George to disinherit *his* kids, saying, "I didn't inherit any money and look at me—I'm a very successful lawyer." So George's second wife now has all those millions, and nobody knows who she's going to leave them to when she dies. Of course, Leo Baekeland had left his grandchildren money.

### Brooks Baekeland

Henry Gassaway Davis was a powerful and charming figure who had always dominated us all. It was he who engineered the disastrous sale of the Bakelite Corporation to Union Carbide, just before the mightiest rise in the history of the chemical industry, which topped in 1946. During this time Bakelite, if my father wanted out—which he did, and was the whole point—ought to have gone public under a new president, after which the family shares could have been sold publicly and reinvested in something like the young IBM. But all that makes no difference now. What happened was that he made the worst choice possible.

It was fate that brought together those two child-haters, my father and Henry Gassaway Davis, the much- and so-many-times-disastrously married Henry Davis—including to two Vanderbilt girls. The drunken and violent father who had disowned him used to hold a cocked and loaded revolver to Henry's head when Henry was a boy, and as so often happens—perversely—the mistreated child, instead of having learned compassion, learns or inherits the same species of brutality.

# 3

# MISCHIEF
# IN THE BLOOD

Tony Baekeland's day at Broadmoor began with a nurse shouting to him—and his dormitory mates—to wake up. From the moment he got out of bed, his every move was supervised—going to the bathroom, brushing his teeth, washing, shaving. He could enjoy the luxury of a bath or shower only one day a week.

"Tony remained in a bad way for quite awhile," Dr. Maguire says, "but eventually, with medication and the realization that he was a member of society and part of a therapeutic community, he was able to receive visitors other than his immediate family."

Under the Mental Health Act of 1959, tribunals were created to give patients certain safeguards. Confined to Broadmoor under a Section 65 restriction order, Tony Baekeland was entitled to one review every two years. On August 22, 1974, he was granted a tribunal to review his sentence. It was determined that Tony Baekeland, after little more than a year at Broadmoor, was not ready to leave. Within several months, however, he was moved to Gloucester House, where patients are accorded a few more privileges; cutlery, for instance, is not counted after every meal. But after a short time at Gloucester, it became clear that he still needed the more protective atmosphere of Cornwall House.

All the houses had small courtyards, called "airing courts," where the patients could walk, but the airing court at Cornwall was distinctive—a patient, using his own money, had planted it with flowers and bushes. Now Tony Baekeland would once again be walking there.

"In the airing court," a patient has written, "you walk round and round, lost in your own private thoughts. There are various games you can play to make it less boring, like counting the stones on the bricks on the wall or counting the number of steps it takes you to get round the court. But it's all exactly the same, day after day."

## TONY VAN ROON

I was a nurse at Broadmoor for some of the time that Tony Baekeland was a patient there. I left in September 1979 to take up a post in Coventry.

I think Tony was in Cornwall House when I worked there. Of course, he might have been in Dorset, the long-stay ward—I also worked there. It was one of the first wards to be upgraded. Well, they stuck some paint on the walls, but they called it modernizing. I know he wasn't in Norfolk—maximum security—which is where I worked the most. No, the contact I had with him was in Cornwall.

What's it like in Cornwall? Well, you go in through the front door, and immediately to your left is a stone staircase going up to the second and third floors. If you go past the stairs and go right, you're in Ward One, which is just one very very long gallery.

The first door on the right is the charge nurse's office, and then all the way down on the right are the cells. They were the usual sort of prison-type cells. The only difference was there was only one in a cell. On the left there are windows looking over the terraces, and occasional sort of bathroom areas and toilets, and then, further down, a huge sort of communal lounge. The second floor is just a duplicate of the first floor.

On the right-hand side of the lounge was a snooker table and a card table, and on the left-hand side was a curtained-off area with rows and rows of chairs, easy-type chairs, with a television sort of on a platform in the front. And these were very drab and very dark areas.

The third floor, Cornwall Three, was what we called a dead ward—it was only used at night, for sleeping.

In the morning the breakfast would be cereals, bread, eggs, and on Sundays bacon and eggs or baked beans. A very very basic breakfast.

And then at lunchtime there would be sort of a standard meat and two vegs. No soup to start with, just a main course. Then in the evenings it would be sort of a hot-type meal. In Cornwall they could order one night a week from a local fish-and-chips shop, and it was brought in by hospital transport. It was offered to every house one night a week on a rotation.

One of the things I found about Tony was he was always on his own. He never really had that much to do with nursing staff. You have to understand that the nursing staff at Broadmoor is less therapeutic and more custodial in role. That's not how it's supposed to be but it's how it is. That's one of the reasons I used to grit my teeth, you know—because we weren't known as nurses, the patients either called us "sir" or "screw." So it was difficult for a lot of them, particularly those who were isolated anyway, to sort of break through the lines and actually have a lot to do with nursing staff.

I had quite a few chats with Tony but they very rarely got into too much depth because he suddenly would realize that I was a part of the system and he was frightened by the system. I mean, *I* was frightened by the system, and I worked there! In fact, I was petrified of it. I mean, Broadmoor is a hospital but it's not that healthy a place.

Another thing I always felt was that there was a lot of remorse in Tony about what had happened, and because of that he had to be constantly coping and coming to terms with the situation he was in. I think that he sort of thought, "Well, here I am now and I'm here because I did this," but he could never understand why he did it— which is the key thing with a lot of people who I met there, they couldn't understand *why*. Quite often I would see Tony just sitting there and appearing to be miles away.


## Letter from Antony Baekeland to Rosemary Rodd Baldwin, December 21, 1974

                                                          Broadmoor

Darling Rosie,
I wrote to you about a month ago. Did you ever get the letter? My whole life has changed completely—I have become a totally new person—by "new," I mean the way I used to be a long time ago. But then, I never really realized what I had, which was love and happiness, so I lost it through ignorance and selfishness. I spend hours, lovely happy hours, thinking of my friends.

Mummy was such a very wise person—I only began to realize who she really was a while ago—she was such a master of the understatement. I owe everything to her and love her so, Rosie. I was eating a tomato at teatime a few weeks ago and I suddenly realized that she is not dead at all, just very, very mysterious.

Love,
Tony


GLORIA JONES
Where *did* Barbara come from? Boston? And didn't she go to Hollywood or something? She married very young, I think.

NINA DALY
Barbara met Brooks in New York. He was going to graduate school and he met her and they started going out right away and it didn't take too long before they got married. Brooks is the most charming person. I used to feel badly that he didn't have some kind of important job. The grandfather did. And the grandmother was a brilliant woman, too—Bonbon. It's a brilliant, brilliant family. Brooks's father was a businessman. Perhaps Brooks was spoiled a bit. He might have been, you know.

BROOKS BAEKELAND
The fact is, I took a little girl from nowhere but who was smart and ambitious and had flair, and put her on the public scene. I educated her, taught her to draw and paint, and I supported her social ambitions. Socially, she was a most gifted woman—and exemplified all the things my grandfather most despised. I, personally, was a social zero. I was completely devoid of social ambition, it meant nothing to me. But Barbara's happiness, for many years, did, so I played along, and in the end, long before the end, became disgusted with myself for having wasted my own gifts that way. Of course, I also loved her, and I have always felt protective of the women in my life. I still support her mother.

NINA DALY
Nina Lillian Fraser was my name. But my mother never called me Nina, she called me Lillian. I like Nina a little bit better. It's shorter.
We were five children—three girls and two boys. The oldest was a

boy and then I was next. And then there was another boy, and then my sister Alice was next, and then in five years my mother had Genevieve—I adored her, I was seven years older than her—Genevieve Agatha Fraser. Irving died in the war. And then Ralph eventually died. Alice and I are the only two living now. She looks quite a lot like me. She used to have red hair a little darker than mine.

My mother stayed home, you know—took care of the house. It was in the country, in West Roxbury, up near Dedham. We usually had a maid do the chores. And my father worked on the railroad, one of those big railroads. He was an accountant and something else there he did.

I had two grandmothers living, and one grandfather, and one great-grandfather. But I don't remember my great-grandfather.

I certainly do remember my two grandmothers. Oh, I loved them both. There's one I worshiped. I used to think she was a saint. On my mother's side. Mary Margaret was her name. Guess how many children she had! Fourteen. I didn't know many of them because they were spread out. Fourteen children, and everybody worshiped her. She was so handsome. We used to comb her hair, I remember. Then she would part it in the middle, and she would take it down and turn these two pieces in the front *in*, and then she'd get those in the back and put them in a little tug. Sometimes I used to ask her, let me do it.

I met my husband Frank up in Boston. It was wintertime, and he had bought a Stutz Bearcat car at the end of the summer, and I was so furious I said, "You're going to freeze to death," so then he went out and got a raccoon coat to wear in the open car.

I was married at eighteen, and I was a mother at nineteen. I was awfully sick, though, after my son Frank was born. I had a terrible breakdown. It was a difficult birth, you know. I was only nineteen and he was a big baby. He weighed ten pounds. Barbara weighed ten and a half. I had her when I was twenty-eight.

She was so beautiful. She was seen by an artist somewhere. He got in touch with her and then he painted her. And she did quite a lot of that work. She was a model. She was in *Vogue* and *Harper's Bazaar*.

She was very bright. She took French lessons when she was little, I think. She was supposed to go to college but something happened and I forget now what it was. She should have gone. Too bad.

I went to visit Tony in Broadmoor so many times, and every time I went there I just loved it. It was up a high hill. I always took a taxi. But I walked it once. I'd take him bags of food. I'd buy a big bag of fruit—oranges and grapefruits, anything that was in season. And I'd sometimes take him steak. You could cook if you cleaned the kitchen up. And I'd always buy two, so he'd have one for a friend. He was so natural and so loving. He used to talk about almost anything. He used to talk about his dreams.

## MARJORIE FRASER SNOW

Nini just doted on Tony. Of course, I don't know the whole story, I don't know why Tony did what he did, because I wasn't close to Barbara those later years. I think of her often. What a tragedy.

Barbara was my cousin. My father, Irving Fraser, was Nini's brother. He died when I was three months old. Barbara and I had a great many wonderful experiences in our growing-up years. She was almost, in many ways, a sister to me. She was a lovely child, she was really one of the most beautiful girls you could ever see. Her coloring was absolutely gorgeous, and of course that beautiful red hair. She was a very popular child and always had a lot of personality.

We lived in Westwood and they were in West Roxbury, in a lovely section, way up on a hill. They had a lovely large house, with a very large porch with columns or pillars going up.

Barbara had her own room, and lots of beautiful toys and dolls. I know she attended public schools at different times but it seems to me there was a time when she did go to a private school for something, I can't remember what.

I remember she liked to wear mostly casual country-type clothes, as we all did then—tweeds and cashmere sweaters and skirts, and loafers or saddle shoes. It was sort of a uniform in those days.

We both loved horses and riding and dogs and dog shows. We spent a couple of summers together on the Cape, around Dennis. Later Barbara with her own family—Brooks and Tony—rented further along the Cape, in North Truro. One of the houses they rented was up on Corn Hill overlooking Cape Cod Bay. It was a very nice house. Contemporary. All glass in the front.

Barbara loved to swim. She took chances in the ocean—she wasn't afraid of anything. In fact, the two of us nearly drowned at one point off of Plymouth, playing in the surf when the Coast Guard had told everyone to stay off the beaches because of a storm at sea. And that didn't bother us at all. We went out into the surf because of course the waves were so tremendous that it was wonderful, better than the usual-size waves. But the undertow was fantastic.

We started to go backwards two strokes for every one forward, and

Barbara started to panic a bit, she started to scream, and I reached out and said, "Let's take each other's hands and pull together." And we did and we gradually inched to where we could find a toe on the sand, then we collapsed. And of course the Coast Guard had been called, because Nini couldn't see us in the ocean from the upper porch because the waves were so big, and of course our bathing caps had been ripped off. We received quite a talking-to from the Coast Guard officer for disobeying the rules.

### ETHEL WOODWARD DE CROISSET

One day, in the early sixties I think, Barbara was staying with me in my house in Spain—years before all the terrible things happened— and the sea was quite violent. She was doing some *skinautique,* some waterskiing, off the beach there. *I* would have been afraid—I'm rather a fearful person. She was in a bikini, and there was nothing to protect her at all, with all these boats everywhere—she could have had her leg cut off by one of the propellers. But Barbara had absolutely no sense of fear. She was a violent person, you know. She perhaps as a young woman *used* her violence to get what she wanted. It was her character.

### MARJORIE FRASER SNOW

Barbara was hoping to go to Bennington. Her plans were sort of made in that direction. But then of course her father died and her plans kind of changed.

Barbara and Nini moved to New York. I remember having dinner with them at the old Touraine in Boston the night before they left.

A bit later, an illustrator by the name of McLellan Barclay saw her someplace and I think said something to the effect that she was one of the ten most beautiful girls in New York City that he had ever seen. And on that basis, I believe, she was offered a screen test or whatever they call it—not your usual-type screen test, better than that—and she and Nini went out to Hollywood together.

### BROOKS BAEKELAND

I believe she was given some small normal contract—the kind the studios get everyone to sign to hold them—while a screen test she made with Dana Andrews was being evaluated.

## Marjorie Fraser Snow

Barbara did not care for Hollywood at all, and she and Nini came back to New York. They had their car shipped back by rail—they just wanted to get out of there!

I think they stayed for a short time at Delmonico's when they got back, and then they lived for a time on Central Park South and then they had an apartment someplace on Park Avenue. I visited them there and we would drive up the Hudson to the Sleepy Hollow Country Club—I think that's on the Rockefeller estate. It was a lovely place to ride, with a lovely indoor riding area.

## Barbara Hale

When she met Brooks, she'd been having this big romance with John Jacob Astor. The fat one. I met him later and I said, "Oh, *you* knew Barbara Baekeland!" and he was furious. I don't know why. I guess he just thought it was none of my goddam business, you know.

## Phyllis Harriman Mason

Mrs. Daley almost got Barbara married off to John Jacob Astor. Barbara was supposed to get the famous emerald ring. I felt that Mrs. Daly was responsible for all Barbara's flights of fancy. She had brought Barbara up to be a duchess.

## Elizabeth Archer Baekeland

Nini was trying to get Barbara into society—and into what she called "the mun." My mother-in-law, Cornelia Hallowell, used to comment on how Nini would always refer to money as "the mun." I mean, to Cornelia money is money, it's not "the mun." There is no pet name for it. The Baekelands put all their sort of dislike of Barbara's background onto Nini. Well, she *was* very obvious. Barbara had a lot more polish.

## Elizabeth Blow

I think there was a part of Nini that probably did want to exploit Barbara. Here she had this really extraordinarily beautiful and talented daughter. They were sort of like little adventuresses coming to the big city, because they came from—where *did* they come from?—no, not Boston proper at *all*—they came from West *Roxbury*, which is, you know, really the wrong side of . . . I mean, nobody comes from West Roxbury, Waltham, places like that. Nobody ever even talked about them. I mean, they didn't *exist*. Even Newton was a little bit going too far out of the magic circle already, and Newton Centre was considered *very* déclassé—it certainly was in *my* day. So Nini and Barbara, these sort of lace-curtain-Irish type of people, weren't in the picture at all.

I mean, I was born in Boston and entered into this kind of society from the time I was five years old when you started going to dancing school in the Somerset Hotel, the Somerset ballroom with the gilt chairs. In those days it was Mr. Foster's Dancing Classes—the little girls were all dressed up—and you proceeded through that. Then you went to the subscription dances, and the last subscription dance was the most elegant and the most exclusive—it was called the Friday Evenings and there you had your first glass of champagne. And then you came out.

### KATHARINE GARDNER COLEMAN
Barbara never played up the Boston side of it at all. My father was Bostonian, as you may know—G. Peabody Gardner. Now, Brooks's mother married an extremely nice man from Boston—her second husband was a terribly terribly nice man and a great great friend of my father's. Daddy thought the *world* of Penn Hallowell.

### LUBA HARRINGTON
Barbara came from very ordinary people. Now the Baekelands maybe weren't so great, but it's a better family. Barbara took over a good friend of mine, Domenico Gnoli—an artist, a marvelous artist—just because he was from a good family. From one of the best families in Italy, as a matter of fact. The *Count* Domenico Gnoli. So she latched on. And when he died—he was only thirty-four—liver cancer—she was running around at the church receiving people, because she felt they were important. I mean, she was acting like a close friend of the family, and she never even knew his mother, never knew his sister. That's how she was—she was a latcher-on-er.

Do you happen to know the derivation of "snob"—s-n-o-b? I used to teach linguistics and crap like that at Yale. In Italy, in, I don't know, maybe the thirteenth, maybe the twelfth century, a lot of nouveau-riche Italians tried to get their kids into the schools where the noble families sent their children by offering the schools a ton of money, so finally what the schools did was start a new category which the nobility called *sensa nobilita*—without nobility—because not only weren't these nouveau-riche noble, they didn't even have the instincts of nobility.

## BARBARA CURTEIS

Barbara adopted this irrepressible redheaded Irish persona to cover up whatever deficiencies she thought she had. She didn't know things that everyone else knew or that she assumed everyone else knew and that in fact they probably did know, and she couldn't entirely catch up with the head start that the people she wanted to know had on her. And this persona that she'd adopted eventually took over.

## BROOKS BAEKELAND

When Barbara left Hollywood and came back East, she did so expecting to be sued by the studio but not giving a damn. She was—joy to Mama!—now considering giving in to John Jacob Astor's strenuous and stertorous courting. Have you ever seen a picture of him? He looked very like Louis XVI and was dubbed by *Time* "The Pear-Shaped Prince of the Idle Rich." His father went down with the other gentlemen on the *Titanic*, singing "Nearer, My God, to Thee."

But after the screen test, the studio decided not to try to keep her. Miss Daly was not, they could see, of rich thespian ore. In fact, she would have made the worst actress in the world.

## PEIDI GIMBEL LUMET

It was a terrific aging actress role that Barbara Baekeland eventually played. She couldn't get over the fact that she'd been John Jacob Astor's girlfriend for a minute. It was a theme, it was consistently there. It was her notion of herself and that's what her behavior was based on.

## BROOKS BAEKELAND

I am not sure why Barbara changed her mind about John Jacob Astor. *I* may have been the innocent reason. In any case, he was still married at the time to Tucky French. He married various tarts, but Tucky was not one of them. Hers was a family as "distinguished" as his own. But it was at this time, according to Barbara, still—or again—a dewy young photographer's model, living with her mother far above their means at the old Delmonico's, that John Jacob Astor made her an offer of three million dollars—money in those days—if she would wait for him until he could get a divorce from Tucky French.

Now, I do not remember the exact order of events—whether Barbara turned down the bribe before or after she met me. I was a pilot trainee in the Royal Canadian Air Force at the time, and had been invited by my sister Dickie, who lived in Ridgefield, Connecticut, with her first husband, to come for the weekend—I had a leave—and meet a pretty girl who was a "poet."

## ELIZABETH ARCHER BAEKELAND
Dickie and Barbara had probably met in Hollywood. Dickie, you see, was in the movies, too. She was in *Cover Girl* with Rita Hayworth and Gene Kelly. They wanted her to stay on but she hated it, she hated it as much as Barbara did. Dickie was quite impressed with Barbara. I mean, they'd be bound to like each other, because they were both very verbal and bright and very beautiful. And later, as a matchmaker, she had Brooks and Barbara for the weekend, and there's no question—that weekend was momentous.

## BROOKS BAEKELAND
I found a remarkably beautiful and staggeringly self-assured young woman whose pretentions to poetry puzzled me when I plumbed them. She thought it would be wonderful to be a poet, but she had no training in words, and I hurt her feelings by calling what she showed me "marmalade."

To skip a banal story of sex and still embryonic violence that might interest the readers of a woman's magazine, during a heated zigzag from Ridgefield to the Adirondacks to the lacy-fluffy abode of mother and daughter at Delmonico's to, finally, Pinehurst, North Carolina, Miss Daly strongly intimated to me that she was pregnant. I took her across the border, to Bennetsville, South Carolina, and for two dollars—the court fee—and ten dollars—for a wedding band—I made her into Mrs. Brooks Baekeland and myself for the next thirty years into "Barbara's husband."

## ELIZABETH ARCHER BAEKELAND
I heard John Jacob Astor followed them all the way down to South Carolina, trying to prevent Barbara from marrying Brooks. But she was madly in love with Brooks, *and* she thought he had a lot of money—a lot more than he had, I imagine.

BROOKS BAEKELAND

I soon realized that, whether Barbara was pregnant or not—and she was not—I had not married a soul mate but a powerful and ambitious antagonist. She was a far more brilliant and a far stronger personality than I ever was or could be.

Shortly before I met her, though I did not know it until long after, Barbara had been a patient of the psychoneurologist Foster Kennedy. Because of my disagreements with my father—essentially the strain that is set up in a young man of overly passionate nature between his desire for freedom at any cost and his desire not to bring dishonor on his name—I had been "introduced" to Foster Kennedy earlier myself. Besides my grandfather, he was the first intelligent man I had ever met—I mean known on an intimate basis, could talk to, could make myself understood to, could seek and take advice from. It was an almost rhapsodic experience. He asked me out to dinner to meet people like Jerome Kern, Robert Oppenheimer, Wystan Auden, and a galaxy of British diplomatic and military stars—his half brother was the British Chief of Staff, Sir John Dill.

Meanwhile my father was tremendously impressed and puzzled by the fact that the man who charged the highest psychiatric consulting fees in the world was charging him nothing for seeing me—and telling him nothing, either. It was Foster who said to me one day, "Brooks, there is something very big and important going on. You should be a part of it. Go up to Montreal. Get in the Air Force. I know the Air Marshal. I'll ring him." And that is how it happened. I left almost overnight.

I asked Barbara not to come to Canada while I was still in training, but she came anyway. I did not go to meet her. My then very close and dear friend the poet Howard Nemerov, one of nature's gentlemen, met her instead and comforted her. I ignored her. I mistreated her. I did everything I could imagine that would put a girl off, but I had forgotten her persistence.

It gives me pleasure to think for a few minutes now about Barbara as she was in those first years, during my training and subsequent instructorship in Canada. She kept insisting on following me about on my postings, first as a trainee in #13 Elementary Flying Training School, St. Eugene, Ontario, then at Uplands Advanced Flying Training School at Ottawa, then at #1 Instructor's Flying Training School at Trenton, Ontario, and then in a long series—Aylmer, Gananoque, Kingston, St. Hubert's in Montreal, Quebec—where I taught the death-defying youth of the British Commonwealth, plus a good bit of Texas, how to dogfight and kill with machine guns, rockets, bombs, and lousy jokes—we could have ended the war four years earlier with *those*, properly employed.

Barbara stayed in local rooming houses, even at one time above an undertaking parlor—the smell reminded me of Bakelite. I had a forty-eight-hour pass every two weeks. I was nuts about flying, about everything I was learning and doing, but I was not nuts about my wife.

One of the things that most put me off about the beautiful ex–Barbara Daly was her convertible Chrysler and her mink coat and her empress's airs, which did not go at all with my disguise as a minor Prince Incognito, Aircraftsman 2nd Class, and "one of the mob" fighting Hitler. I was all for Democracy. She was soon ordering around my commanding officers. She already knew "how the world works." I did not want to know. I hated the very fact that that *was* how it worked. I loathed her for her political acumen. You can imagine my embarrassment when I came home once, after two weeks, to my humble hovel, wherever it may have been at the time, to discover Barbara giving a cocktail party—the first person I saw on opening the door was the man before whom I cringed and saluted every other day of my life, my C.O., suddenly converted into a genial and subservient "friend" calling me "Brooks" instead of "Baekeland, AC$_2$"—a man whose social inferiorities would have embarrassed a Gila monster. I wished that my new wife might just vanish back into the meretricious world she had come from.

Anyway, there were always those two weeks before we were able to couple on bumpy mattresses and cow the local population with her airs of Catherine de' Medici. And it was horribly boring for her—I mean all those blotchy, overworked, overbabied, gingham-dressed other officers' wives at tea in the intervening fourteen days.

Since I soon saw that the poetry was not going to work, I began to try to teach her how to draw and do watercolors. As a teacher I took my job seriously and, standing behind her—as I did through the rest of her whole artistic career—I gave her the ideas, the suggestions about form, theme, color, etc. She did have talent and ambition, but she had no imagination. What she had—and what may be more valuable to an artist—was passion. But she had never had a Conté crayon or a brush of any kind in her hand before. You can see in Nina Daly's apartment in New York that what Barbara did with that ignorance and passion was not so bad at all. The romantic spirit.

And in the long summer evenings in that north country, after a crummy but lovely dinner in some awful village greasy spoon, we would go walking for miles out into the Canadian countryside—wilderness, or semiwilderness in those days, with me trying to walk on the rails of some abandoned railroad line and reciting "Gerontion"— I was mad about T.S. Eliot then, think him an old fart now—and, above us, in the satined evening sky, the Night Hawks sliding straight down with that amazing BOOOOOM to impress their girlfriends. I trust they were! *I* was.

What tied me to Barbara for all those years? Pity. I still feel sorry for her. I still feel guilty. I still feel protective.

## Official Visitors File, Broadmoor Special Hospital, September 18, 1975

VISITOR'S NAME: Dr. and Mrs. Justin Greene, U.S.A.
RELATIONSHIP TO PATIENT: Friend and ex-doctor
SUMMARY: They are both concerned and showed sound appraisal of the overall situation. They knew Tony as a small boy, and Dr. Greene saw him professionally on some occasions where he had most likely formed the opinion that Tony was dangerous to his mother. This present visit was essentially informal. He described Tony as overcontrolled, there being several incidents where he overreacted to situations in a nonviolent way. Dr. Greene recounted two occasions as a child where Tony became overexcited and ran away and there was some difficulty in finding him. Dr. Greene thought his violent outbursts were specifically directed toward his mother and did not think he was likely to be a danger to others.

I discussed our intended transfer of Tony from Gloucester back to Cornwall House and asked the Greenes when they saw him later in the afternoon to explain that this was a therapeutic move rather than in any way punitive. They agreed to do this.

## COLM BYRNE

When I knew Tony, he was in Gloucester House. I couldn't say I knew him that well—Gloucester House when I was there had ninety-six patients.

The patients at Cornwall House, where he had come from, were, let's say, much more disturbed. Cornwall House was commonly referred to as "the monkey house." That was because largely the patients in there were diagnosed as suffering from schizophrenia, whereas the patients in Gloucester House tended to be fairly controlled for a long period of time, more stable—there wasn't a great deal of what we call psychotic behavior in Gloucester House in comparison with Cornwall House. Cornwall House was much bigger as well. Gloucester House was referred to really as a semi-parole block because it was much more easygoing.

## Official Visitors File, Broadmoor Special Hospital, November 27, 1975

> VISITOR'S NAME: Mrs. Nina Daly
> RELATIONSHIP TO PATIENT: Grandmother
> SUMMARY: Maternal grandmother still seems less disturbed by her daughter's death than by the fact that her dear little Tony is in trouble. She seems just as mad as the rest of the family.

### BROOKS BAEKELAND

Nina Daly is a Fraser—no nuttiness there that I ever discovered. I had a very close, often Rabelaisian relationship with her. She was the best part of my marriage. She had an enormous sense of humor, no education, silly values, and indomitable loyalty.

### HELEN DELANEY

Nina Daly is a harmless enough creature. Her values came from Cholly Knickerbocker and the Catholic Church—mostly from Cholly Knickerbocker. But on her husband's side of the family there was real mayhem. It's what you might call a frail line.

### BROOKS BAEKELAND

The fact is, the turning, bending, hinging energy in the stories of human lives is given off by very intense and often very queer people who are no longer alive to play mischief, though the mischief still breeds. There are two kinds of mischief in this regard. There is the mischief in the blood—when it is there, as it was certainly in Barbara's father Frank Daly's family. Frank Daly's own father, Barbara's grandfather, was a violent and aberrant man, and so had been *his* father, Barbara's great-grandfather, by all report. And Barbara's paternal grandmother was a "case" who mooned at the piano all day and never did any housework or house management—a kind of Zasu Pitts creation.

And then there is the other kind of mischief—the mischief that produces more mischief by cause and effect, action and reaction.

### ELIZABETH ARCHER BAEKELAND
Barbara's father committed suicide—I don't know why, I don't even know *how*, unfortunately. And her brother committed suicide. I remember Fred Baekeland saying, "Isn't it extraordinary that the whole family has committed suicide."

### HELEN DELANEY
The suicide of Frank Daly, Sr., was observed by Frank Jr. through the window of the garage. Frank Sr., who had lost what money he had in the crash, was gassing himself with carbon monoxide while pretending to be working on his car—it was a Pierce Arrow, as I recall, and he was underneath it and the engine was running. Frank Jr., walking back and forth before the garage window, watched his father die. The insurance company was suspicious but could never prove fraud. Frank Jr., Barbara, and Nina Daly each got about sixty thousand dollars from the insurance company. This was in 1932, mind you. That would be at least six hundred thousand each in today's currency.

### SYLVIE BAEKELAND SKIRA
The son Frank later died in a car accident, supposedly on purpose—I don't know. How does one decide that somebody has gone into a tree on purpose?

### HELEN DELANEY
One day Frank Jr. whipped around a curve in Cohasset, Mass., I think, and just drove at high speed into an elm tree. The official story was that the steering mechanism had malfunctioned. I know he had been drinking for some time.

He was a front-and-center-look-at-*me* kind of guy—just like his sister. He loved to raise Cain in public. I forget what he actually did for a living but I do remember that he was trying to crack the detec-

tive-magazine market. I don't think he had much luck. His wife was
the quiet-little-woman type, so there was friction there as well. They
had two nice little boys.

## BROOKS BAEKELAND

Barbara and I inherited that fatherless family. She performed all the
brave and wonderful human prophylaxes. I begged for money from
my family. I resented bitterly having to ask my fascistic father for
anything, but I did not mind being in debt to my marvelous grandmother—I could even glory in that, because our spirits, hers and
mine, were always in tune. The problem, the Socratic problem, of
value—how can it be established? proved?—controlled her life as
much as it did mine. Both Barbara and Tony were wrecked on those
stony shores. They became raiders—or rather, she was to begin with.
They were arrogant. They were destroyed. These are not merely abstract questions. Those who have seen Nemesis in their stories were
right indeed. It works in all our lives. It worked with a terrible ob-
viousness in theirs. A swift, destroying sword.

If one seeks to pin down the source of Tony's violent instability,
one mustn't entirely blame the Dalys. I think there was mischief in
the blood on both sides—the Baekelands as well. I have in my notebooks a quotation that I copied down from Robert Gittings's *Life of
Keats*—I was in India at the time: "Suffering had laid cruelly bare his
abnormally passionate nature, unbalanced since his boyhood, always
in extremes."

Was I thinking of Tony when I copied this? Certainly not. I was
thinking of me!

Someone, I now forget who, told me years later that when Foster
Kennedy heard that I had married Barbara Daly, he said: "God for-
fend that they have a child!"

# 4

## MOTHER'S MILK

As gradually Tony Baekeland became a member of society at Broadmoor, he could choose from among the several occupational therapies available to patients: toy-making, pottery, carpentry, metalwork, printing, radio-making, basket-making. He preferred drawing and painting. "He gave me one or two things—paintings of flowers and things like that," Dr. Maguire recalls. "We have to be very careful about paint because in some cases it's very toxic and patients can harm themselves."

Tony Baekeland soon improved to the point where he was reading university-level books—among them, a volume on abstract mathematics. He wrote to his father that he was happy, had "a home and new friends."

Old friends—and friends of friends—began to visit him. There was as well a community group called the Broadmoor League of Friends, two of whose members—a retired army doctor and his wife—took a particular interest in Tony.

"Colonel Verbi was at one time in the English army," Dr. Maguire explains. "He was a wonderful friend to Tony. He and his wife had the time to visit. Tony was so fond of them he gave them a number of gifts—I remember particularly a figure of an elephant.

When Mrs. Verbi died some years ago and I went around to their house to call, Colonel Verbi gave me—to give back to Tony—the things that Tony had given to his wife. And, when Colonel Verbi died, he left Tony a silver ashtray in his will."

Toward the end of his third summer in Broadmoor, Tony received word from his father and Sylvie in France of the birth of a half brother.

## Letter from Antony Baekeland to Sam Green, August 29, 1975

Broadmoor

Dear Sam,

My time has been of great profit to me: I have learned a great deal about people, myself, and life in general. I now realize that for many years I had been living a totally false life and it finally ended the way it did because the burden I carried just became too great to bear. Anyway, for Mummy's sake I have decided to make a new person of myself and I have found great peace and happiness. I realize now how much I always took my mother for granted (and the other good things in life) and how selfish and blind I was in many ways.

My father and I are good friends now. I have a little half brother whom I have not met.

Yours with love,
Tony

### BROOKS BAEKELAND

God, not I, is an ironist. Barbara became pregnant only twice in her life—not counting an "occult" insemination in Mallorca by Sam Green, between two chairs across a room, with the aid, I suspect, of mucho hash—and for both she had to have an operation to untip her tipped uterus. The first one—I was flying then in Germany in early 1945 or late 1944—was miscarried. The second, in the autumn of 1946, was Tony.

## H.R.H. Princess Elizabeth of Yugoslavia

She told me that she was one of those rare cases of women who can only conceive a child during their period. I mean, it's not biologically possible, is it? And she wound up conceiving her own killer.

## Marjorie Fraser Snow

I believe when her brother was killed she was carrying Tony and they were afraid she might lose the baby she was in such a state.

## Notes from a Psychiatric Consultation on Antony Baekeland, New York, March 12, 1971

He was born in August 1946. The labor was very long; there was no anesthesia; and high forceps were used.

## Brooks Baekeland

When Tony was born, I was living at 1220 Park Avenue, in a three-room apartment with Barbara and her mama and, in insidious progression as the next years passed, her widowed sister-in-law Edna and her two sons. Little did I realize that I would be supporting the Dalys for years and Nina Daly for the rest of her life. We also had an incontinent, decerebrate toy poodle which had come with Barbara and her mother from Delmonico's. It peed everywhere and was called Negus. Finally we moved to 136 East Seventy-first Street, the large house that my grandmother had bought for me.

I was a graduate student in mathematics and physics at Columbia. I was the original student who did not go to lectures but discovered the texts from which those supposed gods, our professors, were themselves simply copying out on the blackboard what we, the helpless students, tried to scribble down and understand as fast as we could. I bought all the books and I worked out every single problem in every single book.

## Peter Gimbel

I'm awed by intellectual prowess, especially in the physical sciences, and on *that* score Brooks always awed me. He had the highest academic record of any predoctoral student who ever went through Pupin—that's the physics building at Columbia—up until whatever time that was, late forties or whatever.

ELIZABETH ARCHER BAEKELAND
Brooks was within one week of getting his Ph.D. in chemistry at
Columbia, and he just *left*. He left, he said, because he was sitting in
class and he had taken all day to do the answer to one problem and
this guy came in and did it in fifteen minutes—unless he could be
the best he didn't want to do it at all.

ELIZABETH BLOW
I know there was opposition in the family to Brooks's quitting Columbia, and I think I heard that they even reduced his income
because of it. But meanwhile he had decided to become a writer.

## From the Diaries of John Philip Cohane, Unpublished

*Monday*. Thanksgiving we entertained on a reasonably extensive
scale—thirty or so people late in the afternoon for cocktails.
Yvonne Thomas and her budding daughter Gwenny; Oscar Williams, the poet and anthologist, who gave me a recording of his
dead wife Gene Durward reading a selection of her own
poems—splendid poems, badly read; Jack Astor; Barbara and
Brooks Baekeland—Brooks is currently at odds with his father
who isn't speaking to him because he deserted physics for
writing.

BROOKS BAEKELAND
I enrolled in a short-story-writing class at Columbia to "titrate"—
loosely: offset, neutralize—my studies in mathematical physics. I
used to get off the Fifth Avenue bus at Seventieth Street each day
when returning from my classes and sit for an hour or more in front
of the fountain in the Frick Museum to wash all the chemistry and
physics off me.

ALASTAIR REID
I was teaching at Sarah Lawrence when Brooks's short story—I think
it's the only story he's ever had published—appeared in the college
literary magazine, *Inscape*. The faculty adviser to the magazine was
Brooks's old roommate at boarding school, Ambrose Gordon. In fact,
it was at Ambrose Gordon's house near Bronxville that I met Brooks

and Barbara for the first time. She was raw-faced, large-boned, but I found her very attractive in conversation, in her enthusiasms and her suddennesses. She was much looser than Brooks. He was terribly aloof, very conscious of his own elegance—he dressed with almost finicky attention. What would be that thin elegant look that we have now—it was his. He exaggerated his own thinness. He was balding and he looked as though he polished his head. I mean, he had an incredible arrogance, a kind of personal arrogance.

I think Ambrose Gordon had invited me to dinner that night so I could say to Brooks Baekeland, "I read your story." It's been about thirty years since I read it, but I do remember that he was clearly into a certain kind of wordplay that was pretty fashionable. He talked about Queneau, whom I hadn't read then but have since. Raymond Queneau, the French puzzle-maker—word games. Brooks invoked people like that and Karl Kraus, and I remember being annoyed because he was clearly bent on naming writers that other people hadn't read. He gave the impression that he was a mysterious and secret writer—an impression which I may say he kept up as long as I knew him, into the sixties, because when I met him about ten years after this, he was still, you know, secretly and mysteriously writing something which—there was no question about it—was a masterpiece. He chose to arrive at the top in his own mind. I mean, his story in the Sarah Lawrence quarterly was clever, but that's all. But then, I never thought of Brooks as a writer—ever.

HELEN DELANEY
As a work of fictional art, Brooks's short story may leave something to be desired, but as naked fantasy it is simply astonishing—both as a psychological self-portrait and, amidst all the giddy hilarity, as a sinister foreshadowing of Brooks's future behavior toward women.

## "Milk," Brooks Baekeland, *Inscape,* Sarah Lawrence Literary Review, Spring 1955

Bitterbaron Bentley was bewitched with Bach and Baby-blue eyes; and Balls and Bangs and Bungs and Balloons and Baboons; and Buttocks and Beadles and Beerbohm; and Baubles and Bassets; and Bigness and Biting and Birthdays and Bishoprics; and Blushes and Blurbs and Blow-holes; and Bliss; and Boudoirs and Buns and Borscht and Bow-wows; and Beautiful Bouncers; and Bubbles and Boxers and Boys; and especially with Brut and Bon-ton—just to mention a few things that bewitched him.

How could Knipples (J. Frederick Knipples: "Freddy") resist his excellent advice on diet?

He couldn't, of course.

The thing was that Freddy had been losing weight, due to the wrong flora (improper bowel management), and, meeting Bently at the house of a fashionable hostess—where her small dog vomited yogurt in his lap—Freddy lost no time in seeking the debonair Bitterbaron's advice. Under the circumstances the advice was uncommonly pithy: raw mushrooms and mother's milk—a quart a day, minimum. Bitterbaron gave the name of a good wet nurse and advised stepping up the dose until the final figure of a gallon, or four quarts, was reached in three months, which would require two and possibly three nurses, that is, six tits at the outside.

"They run about 2.7% on butterfats and very high in protein," said Bitterbaron, jotting down the information for Freddy. "So you'll probably feel a nice sort of glow after a while, but I think a little roundness will be becoming to you, Freddy."

He pinched Freddy's breast.

"You're much too thin. The mushrooms will give you what I call Adventure Tone. It's not quite like Muscle Tone. It's better, rather more adventurous.

"You'll be a regular wild boar, you naughty boy!"

They both laughed delightedly.

Well that's how it started—the diet, I mean.


Freddy was small and blond and he bit his nails down to the quick. He had thinning hair (he was painting the scalp with iodine to "stimulate" new growth, and the iodine looked like a birthmark), and his eyes were like two pleasant, disqualified marbles. Freddy needed love—all the time. Those blue, vague, marble eyes of his showed it. They were like the eyes of a woman after childbirth. Of course he wore the fashionable black "loafers" with tassels (the smart, expensive ones), dark-gray flannel suits (Brooks Brothers) and gray socks with blue piping, and he never sat without crossing his legs gracefully and smiling: and he had the world's most happy, charming smile. Freddy had no problems—if you except his flora—and he had oodles of money to play with. Only he hardly realized it himself. He just took it for granted, and he was terribly generous with it with all of his friends. His father, Argon Hoegfeldt Knipples, and his grandfather, Karl Peter Knipples, built up the Knipples family shipping business which had left him and his mother very well off when Argon died. And now there was only himself left, the last of the Knipples, going on thirty-six, adjusting nicely.

Of course, it can't be denied that Freddy missed his mother frightfully, but that too was something he took for granted. When he talked about her—as he did constantly—it was with such a charming and loving naiveté that it hardly seemed like a mourning, but more like a tribute to her invisible concern and protection. Freddy was as gentle and as faithful as a girl. Many people never realized that his mother was dead. He still referred all his choices and delights to the invisible aegis of that gentle ghost whom he spoke of to everyone—even to chance acquaintances—as "Mother." It was as though he took it for granted that everyone had met her or known her at one time, and all loved her as he did. Some people really felt they did, no doubt. And it was hard not to believe that she had been the most perfect of women, though probably unhappy with Argon H. Knipples, empire-builder, and to that small extent—because of her unhappiness—perhaps imperfect, as even towards the rude and bestial empire-builder a good woman has duties. But let us not look into this too closely, as it is likely to be unpleasant. That Freddy did not like his father, whom he referred to as "that brute," we know, and that is enough—perhaps too much.

Naturally then, in the light of all this, Freddy must have asked himself what Mother would have thought of going on a diet of mushrooms and mother's milk. He remembered that she had lived for several weeks once on nothing but tomato juice and yogurt—on his suggestion—he loved her when she was slim—and they had both been very excited by the results. Of course, human milk was a different matter. He loved milk, but he wondered if woman's milk would be as delicious as a cow's milk. After all it was pretty silly to nourish a prejudice in favor of a cow; rather perverted when you come to think of it—like that boy in *The Hamlet*. *That* was something to think about! He'd never thought of it that way, of course, and now that he

did, he wondered why everyone didn't drink mother's milk instead of the milk of those great horny, bellowing animals that
frightened him so. A mother's milk must be delicious or it
wouldn't be human. . . . Was that right? He wasn't exactly sure
what he meant, but that was close to it. . . .

Naturally this line of thought—with the debonair Bitterbaron's moral backing and solid, scientific reasoning—put
Freddy into quite a state of delighted anticipation. Bently was
kind enough to make the arrangements for him (the amount of
milk needed was the thing to make sure of), giving Freddy's elegant apartment as the address to the wet nurse and making the
first appointment for him.

The first appointment was for a Saturday afternoon—a mati-
nee, so to speak. Freddy was extremely nervous and he spent the
whole morning foolishly arranging and rearranging the flowers.
(Yellow and pale-mauve Irises and bruise-purple Lady Slippers.
For some reason the Lady Slippers always gave him a vague
thrill. He called them "you smutty little darlings" and giggled at
the ridiculousness of what he had said.)

When the doorbell rang, he was primping a little in the bedroom.

"Coming!" he sang.

He ran, flinging his elbows out a little, and he was panting
when he opened the door. His face was a little red, but he had
on his most charming smile, and he apologized profusely for not
coming sooner. He offered to take the lady's coat, very gallantly
and affably, which she allowed him to do without any lack of
aplomb, only saying:

"Yo name's Mist' Freddy Nipples?"

She was a big, genial woman with hands like first-baseman's
mitts and a bosom like the State Capitol.

Freddy glided under breasts, clutching her hat and coat, and
hung them up, chattering to her.

She caught sight of him.

"Thas' a funny name—"

"It's K-nipples, not Nipples, dear. You can call me Freddy if
you want, though."

"All right, Mis' Knipples—ah mean, Freddy," she grinned.

"You all min' paying me in advance, Mis' Nipples—I mean,
Freddy? I always ge's paid first. I don' want . . ."

"Oh sure, dear."

"My name's—"

"Yes, I know. Bee told me. Is that all right, Mary?"

He smiled and stuffed a bunch of bills into her hand and started off towards the kitchen with his hands tensed a little away from his sides as though he were dangling little weights on strings from the ends of his fingers.

"Yas, Mis' Nipples! Yas, this is just fine! . . . I'm coming."

She stuffed the money into her purse.

"My real name's John, of course, but Mother and I both hated it. It's so common—Mother passed on, poor dear. I was named after my Uncle Fred. He used to wet the bed."

He giggled.

Mary looked around as she followed him across the large, airy living room.

"Sho mighty nice place, Freddy. Where's the baby at?"

"What baby, dear?"

"De baby I gonna give 'is lunch to."

"Oooo, darling, there's no baaaby!" he howled. "That is, I'm the baby, darling. *I'm* the baby!"

Mary stood rooted to the floor.

"You de baby?"

"Didn't Mr. Bently tell you about it, darling? . . . It's for *me*," he wailed, delightedly.

"My milk's fo' you?"

"Well, you see, dear, Mr. Bently's a very, *very* famous man, and he says I need the kind of milk—that is—human milk. See, he's a dietitian, dear. He knows all about it. It's because of the butterfat, he says. I'm taking mushrooms too. All you have to do is put it into a bottle or something—you know—whatever it is you do . . ."

Freddy waved his hands and smiled charmingly.

"Put it in a bottle? Mis' Nipples—Mis' Nipples, I din' come fo' no—"

"Oh dear, Mary! How perfectly, excruciatingly exasperating! Now everything's gone wrong. And Bee said—here—wait . . ."

He plunged his hands into his pockets and took out ten dollars and held them out to her.

"Here! Now, for heaven's *sake*, don't be a foolish old thing!"

He pressed the money into her hand. She now had about

twenty dollars. It was sinking through her head that at twenty dollars a quart, roughly speaking . . .

"All right . . . all right, Mis' Nipples. But I don' put any milk in any li'l bottles—so, if *you* don't mind, then *I* don' min'. You jus' gonna take it de way she comes, Misteh!"

"You mean—"

"Yas, Mis' Nipples."

She was grinning from ear to ear.

"You gonna be ma baby!"

She went off into roars of laughter, exploding and giggling and shaking all over uncontrollably, and Freddy joined her.

"Darling!" he screamed. "Wonderful!"

"Freddy!" she howled. "Mis' Nipples . . . Oh, ma achin' back! . . ."

And they both danced around the room, holding their hands to their mouths, rocking with laughter, and looking at each other, like a playful, pink mouse and a wild elephant.

Mary began unbuttoning her blouse, showing two enormous, velveteen dugs, lying on her stomach. With one great hand she reached out and grabbed Freddy by the arm and pulled him to her, sitting down on a chair and pulling him down on her lap at the same time. Before he even had time to protest (struggling would have been useless, and he knew that) she shoved his face into the right dug, forcing the stiff, leathery nipple into his open mouth. He tried to pull his head away for a bit, but she pushed it back, forcing his face into the warm, yielding flesh, and then he began to nurse, crossing his feet back and forth and closing his eyes. He had his left hand up on her shoulder, and with it he made a fist, holding the thumb inside. Every once in a while he opened it, and then he closed it again, sucking.

As I said, that's the way it started, but that's not the way it ended.

At the end of the nursing period, with milk drooling down his face, Freddy would sit for a while, while Mary rocked, grinning. They always had a little banter and made a joke of their relationship. She would call him "baby" and he would call her "Mother," both chortling or howling with outright laughter. But when she left, he would go into his bedroom and fall onto the bed in a profound, dreamless sleep. She came by every day, and finally when she could no longer supply the growing demand, she brought along another wet nurse who took turns with her, and then Freddy had two mothers, and the wet nurses in good cheer shared the "baby," drowning him in pap. He gained twenty-five pounds, learned to suck his thumb, wet his pants and do other things which the wet nurses thought terrifically funny, even helping him sometimes, howling with laughter. It was a gay and noisy threesome. They spoiled their baby and were spoiled in their turn. Freddy had never been quite so happy before.

When the third nurse was brought in, Freddy was suckling most of the time, and he always had drinks set up so that his mothers could get high, and the party often grew frolicsome. But they always treated him like a child, and he steadily slipped deeper and deeper into childhood, sometimes being unable to speak for long periods of time during the day, only laughing and playing with himself.

He never left his apartment anymore, spending most of his time in bed or on the laps of his mothers.

Freddy might have rocked gently forever on the Mare Lactosa, gulping and drowning and blubbering deep in tumescent warmth, flowing backwards protoplasmically into the vaginal darkness of memory (or out of it, who knows), if the whole thing hadn't gone too far. But the mothers were jealous, and there were times when they tried to snatch him away from each other, the liquor firing their natural possessiveness.

"Give him . . . to me! It's my turn!"

"No—"

"Give—him—I—say—give . . ."

"No, no! Stop that now, I say! Cut it out! I got him!—"

"Oh, no you—haven't—"

"Ugh—"

"Mary, Mary! Help me. Hey!"

And so they tugged at him and pulled him and tore at his pudgy, sweet body, hugging him and clutching him to their enormous, velvet dugs, stuffing his pale, panting face between them into the terrae incognitae of progressive suffocation. The harder he gasped for air, fighting their great strength with his puny one, the harder they clutched him and hugged him into the cruel, nostril-clogging meat of the Mammary Glands. It was as though by pulling him hard enough, he might be pulled right inside and the warm doors of protectiveness closed after him for ever more.

And so it was that one day, after such a steaming, grappling tempest of desire, he went suddenly limp in the arms of Mary, who held him, tiny like the Christ of Michelangelo's *Pietà* in her lap, and the three weeping mothers saw their child was still. And although they all tried blowing breath back into his little lungs, tearing him again to be the one to bring him back to life, hugging him and clutching him and sobbing and bending over him, it was no use whatever. His lungs were full of milk. It ran miraculously out of his mouth, out of his ears, out of his eyes. His very blood was no longer red but white. And when the mothers saw this, when they saw that their baby was dead, they held him for a while, looking at each other in amazement. And then they dropped him, and he sprawled like a broken doll on the great big bed in the bedroom, still drooling a little out of his mouth.

## Notes from a Psychiatric Consultation on Antony Baekeland, New York, March 12, 1971

During his infancy, he is said to have screamed a good deal. His mother states that his father refused to allow her to pick him up and insisted that he be kept on a strict schedule, "even though he screamed bloody murder."

## MARJORIE FRASER SNOW

Barbara was a very conscientious mother as I remember. I had no children myself at that point. We used to wheel Tony over to Central Park in one of those stroller-type things—once, he got out and started walking along the edge of the sidewalk and I said, "Barbara, that's awful dirty there for him, we'd better get him back into the little stroller," and she said, "If you keep him isolated from all kinds of dirt, he'll never build up antibodies to prevent any disease that may come along." Of course in those days that was rather an unusual way of looking at it—today I think it's accepted. So she understood and knew exactly how to raise him, I felt.

PATRICIA NEAL

The whole atmosphere of Broadmoor reminded me of a play I was in—*The Children's Hour*. I don't know why that just shot into my head but it did. Maybe because there's a school in the play. James Reeve, who painted my portrait, said, "Why don't you come along with me to visit a friend?" He told me that the boy had murdered his mother—I didn't get their name. It seemed really horrendous, but he wanted me to come see him. And I wanted to—I'm loving. So I went and we had tea with him and he was very glad to see us and very polite and well-mannered. He knew I was an actor. James had told him he was bringing me to see him. We sat in a big room with a lot of other people. And he was charming. We made jokes. There was a lot of laughing. Anyway, on the way home I realized who he was. It suddenly dawned on me—Baekeland! Because his aunt is a great friend of mine. I said to James in the car, "I'm sure he's the one!" and when I got home I called Elizabeth Baekeland and I said, "Elizabeth, you'll never guess who I just saw! I just saw Tony." And she said, "You didn't! You didn't! You didn't!" It was like she got frightened.

JAMES REEVE

Elizabeth Baekeland lived in London and never once went to see Tony in Broadmoor, which was disgraceful. And one in the eye to her when Pat Neal rang up, you know, saying she'd just come from seeing him in Broadmoor. I mean, that must have set her back on her haunches! I asked Pat to come because I knew it would give Tony great pleasure, it would sort of bolster him up in the eyes of the others—it's frightfully important when you're in that sort of place to seem to have interesting friends.

## Letter from Antony Baekeland to Miwa Svinka-Zielinski, Undated

Broadmoor

Dear Miwa—
James has come to see me twice. He brought Patricia Neal, who I was very anxious to meet as I have always admired her. She was so very nice—I know you would like her.
    James brought me sketching materials on his last visit. He

showed me photographs of his paintings done in Haiti and they
are macabre and interesting—I liked them very much. I haven't
had too much of a chance to do much drawing because the
dear materials you brought me are still in another part of the
hospital.

All love to you,
Tony

## Miwa Svinka-Zielinski

I got him lots of crayons and paper so that he could do something,
and they did not give them to him. I asked one of the psychiatrists
there about this and he said, "That takes him from reality."

## Tony Van Roon

Tony worked in the handicrafts shop—it was sort of something that
he wanted to do and it was backed up by medical staff. Everybody—
nine times out of ten—is put out on work detail, it's supposed to be
on therapeutic lines. Handicrafts was very much a sort of time-pass-
ing area. Tony used to go over there to paint. It would have been
very difficult for him to do actual painting on the block in Cornwall—to do that he would have had to have been on what they call
"house parole."

From my point of view, I saw him as a fairly sort of stable person.
That's not saying that he didn't have a mental illness, but that he
appeared to have accepted the environment he was in and just got on
with everything from day to day, but kept a wide berth of most people, particularly anybody in authority. I think that becomes a way of
life in that environment. You think, "Well, is that screw in a good or
bad mood? If he's in a bad mood I'd better not say anything 'cause I
might get a kick on the ear or whatever." I think the way of thinking
of most people who had any sense was to just keep a low profile,
because once you started sticking up for your own rights and other
people's rights, not only was it ignored, but it was thrown back in
your face quite often by excessive use of medication—which was always justified by medical staff. I'm not saying that the medical staff
colluded. What I'm saying is that all it took was for a sort of senior
nurse to say, "This patient is becoming a bit psychotic," for the doctors to justify upping the medication.

### PATRICIA GREENE

The first time we visited him, it was a very shocking experience—he looked so bad. He was pretty shabby, and we got him some clothes— a pair of pants and some socks—and we brought him stuff to eat.

The second time, we found him much better—there was a year between visits. And this time he was paunchy. We asked him what he wanted and he said he wanted music, classical music I think it was, and I said I thought he ought to have some shirts—we felt it would pick him up a little.

You know, Barbara had brought him to see my husband professionally. At the time Justin didn't tell me. He would never speak of friends or their children if he were treating them. Several times I met people in his waiting room and I was surprised. I saw Barbara there once and I was totally surprised.

I don't really remember how we first met the Baekelands, whether it was on the street with the children or whether a friend introduced us. I just remember being enormously impressed with Brooks and Barbara. He was cold and dark and she was warm and light—it was like they were Yin and Yang. I thought they were the most fascinating couple I'd ever seen. I remember Barbara with a big fox fur hat. She said, "It's just my skiing hat." To me she was glamorous, and that hat was the cat's meow!

And she rode horses. She'd get up at six in the morning to go off and ride somebody's Irish hunter in the park. Brooks said to me once, "I can tell when she gets up in the morning—the bed goes up like that and she's gone." So that's what I remember—that she would get up at six to ride a fiery horse in the park and Brooks would let her go.

There was a painting of Barbara in their house, painted before she married Brooks. In the painting she had her hair back and very red lips and a very décolleté dress and I remember studying that and wondering if that was the real Barbara or not.

### ELIZABETH BLOW

The first time I ever saw her was at one of the Art Students League balls, which in those days were great events—sort of like the Beaux-Arts balls in Paris. Everybody went to a great deal of trouble over their costumes. This one was a literary ball, the theme was literature, and I wore an old beautiful red velvet skirt that was made in tiers of French ribbon and a black bodice—I was *Le Rouge et le Noir!* A lot of the men didn't know what to do for their costume so they just put a towel around their heads and made their faces up with some kind of dark brown paint and went as Hindus. Fred Mueller, who I was engaged to, was very blond and Germanic-looking, and he went as a Hindu—he looked absolutely marvelous. And I think Brooks was dressed that way, too—he was tremendously attractive, just one of the handsomest men I've ever met in my life.

Anyway, when I went to the ladies' room, there was this beautiful girl there. She was *not* dressed in costume, she just had on a perfectly ordinary dinner dress. We got to talking and she told me she'd just had a son. And she talked about her son—she was very happy, she was thrilled to death.

We saw the Baekelands a lot after that night, mostly in their house. It was a rather conventional house, considering the personalities *in* the house.

HEATHER COHANE

My husband Jack told me this story about the Baekelands. It was long before I knew either of them. It must have been about the time Tony was born. They were all having dinner in some restaurant—Jack and his wife before me, and I think Aschwin Lippe and maybe *his* wife, Simone, and Brooks and Barbara—and they were playing this game: "For a million dollars would you eat a pound of human flesh? Would you go to bed with the first person you met after going through a revolving door, for a million dollars?"—and so forth.

Brooks must have answered yes to *that* question, because Barbara was saying to him as they left the restaurant, "Oh well, if *that's* the way you feel, *I'll* just go off with the first man that comes along in a car!" And she dashed into the middle of the street and flagged down a car with four young men in it. She jumped in and it took off. And of course, Jack and his wife and Aschwin and Simone and Brooks were left there with their mouths open, watching her disappear.

A couple of hours later she came home, having evidently got rather cold feet. Barbara was very beautiful in those days, so I mean, that was quite a crazy thing to do in New York City, a *dangerous* thing to do in New York City. Very crazy and very dangerous.

## From the Diaries of John Philip Cohane, Unpublished

*Friday*. Dinner tonight at the Baekelands—Ben Sonnenberg, the publicity agent, and his wife; a supposedly brilliant psychia-

trist, Sandor Rado; Geoffrey and Daphne Hellman—he writes
for *The New Yorker,* she is a strange faunlike harpist. Afterwards
Betty and Fred Mueller dropped by, and we spent most of the
time trying to get free advice from the psychiatrist.


ELIZABETH BLOW

When Fred and I had our first child, we were living down in Greenwich Village in a very tiny apartment. Then we moved to Fiftieth
Street and Second Avenue, to a railroad flat over a liquor store. Then
we were going to have a second child so we had to move. And Fred
found this incredible house on Seventy-second Street, which we
rented for only one hundred and sixty-five dollars a month from this
couple who were going to England for two or three years—he had a
Rhodes Scholarship.

It was mammoth—five floors—and Fred, poor Fred, would come
home from work and haul himself up to the top floor, the old maid's
quarters, which he was redoing so we could rent it out. Whoever
rented it was going to have to use our staircase.

We ran an ad and a very nice lady and her daughter-in-law, a
widow, turned up and they were absolutely delightful. It came out as
we were talking to them that the older woman was Barbara
Baekeland's mother. She was lovely-looking, and over the years she
has never changed very much. I mean, she had nothing of the sort of
smashing looks of her daughter but she was very pretty, very kind of
birdlike, always very nicely dressed. She always had a sort of prim
and proper look about her.

I think we charged them one hundred and sixty-five dollars a
month. They made the place absolutely charming. The sitting room
in the front they fixed up with great taste, and the little kitchen that
Fred had put in. They didn't entertain very much, but Barbara came
over a lot to see her mother, and that was how I really got to know
her so well. And of course Tony would come over all the time to
spend the afternoon with his grandmother. He adored her. And she
adored him. And whenever Brooks and Barbara would go away for
the weekend, he would come and stay over.

Nini was a fascinating person at that time because she was quite
neurotic, you know. She never could sleep very well, she had to have
all the blinds pulled down—there couldn't even be one single ray of
light coming in—and still she could not sleep a wink. I remember
her thousands of times leaning over the banister. I would say, "Hi,

Nini, how *are* you?" and she would say, "Oh hi, darling. Didn't sleep a wink last night—I'm a wreck." She was always saying "I'm a wreck."

As far as one could see they were a very happy little family. Brooks and Barbara appeared to be the ideal couple with this charming little boy whom they both loved—no, I don't think *too* much, you can't love someone too much. Of course later it did become too much.

### ELIZABETH ARCHER BAEKELAND
One summer I visited Brooks and Barbara on the Cape, Ballston Beach in Truro. It was once my stepfather's beach—Ozzie Ball, Sheldon Osborn Ball. He owned from Truro to North Truro, two miles of oceanfront. Zeckendorf offered him three million dollars for it, but he *gave* it all to the national parks.

Tony and I played together all day. He was so bright, he was way ahead of his class. I mean, I could spend the whole afternoon with him and have fun, and I'm not a child lover to that extent. I mean, I treat children like grown-ups—if they don't give me the same thing as a grown-up, I don't want to be with them. And Tony could give me the same as a grown-up—you know, opinions, feelings, wonderful observations. I would say his best time was up till the age of about four.

One afternoon, he and I watched a praying mantis on the boardwalk, and then he sat and drew the mantis and then he drew some birds—really wonderful. And later that night when Barbara was putting him to bed, I heard her say—it was over the partition that divided the rooms—"Tony darling, who do you love more, Liz or Mummy?" And he said, "Mummy, of course." And I thought, if at *four* she's giving him that kind of signal . . .

### DODIE CAPTIVA
I knew them from the Cape. I can't say I knew them intimately. I mean, I knew them about as well as people do when one lives there year-round and the other comes for the summer.

I used to go once a year to visit New York and I was walking up Fifth Avenue, north of Rockefeller Plaza, daydreaming, when I suddenly caught sight of something familiar out of the corner of my eye—a woman and a small boy. He was five, maybe six—little enough to almost have to be held by the hand. They were strolling and looking into store windows, and when I came abreast of them I

Leo Hendrik Baekeland                    Céline Swarts Baekeland, 1912

The Baekelands, 1915. From left to right: daughter Nina, Céline, Leo, and son George

*Left:* Leo Hendrik Baekeland's laboratory at Snug Rock, Yonkers, New York, c. 1909

*Above:* The main house at Utowana Lodge, the Baekeland camp in the Adirondacks

1

2

3

4

5

6

GEM
RAZOR

10

7

8

9

Objects made of Bakelite. 1—Jewelry. 2—Toilet seat (half section). 3—Ashtray and cigarette holder. 4—Cream deodorant container. 5—Razor box. 6—Milking-machine part. 7—Phonograph record. 8—Telephone mouthpiece. 9—Radio. 10—Bazooka part, bullets, subway straphanger.

Brooks Baekeland in the
Air Force, Canada, 1942

Barbara Daly Baekeland
at about age seventeen,
Boston

Barbara in Hollywood,
1941

Brooks and Barbara at the Stork Club, New York, February 10, 1943

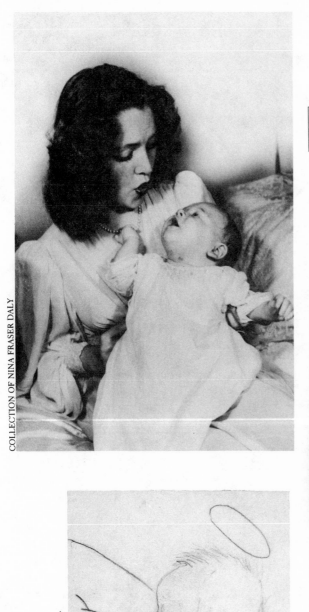

Barbara and Tony,
1946

Barbara and Tony
in New York

An early drawing
by Tony

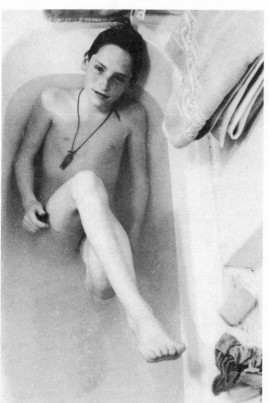

*Above:* Tony at his grandmother Nina Daly's

*Left:* Tony in Paris, 1959

*Below:* Barbara and Tony at Cape Cod, 1949

·looked at the reflection in the window and saw that it was Barbara and Tony. They were so enraptured with each other—whatever they were doing, whatever the conversation was—that my red flag went up!

## SARA DUFFY CHERMAYEFF

I was in Truro with my parents, I was sixteen years old and I had just learned to drive and I didn't have anything to do, and one night my father and mother said, "Now Sara, pull yourself together and *do* something. Now what can you do?" And what came up was that I could make a little children's camp. Well, it turned out to be a big business—I ended up with, like, fifteen children. I charged ten dollars a week. I made a lot of money—for *me*. My mother had this station wagon and I used that to pick up the kids. I took them to Gull Pond on the Truro-Wellfleet border—we took Oreos and apple juice and we'd go swimming. You know how people always say, *"Those were the days, I remember those days,"* but I *do* remember. I mean, now Gull Pond looks like, you know, Ocean City, Maryland, but when I went there with my little group, there wasn't a house on it.

Originally I had Edmund Wilson's little daughter, Helen Miranda Wilson, who's now a quite established painter, and Daphne Hellman's three children, Daisy Hellman, Digger St. John, and Sandy Bull, who became quite a big rock star. And one day Daphne when I was drumming up business said, "Some people called Baekeland have rented a house on Castle Hill Road, and they have a little boy." So I drove right over there and this woman in a brown bikini was washing the car. She was *gorgeous*. I mean, she was just everything, I mean the most . . . I mean, I don't think Marilyn Monroe had come alive yet—right? I think this was before Marilyn Monroe. I was sixteen and Tony was seven, so it was 1953—was Marilyn Monroe in business in '53? I don't know about whether she was there in history or not but for *me* I had just never seen anybody as glamorous as Barbara Baekeland. And I followed *that* star for many years.

She agreed right away that I could take Tony in my little bathing-suit group. He had sort of a batik bathing suit and he was redheaded and oh gosh . . . He was always my favorite. And one day a little later on that summer Barbara or Brooks took me aside and spoke to me about Tony's stutter, and I said, "He doesn't stutter." So they said, "He doesn't stutter with *you*?" I said, "Not at all." So at that point they hired me on as a baby-sitter for whenever they went out in the evening or went away for the weekend.

### DAPHNE HELLMAN
Once at their place on the Cape when I was there for dinner, Barbara and Brooks got Tony to read the Marquis de Sade out loud. He didn't read particularly well. He was doing it because he'd been commanded to. It struck me as very peculiar. Maybe it was to help him get over his stutter. Maybe it just seemed peppier than having him read from *David Copperfield*!

Barbara was the social one and Brooks was the curmudgeon. I remember one day I came upon them walking in the rain at night having some terrible fight. I guess Brooks flirted a good deal. Of course, Barbara was always hitching a ride with the milkman or somebody and being absolutely charming with them. She really was able to absorb people's flavor and get pleasure out of them.

### BARBARA HALE
Bob Hale and I went up to Truro to visit them. I'll never forget sitting on the beach and seeing Ben Sonnenberg trotting along in his Georgian manner—looking perfectly awful, you know, in a bathing suit. He saw that there was this perfectly beautiful redheaded girl sitting with me and he came up to us and said, "Wouldn't you like to share my little picnic?" Well, he had this very elaborate picnic basket such as you've never seen in all your life, filled with pâté and lobster sandwiches and stuff like that—this was his pickup deal, and from then on Barbara saw a great deal of Ben Sonnenberg in New York. I remember Brooks came down to the beach with Tony and joined us.

### DAPHNE HELLMAN
Tony and my daughter Daisy as little kids on the Cape were inseparable. I remember them crowing like roosters on the roof of this rough-and-ready house that Brooks and Barbara rented one summer right on the beach. Crowing was just something Tony and Daisy did at that time. It was very annoying to everybody. Barbara and Brooks got sort of fed up.

### DAISY HELLMAN PARADIS
We used to get into mischief together, at Ballston Beach, and go and raid the local farmer's garden. Once, we took our clothes off in our

garage and when cars came we jumped up and down and yelled, you know—and my father came by and he was rather amused.

I never had great feeling for Barbara at all, to tell you the truth—as a child, I didn't like her. I couldn't put it into words at the time, of course, but it didn't seem to me she had a whole lot of affection for Tony. Or for me, you know—or for kids in general. She was somebody who was always sort of saying "Oh *darling*," you know, this and that, but there was something sort of not so real there. Artificial maybe.

Tony wrote to me a couple of years after he killed her. I didn't answer because I really didn't know what to say, you know. Jesus Christ! What do you say to somebody who's killed his mother?

### HELEN MIRANDA WILSON

I remember very little about him—that he had red hair and freckles, that I played with him when I was very young, with him and Johnny Frank, the writer Waldo Frank's son. I'd better identify him as Waldo and *Jean* Frank's son, because Waldo was married a number of times. Johnny's now a paramedic and ambulance driver in San Francisco. Anyway, we all used to play together in the summer, and Tony Baekeland was a real brat and a bully. Yeah, a bully—and I was a pretty hefty little kid. You want me to tell you what I really remember about him? It's pretty funny actually. I remember us playing up in the woods and somebody went to the bathroom—I think it was him—you know little kids—and I think he scooped some up in his hand and chased me with it. That's it, that's my recollection of him.

### JONATHAN FRANK

Tony and I were real close when we were little kids, up till we were eight or nine. And we were both terrible! In fact there was another boy, Johnny Van Kirk, and the three of us were inseparable—we were called the Terrible Trio. The grown-ups used to call us that. But it was a fond name, even though I'm sure we *were* terrible.

### JOHNNY VAN KIRK

My mother used to make up stories about us—"Black Johnny," "Yellow Johnny," and "Terrible Tony." It was a threesome.

The only reason for the "Terrible Tony" was because he was always off on some very imaginative rant or other. He had a fantastic imagination, he just knew no bounds. Tony was not ordinary. No, I would say he was extraordinary.

He was certainly the wildest of the bunch. I spent a lot of time at the Ballston Beach parking lot with him blocking off large sections and flooding them with water from his house, making vast, swamp wonderworlds between the parked cars. He was always inventing mad games for us to play. Johnny Frank and I would go out and buy toy trucks and guns and stuff, but Tony would invent them right out of his head. Mostly fantasy games, role-playing games. And he had a capacity for involving you in them—you would forget your inhibitions and become a part of it all very easily.

He even convinced us that if we would rub this strange funny clay from the dunes on ourselves, we could fly. We'd literally spend hours running down the cliff and jumping off as far as we could, convinced that we had flown a little further each time—with a little more clay! And it was Tony's ability that really allowed us to do this. There was a kind of persuasion that he had. He was very forceful at that age. And it was a good time.

# 5

## FUN AND GAMES

Once a week Tony Baekeland, along with five of his fellow patients at Cornwall House, was escorted to the canteen, where he was free to purchase, among other things, candy, cigarettes, soap, coffee, and tea. A patient was not allowed to handle cash himself; rather, all purchases were charged to his hospital account, into which his money had been placed. Each month he received a computer printout of the status of his finances.

"Tony could be very kind to others," Dr. Maguire says. "In fact, I had to protect him from being overgenerous. I initiated a request for a protector through the Court of Protection, which is a branch of the Supreme Court in England, and Tony's money was eventually placed under the protection of a court-appointed guardian, who inquired into his needs and then apportioned the money to him. Usually it is given in a yearly sum, but I convinced Tony's guardian to give it to him in six-month installments. He was also receiving an allowance from his father, and there was quite a lot of money from other sources as well, including income from investments in New York."

By the beginning of 1976, Tony Baekeland had adjusted to hospital routine, both social and therapeutic. "He had a chronic illness, of course," says Dr. Maguire, "but he fluctuated—he had ups and downs. His true basic personality would show through every now and then. His kind of illness was not strictly an illness that depends on the environment. It was genetic.

"Tony was well read," Dr. Maguire adds, "but he had something a lot of schizophrenics have—a kind of pseudointellectuality about things. I've been involved with schizophrenics for a long time, because they're not boring—they're very interesting, in fact. There's a certain truth to everything they say. I find this fascinating, because it all *seems* so true, yet they can't function normally. And when they commit criminal acts, they always, in some way, manage to tell the world what they're going to do before they do it."

## TONY VAN ROON

I knew that Tony Baekeland was fairly solvent but I didn't know he was, you know, exceedingly rich or anything. But what I would say is always the sociopathic element in Broadmoor would take great advantage of people who were like that and would be their friend until there was nothing left. I do remember that when he went to the canteen he certainly always made adequate allowance for what he'd need in the week. But the thing was, as soon as he got back to the ward, people would say, Well, you don't need all that, why don't you give me some, and he was really a very nice guy, you know. So the problem was he would give things away, particularly if he saw somebody who was less fortunate.

## PATRICIA GREENE

He was always very sensitive as a child. He was a will-o'-the-wisp child, in a way—now you see him, now you don't. At his parents' dinner parties he would fly in and out, like quicksilver.

He would come to our house, but our children would not so often go there. He would come to us because we were more of a family, I think, and he rather liked that. I think Brooks and Barbara were rather social. I think they were *quite* social. He went to his grandmother's when they went out at night—I would see him walking down the street with his parakeet in a cage and his pajamas over his arm.

One Halloween I took him around the block. We made our costumes in those days, we didn't buy them, and I made one for him. Then I went around with the children. They were quite small. I remember Tony was overwhelmed with the excitement of it. And he ran off through the night, down the block, and I was quite alarmed because he just disappeared. We chased after him and finally caught up with him and he was just running, running, running, in a wild manner. And then we all went around the block together. The block was very nice in those days. At the Paul Mellon house, the butler answered the door and offered us apples on a silver tray. Those days are gone forever.

I remember Tony had some mice or something in his room, and of course he had the little bird, and I suppose he had fish. And when he would come to our house he would look at *our* animals—we may have had a white rat that impressed him, too. That was more of his link with my boys than anything else.

There was a vacant lot across the street from us—they had torn down the building—and I think there were rats which intrigued Tony and our boys, and I said, "You'd better stay away because you might get bitten." Our boys pretty much stayed away, but I think Tony used to go through the boards again and again and poke around and I think that upset Barbara, because I remember her speaking to me about that as a concern—how she could keep him away from the building. I guess Tony just had this enormous interest in any sort of animals.

## From *A Family Motor Tour Through Europe,* Leo Hendrik Baekeland, Horseless Age Press, New York, 1907

My two children are great lovers of animals, and if I let them have their own way, their not too small collection of dogs, rabbits, cats, guinea pigs, birds, etc., would soon increase to the size of a little menagerie. . . . When I finally heard that my boy, George, had been bargaining for a live and healthy ferret I decided that it now was time to compromise on some gentler representative of the animal kingdom, so I finally consented to tte purchase of two tiny Bengalese finches. Housed in a little cage, they were from now on to become our traveling companions.

## PATRICIA GREENE
One of the first times I met Barbara, she said, "Oh, Tony's raising moths in my closet." And I thought that was enchanting, so I looked and, sure enough, in a shoe box he had some moth cocoons, and she twinkled and was merry over that. I must say I adored her for that—*I* was always saying, "Get the moths *out* of my closet!" And *she* had mink coats and very expensive clothes in hers.

We invited Tony to our place in the country mainly because one of our sons had gone over to see some of his moths and was intrigued. You see, Tony was really just the boy-next-door type thing. The second time he came to the country, he developed warts from the frogs. There's apparently a little virus that they carry. I think Barbara was pretty horrified at that. He didn't come again.

You know, he did some drawings at our house in town. I must say they were quite different. Most boys were drawing rockets or airplanes and things like that, and he would be drawing more imaginative stuff—fanciful animals.

Barbara used to do paintings of insects. Very large. Mostly representative. They were very good. I remember she worked very hard one summer on Cape Cod, and she came back with an exhibit in the fall. I remember meeting her before the show and she said, "I'm a wild woman, I've been painting like mad all summer, I just couldn't stop, and I'm on my way to the hairdresser!" And her hair *was* standing out. She *was* a wild woman.

It was a charming show. You walked up some stairs in this very small gallery and Barbara was greeting people. I have a mental picture of her standing with her lovely hair and her lovely complexion and pretty dress. She had little white kid gloves on. I was impressed with that—white kid gloves! She was soft. I can see the little white kid gloves around her little plump hands—she wasn't plump but she gave the impression of being so. I commented on the gloves and she said, "I don't like to touch all these people, I guess." So that was a sidelight I remember of her character. Of course, people did wear gloves in those days.

## MARJORIE FRASER SNOW
She studied under, I believe, Gonzalez, I think on the Cape and also in New York at the Art Students League, and also under Hans Hofmann. I think she had a one-man show somewhere in New York. I think she got very fine reviews, as a matter of fact. I know she had one on the Cape. And Nini was so proud of her!

## PATRICIA GREENE

Barbara was very proud of her mother for taking a job at the Museum of Natural History. Mrs. Daly apparently didn't have to work at that point, although at one time I know she had rather a hard time making ends meet. It must have seemed like a dream to have Barbara marry all that plastic money! But later on, Mrs. Daly said she was bored just sitting around and she wanted to do something. Of course Tony was delighted when she went to work at the museum—after all, the Museum of Natural History! That was right down his alley.

I just took it for granted that he'd be a naturalist. I thought he'd go on and pull himself together—you know, that he'd get to be a rather eccentric naturalist of some sort. Or a painter.

## JONATHAN FRANK

When I visited Tony in New York, we used to cut out to the museum where his grandmother worked. Basically there was sort of a loose connection because we would report to her but we were pretty much on our own—and we were really young at that point.

We used to play outdoors a lot and I'd say we preferred it that way. At night we would escape to the bedroom and we had a game where we would climb up on a cupboard way up high and then jump down on the bed, pretending that we were pterodactyls—you know, flying dinosaurs.

## NINA DALY

I went looking for a job and I got one in the gift shop at the museum and we got a vacation in the summer for two weeks and we got holidays. I really enjoyed it. I would have liked to have done something else after I finished there. I would have liked to have worked in some store or something, if it had been a nice store. Anything to keep busy, to get out of the house in the morning.

Tony would stop in and see me an awful lot. I loved that. He used to come and spend about three nights a week with me, too. It was to keep me company because I was alone, you see. And I had lived with them for a while, because I hadn't gotten used to living alone. You have to get used to it if you're not used to it. My sister used to come and stay a lot with me. She never had any children, so she used the family's children. She loved children. I love children, too. I miss them now.

Tony went right nearby to the Buckley School. He liked it there. He was doing great. He was a good student, he always read and read and read and read. When he was in Broadmoor, he'd write me for some books he wanted and I'd send him some Shakespeare and others.

## "Comments" on Antony Baekeland, French Class, Buckley School, New York City

When he wants to, Tony can produce really beautiful prose and poetry in French as well as in English. The job of getting him to want to do this is tremendous at times, but the result, when it is good, makes whatever has gone before seem worthwhile.

Despite everything that has happened this term I still feel that Tony is one of the finest boys I have ever known. If he can realize his full potential he will be *the* finest.

### PETER GABLE

I met Tony in the second or third grade at Buckley, which was a very competitive school academically. He was not a peculiar child to another child—to *this* child—but he was certainly different because of some of his enthusiasms and abilities. I mean, he was uniquely brilliant—brilliant in ways that another child wouldn't appreciate, I think.

His artistic abilities were spectacular—he loved to draw birds, you know. He was a baby Audubon. I remember once we were out playing in the park—we were old enough to be unchaperoned, eight or nine or something—and I captured this pigeon. I don't think it was an entirely healthy bird, it was a basic Central Park shit-on-the-statues pigeon, and Tony took it from me and tucked it under his coat, and we rushed it back to his house on Seventy-first Street, and it was there for some time, flying free—first in his room and then having the run of the floor. The pigeon rather liked us, as I recall. In any event, it ultimately either conferred lice upon us or there was some fear that it would or whatever, and it was dispatched, I don't remember how. But I certainly remember Tony's sketches of that pigeon, in either pencil or pen and ink.

Every day after school we'd go home together to his house and stuff. You know, he was my best friend, and *his* house was more entertaining than *my* house. I mean, he had an area in his room where he raised orchids. I think that was a passion of his father's. I remember a rather enormous fishtank-like proposition with a controlled environment, in which these exotic flowers grew.

I remember his mother as being striking and a flamboyant and vivacious person. She was certainly more animated than the mothers of other friends. I mean, when you're a child, what do you know of the adult life? You know your parents, their friends, your teachers in school with whom you probably have some sort of distant relationship, your baby-sitter, the elevator man—in those days everybody had an elevator man; when I was a child the only adult you addressed by his first name was the elevator man.

I certainly perceived Barbara Baekeland as being extraordinarily *something*, you know. I also remember what I perceived at the time to be a rather stormy relationship with her husband. Oh, they would fight, they would fight. I can remember hearing them. Tony and I both sort of listened, though we probably couldn't hear the exact words that were being spoken. My mother and father were having a rather rocky time, too, so raised voices amongst adults in a household was not foreign to me, I didn't think what I heard over at the Baekelands was that strange, you know. But the volume!

Tony's father I remember as being austere and uninvolved—very much of a shadow figure. He once took Tony and his mother and me for a picnic one Saturday into some countryside. I remember so clearly being in the back of the car—he kept a Mercedes convertible at the time, I think—a sports car—the top was down, it was a beautiful fair-weather day, and Tony and I were bundled in the back. We buzzed up to where there was a beautiful glade with a pond and I guess we had our lunch and then Tony and I wandered off to play. But the interesting thing is that this and one other time are the only occasions I can remember—and Tony and I were close close friends for several years—when I was in the company of both his parents.

When summers would come, Tony would disappear to some foreign clime until fall, then we'd both be back in our short trousers and blazers, hiking off to school.

### SYLVIE BAEKELAND SKIRA

Brooks and Barbara were two very powerful people who had their own fight together, and the little boy was sort of a puppet in between. He was trained by these parents to be brilliant. You know, you can teach a child to say the Latin word for "monkey" as easily as to say "monkey," and he was trained that way. I'm completely against it.

Even when the son was in Broadmoor, Brooks was ordering him,

"You have to show remorse!" The son would say, "Absolutely not! *You* have to." There were letters, there were letters constantly. One would say, "*You* killed Mummy!" Which is a point of view. And the other one would say, "You didn't hit your mother with a banana, you hit her with a knife!" So. The thing that Brooks could never understand is that his son never showed him that he felt the slightest remorse. *That*, Brooks couldn't understand.

## Mishka Harnden

I'm sure Tony was born fairly unstable. On the other hand, all of what he went through when he was a kid certainly scrambled him for good. He was like that dog they had, you know—he was a slightly larger Pekingese. "Tony, do this! Tony, do that!" "Yes, Mother." I mean, Tony Perkins in *Psycho*—you know? I mean, it gets to be that close.

## Yvonne Thomas

The way she would praise him and show you everything he'd written or drawn! Both of them did. They wanted the boy to be a genius. That's what struck me. And made me feel uncomfortable. I felt uncomfortable with the boy because I felt *he* felt he had to be something.

You know, when you impose yourself on your children like that, it's because you want them to be more than *you've* been. I think they were very ambitious and that nothing had happened with their ambition. She was always talking about what they were *going* to do. They wanted to do a coup of some sort, either in literature or in . . . I thought they were silly. She represented something sort of social— purely social—to me. I thought the way she entertained and her conversation and that crispy sort of voice were affectations—everything was something that didn't interest me that much. Especially at that time. Now I don't care, you know. But then I was very strict— everybody was—about exactly the style that you chose to be. I became an Abstract Expressionist painter and it changed my life—it changed a lot of my views, a lot of my values. I didn't see too much of the Baekelands after that.

But oh, the son was shining as a little boy! But then when he turned into adolescence, one didn't hear so much.

## WILLIE DRAPER

Tony was the *most* brilliant and the *most* refined—and the most creative and the most sensitive—so he built the most walls the most quickly and his ability to communicate his feelings was lost the quickest. Tony right from the beginning was a marked man. I knew him at Buckley, I knew him the whole damn time. I mean, just the whole way through, you know, we were tight. But then I phased him out of my life because he was too negative for me, and my sister Checka filled the spot, she was going through more similar things.

Tony and I got stabbed trick-or-treating and stuff together—I can't remember whether we actually got stabbed or whether we almost got stabbed. These roughnecks followed us back from the park and they cornered us, and we were ringing the bell at Tony's house and nobody was coming down. Another time we had our bikes stolen in the park and some policeman took us around in the patrol car and everybody pointed at us like we were criminals.

He had—*both* of us had—very intense mothers, you know. I loved Barbara. I mean, *she* loved *me*, first of all, and part of the time Tony would be really jealous of me because—you know how it is—he'd get along really good with my mother and I'd get along really good with his mother.

Barbara was very loving—it's just that she was so intense emotionally, and her moods would change, based on her relationship with her husband and her whole Celtic character. She was just, you know, a wild woman. Sometimes it was just . . . it was frightening.

But Tony was a great guy, a great guy—he burned with such a pure flame.

The biggest mystery in my life is *why* we choose what we choose, because we do choose—in the end we have total responsibility for what happens to us. And, you know, what ignorance is it, what is the mechanics of what makes someone like Tony who has all of this potential . . . ? I think it's emotional starvation, myself—I mean, it really has a lot to do with just very basic things.

## SARA DUFFY CHERMAYEFF

I saw Tony every day, every single day when he was at Buckley. I'd gotten married when I was twenty, to Ivan Chermayeff, and we lived just a block away from the Baekelands. Barbara was very happy for me—I mean, she liked Ivan because he had, God knows, the scent of success on him. She gave me for my wedding present some very pale emerald earrings, which were very like the rings she used to wear—she told me they had been Brooks's grandmother's or something and that she had had them reset—two emeralds with two pearls. I mean, I was her darling baby-sitter, right? And, I suppose, to give her credit, which I *don't* like to do, 'cause I'd like to *kill* her, I suppose she really thought I was a lovely girl. You know, because I adored her—anything that she said went with *me*.

Ivan and I had this funny railroad flat on Seventieth and Lexington, right over the bus stop, and every day, from the time I was twenty until I was twenty-three, Tony came to me on the way home from Buckley, because Barbara might or might not be home. I mean, I lived just that far away from them—I was *right there*. At three o'clock in the afternoon he'd come in the back—he had a little strap with his books and a little hat. He had a key to my house. Ivan was at work and I'd be trying to write my novel and trying to clean up my house and trying to think my thoughts. And we'd go home to his house together.

It was everything I ever thought would be the perfect house. You came in and the dining room was there—I must have had a million meals in that dining room—then you went up the stairs and Barbara took you in to a sort of faun-colored library, quite a small room— and she had those green rings dripping off her fingers and her feet hanging off the ottoman like nobody's business. And back there was her bedroom, with lace all over the bed. She was often in bed, with all sorts of men sitting around—Harold Rosenberg, Saul Steinberg . . . I never saw Brooks there. She had a salon. And I mean, all I thought was, That's the way to live!

Tony's room was on the top floor. It had a skylight and a little tiny sort of wire balcony. I sure remember his room in that penthouse on Seventy-fifth Street that they moved to later on! I mean, in *her* room up there, she had the leopard-skin bed, the seven thousand Chanel suits in her closet—right?—and then there was Tony's room—the maid's room!

I don't remember when it was, but I began to see that Tony was just breaking to pieces, that they were killing him. They were a perfect couple, for that—to destroy the boy.

Oh, I can remember her movements when she would say—she would always say—"I've found this *marvelous* . . ."— right? That was a word she used all the time—"marvelous, marvelous."

Last spring it was a beautiful day and I went down to the Strand

Book Store—they have books on the street down in front, many many books—and I bought *The Letters of Madame de Sévigné* that I've always wanted. And I didn't notice it for a long time but some time later I saw that the book was signed "Barbara D. Baekeland, 1942—New York." It must have come from her books in the penthouse that were sold after she died. I mean, how bizarre!

And then I thought, God, in 1942 she was already collecting *The Letters of Madame de Sévigné*! Now I don't even know if she ever read them. *I* have them now and *I* haven't read them. She obviously already had something in mind. I mean, Madame de Sévigné had a salon—she was in contact with the cream of the French intelligentsia of the time.

She—they—they were really false, the Baekelands. False. False to everything. When I first saw them as glamorous, I guess I wanted to be false, but when I began to understand how *Tony* felt, I saw them as—terrible, both of them. *Both* of them *terrible*. I mean, I feel they never attended to what was serious—neither one of them *ever*. They just took on this idea of what was *life*. What did they have in mind? Imagine, I mean, going to live on the Île Saint-Louis! Who did they think they were? The Murphys?

I mean, when I knew Tony I was only ten years older than him and I didn't have any children of my own. But once I had children and I knew the responsibility that it takes to bring them up, I realized what total bullshitters the Baekelands were, with their *goddam* salons—well, it just isn't fair. I mean, I resented my parents—everybody resents their parents in one way or another, I suppose, right?—but, boy, I survived, and when you get down to it, you have to hand that to your parents in a weird way—right? They didn't *kill* you. And the Baekelands *killed him*.

And he was a wonderful little boy. I was a very romantic young girl and I had read D. H. Lawrence's *Rocking Horse Winter* and, you know, that's what he was—he was like a little literary boy, he was like all the boys in English novels. And that's what she had him be. He'd be brought in on a string and shown. She just didn't leave him alone. Not for one second.

I went to Broadmoor to see Tony with Missy Harnden, who I knew from when Ivan and I had a house in Cadaqués for five years, and all he kept saying was, "I'm free, I'm free now, I'm free." He said it to both of us—"I'm free now."

## Letter from Antony Baekeland to James Reeve, February 12, 1976

Broadmoor

Dear James,

I just got your letter which came with a lovely *Audubon* magazine from my grandmother, Mrs. Hallowell. Full of photographs of birds and flowers and forests in the U.S.A. This morning we had group therapy and it went very well. I feel so wonderfully well these days—my grandmother Nini will be very pleased with me.

You must be happy to be with your mother—when do you move into your new house? I have decided to be a writer like my Papa.

Poor dear Una Verbi has had to be put into a home—her mind has gone and Val feels terribly, of course, that he has abandoned her. He came yesterday in tears and stayed an hour. They both have become such good friends—I will be sad not to see her again, but who knows?

James, please give my regards to your mother. And do try to write if you find time in your busy days.

Love,<br>Tony

JAMES REEVE

The really disturbing thing was this mother bit. You see, in his letters to me he always said to give his regards to my mother. *My* mother! I'd probably mentioned my mother to him in passing but no more than that.

I had this recurring nightmare that he'd be let out. He had told me once, certainly, how lovely it would be to come and stay with me in the country, down in Somerset, and this haunted me, because what was I going to do if for some reason he *was* being let out and he said, "I want James Reeve to come and pick me up?"

I suppose I would have done it. But I remember being warned that he could be frightfully dangerous. I mean, anything could have set him off, poor chap.

When you went to see him, you went in through a great big massive gate. Then there was a little door, and sitting behind a desk was a man who took your parcels if you'd taken presents, and there was a ledger where you wrote your name and you said whether you were a friend or a relation. And then you walked through this tiny cubbyhole and there was another door, and you were let in, and then there was a huge great courtyard. You walked down one side of it, like a sort of cloister, and there was another locked gate, with a guard standing there who opened that, and then you would go down a corridor where the kitchens were, and this corridor went on endlessly. And finally there was this great big mausoleum of a room with a stage, a piano, windows, and dotted around were these sorts of little tea tables where we would sit and have our tea. Two or three guards sat on a bench, watching. If your back was turned to them, you could have slipped anything to your friend or relation, and taken anything back. Which was extraordinary!

I wondered to myself where Tony had got the clothes he was wearing, because they just weren't the sort of clothes he would wear. Not that they were rag-and-bone-men's clothes, they were just what my grandmother used to call "lower orders" clothes. They didn't fit well on Tony. I mean, he was rather distinguished-looking in his sort of slovenly way. The materials were all wrong—I mean, nylon jackets and things didn't look right on him. The impression was that the clothes were just castoffs, from a murderous plumber or something, who happened to have died the night before.

One always had the feeling he could very easily have supposed that one's interest in him or visits to him were just out of a sort of macabre fascination. And this is why one had to tread a very careful line jollying him along. I soon discovered that if Tony had a visitor, he didn't want to sit there and talk about Broadmoor. I respected that. He wanted to have news of the outside, which was a shame, because I was dying to ask all sorts of questions, like what were the bathrooms like, what were the dormitories like. And were the beds comfortable. They obviously weren't. But you couldn't ask him. He hated that. And actually, any morbid curiosity may have had a place the first few times I visited, but then it evaporated, I can tell you that.

Whenever I wrote to him, it was difficult because one didn't want to dwell on his side of things, so naturally one would just talk on about one's life. In one of his letters to me—here it is—one line says, "I wish you had done what I had suggested, i.e., come at two o'clock." Actually I remember that day. I deliberately hadn't come at

two—to cut short the thing. "So we could talk at length," he wrote.
Which meant, of course, two hours. "Also so I might have shown
you the really beautiful pictures of my mother which I felt would
have interested you. I don't think I told you, but she was a great
Artist." With a capital "A"! "And I'm trying to find some of her
remarkable paintings which were lost with the other things at 81 Cadogan Square." It's all so complicated, isn't it? I mean, you pick up a
letter to look at one sentence, and three others are underneath it.

Well, my friendship with Tony was a bit different. Visiting someone in an institution like that is not like having a friend, it's like
looking at an animal in a cage. I mean, it has to be!

Every time, I had to screw my courage up to the sticking point to
visit him, because, I mean, I also had my personal hangups about
the place. It reminded me of Rugby, where I was sent, which is
about the nastiest form of public school in England. It wasn't what
the authorities did to us, it was what the other boys did that was so
appalling. They used to roast you over fires when you arrived and
were sort of a new creature, and they used to heat up the backs of
those old-fashioned metal hairbrushes and brand your bottom with
them. Three boys committed suicide while I was there. It was a Victorian institution very much like Broadmoor. So it nearly made me
sick going to visit Tony, because even all the smells were the same—
sweat and urine and cabbage water and damp walls and blocked
drains and uncouth lavatories.

And then I would find this pitiful, wan, pasty-faced creature with
the bitten nails and the light-red oily hair. It was *not* attractive. Nothing attractive about it. Not that life should be attractive all the time, I
know, but it would have been nice to find one ray of light there.

The thing that used to shatter me was his having to be got from
being asleep. He shouldn't have been allowed to go to bed in the
afternoon—except, you see, a lot of the time he was drugged. It was
very obvious sometimes that he was drugged up to the hilt. This is
the pitiful thing—they'd rather the patients were quiet, so they'd
rather they just went to bed in the afternoon. They haven't got the
skilled staff to look after those difficult creatures. If each one of those
prisoners had had an interested psychiatrist, it would have been a
very different matter.

I remember going in the autumn once and all he wanted to know
was what the countryside looked like. Pitiful, really. And so few people visited him. That was the thing that I found unforgivable. So

many of the fashionable friends never went near him. They couldn't
be bothered! I suppose all that circle was just vapid butterflies. How
else do you explain it? They were all a lot of Fitzgerald dustbags!

## From the Diaries of John Philip Cohane, Unpublished

> *Saturday.* The night before last we gave an "artists" party for
> Jack and Drue Heinz—Brooks and Barbara Baekeland, No-
> guchi, Marcel and Teenie Duchamp, Barbara and Bob Hale.
> Barbara Hale and I presented over two hours of enthusiastically
> received pantomimes during which I engulfed over half a bottle
> of brandy which, on top of a stupendous bottle of Musigny '49,
> gave me my first hangover in months. At one a.m. everyone—
> including Marcel—was dancing gaily to Jelly Roll Morton—at
> 3:30 finally fell into bed.

### DRUE HEINZ
I knew the family early on in their life in New York, when the little
boy was about seven years old and his father was writing a scientific
thesis. They were a charming, intellectually inclined family, who
seemed at that time very "together" and set for a happy life.

### ALASTAIR REID
Barbara invited me to a cocktail party soon after meeting me at Ambrose Gordon's. Their house had an enormous paneled living room
and I realized then that they must be impressively wealthy. Clearly
she collected people, because she talked about having a salon and so
on, and she had picked the people who were there that night. She
was certainly capable of having a salon, she was just exactly the kind
of person who should have had one. She sparked, she was the center—people paid attention and she paid attention to them, too—
enormously. And Brooks was very laconic and, you know, cool and
hanging back, while she did the whole thing for him, and I could see
that he had acquired her because of her vivacity.

### JAMES KINGSLAND
I never knew quite what Brooks was doing, he was always doing
something—either writing a novel or dabbling in mathematics. It

was occasionally referred to lightly at dinner parties but I assumed that it was nothing very serious other than keeping him occupied during the day. Later on he went into exploring and stuff like that. He was a guy with a lot of ideas and energy who was looking for things to do.

### SYLVIA BAEKELAND SKIRA
It seems to me that Brooks has had the great problem of finding his own field, which he hasn't. And Barbara was certainly an excuse for his not having done anything particularly with his life and with his talent. He liked to say that he couldn't do this or that because *she* had to be going here and there.

### CÉLINE ROLL KARRAKER
Barbara changed tremendously from the time I first met her. Brooks, sort of like my grandfather, didn't like that life—and yet he was not strong like my grandfather to keep his own life.

### ELIZABETH ARCHER BAEKELAND
I can remember being at their house once when Barbara was carrying on in her very social way. And when I left, Brooks followed me out, he said, "I'm so sick of all this." You see, he was already fed up with it, but then he gave in—it was comfortable, it was easy. He became just like Barbara in some ways because he said to me one time, I remember, "I was shooting with the Duchess of Sutherland," and I said, "Who's that?" and he said, "You've never heard of the Duchess of Sutherland? Why, she's the richest woman in Scotland!"

### FRANCINE DU PLESSIX GRAY
The Baekelands entertained like no one else in New York; they had a kind of largess for it. It had a kind of European touch—there wasn't this ghastly long cocktail period, you know. It was orderly, and it was beautifully catered—marvelous food and marvelous wine. And it was very lively, it was more like a Parisian salon in a sense—there was a combination of money and intellect. In America, especially at that time, in the fifties, people didn't know the difference between Isadora Duncan and Inigo Jones, you know. I mean, the W-A-S-P ruling milieus were just rather illiterate, you could *not* have an intellectual conversation.

The Baekelands gave Cleve and me a fabulous engagement

party—just maybe twenty, twenty-four people—and afterwards, I remember, we played a kind of game where there was a curtain raised
to a certain height and the women sat in the back of the room and
the men took their trousers off—we got to see their BVDs and so
on—and they did this kind of chorus-girl dance behind the curtain
and the women had to guess whose legs belonged to whom—you
know, which are my husband's legs! Then they switched—the men
went on the other side and the women did it.

## ELIZABETH ARCHER BAEKELAND

There were always a lot of games. If the evening wasn't going well,
Barbara always had a great feeling for what to do to sort of pick it up.
She was a wonderful hostess. I never went there without having a
good time—*ever*.

The turning point in Barbara's social life came, as far as *I'm* concerned, when she met Marjorie and Fairfield Osborn. He was the
head of the New York Zoological Society and also the head of the
American Museum of Natural History—they were very well-con-
nected culturally, socially, everything, absolutely, and from then on
they were her closest friends. They adored her and they introduced
her to all of society, including Prince Aschwin Lippe, Prince
Bernhard's brother, and Barbara was just adored by all these people.
The Osborns got her going on the fast track.

I remember Barbara saying to me before one of her parties, "Now
you've got to look your best tonight, Liz, because all the most beautiful women in New York are going to be here." I remember Patsy
Pulitzer—she was a model, *very* beautiful. And Tennessee Williams
was there that night.

## BROOKS BAEKELAND

I had Dylan Thomas in my house. I was supposed to keep him while
he was in New York. He was a great poet but I bounced him out. He
took a Huntsman's shirt of mine with him—much too big for him.
My house was always buzzing with beautiful, silly, tipsy people.

## JAMES KINGSLAND

They entertained constantly. At the time we were all much younger
and one didn't think of them in terms of, you know, being marvelous
parties—one just used to go there and get mildly smashed, have a
good time, and go home. Later on I think Barbara realized that she

was giving good parties and became more self-conscious, and that's when you started seeing the likes of Salvador Dalí and stuff like that around, which I personally didn't find as amusing. I think she became very conscious of who people were in the public eye. There were also a number of foreigners coming through with handles of one sort or another.

It all goes back to the thing of people's weaknesses, and social climbing was certainly a *faiblesse* of the Baekelands'. These days they call them alpinists. Brooks I think had less social pretentions than Barbara—well, obviously, because he had the advantage there with her.

### ELIZABETH ARCHER BAEKELAND

She came to a party of ours once—at the time I was married to John Squire, my third husband, and we lived in a fifth-floor walkup. When I called to invite them, Barbara said, "Well, if you want us to come to a party, you have to ask us at least two weeks in advance." So I set a date a few weeks after that, and Barbara called up the day of the party and said, "I'm terribly sorry but we were out until three this morning and we're going to have to leave your party early tonight." So I said fine, I didn't see anything wrong with that. But John was furious, he said it was rude, that if she wanted to leave early she should just leave but don't call and say it's because she was out too late at somebody else's party—as if ours wasn't important.

Anyway, they came, and it turned out that a friend of John's who was with Pan American in Lisbon came with his wife, a Portuguese countess who was absolutely stunningly beautiful. And Barbara was galvanized. And then Muriel Murphy arrived with some man—none of us knew who he was and we didn't really catch his name. And when he left we all said, What beautiful shoes, did you ever *see* such beautiful shoes! That was all anybody noticed. Somebody finally realized it was Stanley Marcus of Neiman-Marcus. Anyway, Barbara was having a ball—she was dancing around with candlesticks. And at one point later on she was sitting on the floor and I remember John suddenly reached out his hand to her. He said, "Barbara!" She thought he wanted to dance with her so she jumped up, and then he just escorted her to the door, saying, "It's eleven o'clock, you're going home." She said, "But I don't *want* to go," and he said, "Oh no, you're very tired, you stayed up so late last night. *You're* going *home!*" And he put the coat on her. I was dying of embarrassment. The next day I called and apologized but Barbara said how impressed she was by John—she said she hadn't known he had that kind of guts.

Later that day the countess called to thank us and mentioned that Barbara had called and asked her to lunch—I mean, not even asking John and me! It was then I began to really see the light with Barbara.

I'll tell you another thing. I hadn't seen them for a long time and I was at some opening at the Metropolitan Museum and I saw Brooks and he said, "Barbara's upstairs," and I said wonderful as Brooks and I hugged, and I dashed all around till I finally found her and we kissed, you know, a peck on the cheek, the way you do. And then suddenly I saw her face go completely blank on me, and she's looking over her shoulder at Janet Gaynor and her husband Adrian who were arriving—can you imagine! I mean, she dropped me like a hot potato and went right over to them—never thought of introducing me. I was left just standing there, so I just turned on my heels and walked away. After that, I didn't even really want to talk to her. I was sorry at losing her friendship, but she had gone on to things that I wasn't willing to follow.

HELEN DELANEY
Have you ever heard of Sarah Hunter Kelly? She was a famous decorator, and she and her husband lived next door to Brooks and Barbara on Seventy-first Street. What divided them was a wall—luckily a thick wall, so Sarah never heard all the hollering and screaming that went on, and that's why they were able to remain friends. It was Sarah Kelly who introduced Barbara to Europe, and of course Barbara became a Francophile—she had what you might call terminal Francophilia.

From the New York Times, "A Lifelong Taste for Good Taste," Jane Geniesse, April 9, 1981

"I was absolutely determined to go to France," said Mrs. Kelly. Visits from a dashing cousin who lived in France, she said, set her on her "grand plan." "I thought she was immensely elegant and I wanted to live just like her," Mrs. Kelly said.

But if she liked living well—which fortunately she and her husband had the means to do—Mrs. Kelly also attached great importance to the cultivation of creative people. "I liked the writers and artists and I liked to paint. But I also had this yen for houses and fixing them up," she added.

The Kellys were soon part of the same group of young Americans as Scott and Zelda Fitzgerald and Sara and Gerald Murphy.

## NINA DALY
Mrs. Kelly used to come over to Barbara's house. I've been over there to her place and the inside is just like a museum. Barbara always called her her second mother.

## Letter from Barbara Baekeland to Nina Daly, June 1, 1954

Portofino

Dearest Mother,

You seem awfully far away and by the end of the summer I suspect I will be glad to get home. Europe has charms but traveling certainly gives one a certain perspective and a realization that we're a pretty wonderful country after all.

As things stand now we're living quite cheaply but Paris was a lot more expensive than we'd figured and this apartment is not cheap. But it is completely adorable. I wish you could see it. A tiny duplex where everything is perfection. You would love it and this village but we plan to take scads of pictures so that you'll have a very good idea of what the place is like.

Tony seems to be very happy here and certainly enjoys our American-style breakfasts. Most evenings we eat out in the Square under trees where we can watch the life of the town as we dine. Then home to bed to read and sleep and to look forward to another day much like the one before. Tony and I have been going in the afternoons to a really sweet little beach called Paraggi where he occasionally meets other English or American children and has a happy time anyway collecting sea-polyps— urchins and the like.

Brooks has settled down to a pretty good writing routine and I intend to start painting next week. This place is crammed with material and Tony's fishing and bug hunting should afford me ample time.

All for now, dear. My how I do miss you. I'll try and write at least once or twice a week.

Do write and soon—B.

## Letter from Barbara Baekeland to Nina Daly, July 7, 1954

Dearest Mother,
Well here we are in Austria and have been for some ten days and I with nothing whatever to do have just now found the time to write.

The country is really beautiful—idyllic. The village adorable with a really beautiful 15th cent. church and darling narrow winding streets with flower boxes everywhere and the traditional peaked roof that one always associates with Germany.

The service here is really first-rate. The hotel is run by a Countess Schall and the *bar-man* is the son of the ex-Austrian chancellor so this will give you an idea of the level of taste. It is costing us about $33.50 per week apiece for 3 meals and our beautiful room. And when I say the food is excellent I really mean it!

I am still in no mood to paint. I have all the wrong things with me and am enjoying too much all the leisure and relaxation. And as I don't know when or if ever I shall live in such ease again I am not going to create work for myself.

It rains heavily today but we are quite snug and content despite the weather.

Do write all your news. Love from all of us.

B.

## Letter from Barbara Baekeland to Nina Daly, July 27, 1954

Dearest Mamashka—
There has been such a deluge of mail coming from you these past days I can barely keep it all straight. This morning arrived your letter regarding windows, dirt, etc.

This will be extremely short as we were up until 5:30 a.m. with the Archduke Franz Josef and Princess Martha and I wakened at 7:30 a.m. and as a result feel slightly shattered. They are delightful and we had a very happy time.

Tell Mimi Cohane that Nancy Oakes de Marigny is expected today. Also expected is Patino the South American tin financier whose daughter eloped a few months ago and then died in Paris of a cerebral hemorrhage. Tell Mimi I shall give her love to Nancy.

All for now. You've been an angel to do all those odd jobs in the house for me.

Love & kisses,
B.

P.S. It won't be long before we all see each other once again.


## Letter from Barbara Baekeland to Nina Daly, August 9, 1954

Dearest Mum—
Just one quick last note to answer all your questions and then a silence until we see you at the dock as this last week will be hectic and during the sojourn in Venice and Florence we'll not have time.

Have just had a final fitting on a tweed suit I had made here for the staggering sum of $36.00 *including* a good English tweed. It's very nice and will be very useful. Brooks has also had a jacket made. It cost $28—in the same material though a darker shade.

I hope you will be able to come to Camp with us. You will need the change.

What would you like from Europe? We are bringing back very little but you are a must and I would like to get you something you would like.

Tony enjoyed having Daisy Hellman here but has made even better friends with a little English girl who is here for her health—ten years old and really a charmer. She reads 2 books a day and had taught herself to read by the time she was 3. A remarkable child with a mother who is completely a darling. I can't bear to think of not seeing them all again.

The Archduke and Duchess have left after making me promise to call them in New York. They were both very taken by me and I liked them a lot.

We've had a very entertaining time here and it will be a real wrench to leave. I hope we shall be able to come back one day.

Tony is marvelous and has had the time of his life.

All for now. Love and kisses to you.

B.

## BROOKS BAEKELAND

The summer of 1955 I rented Villa Balzac from Drue and Jack Heinz at Cap d'Antibes. Ben Sonnenberg came in his Rolls-Royce and spent some days with us there. We sat up all night long high up under a great moon in Drue and Jack's ultra-Hollywood bathroom, which was the chicest room in the house and furnished like a living room, with a lovely terrace overlooking the mercurial sea. Ben got into the great autobiographical let-it-all-hang-out story of his life, which I had the impression he had never done before but did for "two kids whom I love." He called me "the remittance man." There is a great link between divided generations—especially when there is no familial responsibility.

That summer our neighbor was André Dubonnet—of the drink—who was being robbed by one of his servants. My playmate was Freddie Heineken—Baron Heineken, who was kidnapped and released a couple of years ago. Tony's playmate was Yasmin Khan, the daughter of Rita Hayworth and Aly Khan, and his kindergarten was Eden Roc, where he was sometimes left for lunch and a swim on his own, cosseted by divorced and lonely ladies from Wallachia and Waldavia.

Somewhere—at Gil Kahn's, I think—I had met Greta Garbo and was surprised when I asked her to come to Villa Balzac for a drink that she readily accepted. About fifteen others were to come, too.

She was asked for seven. At six, I remember, I was reading in a hammock and my maître d'hôtel was in his shorts watering the garden—we had a cook and chambermaid, too—when someone came out to say that Mademoiselle Garbo was there, one hour ahead of time. Without her great friend George Schlee. Alone.

Barbara was upstairs in a perfumed bath. Before I could even get my wits together, Garbo came out and apologized for being early, saying she was shy and did not want to meet anyone, she wanted only to spend a few minutes with me. So we had a drink and made some sort of conversation and she went, and I was left with the image of the finest *poitrine* under the gauziest shirt I had ever seen. She must have been close to fifty!

All those foolish, social years. My Barbara loved it all so—and she was so good at it.

## Patricia Greene

The last I saw of Brooks was just before they moved abroad. I think I was walking the dog and saw him sitting in his car, and I got in and sat down, and he said he thought he'd like to live in Europe, it was a much nicer life.

## Alastair Reid

In 1957 I was going to Europe on the *Liberté*, I was traveling Cabin or Tourist, whatever, and Brooks and Barbara were in First Class. They told me they were planning to stay in Europe for quite a while. I got to really know them—I mean, inevitably—on the high seas. They invited me up to their cabin for drinks a number of times, and dinner. And Barbara was always calling up and coming down to whatever class I was in, whereas Brooks, it seemed to me, was making the point that he was in First Class. It was then I began to dislike Brooks intensely.

I was going to Geneva to work on the libretto of an opera with a composer. Then I was going on to Spain, where by that time I was spending half the year, translating Suetonius with Robert Graves and living at his place in Mallorca. I worked with Graves a long time, until I had an almighty quarrel with him, this rather savage falling-out. In 1961 I ran off with his girl, one of his "white goddesses," and we stopped speaking abruptly. Margo, Margo Calas, she was called. Very beautiful. She eventually married Mike Nichols, and then divorced him—she was the wife before the present one.

Brooks and Barbara had taken a place in Antibes for the summer where they said they had spent some time a couple of years before, in a very grand house, and they invited me to stay for a couple of days.

And I did—I stayed with them for three days. A very nice house, just around the edge of the town, on the bay. There was a great thing made of drinks, I remember—you gathered on the terrace, and that was when you began to talk. And they always had a good dinner, too—they had a good cook and we ate well.

Tony was a little nipper then. A pleasant little boy, small enough to be enthusiastic. He and I played with rubber rings and rubber boats at the sea. I noticed that Brooks talked to him as if he were a grown-up, always—there was the impression that he didn't want any baby stuff. I didn't feel that there was too much connection between

Brooks and Tony. Barbara, on the other hand, was affectionate with him, and one felt relieved that there *was* a connection between her and Tony.

We all used to go down to Eden Roc to swim, and one morning as we were sitting around the hotel pool overlooking the sea, and taking the sun, Brooks told me an extraordinary story about when he was a P-47 Thunderbolt pilot in World War Two. It was the very last days of the war, and he was flying over Germany at about four hundred miles per hour—and suddenly, he said, he just saw a green slope ahead of him, and that was the last thing he remembered.

### BROOKS BAEKELAND

I got lost when very close to my target and doing about three hundred and fifty miles per hour as I climbed up a long hill. I crashed, in Schweinfurt, near Regensburg, and was reported dead, because I had no memory—couldn't even identify myself—and because 13th Tactical Air Command pilots had already photographed the top of the long hill where my P-47 exploded and distributed itself—and set fire to the mountain—for one and a half miles, and my young wing man had seen the whole thing, and there was no possibility that I might have survived. When I came to, undead, I found myself (who? I had no idea who I was, or where or why or how) supported by two old German farmers who carefully led me—bleeding and with a fractured skull, two broken shoulders, a smashed left cheekbone, and one zygomatic arch crushed in, and all my clothes blown off—down off that golden hill into the cold, dark valley. I was from there taken in a German jeep by four soldiers to a military hospital. And all I remembered was that up on the hill I saw fire and smoke, and the irrational thought came to my mind: Something has happened to my mother.

### ALASTAIR REID

Brooks and I always had a good time in conversation—whenever you talked with him about something you could actually lose yourself in, as we did during those days I spent with them in Antibes. Of course, that whole idea of *wanting* to be in Antibes in the first place . . . They were like the Murphys then.

### BROOKS BAEKELAND

Our lives became more and more Europeanized, and I—by accident and by choice—was becoming something of a European myself. I had a strong French background from my French-Belgian grandmother, and I had quite a lot of experience already with France, before, during, and after the war. I also read French.

From 1954 on, Barbara and I began to live more and more in France—also in Austria, Italy, and Spain—and this underlined with a terrible clarity my father's betrayal of his origins. Barbara had already learned—and climbed—all the rungs of power and *réclame* in New York—*tout pour parade,* as a French cook of ours once said to me—and we were beginning to lead that life that people later compared to Gerald and Sara Murphy's.

# 6

## RUINED ROYALTY

If Tony Baekeland had participated in afternoon occupational therapy, he would be returned to his ward at four-thirty—which would leave him with three hours to fill before supper. Although various sports such as football, soccer, tennis, and baseball were available to patients in the late afternoon, Tony preferred watching television or listening to his tapes. "I was always encouraging him to play sports," says Miwa Svinka-Zielinski, "but he was reluctant. I told him that going out for one of the teams might contribute to an eventual diagnosis of his being cured, and he said he'd think about it."

Sometimes patients mobilized themselves to the point where an entrepreneurial skill emerged. "Surprisingly, in an environment like Broadmoor, very imaginative things *can* go on," a staff member comments. A group of patients, including Tony Baekeland, once got together and ingeniously brewed beer in the bathroom area—out of raw material smuggled into the hospital by visitors. "While it was fermenting," one of the nurses recalls, "the patients—to maintain the temperature in the room—kept taking hot baths! Despite all the time and energy spent on this very elaborate enterprise, the patients lost out in the end—they were caught by a supervisor just as the beer was ready."

Ironically, Tony Baekeland's great-grandfather, a determined violator of Prohibition, also brewed his own beer. Found among Leo Hendrik Baekeland's private papers was one titled "A Simple and Rapid Method for Making Beer."

The result was a drink of about three and a half to four percent alcohol, which fermented in anywhere from forty hours to five or six days, according to temperature. "Stronger beer," Dr. Baekeland advised, "takes more time." In Broadmoor there was all the time in the world.

### ELIZABETH BLOW
I think it started going wrong when they sold their house in New York and moved to Europe and then started moving around in a sort of rootless way. They never bought anything, they never had a home in Europe, they just rented houses in various resorts. Mainly, though, they were based in Paris—that's where they knew Gloria and Jim Jones and so forth.

### GLORIA JONES
Jim and I were having a drink at the Ritz bar, we'd just come back from the bank or something, and she just came over and said, "Hello, I know who *you* are." Like that, you know. And then we saw quite a lot of them, I guess, in those times, and they seemed all right—they had wonderful parties. They had this little house on rue Barbet de Jouy, 40-bis I think it was, and once a week we'd probably go to dinner there.

I remember she had a bed down in the living room, sort of a Louis Seize lounge where she slept—which I thought was funny, because Brooks had a bedroom upstairs which I never saw. She sort of made a thing about that—that she slept in the living room. And they had two Spanish servants. They lived, you know, very well. She decorated beautifully, and she was a good housekeeper, too.

Tony was young, I think he was going to school in Paris—a day school. Sort of vaguely I remember him coming home with bird cages and birds. He was a nice little boy. Barbara gave him all the attention in the world as a child.

## Letter from Barbara Baekeland to Gloria Jones, Undated

Gloria—chérie—

Sorry about Wed. night. His name is *Sonnenberg* and he is the king of "Hoopla" (his name for his work), the best, and a very wise and wonderful man.

Tony languishes with his drawings and wants to deliver them as soon as you're back. He's wild because I forgot them!

Wuss sends you a purr and a snuggle and says he wants to meet Missy What's-her-name very soon. Call us when you're back.

Also am mad because Brooks returned Jimmie's manuscript before I got a chance to look at it. . . .

A good trip—
B.

### GLORIA JONES

She was a loyal good friend, she was fun, she was appealing. And she really knew how to dress. I mean, she always had one *real* Chanel suit and then two or three made by this wonderful fat lady we used to go to.

### ADDIE HERDER

Barbara used to take me to the openings at Chanel, and we were given proper seats and deference because of her. She also knew a good dressmaker—a charming woman, maybe Rumanian, very talented—who ran up little numbers for us. I think they were fifteen dollars or something, for beautifully tailored summer frocks in linen. The dresses she made us were as elegant as you could get anywhere in Paris. She later became the designer for Hermès. I mean, how would I ever have got to have anything like that if it weren't for Barbara? Barbara knew where to get everything.

I liked her, because she was funny, and wicked, and because she extended her friendship to *me* in a way. It wasn't really friendship, but still, for her, it was something. What I mean is we were not socially equal in the sense that, although we had many of the same friends, I never entertained and I didn't go to all the fashionable watering holes unless I was taken. When I came to Paris I was practically a waif. Barbara didn't know me but I was under the aegis of Gloria and Jim Jones, so I just came along with the package for her. She was also a genuine admirer of my art, my collages, and said so, to other people.

## GLORIA JONES
Barbara was doing the *chasse* when I first met her—you know, hunting. She loved that. She had the costume and everything—you know, for jumping over fences and killing a deer, a boar, I don't know what the hell kind of animal it was. She had a streak of that craziness in her.

## ELIZABETH ARCHER BAEKELAND
She was the boldest rider ever—she'd get on *any* horse and it would be rearing and bucking and Barbara was always just laughing. She had tremendous courage. She joined the hunt that was done out at Chantilly. You had to pay a thousand dollars a year to join and have maybe three hunts, and you had to dress in red velvet with hats and feathers. And she was always in on the kill. Everything Barbara did she did well.

## PAULE LAFEUILLE
Barbara Baekeland was a student of mine in Paris. She was strikingly keen on improving her already fluent French. She used to come to me punctually twice a week, and she studied her lessons better than any of my other students. The sessions we had together were for me time spent with a dear friend. We spoke—in French—of every interest we had in common: literature, theater, music, art, and life in general. Barbara was extremely fond of Paris and got along amazingly well with the French, whose way of life she appreciated and partly adopted.

She was a woman of delicate artistic taste. When she moved from the rue Barbet de Jouy, she chose unhesitatingly the most beautiful part of Paris to settle down in: the section of the Île Saint-Louis called "the prow of the boat," an old and picturesque area teeming with memories of the past. She adorned her cozy seventeenth-century apartment there with genuine antique furniture, beautiful paintings, Persian rugs, and a selection of lovely pastel-colored materials.

Barbara had many glamorous French friends but she also led a very elegant life among the American circle in France. On my part, I knew quite a few of her intimate American friends: Virginia Chambers, Ethel de Croisset, Dorothea Biddle, Kitty Coleman.

Barbara's most characteristic qualities were broad-mindedness, charm, grace, and kindness. My heart aches thinking of her, and that does not help.

I never tutored Tony. I remember her saying how much she adored him and admired his talent as a poet.

## From a Psychiatric Report on Antony Baekeland Ordered by the British Courts, January 5, 1973

Tony Baekeland was happiest at a school in Paris from eleven to fourteen.

### KAREN RADKAI
École Active Bilangue is the name of the school in Paris that I think he went to at one point. It's on the rue Bourdonnais, near Champs de Mars. It's where children from abroad often go.

Tony's parents as such drifted in and out of Paris. I had dinner with them there once, and I couldn't wait to get out of their house—you couldn't have even a conversation with them they were so busy name-dropping.

### KATHARINE GARDNER COLEMAN
They gave very nice dinners. I was living in Paris—I was Kitty Herrick then, the Widow Herrick. And they were renting a house from this wonderful architect friend of mine, Burrall Hoffman, and his adorable wife Dolly. Burrall built what's often described as the finest house ever built in America, you know—Vizcaya on Biscayne Bay in Florida, for James Deering, the industrialist.

At the Baekelands' I met a great many people I never would have seen, ever in my life, anywhere else—some quite fascinating Americans. I mean, that's about the only time I met Ben Sonnenberg—wasn't he the man that had the place on Gramercy Park? And she had the Art Buchwalds there once—I would have given my eyeteeth to have had the Buchwalds for dinner. Barbara had a way of absolutely attracting—well, I mean, *everybody*, men, women, and children.

As you can gather quite well, it was Barbara who was my friend. She was just like that huggable, warm, adorable little dog she had. It was a Peke, and I mean, the hair and the cuteness—everything.

My feelings were perfectly congenial and all that in the beginning with Brooks. He was a good enough host, a good enough guest, and at one stage I thought he was quite a good father. At *one* stage.

He looked just like those Siamese cats they had. Those slit eyes! Well, I'm allergic to cats—maybe that's a part of it, I don't know.

## PAUL JENKINS
The first time I saw Brooks, he was with Jim Jones at this fancy fencing place on I think the avenue Hoches. There he was, fencing away. He looked pretty good, too.

## BROOKS BAEKELAND
I fenced with the French team at the Cercle Hoche, the oldest dueling club in France, both in epée and fleuret. I had already studied saber with the Santelli brothers in New York and was being considered for Olympic training while a freshman at Harvard.

I took Jim Jones to the Cercle Hoche. I took him also to Klosters to ski, but never mind. He had told me that he had been a Golden Gloves champion. I found he couldn't box his way out of a wet paper bag—in fact, he refused to put the gloves on with *me*! He had no speed or coordination or eye and so soon gave up fencing. He was hopeless on skis, too—hopeless in all the Hemingway things he so aspired to. So he *wrote* about them. I did not despise him for any of this—I was touched. I understood one of the springs of a novelist for the very first time: imaginative compensation.

The fact is, he wrote one impassioned, true, and very fine book, *From Here to Eternity*. He ruined his life as a writer—I told him so—by trying to live with the nobs, not only the Hollywood and other big-money sets, but the French aristos. He was horribly flawed by his snobbery and a whole display of social-defense complexes— falsities that marred his work: all the worst American values. Celebrity and the open signatures of wealth—all the things my grandfather laughed at—were uppermost in his life. His *generous* life, I hasten to add, for Jim was a walking heart.

He was a small-town boy from the Midwest. He would have made a perfect target for Sinclair Lewis. His "taste"—a concept so important to Barbara, who was just as big a snob but who had the woman's keener tracking insights—was awful, embarrassing. Barbara and I were as far in taste from Jim and Gloria as Gerald and Sara Murphy were from Scott Fitzgerald. But this, too, is a kind of snobbery.

Incidentally, both Joneses had been completely taken in by Barbara's act of being a Back Bay Brahmin—an act which I sometimes regarded tenderly and sometimes with contempt but which I still financed, to my ruin. The Joneses meanwhile thought of me as a parvenu—I was the shy and quiet one.

Jim was actually as shy as a girl. He was a very intelligent, kindly, feeling, sensitive man. A girl. A girl that snarled. The idiot world was "took in" by the snarl. I loved Jim.

### WILL DAVIS

I thought Brooks was pretentious. Barbara, too. They were trying to model themselves after Caresse and Harry Crosby but they just didn't have the equipment. You know, the English have a phrase for people like Brooks and Barbara—"light, dangerous people."

I liked Barbara all right—I loved her laugh—but I didn't approve of her. I mean, I'm very conventional about women. I essentially like them to behave, and Barbara didn't know how to behave. She was a madcap.

I started to flirt with Barbara the first time I ever met her. Brooks and I were sitting in the front of this cab and Barbara was sitting in the back between Jim and Gloria Jones—this was in Paris, in the spring of '61—and I had my arm around the back of the front seat and I started to let it go up and down Barbara's legs while having a conversation with Brooks. Jim and Gloria both thought this all extremely funny, and Barbara herself was nearly hysterical with laughter. What I was saying *was* reasonably funny but of course Brooks didn't understand why they were all breaking up like that.

Oh, she was very pretty, very pretty and good legs and stuff like that, but the more I saw of her, the less I was drawn to her *that* way. What she had was, she had more energy than anyone I've ever known. You couldn't tire her out—no matter how late you stayed up at night you could *not* exhaust her.

### DUNCAN LONGCOPE

I had been living in Paris for perhaps a year before I met her. But I had once seen a very good-looking woman with a Pekingese in the café opposite the Brasserie having a *tartine* in the morning. I thought she was English. We didn't speak or anything. And then later a friend took me to meet the Baekelands, and, I mean, there she was—Barbara.

She had a real *élan vital*. She could carry an evening despite whatever mood Brooks was in. You never knew—usually he played along, he was a decent enough social type, he didn't sulk and stuff—whatever his particular position may have been at that moment in regard to the rest of the female world.

They liked to walk quite a lot, I remember. I often saw them walking on the *quais*, and they were quite charming on those occasions. I walked with Brooks now and then myself, and it was possibly on one of those walks that he told me he had his mail sent to another address in Paris, I supposed so that he could have his privacy.

### EILEEN FINLETTER

Brooks was always very secretive, and more than a little somber, while she was gay and happy, but they looked good together—they looked rich and self-assured. I used to see them at the Joneses, who had kind of an open-house thing every Sunday night—mostly Americans, a lot of Hollywood people, a lot of writers. One night the Chief Justice of the Supreme Court appeared—Earl Warren. Sometimes Jim would read a chapter from his latest book, and Barbara, I remember, would sit there looking up at him as though he were God or something. She'd say, "Oh, how *beautiful!*" I mean, she'd gush, and it would drive me crazy.

### ADDIE HERDER

I remember Barbara at the Joneses reading a wonderful story to us that *she'd* written, about a trip where she and Brooks and Tony went walking somewhere in places that were not urban—some kind of exploratory hike—and how on this excursion there was a struggle between the parents for possession of the boy.

### BROOKS BAEKELAND

I found a great many stories in Barbara's London apartment after her death—with her writing teacher's comments on them. The only thing I saw that had not been written by *me* was her so-called novel, which was frankly pretty lamentable—and so designated by her instructor in his tactful way. Barbara, while she had the most essential thing for a writer—passion—could never have been a successful one. You have to brush your teeth, put away your clothes, make your bed, pay your rent . . . you must have some respect for order. Good writing is damned difficult. Spoiled girls don't do it.

## EILEEN FINLETTER

One Sunday at the Joneses, Tony was standing next to Barbara behind the bar, which was high, like a church pulpit, and she had her arm negligently draped around his shoulder and she said to me, "Oh, what a lovely day it's been! Tony and I spent the entire morning lying in bed reading the papers." And since my own son was about the same age as Tony, I was shocked, because I thought, My God, if I did that to *him*—I mean, in front of a roomful of people. She wanted me to have the impression that it really *was* in bed. And Tony didn't move, he just stood there smiling. And I thought, That's odd.

## PAUL JENKINS

Barbara Baekeland had a glorious side to her nature, too, but one night at the Joneses' I saw something from another point of view and my anger just surfaced from that, from suddenly sensing the son's curious kind of despair. What was his name again? He was kind of like a wild James Dean.

Barbara and I had crossed swords before on a couple of occasions. She came to an opening of mine once and made some frivolous remark, and you know how tense you get on those occasions. I thought, you know, basically, that she was an undermining person. But she was a frequent guest at Gloria and Jim Joneses', which is where I held forth, and when she came in I always felt guarded to some extent after the flip kind of way she'd treated me and so I gave her a wide berth. But on this particular occasion I just let her have it, there was nothing in me that could *refrain* from letting her have it. I can't quote myself, I can't even paraphrase myself—it was just a concentrated salvo of what an insensitive and *dangerous* mother I thought she was.

I can only confide one other thing. Having been brought up in a particular way myself, I probably saw a mirrored reflection of my own mother in Barbara. And although I didn't see much of Tony, the brief moments I did, it was very vivid to me that he was trapped in something that there was no . . . I would look at him and I'd think there but for the grace of God went I—although I don't think I would have gone to the length Tony did. Of course, *my* mother was also out of reach.

I remember when my mother came to my first opening and we

went to the Cedar Tavern afterwards, Marisol came up and bent over and said, "And how iz zee dominating mozzer?" Then I got into a fight with somebody at the bar who had made a remark to my mother as we walked past, and he just happened to be Charlie Egan, the art dealer—he was the first to show Bill de Kooning and Franz Kline. Anyway, I slammed him into a cigarette machine. But usually at the Cedar Tavern *something* happened, somebody got a beer in their face or something like that—so it was a good climate in which to rid yourself of the frustrations and ignominious vicissitudes of being an artist.

Anyway, that night at Jim and Gloria's I could see that Barbara was doing something bad to someone who had no drive, purpose, or focus. Her son was what I would call a psychological object for her. It was very strongly clear to me that this young man was being psychically exploited to the fullest extent. He was a human sacrifice, to Oedipal emotions. It's what I would call incestuous betrayal. She might have never touched him and yet you could tell he was being smothered alive.

### SUE RAILEY

I felt that he never had a chance—perhaps his father really didn't bother enough about him and his mother bothered too much. I think that if Brooks had been a different type of father, maybe . . . But that's a big maybe.

I met them when they first came to Paris, I can't remember what year that was. I lived there for thirty-three years. My husband went over there to our embassy and he fell in love with France and when it was time to be sent somewhere else he said he'd never leave Paris and he never did till he died. We saw a lot of Brooks and Barbara. They had a very quick, easy contact with people. And a marvelous house, a little pavilion. It was like a doll's house, in fact. They entertained a bright group. I would think that they would have felt that they could easily have been Sara and Gerald Murphy.

### BROOKS BAEKELAND

The Murphys—no, Barbara and I were not that way, although I understand why people who are romantic and like tradition would see us that way. Gerald and Sara Murphy had no energy. They entertained people who did. They sucked up others' energies and taught them—the brutes—style, fifty years ago called "manners." All their guests acknowledged the lessons. I may say that Madame Ethel de Croisset falls into the same class—a benefactress to brutes and to princes.

These are exquisite people. Barbara and I were never exquisite—cultivated, Proustian. We were a bit mad, especially my beloved Barbara. *Mad.* I was mostly smiling, not behind the arras but in a window seat, watching. But Barbara gave penny for penny.

The comparison between us and the Murphys comes from our being spoiled and loving the arts and being in France after a war. We never were that stable—purring, gracious, collected, surrounded by our domestics. We could have been. Barbara never understood that in order to pay for something you wanted tomorrow you might have to give up something today. Order. She never had understood order. We were *not* the Murphys. We were more like ruined royalty. We were two gulping bankrupts. I tease—or rather, I repeat what I used to tell her. Barbara could have given lessons to Jackie Kennedy. She had spent all her insurance money from her father's death, then all her mother's, and now she was spending two thirds of *my* money.

THILO VON WATZDORF
They were traveling all over the spas of Europe, the places where one should be "seen," when I first met them. They had this white Mercedes 190SL, with a cat in the back and Tony in the back, and they were traveling through Europe for months on end.

They rented this place in Ansedonia, where my mother and stepfather had a house on the Dutch royal family's property—my stepfather, Aschwin Lippe, is Prince Bernhard's brother. The Baekelands got their house through an eccentric Englishwoman named Rosie Rodd, now Rosie Baldwin—there was a whole tribe of English there, friends of Rosie's and friends of her three beautiful daughters'. I must have been sixteen that summer, a couple of years older than Tony. He gave the impression of being the typical case of a son of well-to-do American parents who just played all year round. He seemed to me to be very shy, very much of a loner, and I sort of romanticized about that because I felt that there was something so crazy in the structure of his life. I could never even figure out where he went to school, or if he ever did.

MICHAEL ALEXANDER

They lugged him around from place to place, they were always sort of getting a house here and a house there. I met them in Ansedonia with my friend Rosie Rodd. Tony was just a sort of nature boy then. I can tell you that nobody thought he was a violent person.

I used to go and see him in Broadmoor, poor dear. It's not an unpleasant place, I assure you. It's not exactly a hellhole. Oh, maybe some of them do go a bit berserk from time to time, but you don't get the impression of one big roaring madhouse. They all look like perfectly harmless people. However, that's not the point, is it? Tony, between you and me, was perfectly happy there, all things considered.

## Letter from Antony Baekeland to Rosemary Rodd Baldwin, Undated

Broadmoor

Dear Rosie,

Great and wonderful things have happened in my life—the Sun is coming back to me and I am so happy and well. I feel as if Mummy had really never left me at all.

I have stopped being desperate to leave Broadmoor: I find I am learning so much every day here and I know that when I am ready I will go. And I have made many good friends here.

Insects look all right again, grass, flowers, and trees. I still tend to go rather astray in my reading but it's getting better. Rosie, please write to me soon and tell me all your news. I miss you a lot.

Love,
Tony

ROSEMARY RODD BALDWIN

I had the first house ever built in Ansedonia—me and my three children and my second husband, Mr. Rodd. He was Peter Rodd's brother—do you know who I mean? Marvelous-looking. Peter was married to Nancy Mitford, and he was the model for the character Basil Seal in Evelyn Waugh's *Scoop* and *Black Mischief*. My mother-in-law, my darling old mother-in-law, threatened to take Waugh to court—there was *such* a hooha. Waugh was terribly rude about *me* in that book of letters of his. My children were absolutely hopping mad—"Mummy, can't you do something about this?" But I really couldn't care less. First of all, it's lies. He says in a postcard to Nancy Mitford: "I did not find Mrs. Taffy a lady." Well, *I* am Mrs. Taffy, because my husband was Gustavus King of Sweden's godson and namesake, so he was always known as Taffy—Taffy Rodd. But you see, I never met Evelyn Waugh in the whole of my life! I was dying to, but my husband would never have him in the house. Not so very long ago a man who was writing some sort of book asked me, "What did you feel like when you read that Evelyn Waugh said he didn't find you a lady?" And I said, "Why *should* he have found me a lady? I didn't ask him to. And what would I have done with one if he had?" In another letter Waugh runs down the film *La Dolce Vita*, which I acted in with my children—I was the medium—to make some money, because we had *no* money.

You see, my husband's father, Lord Rennell, had been for years the English ambassador in Rome, and we were the only unofficial people living in private properties for the first few years after the war. We had Palazzo Rodd, on the Via Giulia, and for holidays we went to Ansedonia, to Casa Rodd, and when we got hard up we rented it.

Look, I launched Ansedonia and Porto Ercole. Yes, really. I started the whole thing. I lent money to fishermen to build tiny flats and then I opened a restaurant which was the biggest fun on this earth—which, alas, doesn't exist anymore. And I found the property for the Dutch royal family, and then that's how it went—all the rich and famous came. And it was ruined for me—I can't bear going back there. So then I left for Turkey, and that's another part of my life.

I met the Baekelands when they wrote me asking to rent a house in Ansedonia. Practically all the houses had been taken, but I got them the house of Princess Boncompagni. *They* thought, of course, it was going to be one of those frightfully smart Cadaqués or South of France houses; in fact, it was a small bungalow built by the local builder. Anyway, during all this I had the most extraordinary correspondence with Brooks, whom I had not yet met. One day, for instance, he wrote me that he didn't want two servants, so I said, "You won't have two servants. I've got you a cook, that's all, and her husband will just sleep in her room, naturally." He wrote back saying, "I don't want the husband sleeping in the house because he's bound to

eat some of our food if he does." *I* wrote back and said, "Listen,
there's one bed, he'll spend the whole night making love to her, and
I assure you it'll be only the matter of a cup of coffee in the morning." And I had a letter back saying, "I don't give a damn if he makes
love standing up, I don't want him in my house!"

So the Baekelands arrived, and almost immediately they said,
"Mrs. Rodd, we must tell you we're very disappointed in the house,
it's not at all what we wanted." Well, I thought then that they were
the sort of Americans who would never be happy in Ansedonia. So I
said to the child, who was wonderful-looking, like a faun—the most
adorable little boy that's ever *been*—"Tony," I said, "why don't you
go on up to my house and meet my children?" and he rushed off
while his parents and I sat down to sort things out. And when he
came back, he said to Barbara, "Mum, they've got the best library
I've ever seen—*please* let's stay here." And on *that* appeal the
Baekelands remained in Ansedonia, and after about a month I was
able to move them from Villa Boncompagni to Villa Nistri.

## Letter from Brooks Baekeland to Gloria and James Jones, July 18, 1959

> Villa Boncompagni
> (Villa Nistri after July 28)
> Ansedonia

Dear Jim: Gloria:

We are getting squared away finally ("you squares!"). . . . We
have found a comfortable villa on the water . . . rented from
Pieri Francesco Nistri, a famous pal of Il Duce and a great War
Criminal; but I love him. It turns out that we are sitting in a
nest of Etruscan remains: in fact, two hundred yards above us
through the gorse is the ancient city of COSA, an Etruscan,
then a Roman stronghold, where the American Academy of
Rome has had a bunch of archaeologists digging for nearly a
decade. . . .

We swam off a small island here the other day, just made it
back in a sudden storm that came up, but the island was worth
visiting to Tony. Millions of seagulls and some sort of native
partridge are nesting on it. . . . What would interest you most, I

think, is the underwater archaeology around here. There are rocks, small islets, islands and reefs all ready and waiting to wreck ships. There must be plenty of dead galleys and galleons lying on the bottom around here. Do you think you would be tempted to pay us a visit at some time convenient to all of us in August or September? . . . I'll be in touch with you. Are you having fun? How's the baby?

Love,
Brooks

KATHARINE GARDNER COLEMAN
I went down to Ansedonia to visit them that August—in rapid succession they had these two older women to stay, Sue Railey and me. I was one of the two old crows that went down—I mean, Sue and I were nine or ten years older than Barbara. Anyway, I stayed for a week, a good fat week, you know—ten days—and that was exactly the summer when Prince Bernhard came down with his equerry to look over the Borghese property that was for sale.

We went out on all these glorious picnics in this Italian fishing boat that Brooks had rented, and there'd be every kind of possible combination of people packed in. There was one time that I got very upset with Barbara, very very upset because she was showing off and diving from the top of this boat where if you didn't do it quite right and your foot slipped or something you could just crack your head open on the edge, and there were boys, young people, around who wanted to copy what she was doing. There was an Italian diver in the group—one of those professional people who go underwater and carry a knife with them, you know, and he and I got together and said we didn't like what Barbara was doing at *all*, it was very dangerous what she was doing, she was reckless, and finally we both prevailed upon her not to do it, but, I mean, it took *him* plus something of *me* to put a stop to it. And Brooks didn't even seem to take any of it in.

One time I got perfectly furious with Brooks—and told him so—because he said, "I've got something pretty darn interesting to show you. Do you want to see Tony's diary? He's written some things about a little girl he met." I said, "I not only don't want to see it but I don't know how you can feel you have a right to take something that is your child's private private thing. . . ." But on the whole he seemed utterly devoted to Tony that summer. He was teaching him how to snorkel—it was when snorkeling was just coming along. And Tony was just a cunning little boy who was a little bit extrasensitive and very interested in animals and nature. What he really did *not* like was his mother's society—or social life, if that's what you call it. We'd all be sitting around and he'd say, "I don't know why you want to go out tonight, Mummy. Look at Mrs. Herrick"—which is what my name was then—"*she* doesn't want to go and meet the Marchesa of so and so and so and so and so and so."

DAPHNE HELLMAN
Brooks and Tony both were sort of in despair over the social life but Barbara kept escalating, she wanted to see more and more titles—princes and duchesses down through barons and even *sirs*.

## Notes from a Psychiatric Consultation on Antony Baekeland, New York City, March 12, 1971

He recalls being most happy when he spent entire days by himself. He states, "I was taken by my parents to all their friends' houses, so I really grew up more in my parents' generation than in my own."

NIKE MYLONAS HALE
When Bob Hale took me to meet the Baekelands in Ansedonia, we weren't married yet, and I was quite young, and, you know, Brooks was very flirtatious. He carried me across the threshold, and that infuriated Barbara. The next thing was, she was saying to me, "Why don't you go down and play with Tony?" Now Tony was about twelve, you know, and I was twenty-five! Well, Barbara didn't like me at all. She was great friends with Bob's first wife, Barbara Hale.

Tony was on the rocks playing with crabs, sort of pulling them apart, which Bob thought was very creepy, but I didn't think so, I think that's what little bbys *do*. Of course, in hindsight it *is* an awfully creepy little episode.

They didn't really pay much attention to Tony. I mean, it was typical that he was down on the rocks alone. I think one of the things that must have been very difficult for him was that Barbara and Brooks were *so* dramatic—*always*. Both of them had so much drama that you couldn't sort of survive around them.

## From the Diaries of John Philip Cohane, Unpublished

*Wednesday*. Ansedonia is somewhat barren, the villas are too close together, the mosquitos at times are devils, but it was a thoroughly pagan, never-to-be-forgotten Tuscan summer.

There is a breathtaking ruined temple on a hill; the view is stupendous, up and down the coast in both directions, but Heather is still convinced she saw a somberly clad sinister ghost sitting on a low wall of the temple at eleven o'clock one morning and it was hard to drag her back again at any hour.

By coincidence Barbara and Brooks Baekeland, son Tony, Millie their deaf Pekingese, a rooster and a Siamese cat turned up two days after we arrived, settled into a villa a few hundred yards away from the one Heather has rented for us, which belongs to Prince Antonello Ruffo di Calabrio, whose sister has just married Prince Albert, the Belgian King's brother. The Baekelands have added greatly to our stay. Later Simone Lippe with Thilo, one of her two sons, and Alexis Lichine and his wife also dropped by.

## From *A Family Motor Tour Through Europe,* Leo Hendrik Baekeland, Horseless Age Press, New York, 1907

Everything around us was so harmoniously peaceful and the Italian landscape so serene with the freshness of nature! Yet, wherever the eye wandered, ruins evoked visions of a fugitive splendor, which had been in all its glory during ages long gone by, when human ambitions and human might tried to rule this enchanting corner of the world.

## Letter from Barbara Baekeland to Gloria and James Jones, August 1, 1960

Ansedonia

Dear Gloria & Jim—

. . . Our beds haven't had a chance to cool and this certainly hasn't been what I'd call a tranquil summer but it's been fun. . . . Yesterday a large contingent dove for gem coral. We almost lost one languid Englishman—very exciting! Tony brought up one perfect amphora and we have masses of fragments. . . . Why don't you write to Klosters *right away* for reservations for skiing. It would be fun to be there together.

Have started painting but it does not go well.

We miss you—

B.

### ROSEMARY RODD BALDWIN

The following summer, 1961, Brooks and Barbara rented *my* house, and we did the most fantastic things together. *Long* before the Kennedys started their great river travel, we were going down rivers, these marvelous Etruscan rivers in Italy. And millions of people came and stayed with us—old, young—Lucy and Alan Morehead. . . . And Tony was wonderful. My servants all adored him. He used to train crickets to sing in different keys. I remember when he was going back to school in America he gave me two crickets which sang in totally different keys and I absolutely nearly went mad, I couldn't get to sleep at night. He always had all these animals—partridges, turkeys, and everything you could find outside. He would take them up to his room and study them, and he would draw the most beautiful drawings of them.

Now this second summer there were terrible scenes between Barbara and Brooks all the time. She was being difficult and impossible, and Tony, whose room was right over their bedroom, heard all these rows going on. You see, Brooks was the passion of Barbara's lifetime and that summer he was having a walk-out with some debutante that he'd met. And that was, *I* think, the beginning of the unhappiness—that primeval flutter.

FRANCINE DU PLESSIX GRAY

When Brooks and Barbara asked us to share a house with them in
Ansedonia, it seemed like such a good idea because I'd been very
tired after the birth of my first child, and I was expecting a second,
and Cleve and I had rented out our own house in Connecticut for
the summer, to a couple who gave us wonderful money. And with
that money we were able to share the fee with the Baekelands. I
mean, it was a way of resting and not having too many responsibilities—and we *thought* we were going to have a lot of fun.

It was a very large house, we each had a big section to ourselves.
And there was a large staff. It was Rosie Rodd's house, the haunted
house. Totally haunted. Really. Cleve trusts ghosts and likes them,
I'm terrified of them, but we both felt it. I refused to walk in the door
alone. He had to come with me.

CLEVE GRAY

It was a very strange house. It had a very long, very dark corridor,
and I would say that around six in the evening you started feeling
these swooshing presences—it's the only way I can explain it. And at
night, after dinner or whenever it might be, when we went up to our
room, we both couldn't get into the room soon enough and shut the
door, because there *were* these . . . these . . . these *things*. I think
the Baekelands both accepted the fact that it was haunted.

I used to wake up at dawn and hear this absolutely beautiful Arabic
song, it seemed to come from the garden, and one day I said to
Barbara, "The gardener has the most marvelous voice." She said,
"Do we have a gardener? There's no gardener here." I said, "Well,
the man who comes every morning very early to the garden and sings
this Arabic song." Well, she got all upset. She said that Rosie Rodd's
lover, an Arab, had disappeared about six months before, in Africa—
he had been an agent with the British government and had apparently been murdered—and she said that it was he who was haunting
the garden. Well, that isn't my kind of ghost. Except that I did keep
hearing that song.

FRANCINE DU PLESSIX GRAY

The house was right underneath the walls of one of the great
Etruscan towns, called Cosa. When we were residents at the American Academy in Rome in 1979, almost twenty years later—which is
the place which has done all the digging—we were often in the com-

pany of one of the world's great archaeologists and classical scholars, Lawrence Richardson—a very very British-type American, very elegant. And the kind of man, the kind of Victorian rationalist, who you would think would absolutely dispel the idea of the existence of ghosts.

Larry came to dinner one night at the Academy and we started talking about ghosts and he said, "My dear, I've lived with them from the time we started digging—Cosa is *filled* with ghosts. Of *course* you heard ghosts in Rosie Rodd's house! That whole *wall* is an acropolis. What did you expect—there'd be no ghosts?" He kept us up to two a.m., and I thought of this whole haunting of this . . . of this doomed couple by ghosts who were now being certified by this great archaeologist. That's a very interesting metaphysical symbol.

That summer the Baekelands went out every single day on this yacht that they chartered from a local fisherman. And they just sat and drank masses of wine and jabbered and gossiped with this duchessa and that principessa and yet another contessa this-and-that. We did it twice and we never did it again—two boat trips and we retreated completely into our shell.

Luckily we had for, oh God, a few lire a day, a local girl who took care of the baby—which is another thing we could never have afforded in the States—and twice a week we drove to a marvelous town called Setonia where there are these sulfur waters which heal everything and which make you sleep beautifully and so on. We also made an extensive tour of the Etruscan places because Cleve was buying black Etruscan ware and Brooks used to help him find it. We got museum pieces for practically nothing and we brought them back wrapped in our baby's diapers. And Cleve would do watercolors, and I was painting, too, at that time—this is years before I was a writer.

That summer Brooks was trying to write a novel or whatever. Trying or pretending, nobody *knew*. But I mean, he was definitely bitten by that terrible American neurosis which *I* think should go into medical dictionaries, which is somewhere between obsession and paranoia—novel-writing, the idea that you've got to write a novel in order to prove yourself. And Brooks seemed to me to be absolutely tainted with that disease. Well, you see, he was a romantic, and he wanted to write a romantic book—I think he wanted to be Hemingway.

And Barbara pretended that she wanted to paint but that her life was too busy to allow her to. Of course, she was creating her own mayhem. She had a studio in the garage into which she went *once* the whole summer we were there. Everything was this dispersion toward other people, you know—this trying to make an impression, this thing of having people around all the time, which had to do with her being so terrified of facing herself and facing her own center, her own gravity. It was a totally dispersed energy, Barbara's.

I never found her as entertaining as Cleve did, because I think he was sort of sexually charmed by her. She wasn't my kind of woman. I like women who are intellectually more centered than I am. I mean someone like Ethel de Croisset. I like very rigorous personalities. I cannot *stand* dispersed personalities, and all my close women friends have been women who are more powerful than I am. I need women who are stronger than I am. I'm pretty strong, but I want them even stronger.

And Barbara at that time was all parties, parties, parties—well, the way the Murphys were. You know, I mean, in a way they were Murphys with no talent. Which is a terrible thing to say—Murphys with no talent. I mean, Gerald Murphy was a pretty good painter, you know.

## Cleve Gray

Barbara wasn't a bad painter at all. She was a very very talented person. She thought she could do everything. Well, of course, she *did* everything, but none of it was quite good enough.

Brooks I always thought was extremely intelligent. I remember Peter Gimbel, several years later, saying to me, "Do you think Brooks is going to turn out all right?" And I said, "God, Peter, if *Brooks* isn't going to turn out all right, I can't imagine how anybody will." You see, I was still very impressed with him. He seemed to me perfectly balanced, I didn't see *any* of his imbalance. His ideas were all very sound.

I remember he said to me that summer, "I have a terrible fate in store for me." I said, "What do you mean?" And he said, "Well, I have to remember my family—my grandfather, my father, every member of my family became senile fairly early. There's no question that that's what's going to happen to me, and this is what I dread." But I think this was a romantic idea—you know, that he thought about himself that way.

I remember he made fun of Barbara's chasing titles, but then he got wrapped up in it himself, I guess. I mean, any title—any possibility for a title—she would just go zooming at it. One thing that always amused Francine and me—in the entry hall there was a table and on the table was a bowl and in the bowl Barbara always had scores of visiting cards which would all be left so you could see them—"Duchesse de Croy," "Prince de Lippe," "Principessa de Colonna."

### FRANCINE DU PLESSIX GRAY
And then the bills she was paying or the letters to her poor mother in New York, her poor little Irish mother—the nonglamorous things—were always way at the bottom of the bowl. But always on top were the titles.

I disliked them much earlier than Cleve did. I wanted to wash my hands clean of them.

Remember the ending of Evelyn Waugh's *Handful of Dust*? That's the ending I see for Brooks. Exactly that kind of ending.

Once we were having dinner at the Gimbels' in New York, and Peter kind of grumbled something about how fake the happiness was between the Baekelands. I said, "Oh, but they always talk so much about their happiness!" and he said, "That's just what I mean."

During the time we spent with them in Ansedonia she would hint that they'd had no sexual contact at all all summer. She had some kind of menstrual problem, she was bleeding all the time and refusing to see a doctor, and the bleeding problem was deterring her from having sex.

I don't know if Brooks was fooling around or not. I mean, he would probably pretend he was going off to study some wild plant—he would do it with the utmost elegance. And that was Brooks all over—he was very much to the manor born. He had the most European sense of manners about those things.

But now, the most incredible thing of that summer comes down to Tony. Very often we would have dinner alone with him because I was feeling kind of weak from this pregnancy that was so close to the other one, and the social life bored me, as it always has in my life. So in the evening Cleve and I would mostly stay at home, so we were a lot with Tony, because every time his parents went out he was left alone, and if we had gone out also, then he would have been totally alone. And we had the most delightful conversations with him—he was a total charmer. He was off to Exeter that year.

And not a *hint* of anything wrong in him except for that stammer, which would go in and out. I mean, like many stammerers, he would sometimes talk for half an hour without stuttering. I had a stuttering problem as a child myself, I was the same kind of stutterer—and I had a definite lack of attention from my mother, and a lot of psychiatrists have new theories of how stammering is an attention-getting device, subconsciously of course. And the only, only hint that there was something deeply wrong in him was this.

I should begin by saying the house was crammed with food. I mean, Barbara was the kind of woman who had no sense of moderation, and it drove my kind of abstemious frugal French nature crazy, I having lived, you know, under the Occupation, knowing what hunger was like and so on, seeing these hams and chickens and roasts being thrown out or given to the peasants, and three turkeys being bought instead of one. I mean, the house was so full of food you didn't know what to do with it.

We had brought from France with us baby food for our six-month-old son, because French baby food is notoriously marvelous, so much better than American, and Italian baby food is well known to be not nutritious. Anyway, we had two months of French baby food in Ansedonia with us, packed in vacuum crates—cans of puréed veal and puréed beets and puréed spinach and so on. And about the fifteenth of July we noticed that there were these strange gaps in the rows.

And a few days later the peasant girl who was looking after our son said to us, and I think she began to cry—we had enough Italian to get the gist of what she was saying—"It is Mr. Tony. I have seen him do it. He comes in at night when the baby is asleep and steals the baby food."

Tony was stealing Thaddeus's food! To eat—in this house brimful of food. You see, he wanted to be a baby. He'd never *been* a baby. He wanted to be mothered. Or maybe he wanted to identify with *our* baby, because he'd never had any proper parenting from his own parents, and maybe at that point we were giving him more parenting than they were.

Tony was a complete victim of the whole thing. But a victim of the most curious kind—under this deceitful veneer of affection and praise, this unbelievable and constant praise that went on—"This child is so gifted. . . . Isn't he beautiful! . . . And his painting and his poetry, and his schoolwork!" I mean, every afternoon this child was praised, praised, praised, but deep down he was completely left out of everything.

Ethel de Croisset came to stay with us for a few days toward the very end of our time in Ansedonia, and she saw through all this immediately—and she knows what parenting is. She's been a remarkable parent herself, and *her* parents were marvelous—I mean, Elsie Woodward was an extraordinary mother, and the father was extraordinary, and Ethel was absolutely appalled by the way the Baekelands were bringing up Tony.

## Letter from Brooks Baekeland to James Jones, February 17, 1966

New York

Dear Jim:

I have taken the liberty of writing Ethel, with you as substitute, into my will as the guardian of Tony's person and U.S. Trust Company as the guardian of his property in case both Barbara and I should grow wings (or perhaps a forked tail, in my case) before Tony is 21.

Duties are just about nil except for tender hand holding and the offering of dry Kleenex, but the law demands a "guardian of the person" for all minors. Tony loves you both and just about no one else that I can think of in the fuddy-duddy generation, so that is why.

Affectionately—Love to Gloria,
Brooks

P.S. St. Anton for about ten days, then back in Paris.

# 7

# ASPIRING AND PERSEVERING

Often the Broadmoor staff would "look the other way," in the words of one nurse, when it came to sex. "As long as it didn't get out of hand. Even by day there were areas of the wards that weren't very closely supervised. You only had five nurses on duty for every forty or fifty patients, so you couldn't possibly patrol all the areas all the time."

"I have the distinct impression that Tony did have relationships at Broadmoor," says Michael Alexander. "He was quite happy, so they must have let him have some sort of sex."

James Reeve adds, "Tony only talked to me about things he thought I would approve of, though I often wondered what the story really was. I did try once to draw him out on the subject of sex at Broadmoor, but he was very reticent."

"There is a great deal of homosexuality in the hospital," reports David Cohen in his 1981 book *Broadmoor*. "On the whole, what sexual activity exists seems both rather cheerless and loveless." One patient describes Broadmoor in the book as a "homosexual brothel." Another explains: "If you haven't got any women available, there does come a point when you just burst." One patient offered that he felt rather tender toward another patient simply because "I *am* quite tender."

"The authorities sometimes break up couples after having 'tolerated' the situation for some time," Cohen elaborates. "Fear that they may be split up arbitrarily makes relationships even more brittle."

Broadmoor authorities are at pains to point out that homosexuality is not at all uncommon in sexually segregated institutions, be they mental hospitals, prisons, or schools.

## Notes from a Psychiatric Consultation on Antony Baekeland, New York, March 12, 1971

From ages 11 to 14, he spent the school year in Paris and then summers in Italy. At age 14 he was sent to Phillips Exeter Academy in New Hampshire, but was forced to leave because of his grades.

### JAMES M. HUBBALL

I was Tony's headmaster at Buckley School, a long time ago. I have a vague recollection that when Tony went to Exeter, there was an episode in which he was found hiding in the laundry chute—for what reason I never knew. The last I heard of him was that he was living in London.

### SARA DUFFY CHERMAYEFF

When he got thrown out of Exeter, the evening he came home, Barbara called me and we had a long talk. I don't know what exactly he was kicked out for. She always said, you know, "They don't understand him—he's an artist."

## Notes from a Psychiatric Consultation on Antony Baekeland, New York City, March 12, 1971

At age 15, he ran away from another private school.

## From the Private Diaries of Leo Hendrik Baekeland, February 7, 1910

George is today fifteen years old. At his age I was I believe in the same mental condition as he is with the difference that he has had the benefit of better intellectual environment. I had to do everything by myself and find my own way. The only help I had was the encouragement of my beloved mother.

SUZANNE TAYLOR

Tony was at Brooks School, in North Andover, Massachusetts, with my son David, who told my husband and me, knowing we knew the Baekelands, that Tony had run away from school to go to the Caribbean and write poetry. And David said, "Guess what he was taking with him!" It went all around the school, you see. I mean, he was going off to write poetry, right? And he was taking a hatchet and a flashlight and I think a rope hammock! He never did get there—he was caught at the airport.

KATHARINE GARDNER COLEMAN

I was having lunch with Brooks and Barbara one day when Tony came in from school with his little traveling case. I mean, it wasn't vacation time. He had walked away from, you know, *another* school. And I said to Barbara and Brooks, "Here's some free advice for you." I had boys then that were older than Tony, you see. I said, "You just *cannot* let him come home. Don't even let him *think* that he can come home. He's got to get through, and then at the end of the school year, if the school hasn't been successful, find him another one."

He was just sent to his room and told they'd talk about it later.

BROOKS BAEKELAND

I was very disappointed to discover that the flame of curiosity and intellectual determination—capacity for, belief in, work—that might, for instance, have made a scientist out of Tony was lacking. Whether that was genetic or due to the values he was being brought up in I cannot say. In any case, I had already educated him to the point where he was ahead—in some directions—of his science teachers in the various prep schools he went to.

Two things had become clear—to me, not to his mother—by that

time: one, that he was bright enough—and even talented enough—
to embark on any career one could think of, and two, that he was
bone-lazy. There is a myth that very bright people can accomplish a
complete academic program without ever opening a book, to coin a
phrase. That is false. In fact, the very, very bright open more books
than anyone else. Usually. Therefore my son soon puzzled me, for I
had spent every summer, wherever we happened to be at the time,
tutoring him mornings to bring him back to the surface, as it were,
for his entry in school the next fall. He would always start at the top
of his class and end up at the bottom, with strong suggestions from
the schools that he be taken out.

As he was entering puberty he also began to be a disciplinary problem in his schools—"subversive," "a bad influence," etc. But I went
on tutoring him right up to the time that he and his mother an-
nounced that he wanted to go to Oxford. He had never been able to
finish high school and had even been asked to leave a school with the
academic standards of Avon Old Farms.

## From the Catalog, Avon Old Farms School, Avon, Connecticut

Aspirando et perseverando—aspiring and persevering: the School
motto is more than a figure of speech to members of the Avon
community. The motto is a reminder of the way of life that
governs the hearts and minds of the people who make up the
School. Boys discover at Avon that aspirations *can* become realities and that perseverance is vital to the attainment of both individual and community goals.

## Letter from Antony Baekeland to Gloria and James Jones, Undated

Avon Old Farms
Avon, Connecticut

Dear Gloria and Jim,
Now that I'm more or less installed in school I can write. Getting back here was a bit unpleasant, but everything feels very
normal after a few days. I'm going to see Rosie Styron pretty

soon about those poems. This school is a real waste, so what I might do is leave at Christmas and come to London, go to a Cramming school to see if I get these A-level exams and see if I can get into Oxford next year. Anyway I'll probably "aspire and persevere" at least until then. . . .

Love,
Tony


PETER GABLE

After Buckley, when I was ten or eleven I was shipped off to Choate, where I was a very bad boy. I was sent down from school. I don't remember what my crime was—it was probably being a smart-ass. Then I was sent to some hideous school in Greenwich which has long since gone out of existence, and I stayed *there* for a while— Tony meanwhile was at Exeter or Brooks—and then I fetched up at a somewhat backwater boarding school outside of Hartford. Avon Old Farms School. The beach upon which I was washed up.

And it was quite amazing—the first day of school, who should I see but Tony! And we fell on each other's necks—how have you been and so forth and so on. Now when we were little boys at Buckley, Tony and I had the sort of telepathy that children can have with each other—I mean where whole paragraphs can be left out because you know each other so well, you have a continuity of experience where even the slightest little trigger puts you both on the same track. Anyway, there had been this hiatus of three or four years, and now, the long and the short of it is, the magic was gone. *I* was a little different, *he* was different.

Tony was most decidedly no longer "just another kid." All his brilliance and genius, dimly perceived by me as a child, was becoming more difficult for *him*, I think. I remember him in English composition class at Avon—his vocabulary was quite an astonishment even to his teachers. At Avon if you were bright you stood out, and Tony had a brilliance above and beyond anyone else in the school. Still, I don't think he excelled in his studies.


BROOKS BAEKELAND

When *I* went there, Avon Old Farms was an interesting school. But it was not an educational institution in the usual sense. What had appealed to my father when he sent me there was that the students milked cows, cut trees, worked in the fish hatchery, plowed, raked leaves, bound books, and worked in a carpentry shop. The fact that some of the boys came with a string of polo ponies or an airplane was not what interested him. Not all of the boys went on to college—I suspect most did not, and of those that did, damned few went to Princeton, Harvard, and Yale.

I had an altogether easy ride at Avon—I spent a quarter of my time fencing, an eighth on team sports, and much of the rest on ornithology. And I was admitted to Harvard, where I might have chosen to study Chinese bronzes or cultural anthropology or Russian history or French literature or comparative religion or philology or the art of glassblowing in the Renaissance or architecture from Egypt to the Bauhaus, but since I was a Baekeland, none of these "frivolities" were open to me. What I did, and my family never knew, was audit them all—in those days, for I think eleven dollars you could audit any course you wanted, which meant sit in on the lectures, read the books, make a fuss in class, and even take the exams, but you could not take the credits. At the same time I was taking a heavy course load leading toward a biochemistry major. Why biochemistry? God knows, but I knew it would please my family—or rather, not shock them. I was expected to become a scientist, to do something satisfactory for the family—as for myself, I was as unmotivated as a loose-skinned pup, nine-tenths curiosity.

I was rooming—or rather, dividing a capacious suite in Massachusetts Hall—with the editor of the *Crimson*. He was a wag. He was a dog. I was a cat. But that dog and this cat shared a sense of the absurd and I still remember him with affection. We were grand, budding terrorists. I showed him how to convert all our cotton underclothes into guncotton; how to fill our housemaster's bathroom—bowl, tub, sink—with Jell-O when he was out courting and the icy winter air could come in through the opened bathroom windows and set it for his sleepy return; how to string our underwear on a cotton clothesline converted into guncotton and with the tip of a lighted cigarette make it disappear with a flash behind one of the campus cops' back when he came up red-faced to arrest us for hanging our laundry in the Yard. It was my grandfather, by the way, who had taught me to make guncotton out of my underwear—also how to make an extremely unstable explosive out of ammonia, potassium iodide, and iodine— and so helped me on my way out of my freshman year at Harvard.

I remember having a tin full of aluminum powder dropped down the chimney from the roof of Mass. Hall while I waited in our ground-floor apartment with a match to light it, sending a flame one hundred feet high into the night sky over Cambridge. The list of tomfoolery is long and I could go on. Most of my inventive powers were occupied in such nonsense that first term.

And then, I got the ax. Suddenly I was a totally defeated young man. I never expected to see any of my family or friends again. I was dazed—literally frightened out of my wits. No future that I could see was open to me. I was finished. Honor, Family—such things were important to me then. Who thinks of Shame today?

Pride—some say satanic pride—has been one of the keys to my whole life, and in 1938 it had a great deal to do with my not seeking the advice from my family that I might easily have found, had I only been able to seek it. But the essence of pride is that it never asks for anything, can never admit weakness. It may demand, it cannot beg. In fact, great pride never even thinks of asking! I am positive that it never even occurred to me that anyone might be able to help me.

My father's reaction was—predictably, and he was right—that I had "absconded with funds." I had taken with me eight hundred and fifty dollars in cash, all I had in account with the bursar, which my father had given me to study biochemistry and not for gallivanting out to the West Coast, which is where I decided to go.

I took a Greyhound bus from Cambridge to San Francisco. I stopped off in New York to say goodbye to my mother, who lived in Turtle Bay, and my sister, then eighteen. I did not reveal to my mother that I was leaving "forever" but I did to my sister, who then did an impulsive and generous thing—she gave me a small necklace of cultured pearls.

In San Francisco I lived first on Howard Street. I had discovered Jack London, and I soon began exploring Pacific and Montgomery Streets—the famous "Monkey Blocks" where Saroyan lived. I had never heard of him and drank with him at the Black Cat without knowing who he was. We remembered it all together in Paris many years later when we went to Longchamps and Auteuil to lose our money on the ponies and spent nights drunkenly with Jim and Gloria Jones. At that time the Black Cat was the hangout of strip-tease girls and whores. It was a tough neighborhood. I could hardly take in the education I was getting, it was coming in so fast, but my ears were as long as a donkey's and my eyes were out on stalks.

I met a lot of extraordinary characters out there—truly Saroyan's world and Steinbeck's. They didn't come from nowhere, you know—like all writers, they were just writing what was, and that *is* the way it was in those days.

I could add a lot of stories to theirs. The Duke. "The Duke of Market Street," he was called. A famous fixture in San Francisco. He was the King of the Bums. His only possessions were a magnificent Capehart record changer, the first word in hi-fi almost before hi-fi began, and every opera and symphony that had ever been recorded—this in a fleabag that he shared with a Norwegian sailor who was always out to sea.

He did not want me to become a bum like him. He found me a job as a trainee doing analytical chemistry for a paint company. And then several things happened quickly. One day, courtesy of an old Avon classmate, I received a letter from the general manager of the Cyanamid Corporation, who was also the president of the Chemical Construction Corporation, offering me a job in south-central India assisting two chemical engineers in building a basic chemical complex for the Maharajah of Mysore.

"Duke," I asked—for I could talk to *this* duke, as I could never have to my father the *Grand* Duke—"what should I do? Should I keep on trying to find a night job that lets me go to school by day, or should I go to Jack London's Alaska, or should I accept this great panjandrum's miserable offer of a hundred dollars a month to build a chemical factory somewhere in India?"

He never hesitated. He said, "Make peace with your father and go out to India."

I was able to do the second.

## DR. W. LINDSAY JACOBS
Brooks Baekeland was hostile toward his son and in a welter of confused moralizing seemed to wish him ill, consciously or unconsciously.

He wrote me a letter about Tony, enclosing a cutting from some French magazine. I remember it was a full-page color cartoon made up of three separate sections. The first showed a man sitting quietly in an armchair reading a newspaper. The second showed a little boy pointing a space-ray gun directly at the man, with all sorts of yellow stars shooting out—it looked like the finale of a Fourth of July firecracker display. The last section of the cartoon was just a pile of ashes on the chair. And Brooks Baekeland had written on the side of the cartoon: "Sometimes this frightful realism comes too close to the heart of the thing."

### BROOKS BAEKELAND
In the end—long before the end—I saw Tony as a kind of personification of Evil, and I knew him better than anyone in the world and he knew that I did—as Caliban knew that Prospero knew Caliban. But to whom could—would—I have said that? No one. I told him— oh, I told *him*. And he understood. He knew that I loved him, too. And he loved *me*—too much according to some of his homosexual friends.

### SUZANNE TAYLOR
Angel, who cooked for the Baekelands two or three days a week, also came to us two or three days, whenever we were alone—she wasn't good enough to cook for company—and she used to tell us an awful lot about the Baekelands, naturally. She told me, "I don't know what's going to happen to Tony because when his parents are away he picks up older boys on the street and brings them home." He was about fourteen then.

### DR. THOMAS MAGUIRE
Tony's first homosexual relationship was at the age of eight.

## From a Psychiatric Report on Antony Baekeland Ordered By the British Courts, January 5, 1973

> In adolescence Antony found homosexual interests and had some physical experience at boarding school. He regards himself as attracted to both sexes.

### PETER GABLE
One Christmas break at Avon I came trundling down to New York and I stayed with Tony. His parents were living in Paris most of the time by then but they had this penthouse *pied-à-terre* on Seventy-fifth Street and Lexington, with lots of terraces. It was just kids down for a long weekend. Tony had a party, a little gathering. I remember

there were a lot of very cute girls there. Girls appreciated Tony's looks and his wit or his manner or something—they rather liked him. And he seemed to reciprocate their enthusiasm. I mean, he had, it appeared, as much enthusiasm for girls as anybody else, certainly as much as I had. He seemed to be as hotly in pursuit of the almost unachievable piece of ass as any of us. He became attracted to a friend of a cousin of his who I was going out with. God she was a sexy little girl—long brunette hair, curvaceous, quite something to warm the cockles of your heart on a cold winter's night in a boy's boarding school in Avon, Connecticut. And this girl and Tony formed some sort of vast friendship for six months or so. Her parents lived somewhere in Connecticut—Westport, Southport, Eastport, Northport—and there was a weekend that we all spent unchaperoned in their house, which I remember as being beamy, with a large fireplace and lots of stone. We built a fire and drank a bottle of Cointreau or something, and then we toddled off to bed. Now these were the years when girls' knees stayed wired to each other. So neither Tony nor I expected, nor did the girls anticipate, that anything of a particularly prurient nature would transpire. We did end up in the girls' room, where there were two double beds—Tony and his girl in one and me and my girl in the other, all of us clothed to some degree. And what did we do? We went to sleep!

The point of all this is, we're now fifteen years old and Tony is pursuing females. Another year or so and I begin to discern that he has something less than a burning interest in them. I'm trying to remember exactly when it was that I decided that Tony was *not* masculine. There was a period there, in his late teens, when I simply felt that he was neuter. It could well be that he was by then actively pursuing homosexuality—I don't know. As I said, at Avon we basically went our separate ways. But there was this one guy there, Mike Perkins. He was tall, dark, and incredibly handsome, and he was a real sexual enthusiast with women—I mean, I knew many of his girlfriends. But looking back now, I have the feeling that maybe he and Tony were more than friends.

NANCY PERKINS WALLACE
Tony and my brother Mike ran away from Avon together. They went to Puerto Rico. They were out of school for quite a while. They lived on beaches and that sort of thing. According to my brother, who is *not* homosexual, Tony had male lovers while they were there.

## HENRY H. PERKINS
Mike never told *me* about Tony's male lovers, you know, but I'm such a butch guy myself, my brother knows I don't like to hear stories of that stuff. I just remember they had no money, they slept on the beach, and they were bitten by fleas—they held out for a week or something, and then they, you know, came home, like any other little kids that have run away. After that, Mike began getting very involved in Tony's life, both here and in Europe.

They had airs, those people. Of grandeur. The Baekelands had the French parlor routine. And the salon, *oui*. And Tony had all of that, too, you know, and that's what I think was somewhat fascinating to my brother. I think that he was somewhat seduced by that.

## DUNCAN LONGCOPE
Tony had an American pal called Mike, quite a nice young man, dark-haired, very handsome as I recall, and they used to do the boulevards together, and according to this woman I knew who used to tell me stories about Tony's life on the Île Saint-Louis, it was the same thing every night—I mean, either two boys or two girls would come back with them, to this place of Brooks's that Tony used. Brooks, you know, had that other apartment on the Île, I think it was on the rue Regrattier—a studio where he wrote. And Tony at a certain time had the use of this studio.

## BROOKS BAEKELAND
For my part, I was sorry for him, sorry that he was homosexual—very sorry indeed—but I do not have most people's knee-jerk reactions to such things. It rather tends to make me think and wonder why, how, people like Tony who are not really effeminate—except, clearly, by imitation when in the company of others of their kind—become imprinted, diverged, into such channels.

In any case, in England, where he went after Avon, he met some very swishy titled young men, went to a Savile Row tailor, charged up what would now be ten thousand pounds of tailor-made clothes—he hadn't a bean, but Daddy would pay—and said he wanted to go up to Oxford with his friends.

He and his mother made a strong case for this remarkable request. Influence was to be used through the head of All Souls, now dead, "a charming man," etc. That the boy had not even finished high school and was essentially uneducated did not seem to them to be a reason why Oxford would not be delighted to have him.

I was finally able by various machinations plus my son's high IQ score and the charming and civilized impression he could make—I am not being ironical here; these things still counted in certain places—to get him provisionally accepted at St. John's College, Oxford, provided he could pass his O-levels—A-levels? I forget—after a bit of cramming, which shouldn't take more than a few months for a person of his intelligence, everyone agreed.

I hired a young Oxford student to come to Cadaqués, where we were to spend the summer. The task was for Tony to learn enough Latin to pass the examination in that subject, which, with a founding in French and some Spanish already learned by ear, should not have been too difficult.

But the tutor was corrupted, confessed the hopelessness of the situation to me, and left. No work had been accomplished at all.

Tearful scenes with Mama and Papa, promises of reform. So that autumn, kindness of Michael Alexander, Tony went to live in London and was put into a cramming school.


MICHAEL ALEXANDER

Tony stayed with me for about six months while he was studying at Davies, Laing & Dick somewhere up in Notting Hill Gate. He lived in my basement and he looked after himself. That was when the father-son relationship was at its most, how shall I put it . . . Brooks was trying to turn Tony into something other than a sort of layabout with homosexual inclinations. He was trying to turn him into a man—shall we put it that way? He was putting a lot of pressure on Tony, who I must say did not seem to be at that stage the ideal American boy.


BROOKS BAEKELAND

To make a long story short, the cramming school wrote to tell me that I was wasting my money. The lad, they said, was not even coming to his tutorial appointments, much less doing any of the work assigned to him.

But he was having a fine time with his swishy friends.

About this time I received a letter from Jim Jones reproaching me for not letting my son be a writer.

## Letter from Antony Baekeland to James Jones, Undated

% Michael Alexander
London, W. 1

Dear Jim,
Can you look at these for me and give me some advice? I know how busy you are, but I've given up the idea I had of going to Oxford and I'm going to be pretty broke by the first of the month. I thought you might know where to send them, if they're good enough to send. The one called *"Snow Dream of David Lanyon"* needs editing, I think. Anyway, tell me what you think, and love to Gloria and Kaylie.

Yours ever,
Tony Baekeland

P.S. Can you help me get an agent? Also (I'm out of my mind) do you think I could get *"Jolyon Condemned"* in *The New Yorker*?

## Letter from James Jones to Antony Baekeland, December 22, 1964

10, quai d'Orléans
Paris IV°

Dear Tony,
I have read your three stories with a great deal of interest. I think you write extremely well. Really remarkably well. I enjoyed all three of them very much, simply for that reason. However, I do not think you could get any one of the three of them into *The New Yorker*, which is not only pretty much of a closed corporation, but also very severe in its dictates of and demands for the quote *New Yorker* style unquote.

With regard to an agent, I suggest you call and meet my own agent in London, whose name is Hope Leresche. Her phone is FLAxman 43.11 and her address is 11 Jubilee Place, London, S.W. 3. Hope is an agent for a lot of people among whom is Sheila Delaney whom she helped to get started. If she likes you and your work, and I should think she would, she may be able to help you get started.

On the other hand, trying to make even a bare living out of writing short stories is next to impossible. The kind of stories you would like to write have very little commercial market value unfortunately, whatever their true value. I am only telling you this because it is the truth, because I want you to know what may be in store for you. Despite that, because I did like the stories you sent so much, I would be willing to write your Dad and Mom that I think they should support you—if not richly, at least so you can live—so that you can write. It's a peculiar fact that most parents will support their kids in studying just about any profession except learning how to write. As a matter of fact, I told them that when they were here last time. However, I would not like to write them to this effect unless I was absolutely sure it was something you wished me to do. Also, I don't know how to spell Cadaquez (?). In fact, I'm not even sure they're there now.

With regard to the three stories, I think the first, untitled one comes nearest to being a short story in the old-fashioned classic sense. By that I mean something does happen, the boy does see his mother with a man, and at the end does act on it. However, I feel it is obvious that you have imposed these two scenes on the story as a whole. Each of them is dealt with almost cursorily, with much less of the interesting and affective detail which makes the rest of the story so good. I feel that the ending is therefore too abrupt, unprepared for, and happens too quickly for the reader to partake of it fully. I also think that the arising of the storm, clearly a device to promulgate the ending, could be made more natural, and perhaps more emotionally a true part of the story (as opposed to a device) by having its first signs commence earlier, when the boy is climbing on the island, so that when he sees the man kissing his mother, it is during the first beginning winds rustling the trees and grasses while he sees them. Then let it build up slowly to the rest of the story to the end. It would of course be easy to overdo this thing of the storm, but if it is done naturally without being pointed up too much, I think it would clear up all the criticisms I have and this feeling of abruptness of device laid on over the top. I would think, too, the boy would have some inkling, earlier, that his beautiful mom is not as perfect as he would like her to be. You could play this off against naive younger sister.

Neither of the other two is this close to being technically a short story, though I found them both interesting and moving. Of the two I think *The Snow Dream* is the better, although I feel the ending sort of tapers off leaving one with an unsatisfied feeling. The *Jolyon* one is the least successful, largely because in its latter half there is an undefinable adolescent-bravado quality which the other two, while written *about* adolescents, do not have. I liked the first part with the girls, though.

Please let me know if you want me to write your folks, and please look up Hope Leresche. Gloria joins me in sending all best.

Sincerely,
James Jones

## Telegram from Antony Baekeland to James Jones, Undated

JUST BACK NEW YORK READ LETTER THANKS FOR ENCOURAGEMENT I NEED IT CAN YOU WRITE FATHER AT CASADEVAL CADAQUES GERONA WILL LOOK UP MRS. LERESCHE HAPPY NEW YEAR LOVE TO GLORIA          TONY

## Letter from James Jones to Brooks Baekeland, February 5, 1965

10, quai d'Orléans
Paris IV°

Dear Brooks,

I seem to remember that we are coming down to see you for a few days some time fairly soon, but as I am up in the office and Gloria is downstairs and the phone is busy I cannot check with her just when. Anyway that is not what I'm writing about just now.

Shortly before we went to Klosters Tony sent me from London three stories of his which he asked me to read and comment on. I did this and I quote in part what I thought about them:

"I think you write extremely well . . . Really remarkably well. I enjoyed all three of them very much, simply for that reason. However, I do not think you could get any one of the three into *The New Yorker* . . ."

I meant every word of this, Brooks. I think Tony has the *unacquirable* trait of a writer, which is to make people see and feel things powerfully. I don't think as yet that he has any of the technical proficiency, or the constructive sense, to utilize the talent he has. (Max Perkins once said the same thing about me, and I guess I'm more or less quoting him.) Anyway, it's going to take him quite a while to develop his talent, but I sincerely think he does have a talent, and I think he ought to have a chance to try to develop it.

Tony mentioned in his letter only that he's given up the idea of going to Oxford and was going to be pretty broke by the end of the month. He was hoping I could help him sell one of the three to *The New Yorker*. I of course having talked with you and Barbara knew more than Tony was saying and could read between the lines. I wrote him a detailed analysis of all three of the stories and then went on to explain that it was next to impossible to try and make a living by writing short stories. I also offered to write to you in his behalf, and tell you what I thought about his writing. I feel strongly enough that Tony has talent that I would suggest to you that you give him a chance to work at it, which would mean sending him enough money to live on (and I don't mean luxuriously). I am aware that most American parents while willing to support their kids for eight years to become a doctor, nevertheless take a very dim view of supporting the same kids the same length of time to become a writer. But it takes just as long. What does surprise me is that you, who have worked at becoming a writer yourself and who love writing and writers, find yourself now in a moral position where you cannot give Tony a fair chance to become one himself.

When I wrote to Tony I said I would not write to you unless he wished me to, and while I was in Klosters I got a wire from him here giving me your address in Cadaqués and asking me to go ahead and write you. So I am.

It's not as if you were poor and didn't have the money. And I am not writing you out of any sense of moral issue or empathy for the young. But I've been dedicated to writing all my life, and whenever I see someone who has a chance at writing well I always try to help them get that chance if I can. I think you ought to help Tony. Actually, he has made remarkable strides since those few early things of his I read two or three years ago.

Gloria joins me in sending our love to you both and I hope we'll see you in—what is it, May?

Sincerely,
James Jones

## Letter from Brooks Baekeland to James Jones, February 7, 1965

(44 today)
Cadaqués

Dear Jim:

It was very kind of you to write me. You are a kind man and an understanding man and some other things too—but that's already enough for what I want to say.

First of all I am not quite the horse's ass that you may think, nor so conventional. The doctor writer bit I can truthfully say is unimpeachable, because it is, and has been for a long time, my own opinion. Tactics *(when)* is all I was concerned with, and (much too long a subject) that is conditioned by the mercurial changes still going on in Tony. (I am waiting for him to burst out of Davies's, which I think he will, and then I fully intend to do what you suggest and with blessings that will mean more then than they would have 3 years ago when I had already reached your opinion and when he might have had troubles which could have finished, or broken, the impulse that is growing hard in him. I don't know whether I can make myself clear about this in a few words.)

Secondly, as a matter of principle, although I disagreed with it in almost every aspect (and was overridden, as far as I could tell, by both B & T), I would not gratify Tony by torpedoing his mother's late arrangements for him in England. They will collapse of their own foolishness. The harder Tony's resolve becomes, the better as far as I am concerned—because (for one thing) I would like to see him grow out of his mother and he can only do that by an exercise of male defiance—which I soon expect.

Third—I gave him the signal, permission and money in December. (I gave a lot of thought to your counsel: I say counsel, because I have great respect for your insight. It was a relief to hear *you* say that.) But I made one condition—that he take the occupation seriously and show some signs of it. (Agent, work, etc.) He did and I was pleased. (The efforts were inefficient, but they were efforts.) In London he showed me his stories and I was pleased. I told him so. I have known for years that whatever else he did in life, he would be a writer. I never told him different when I decided that. He has never had anything but praise and encouragement from me in that. (Ask him.) O.K. The next thing I knew, he was in the USA with Mama. The next thing I knew after that was that he was going to go to a shrink and go back to Davies's. I suggested to him that he get away from us— go into the military, get it over with, write his head off (or not if he chose) and spend some peaceful, boring, regular and *distant* years from us. Mama has so indoctrinated him with the blood- thirsty horrors and depravities of military service of any kind that he thought I was trying to punish him. I wrote him no. I also wrote him, however, that I was not going to blow up "Mum." The next move is up to him. . . . He knows that I am on his side, but he also knows that I want it *straight* and as soon as he wants it straight too, he has his ticket. That's his problem.

He's afraid. (Again Mama—the homosexual fear.)

Nothing is ever simple, and this shrink may capture him (keep him in a kind of permanent dependent babyhood). I think not. I have a high respect for this boy who has a head as clear as anyone's I know. He's lucid.

The clock is ticking and I know that his little bomb is going to go off soon. If it doesn't—I'm going to be all confused! I will never have been so wrong in my intuition (I'm not used to that either).

I am sorry to bore you with this, but I owe you something for your long, kind letter and for your interest in Tony. When you said at your house that you weren't sure "he could put words together" (a judgment you made several years before) I decided not to say all this to you. The tactics, however, interest me. The raw meat of frustration, eaten for quite a long period now, may not have been so bad a training diet. I respect writing. I want him to respect it. He is not likely, no one is *likely*, to be another James Jones. But even less is anyone likely to be that if he treats it like an escape or a kind of lark. When he decides to write, he will also lick Mama and everything that implies. Everything (I hope) will come together at once.

Want to see your book. When? My book I think going well. Love you both very much.

The old Puritan

## BROOKS BAEKELAND

My reaction to all this was not simple. I knew that professional writing required amongst other things a tremendous amount of discipline—guts?—and solitude. That Tony was articulate and "a born writer" in every sense but the above, I had long known, and that had already impressed a lot of our other friends. With Michael Alexander's good influence, I was, if not hopeful, not entirely skeptical either.

Again, to make a long story short, it began to be evident that Tony was having a lovely time in London with his swishy friends but was not writing. Whatever else a writer does or does not do, he writes. He cannot help it, it's compulsive. And Tony was not writing.

Thinking how discouraging it all was, I offered him a deal. In retrospect I do not think it was a wise thing, but I thought it might help him then. I told him I would buy whatever he wrote *by the word* and try to get it edited and published for him. Which he had asked me to do, so that the only new thing here was my—rather crass— financial inducement to try to make a writer write—that is, to make him stop leading his playboy life enough at least to finance it. A few hours a day would have done it.

It was really a rotten idea, and I tell you this because it now makes me laugh. Laugh?

And then Tony began to become *persona non grata*—just hints from Michael Alexander—and his sojourn at Michael's ended. There were some damages to pay.

And that was the end of "writing," which is what Tony's mother, having abandoned all hope of his becoming a biologist, had hoped that he would do.

## ELIZABETH WEICKER FONDARAS

Barbara was always highly stimulated by literary people. She felt *those* were the social prizes.

## BOWDEN BROADWATER
Mary McCarthy when I was married to her always thought Barbara
Baekeland frivolous and intellectually pretentious, and I must say I
quite agreed.

## GEORGES BERNIER
The first time I ever met Barbara Baekeland, she said, "Tell me,
Georges"—you can imagine how flabbergasted I was as a Frenchman
to hear myself called by my first name by someone I hadn't known
for more than five minutes—"was Marcel Proust a homosexual?" I
must say I had to laugh, because this was at a time when you
couldn't open up a literary supplement anywhere in the world without reading about Proust—Proust, Freud, and Joyce were the big
three—and this question that was preying on Barbara Baekeland's
mind was of course almost the first thing anybody ever addressed in
Proust.

Ben Sonnenberg had called to tell me there was this *wonderful*
American couple that had just arrived in Paris that he very much
wanted me to meet, whereupon, a few days later, I was invited for
dinner at the Baekelands', whereupon Barbara had immediately asked
me this amazing question.

Then Brooks began carrying on about what a wonderful fertile intelligent mind his son had because he would get hold of flies and
remove one wing and watch what the equilibrium was, and then he
would remove the other wing and see how it worked at *that* point—
and sometimes the legs would be broken, so that was another interesting thing. I found Brooks's attitude extraordinarily odd. You know,
that kind of sadistic behavior is quite common in children, but one
seldom sees a father who thinks it is marvelous. And then after dinner the child himself was produced. I said to myself when I walked
out of their place that night, I never want to see those people ever
again.

I did in fact see *her* once after that. We were both the guests of
Ethel de Croisset at a restaurant near Notre Dame, called Quasi-
modo—Marcel Duchamp was also there. You know, I admired Marcel and I was rather *agacé* that he was wasting his time with the likes
of Barbara Baekeland.

She continued to invite me to their dinners, of course, but I had—
and still have, for that matter—a great technique for stopping these
things in the bud: sudden frost.

## BROOKS BAEKELAND

My technique was flight, although once, in Klosters, both of us naked in a small hotel bathroom, I held Barbara down with my foot—approximate region, her thorax—while she sank her strong, white teeth as deep as she could into my calf. I thought the situation so funny—though I dared not let her up—that I enraged her still more by laughing. I really loved her, you know. This "fight"—and there was one almost every night, sooner or later—came about because I refused to take her to the Chesa Grishuna that evening—again!—for dinner. I believe it took at least a half hour for the adrenaline to burn out of her veins. But before that she was a wild animal, a flaming, beautiful tigress. In thirty years I only hit her once—and that was not intended.

## ELIZABETH ARCHER BAEKELAND

Brooks told me that sometimes in the middle of these horrendous battles of theirs he would say, "Barbara, I have to go to the loo," and she would suddenly calm down and sit patiently while he went to the bathroom, and then resume screaming when he came out. But one time in Paris the fighting was so terrible he just left and went to a very elegant hotel. He got in bed and said, "Thank God, now I'll have some peace," and started reading, and then suddenly the armoire door flew open and out came Barbara—"Darling, I'm here!"—and they had a fantastic evening together. You see, he had told her when he stormed off which hotel he was going to, and she had somehow gotten there ahead of him and said to the desk, "I'm Madame Baekeland," and they had let her up.

## PEIDI GIMBEL LUMET

Barbara carried on fiercely and dangerously for years. There was that headlong pitch of hers, on the down. Once we were in Zermatt together. I was skiing with a Swiss guide I'd skied with in St. Anton for a few years, and Barbara used to sort of come around corners and join us or try to—she was sort of tailing us. And she was skiing too fast for how she skied—she had skied much less than I had—she was sort of going pell-mell. And she broke her leg really badly. I mean, it was very self-destructive.

But it wasn't just the skiing. She was possessed. The house where we were all staying, Brooks and Barbara and Heather and Jack Cohane and I, was sort of a chalet on top of a rise of land, and the

moon was very full. I had the feeling Barbara was just going to turn
into a creature we'd never imagined. There were these transforma-
tions going on at night that you could see. A couple of times she
packed her suitcases and piled them on the *schlittens*—you know,
those wooden sleds—and she'd start to keen and wail, and I think
maybe Brooks went out and got her and brought her back in.

## From *A Walk in Winter Woods,* Brooks Baekeland, Unpublished

How many times they had lain like this on their backs in the
snow at Zermatt and looked up at a full moon. It was she who
had always wanted to ski under the moon, she who had always
dared, and he had followed—not because he had wanted to or
thought it was wise, but in case she got hurt. He had never been
able to stop her from doing anything she had set her mind on
doing.

### HEATHER COHANE

It was always the moon, either the full moon or the new moon. A lot
of people are affected by it. My mother had an admirer who was the
first person I ever knew who was affected by it. He'd be with us and
then suddenly he would lose his temper and rush out, and sometimes
he'd stay away for three days. We would pass him in the street and he
wouldn't even say good morning, how are you. And then when the
moon had gone through its cycle or whatever, he'd come back as if
nothing had happened. And when we shared the house with the
Baekelands and Peidi Gimbel in Zermatt, with the Matterhorn loom-
ing up right next to us, I noticed that with Barbara, too, it was the
moon. It came on very suddenly and she would go very round the
bend.

### BROOKS BAEKELAND

I took a series of questions with me to Zermatt—Chalet Turquino,
Winkelmatten mit Matterhorn, to be exact—that winter of 1963:
How do you get an exploring team into a lofty, jungled, tropical
mountain range that is unmapped? How do you supply it? How do
you defend it? How do you get it out again?

## From *National Geographic,* Vol. 126, No. 2, August 1964

The strain of being first to conquer one of earth's unknown areas shows in the haggard faces of two New Yorkers who parachuted into Peru's forbidding Vilcabamba mountain fastness: Brooks Baekeland, 43-year-old grandson of the Belgian who invented Bakelite, and Peter R. Gimbel, 36, a great-grandson of the Gimbel-Saks department stores. Forsaking life in Manhattan's man-made canyons, they and two companions spent 89 harrowing days traversing the wilderness. . . .

### BROOKS BAEKELAND

What compelled me to undertake such a journey? The fact that no one had ever parachuted anywhere near such altitudes before. But there was another reason, too, in 1963. I had fallen deeply in love with a young English girl—she was fifteen years younger than I was, the daughter of a diplomat friend of mine in Paris—and this had occasioned Barbara's first—of four—suicide attempts when I had asked for a permanent leave from her excitements and expenditures, from her way of life. Faced with becoming a murderer for the sake of freedom, I gave up my English girl and went into the desert, so to speak, for I knew now that Barbara would never give me my freedom. I knew that I was bound to that monster of green-eyed jealousy for life. So I took up exploring as a profession.

The fact is, at this time in my life I did not give a damn whether I lived or died. I still don't, and that has always been a great strength. Many people who know me fear me for that reason. Even dogs are aware of it and treat me with circumspection. But I feel no arrogance in this thing—it is a proof, to me, of failure. That, you will see, is what allowed two people as basically different as Peter Gimbel and I to become partners for a while.

It was a funny partnership—which he never understood. I mean, I was very old, he was very young. In the end he felt—and perhaps he was—betrayed. For some astigmatic reason of his own, he hero-worshiped me—*then*. Later, he discovered the hollowness of his error.

He was then, and may still be, caught up entirely in the balls-around-his-neck Hemingway ethic of grace under pressure. I have always believed that real bravery is of the intellect, not of the balls. But this Hemingway style was very much in fashion then. I openly derided it. Not that I am in the easy anti-Hemingway camp, either. Never was.

"Brooko," said Peter, "we have got to go down there! We have got to see that country." He was always a magnet for challenges. What intrigued him most was the danger of being killed by those wild Indians! As for myself, not being in the bravery game, I needed that excuse to escape Barbara for months at a time.

I was of course also intrigued by a very interesting four-hundred-year-old mystery: what had happened to Manco Inca, Atahualpa's brother, and his two hundred thousand soldiers when they had fled down into the Alta Selva, the backside of the Andes, from the Spanish.

Up in my eyrie at Zermatt I decided that they must have settled somewhere at the southern end of the Cordillera Vilcabamba. They were pursued by the Spanish rabble but disappeared—and then a silence, a silence of over four hundred years. I liked that a lot.

In the prospectus that Gimbel and I wrote for the expedition—we were applying for funding principally to the National Geographic Society, whose owners, the Grosvenors, were old family friends, and to the New York Zoological Society, of which Gimbel was then a trustee—we carefully made no mention of lost Inca cities, etc. That would never have done—would never have gained us the money we needed. So we made it into a scientific expedition. And my argument for this—and which sold our project—was that the island cordillera rose practically from sea-level altitude out of the Amazon plain to heights just short of snow and ice and therefore contained a whole series of climates and therefore flora and fauna from the tropical to the arctic and that, because of the "island's" separation from the main mass of the Andes rising to the West, a variety of unknown species of animals, plants, and insects could—over millions of years—have developed in isolation there. I therefore proposed that we make the expedition for purposes of biological exploration. If I mentioned the disappearance of Manco Inca four centuries earlier in the general direction of this cordillera, it was strictly in passing.

Since we failed to land our biologists on top of the cordillera, the expedition was a formal failure in terms of its main objective. In every other way it was a success. Until such time as a weather freak permitted the cordillera to be mapped by photogrammetry, our map was and would remain the only accurate one of the region. The reason it had gone unmapped for so long is that everyone who had ever entered and tried to traverse it had died—thirteen expeditions had left their records and their bones. It was a place of death. We were the first team who had actually traversed the cordillera and lived to tell the tale.

Our expedition also pioneered a new method of penetrating and exploring otherwise inaccessible regions. Finally, and not least, it developed the "Para commander" parachute, a radical new design based an invention that allowed high-altitude parachuting for the first time. This design became immediately the standard parachute for every army and air force in the world. It had been tested for the first time in early 1963 by Jacques Istel—Peter Gimbel standing by— on twenty-thousand-foot Popocatepetl in Mexico, and I remember well when I received the telegram announcing their success at my H.Q. in Zermatt. The jump was, I think, to eleven thousand feet, which was more than six thousand feet higher than had ever been achieved before.

That I did not find descendants of Manco Inca waiting up there to kill me—well . . . too bad?

Finally, after having been almost murdered by some Machiguenga Indians, we made friendly contact with them and brought three of them to civilization. As for the ruins of Manco Inca's last—lost— city, we had guessed that it would be found on what I called Paddock's Ridge, but we could not get to it and it was invisible from the air. And indeed that is where it *was* found—by Gene Savoy a couple of years later!

I may say, immodestly, that I was the only one of the four of us who made the famous walk out of the cordillera who was happy doing it. I was, due to my background, in my element. Gimbel hated it—his interests, his training, did not extend to botany and entomology, etc. He just wanted "out," while I hoped we might take forever. Jack Joerns, one of the three pilots on the expedition, a Texan, became deeply depressed. Only Peter Lake, a Dartmouth student, maintained his natural gaiety. He was really wonderful— partly, I think, because he had absolute confidence in Peter Gimbel and me. I had guaranteed his parents that I would get him home alive, and I took that promise seriously. He knew it, he knew me, and he believed it. As for me, my strength came partly from the fact that my personal life was in a shambles. I was deeply unhappy over having had to renounce the English girl, with whom I was deeply in love. My career was shattered, and my son, already far gone in drugs and sodomy at seventeen, was obviously beyond change. Do you understand?

Gimbel called me "Ahab"—and our friendship ended with that

expedition. For one reason or another, one of my closest and most treasured friends, a man I greatly respected and for whom I had deep affection, was lost to me. I asked him why on several occasions but never had an answer. But expeditions are famous breakers of friendships—as are marriages. In our case the break was particularly painful, not only because we had been like Damon and Pythias but because we had never so much as had a disagreement—we had always seen all our problems in the same way and quickly reached our solutions. He had many wonderful gifts that I lacked, and I had those he lacked—and it worked! If we had fought or disagreed, my sorrow over what happened to our partnership would have been nothing to speak of.

## PETER GIMBEL

It was Brooks who got me involved—he really enticed me into the thing. My identical twin brother, David, had died of stomach cancer at the age of twenty-nine, at which point I started to examine my own life pretty hard and decided that Wall Street where I had been working was not the world where I wanted to spend the rest of my life. I had met Brooks a couple of years earlier, and now I was looking for something very offbeat to do. In July of 1956 when I was twenty-eight, I had made a dive to the *Andrea Doria* and in a small way, the way it can happen in a bigger way now, I became instantly noticeable—anyway I was called by Fairfield Osborn and asked to join the board of trustees of the New York Zoological Society, and a short while later the president of the American Museum of Natural History got in touch with me and asked me to join *their* board.

So anyway when Brooks came up with the idea for the Vilcabamba expedition I was very excited. I was much more interested in the expedition from the standpoint of pure exploration and adventure, not in the scholarly/intellectual/archaeological kind of thing that Brooks was interested in—he wanted to find the lost city and figure out exactly where the last stand of the last Inca had been and discover the last tomb and so forth and so on. I would have gone in there even if you had guaranteed me that there *was* no lost city—just because of the romance of dropping into a virtually cut-off island of land, because that's what it was—a huge fifteen-thousand-foot-high island rising out of low jungle on all sides. Here was the *unknown*, you know.

Brooks was in Zermatt with Barbara, so we were planning it all by long distance, you might say—by voluminous correspondence. Barbara had broken her leg skiing, really smashed it—a terrible break. So Brooks had—I have to call it an excuse, because it was what he really wanted to do: remain in Zermatt skiing while I organized the whole thing. I mean, he was in Switzerland and the guy doing the dirty work was right here—okay?

I have to give him credit, though—he was a brilliant, brilliant land analyst. He could look at a cliff that was covered with jungle and say, "There's a ledge running there that I think we can traverse." And he'd be right on the money every fuckin' time! I question whether we would have gotten out without him.

Scientifically my evaluation is the thing was a complete failure as an expedition—a failure, a nonsuccess—but that in terms of a strange adventurous exploratory feat it was a success. And I would say that on the *Geographic* staff it was perceived both those ways. Clearly, the drama of our entry and the long trek out outweighed whatever the magazine's disappointment scientifically was, because they ran it as a cover story and devoted quite a lot of space and attention to it and so on.

From *National Geographic,* Vol. 126, No. 2, August 1964

### BY PARACHUTE INTO PERU'S LOST WORLD
*by Brooks Baekeland*
PHOTOGRAPHS BY THE AUTHOR AND PETER R. GIMBEL

Cramped in the airplane with our bulky gear, Peter Gimbel and I looked out of the open door and then, questioningly, at each other.

A year of careful preparation had brought us to this moment of decision far above a remote spur of the Andes of southeastern Peru. . . .

### BROOKS BAEKELAND
That was not *my* "colorful account" in the *Geographic*. My piece—"too subjective"—was totally emasculated and rewritten by a *Geographic* hack for that thirteen-year-old girl who lives in Sioux City, for whom every issue of that amazing magazine is always writ-

ten. I did not give a damn. I had a wonderful summer, mostly paid for by National Geographic Society funds, and my own vanity was not involved.

### ETHEL WOODWARD DE CROISSET

Brooks asked me to have a look at his article for the *Geographic* before it was published. Now it had some very good things, wonderfully described things, in it, but it was badly punctuated, full of misspellings, so I did some editing, you know—just little, simple things to the English, which I did on a separate sheet of paper. Then I gave it to Barbara, whom I happened to be seeing, and said, "Give this to Brooks. I did a little editing." I'd actually taken great pains with it. And Barbara was outraged. She said, "I wouldn't *think* of showing this to him, and don't *you* ever mention it! Just tell him it's wonderful. He mustn't be discouraged." And she tore it up. I felt very bad, I hadn't realized. . . . But it shows you how she protected him, always telling him he was a genius. All of this sort of thing was to *keep* him.

You know, Barbara had a love affair with a Spaniard and it was all for Brooks to realize that she was more attractive than he seemed to think her. She told me that she'd met him in New York, right when things were going very ruggedly. She had suddenly discovered—she hadn't known—that Brooks was dragging around and looking for other women. A little later she found out that he had an affair on with an English girl.

She didn't like her Spanish friend at all—very soon she'd had enough of him. But she played the game that she was going to leave Brooks and run off with him. And she told me that Brooks begged her not to go, that he was very moved and all of this. I think the Spaniard was terrified that she *was* going to go off with him—he faded out of the picture when he heard *that* threat.

She may have slept with him *once*. You know, she was fundamentally an Irish Catholic, brought up very severely in Catholicism, but I think that then she got into this very sort of Café Society group of people, but of rather an intellectual sort, and probably had some false Freudian ideas as well. But she was basically extremely correct.

## Letter from Barbara Baekeland to Gloria and James Jones, Undated

New York

My very much missed Joneses—

There is so much to tell you—I feel I'm back in the trap but I'm sort of beginning to enjoy it. When we first arrived Tony & I were in a state of such despair. I missed you—Paris—some kind of human order—but now that old pals begin to hove to, I begin to cheer up a bit, but my God what an inhuman city it is! . . .

Brooks is still crashing about the jungle. Making only 2 kil. a day—hacking his way through with a machete and probably having a very tough time. In the meantime I see my Spanish boyfriend from time to time but I am less and less interested. He has a kind of warmth and tenderness that is very touching and I think knows me better in 2 or 3 weeks than Brooks does after 20 years, but finally the odor becomes oppressive. I think I'd rather sleep with a stranger—and after 20 years my husband still is! . . .

Anyway I've decided to come back in Feb.—no matter what—and I am going to try to *do* something this fall. Rather like a plant struggling up through a yard of cement but maybe there will be a small flower.

Just came back from a fancy lunch at Pavillon with Ben Sonnenberg, Italians, etc. Life is gay—I'm a new arrival! In fact I find social success can be predicated on the notion that one must *always* have more an air of arrival than of departure. I intend to cultivate this for my gray hairs.

Kisses & hugs. How is Kaylie? Her little face on the balcony as she watched us drive off I see as clearly as if she were in my arms. Kiss her for me.

X
B.

## From the Diaries of John Philip Cohane, Unpublished

*Tuesday.* We went to a teeming late evening party given by Ben Sonnenberg, a wonderful, erudite, close friend who owns the

Stuyvesant Fish house in Gramercy Park, probably one of the best-designed houses in New York, overflowing with incredible paintings and etchings, not to mention several hundred guests including Aschwin and Simone Lippe, Charles and Helen Rolo, Gilbert and Polly Kahn, and Barbara Baekeland, solitary and wild-eyed.

## PETER GIMBEL

Once at Jack Cohane's house Barbara put her arm around my neck and tried to wrestle me to the floor to force me to have it *her* way—she'd gotten angry at me because I didn't agree with her about something.

Here she was, hanging on to me. I didn't try to shake her or push her or anything. I was so mad I just wanted to let her humiliate herself. Finally she started to giggle, because she saw how really absurd it was.

Let me tell you something more about why I felt taken advantage of by Brooks. Having shown up for the expedition as close to the time of departure as was possible—I mean, just in time to help me with the last of the preparations and to go through his parachute training—what did Brooks do shortly after the expedition but leave again for Europe. Leaving me to mop up. And oh God, the mopping up! You can't imagine—information the *Geographic* wanted, returning equipment to the people who supplied us, filling out reports, just a lot of busy work. But believe me, that's very much the way he is. You know, he's never asked me why I feel the way I do about our partnership. Looking back, I suppose he did me a kind of favor, because from that period of my life on, I've never been somebody who's been particularly easy to take advantage of.

## PETER LAKE

Brooks got to be a god on our expedition! No, seriously, for a few minutes he *was*. About two-thirds of the way into the trip Peter Gimbel, Jack Joerns, and I were drinking from the river when we were surprised by some Indians who had snuck up behind us with bows and arrows and were clearly going to kill us—they thought we were evil spirits or something. And then Brooks came up from behind and surprised *them*. Now these Indians didn't have any facial hair, they had long straight black hair on their heads, and they were short, and there, suddenly, was Brooks—you know, tall, bald, with a gray beard. We got this letter about a year later from some missionaries that said the Indians had thought Brooks was some kind of god and that that's why they had spared us.

## BROOKS BAEKELAND
The arrow that kills you is shot by an enemy you never see.

I only killed one human—an old man sitting with his back to a tree by a bridge in Germany. There had still been no Hiroshima, but there had been, I think, the awful Hamburg and Dresden and Cologne. About Himmler's gas chambers, we dewy youths still knew nothing. I had already decided that if I were sent on fighter bombers, to bomb "targets of opportunity"—that is, French and German towns—I would try to destroy cabbages and potatoes rather than young mothers and children.

He was reading a newspaper. He was wearing a bowler hat. We were "attacking" the bridge. My stream of .50 caliber bullets from four wing guns hit him before I even saw him and by mistake, and his bowler hat rolled slowly across the bridge. This was just before the end of the war.

I mourn for that old man still.

## From the *New York Times*, December 2, 1963

### FINANCIER TELLS OF TREK IN ANDES
He and Friends Explored Unknown Areas of Peru
By JOHN SIBLEY

Two New York investment bankers, G. Brooks Baekeland and Peter R. Gimbel, have returned to tame office routine after a grueling 90-day expedition through previously unexplored wilds of the Peruvian Andes. . . .

Why do men do it?

"I don't know," Mr. Baekeland mused. "I'm one of those people who's always driving up a little dirt road."

## PETER GABLE
Tony and I were still in school at the time but we decided that nothing would do but that we go along on the expedition. Why not? We were two healthy, active seventeen-year-olds. So we bearded his fa-

ther with this idea—you know, "What do you think of the notion
that we tag along and fall out of the sky with you and Mr. Gimbel?"
We'd spent so much time fantasizing about how much fun it would
be, what an adventure—I mean, Tony's father was a swashbuckler
from the word go. Anyway, the thing I remember most about his
response was his distinct lack of enthusiasm—not about our par-
ticipating in the project, because, of course, how could a responsible
parent be enthusiastic about that? But he wasn't even willing to play
along with us. He didn't say, "I don't think it's such a hot idea
*because* . . ." or "Gee, that's a great idea *but* . . ." He just said no.
End of case.

I saw Tony only a handful of times after 1963. We really did just
do different things. I mean, I went off to college. In the early seventies sometime, I bumped into his grandmother, Mrs. Daly, on the
street and she gave me Tony's address in England.

## HEATHER COHANE
I went to see him quite a lot in Broadmoor. The first years he was
there I couldn't go because I was living in Ireland and very involved
in my knitwear business and I hardly had time to even visit my children at school in England. But as soon as Jack and I sold our house
in Ireland and went to live in London, I started to go to see Tony
very regularly. Because I loved him and because I remembered him
as a very gentle boy in Ansedonia. Jack would never go with me,
because he suffered from claustrophobia—he was afraid of getting
locked in.

What riveted me about Broadmoor was, you could not tell who
was the inmate and who was the visitor because the inmates were
dressed in ordinary clothes. There'd be, you see, two men sitting at a
table and I'd say to myself, Now *which* one is the madman? And
when the bell clanged, meaning visiting hours were over, I would
jump to my feet to see who the inmates were, because they would be
going off through one door and the visitors would be going out the
other. And I practically never got it right! And this is the thing that
fascinated me, and I decided that we were all mad.

Tony told me he went berserk once at Broadmoor because something annoyed him and that he was put in one of the solitary cells for
a couple of days. He also said that he got beaten up once, I can't
remember why. But a nice thing is he did develop a very good friend
in there, I presume a lover. I don't think the friend had any parents

or anything. It was rather a sad story—you know, nobody to worry about trying to get him out. In fact, he's still there. You see, in Broadmoor you have no hope if there isn't somebody campaigning the whole time to get you out. I remember Tony saying that if he ever got out of Broadmoor he would miss his friend very much.

Once I took my daughter Ondine to see him on her way back to school—she was at a boarding school called the Manor House in Wiltshire. She wanted to go with me to see him, though she was only eight at the time. Jack and I had told her what had happened—I mean, she grew up knowing that Tony had killed his mother.

### ONDINE COHANE

There was a lot of clanging. I'll never forget all those gates clanging behind us. I liked him. He was nice. But I didn't talk to him much because I was upset about having to go back to school, so I just listened. He talked about his inmates—the people in his cell—and what they were allowed to do. He told us the rules. My mother told him I loved animals, so he told me about his chicken when he was small and how he used to take it around with him. I felt very sorry for him. I didn't like to think of him behind all those gates and everything. He wrote my mother later that I was rather a sad little girl, but I was mostly sad to be going back to school.

### HEATHER COHANE

One day I decided that I should take my son Alexander, who in fact was Barbara's godson, to see Tony. He was at a very impressionable age, you see—seventeen—and at Eton, and, you know, there were drugs and all sorts of other things around and available. So I thought it was a very good idea to show him what could happen to you if you did take drugs.

### WILLIE DRAPER

Tony was destroyed by drugs, but the drugs were just the means, not the cause. When I was at St. Paul's School in New Hampshire, he would send me hashish from Paris, wrapped in tinfoil in an envelope. It was a whole different scene then. Nobody at prep school knew anything even about marijuana in 1963. Believe me. *Nothing. Nobody.* But then pot and all the hallucinogens began to be used in very creative ways, you know. Tony and I would pretend to be sea turtles on the beach in East Hampton where his parents used to rent a house sometimes when they came back from Europe for a couple of months. At this point it was only pot, and we didn't do it all the time—we weren't potheads or anything. I mean, you can't even begin to relate it to the way people smoke pot now. We didn't do it as a social thing at all.

ALEXANDER COHANE
We drove down from London one Sunday, Mummy and me, just the two of us, and we went through the main gate and then, you know, he came through into this sort of visitor's lounge. He was taller than me, he was about six foot. Quite good-looking. I mean, a handsome man he probably would have been if he'd been out in the street walking along. We sat down and we just started talking, and we gave him a packet of cigarettes and a whole load of apples and oranges, sort of a selection of goodies—you know, what we sort of call in England "tuck."

We must have been with him about three hours. He talked the whole time. He told us every detail about killing his mother. I wish I'd had a tape recorder with me, because, you know, I've never known anyone who killed anyone else. He said she had pissed him off—you know, done something to annoy him—and that he just picked up the knife in the kitchen and said, "You've destroyed my life. I'm a wasted human being."

He also said to us, "It's ruined my life in several ways to be in here." And he said that it was just absolutely hopeless and depressing to look out at the countryside and not be part of it. Then I remember him very clearly saying, "I feel my mother's presence around me all the time, I love her so much. She's in every tree."

# 8

# POSSESSIONS

After Tony Baekeland had been at Broadmoor for three years, he began to wonder if he would ever be allowed to leave. "He was showing great improvement," says Miwa Svinka-Zielinski. "He sounded quite reasonable on the whole, and he even began to consider what he might do if he got out. He told me he thought perhaps he would teach."

But even though Tony might be feeling better, the legal obstacles surrounding his release were still tremendous. An average stay at Broadmoor is six or seven years, but some patients—and Tony was one of them—are there under restrictions that make it all but impossible to leave. In Tony's case, not only would Dr. Maguire have to be convinced he was completely well, but the Home Secretary would have to concur that a discharge was in the best interests of society as well as the patient. It was not unusual for cases as complex as Tony's to be bound up in red tape for years.

"I've got a patient who's been here for seventeen years," Dr. Maguire points out. "And sometimes a patient may need to stay for twenty." According to a former superintendent at Broadmoor: "Half the patients would be perfectly safe to release but the problem is to know which half." In fact, out of its population of approximately 750, Broadmoor releases an average of 104 patients a year.

Early in 1976, Tony told a visitor, "I would like to come to New York if I could see Dr. Greene instead of being hospitalized." After a visit that Dr. and Mrs. Greene made to Tony that year, they discussed at length with Broadmoor authorities the practical difficulties that would be involved in his rehabilitation: He had no relatives, except for Mrs. Daly, who was elderly and frail, who were willing to take responsibility for him.

## Letter from Antony Baekeland to Miwa Svinka-Zielinski, February 19, 1976

Broadmoor

Dear Miwa,

I have discovered Buddhism and it has helped me tremendously in my attitude to Life. Before, I was forever chasing after things, never satisfied for long and always let down in the end. Now that I have stopped grasping and clinging to the world and the ideas and concepts of the mind I feel free and peaceful as never before. I have completely stopped forcing myself to do things but just accept them now as they come to me. The Ego, that horrible giant-dwarf, which ruled Life like a childish tyrant, forever posturing and imagining and suffering, is melting away like the Wicked Witch in *Dorothy and the Wizard of Oz*. I wish more people could become acquainted with this wonderful doctrine. It is truly a panacea, the end of all suffering.

I will write to Fred Baekeland, my uncle, who is a psychiatrist, and ask him to write to the doctors here for me to see if I can get some treatment. I feel much better than when you last came, and feel that I will soon be well.

I have some dreams to tell you. The first one is that I sense the wish to come home in an intense religious experience. Next, I am naked in a hailstorm in an Indian valley hotel—nobody seems to mind my nakedness and I finally get my clothes back. Then I dreamed that Barbara Hale had cut the back of my neck open so I could breathe, and then I dreamed that I was eating more so that I could come home. I think you must realize what I mean by home. And lastly I dreamed that I was in Paris with Nini buying clothes for my wedding.

I must end here—there is so little to tell you except my

dreams. I write them out in the middle of the night—there is no light, so sometimes in the morning I have trouble deciphering them.

Love,
Tony

MICHAEL EDWARDS
We moved around in much the same group of people in Paris, and in due course, when I decided to move back to London, they—Barbara particularly—wanted to rent my flat at 45, quai de Bourbon. They'd been living on rue Barbet de Jouy for four or five years by then. I had already rented the flat to somebody but when it became available I let them have it—inexpensively, I might add—on the condition that I could stay there myself whenever I liked and that if I needed to have a party there, they would plan to be away that night. This arrangement worked out very well for all of us, and I must say they lived there reasonably happily for a while. The house belonged to Prince Antoine Bibesco, who had been such a great friend of Proust's, and I remember that *that* pleased Barbara.

My flat was the *entresol* of the house and it was perfectly suitable for *me*, but I mean, for *them*, for the two of them living there the whole time, it was a bit small, though I think it was largely she who lived there. Brooks lived there only sometimes. Tony also slept there every now and then but he wasn't around very much that I knew of.

The flat had three rooms—quite a big living room and then a little room next to it which Barbara used as a bedroom—at least I think she did, in due course—and then upstairs it had a little bedroom which was behind a bathroom that was completely Art Deco. The thing about the flat is it has the most marvelous position—it looks out on the Seine on three sides. A glorious view, especially from the bathroom, which is right on the prow.

**Letter from Michael Edwards to Barbara Baekeland, June 15, 1965**

Dear Barbara,
Thank you for the variety of notes and postscripts which I found dotted about the apartment last weekend. I agree with you that

the dining room has been done up very well and I seem to miss the dining room table less and less. The material in the little room should go quite well and I hope it does not clash with the red of the cover. I understand that the work will be completed next week.

I hope that all goes well with you in Mexico, but I suspect that you will be hard put to it to beat Paris in June in fine weather, but I do not want to make you wistful.

Fondly,
Michael

## Letter from Barbara Baekeland to Michael Edwards, July 13, 1965

Tepotzlán
Morelos
Mexico

Dear Michael,
You are *so* right! My heart aches for Paris. For me it is home. But Brooks has now decided that we should sublet the apartment for August. Carolina will, of course, stay on and look after the new tenant.

Brooks was asked quite unexpectedly to join a young French explorer to visit the ruins of Quintana Roo in Yucatán. Brooks thinks the trip too interesting to pass up.

I will try to use the August tenant's rent to do up the kitchen. How did the dressing room turn out?

Mexico is a dream of beauty. We have masses of servants and, after Europe, it is all very peaceful and tranquil.

Love,
Barbara

## JOHNNY VAN KIRK

I ran into them in Mexico. I was walking down the street and I just recognized Tony—the red hair! It was funny. I hadn't seen him for years and he didn't recognize me. I stopped him, and that's how we got together.

Tony had these two boyfriends with him. They were American or British, both blond. That's all I remember about them. Tony had run across some pot and we all went off and got high together in this hotel room, high above the main avenue. I remember it had no windows, just sliding glass doors, open to the street fifteen blocks below. And we sat there on the edge of this sheer drop smoking a joint and talking about the old times on Cape Cod.

The Baekelands were staying with this friend of theirs who had a very beautiful ranch and I went out to visit them there. Mostly I just hung around the pool, talking and so on, catching up with Mr. Baekeland's travels and so forth and Mrs. Baekeland's life in Paris.

## Letter from Barbara Baekeland to Michael Edwards, August 20, 1965

> Baekeland Camp
> Blue Mountain Lake
> Adirondacks

Dear Michael,

My plan is to come back to Paris and to reoccupy the flat where I expect to be in residence for a protracted length of time—at least until the snow comes. The kitchen is one of the things I will attend to the moment I arrive.

We are here, all three Baekelands, with my mother and 36 other members of the family. Much boating, walking, waterskiing—very pleasant. Except that it's freezing here now, all outside communication impossible, lines all down after a heavy storm last night.

*Please, please,* please would you attend to the missing tiles in the bathroom? I cannot bear that scar another day.

See you *very* soon.

> Love,
> Barbara

P.S. My mother, Tony & I leave for New York tomorrow where I will be in residence on East 75th for more or less two weeks. I *think* I've got it rented from the 15th on.

### Elizabeth Archer Baekeland

Barbara used to rent her penthouse out whenever she could, for the
money. There was one period when she was renting it to *me*—by the
night! I was having an affair with a very powerful dramatic big-busi-
nessman, who was married, and I didn't have a place in town and I
wanted, you know, to set up a nice ambience for him, which of
course that *was*. So she would let me have it at a hundred dollars a
night and she would go and stay with her chum Emily Staempfli.

### Elizabeth Blow

A friend of mine—well, a very vicious woman, who really didn't like
Barbara very much—called it a mistress's apartment. It *was* a place
where a man would set up a woman. She had all these things in it—
that big book on the stand with colored illustrations that was open
always at a certain page, that marvelous mirror, the whole decor
really, and the terrace where they gave the marvelous dinner parties.
But it was not a sort of place to *live* in, it was not a home at all.

## Letter from Brooks Baekeland to Michael Edwards, Undated

45, quai de Bourbon

Dear Michael,

As you know, we have been recently looking for a place to buy
here in Paris (otherwise a final return to the USA and purchase
of a country house, probably near East Hampton) large enough
for a real home and not a *pied-à-terre*. We have found nothing
reasonably priced yet and/or with the sort of charm, air, light,
quiet and *quartier* that one wants if one is to become an exile—
even in Paris. Both Barbara and I are anxious within the next
year to settle this living problem once and for all.

With fond regards,
Brooks

## Letter from Barbara Baekeland to Gloria and James Jones, Undated

Cadaqués

Dear Joneses—

. . . Tomorrow we go to Prades to hear Casals play—& leave on Wednesday for Málaga for a week—after which we join our Greek pals on their yacht & cruise around Ibiza and Formentera.

We'll be out of here by the end of the month and will go to Scotland to stay with Nina, Countess Seafield, who owns most of it, and motor down to London . . . and, I expect, be going through Paris on our way to Switzerland about the 15th—will you be there? . . .

Love to you both—

I miss you,
B.

## From *A Family Motor Tour Through Europe*, Leo Hendrik Baekeland, Horseless Age Press, New York, 1907

Most of the time people who travel try to cajole themselves into the belief that they are enjoying themselves, while in reality they are merely spending money right and left in increasing amounts without great satisfaction, or they keep rushing from one country to another in vain search of happiness. I have known such people who from the mere fact of being in a certain city were overcome by ennui, which caused them to move to another place where their implacable tormentor, ennui, followed them as fast as train or automobile could carry them. Such people will ordinarily finish by finding that two or three large capitals in Europe, with very elaborately appointed hotels, agree best with their perverted psychological condition.

### BARBARA CURTEIS
Brooks never provided a stable residence for Barbara. From the time he sold the house on Seventy-first Street, they just had little places—

nookeries of great elegance, to be sure. But there was no room—in
*any* sense—in any of these places for Tony. He didn't even have a
proper bedroom. And Brooks and Barbara were constantly fighting—
it was their only form of communication. Tony once said to me,
"My parents are both very young souls." I found it a perfectly valid
remark, if one excludes the Eastern religiosity of it—he *was* more
mature than either of his parents. Barbara really enjoyed making
those scenes. If somebody said something she didn't like or even if
she didn't like *how* they had said it, she felt morally bound to slap
their face or throw whiskey in their face and rush off into the night.
And of course, every time Brooks threatened to leave her for another
woman, she would try to kill herself.

## Letter from Barbara Baekeland to Gloria and James Jones, Undated

                                                    45, quai de Bourbon
Dear Joneses—
I wonder if I'll ever be able to demonstrate my friendship & love
for you both as you have done for me so many times (I am
ashamed to think about it). Anyway, thanks—it was the full
moon, I guess, because *nothing* on the outside can ever be *that*
bad!

    I love you both. . . .

                                                                    B.

## Letter from Brooks Baekeland to Gloria and James Jones, October 14, 1965

                                                    1, rue Regrattier
Dear Jim and Gloria—
I guess you don't have to hear from me what I think of what you
both did for Barbara the other night. I know that you both love
her, and it isn't for me really to thank you. I would not have
bothered you, except that for the first time in a long time I felt I
was at the end of my rope. I couldn't face all that alone. So it
was selfish too. But strangely enough, when I wondered who *I*

could turn to in Paris, there were only yourselves. It was the first time I had felt quite so lonely in this town. So whatever you feel about me, I must be clear to you what I thought about you. And I knew that you were the only two people in the world almost that Barbara wouldn't mind knowing about what she had done—that I could call on without injuring her pride. I also feel the same way.

By noon the next day, B., sitting up in her bed, had the shy expression of Alexander bestriding Europe and Asia. But each time she gets away with this, the more dangerous it is. If Franklin had flown a few more kites, he'd have become a pork crackling. Someday, if Barbara really believes in this kind of ultimate force over the kindhearted (or guilt-susceptible), she is going to make a miscalculation. They all do. She is not half so intelligent as she pretends to herself. It is that which worries me— that and her effect on Tony. He's still awfully young and tied up.

Anyway, thanks. . . .

Brooks

## Letter from Brooks Baekeland to Michael Edwards, June 25, 1966

Mexico

Dear Michael—

Off again very soon to the jungles. It occurs to me that you can use a few months' rent in advance.

Barbara and Tony skim northwards within the week for a summer of sea-shoring in East Hampton. I go on July 3 to Lima for 2 weeks of wrestling with customs and then off into the unknown again.

Affectionate regards,
Brooks

**Letter from Barbara Baekeland to Michael Edwards, July 10, 1966**

New York

Dear Michael—

Enclosed your check for gas, electric, telephone, etc.

Brooks left for Peru on Sunday. Tony, my mother, and I are installed at East Hampton—pleasant but all too familiar, except for the beach which is superb.

Affectionately,
Barbara

FRANCESCA DRAPER LINKE

One time in East Hampton Tony tried to paint himself blue at my parents' house. He had this wonderful idea about everyone going blue, this beautiful beautiful shade of blue, and how you'd see these blue people at the chicest places, and everyone would *want* to be blue—there'd be signs saying "Go Blue." So he went and bought some dye and then he got in the bathtub and tried to get blue, but he came out kind of a mottled greenish blue, and then we went down to the beach and he put all this seaweed on him, and we walked on the sand and he was Neptune—he was very into Neptune. And later we stayed up all night playing music. It was really a magical time. That was when he was still on the great creative fringe. I mean, we all thought Tony was like a god.

**From a Psychiatric Report on Antony Baekeland Ordered by the British Courts, January 5, 1973**

He had few qualms accepting the notion that he was a very special person. During the time he was in a London tutoring school, he saw a psychoanalyst for four months. Following his discontinuance of this school, his last schooling, he lived something of an aimless existence, writing and painting, living in various places such as India and Nepal, with a lot of time spent in Cadaqués on Spain's Costa Brava, and traveling around on no set schedule.

## Letter from Barbara Baekeland to Gloria and James Jones, Undated

Cadaqués

Dear Joneses—
. . . The Gare d'Austerlitz was an *abattoir* when we finally arrived—God how I loathe masses of French, German, American, Jew, Negroes, everyone. Couldn't possibly have found a
porter and couldn't lift the valise myself. A kind "adjuster of
train wheels" helped me and put me in a first-class carriage! . . .

Love to you both,<br>B.

### KAREN RADKAI

Cadaqués was not far from Paris. You went to Gare d'Austerlitz and
took the night train and the next morning at nine-thirty you were in
Port Bou and you took a taxi and you were in Cadaqués by ten—do
you see what I mean?

Now in those days Cadaqués was extraordinary. I remember the
first thing I saw was a girl on a white horse riding through the center
of town, with wonderful long blond hair flowing out behind her. It
was Lorna Moffat, Tony's great friend—he used to bring her all the
time to my house.

What we always did in Cadaqués is we had a picnic, daily, with
these wonderful chickens and all these fantastic Spanish salads—
chick-peas mixed with tuna fish, you know. My picnics were famous.
The cooking I did outside on the open fire. I gathered the wood on
the beach, one of the way-off beaches. There was thyme growing by
the bushes, so all you had to do, you know, was throw the chicken
with the thyme on a little fire and have a wonderful thing going. And
you'd come home at five in the afternoon and take a nap and then go
out for dinner at ten—that was sort of the life we led, you know.

### LOUISE DUNCAN

The routine is you get up at ten or eleven, you go to one of the two
cafés and put your face in the sun to get over your hangover, and
then you stagger back up the hill at around four o'clock for lunch and
then you stagger back down to the other café.

## KAREN RADKAI

Meliton's was the café where you played chess. My son used to play with Duchamp. He was small, he was only nine. He learned a lot of good chess there. Man Ray used to come to visit Duchamp and he played very good chess, too.

It was a little group, you see. That part was very nice. But the other part I just couldn't stand—there were a lot of psychotic aspects to Cadaqués. The whole town was sordid.

I was first in Cadaqués for Vogue, to photograph Melina Mercouri, who was doing a film there. Diana Vreeland was then editor-in-chief of Vogue and she said to me—you know how fantastic she is—"Get Melina on the beach in a bathing suit with Dalí putting eggs of emeralds and rubies in her hand!" So Melina says to me, "Darling, I can never get into those bathing suits, I'm not Brigitte Bardot, you know." So then I had to go and see Dalí and see if he would cooperate. I'd met him already once, in '51, in Venice, at the Bal de Bestigui, Charles de Bestigui's great ball at the Palazzo Labia, which I was photographing for Harper's Bazaar—Cecil Beaton was doing it for Vogue. And Dalí was so charming and nice then, I can't tell you—just like a perfectly normal human being. Now, of course, he's so corrupt he's close to being—I don't know what, dear—Hitler, you know.

So I went up to his house in Port Lligat—that's the twin village to Cadaqués. You went by the cemetery of Cadaqués to get there, in those days over a dirt road. Dalí had an interesting house, it was old. As I walked in he gave me some pink champagne and he said, "Come with me, I will show you my studio," and he showed me this enormous, strange room, sort of octagonal almost it was. He said, "Here is where I masturbate." He thought I was going to be shocked, you know, but I just paid no attention.

And Dalí set the tone for the whole village.

## Letter from Barbara Baekeland to Gloria and James Jones, Undated

Cadaqués

Dear Jim and Gloria,
. . . This place is surreal and very fake except for the natives who loathe everyone and cast a spell on us all. The morals are

so crappy & awful & hypocritical that you *can't* take them seriously—the cripple being helped in and out of the boat by the mistress of her gigolo husband who loathes them both and tries to attack, each night, the baby-sitter who is Tony's girl and tells him everything. Balthusian symbols abound and *trompeurs* and pleasure-seeking. Marvelous!

I swim in the sea, comtemplate suicide, think that somehow I must do something to justify something and I don't even know what it is!

Anyway it's the classic Mediterranean summer. Not for the likes of me. I need the cool northern fogs & tides to keep me sane.

X
B.

### Elsa Mottar

The whole thing was just so impossible, you know—one just didn't know what to do with Barbara. You never knew what was going to happen next, so whenever she appeared on the scene, everybody's nose would be out of joint. She and Brooks were always flying away from each other and then coming back together again, and it was a totally mixed-up relationship that you could never make heads or tails of. I mean, you didn't know if they were really interested in each other or if they just stayed together because of Tony.

### George Staempfli

I remember one scene at Barbara Curteis's. She had a terrace outside her bedroom, and that's where she gave all her parties—it had a wonderful view of the harbor. And Brooks was there one night and Barbara Baekeland suddenly appeared downstairs and marched into the house and he had to flee over the rooftops—literally! Another night Barbara Baekeland was found wandering around the streets of Cadaqués stark naked.

### Daphne Hellman

I was visiting Lily Auchincloss in Cadaqués and I saw Brooks in an open car, with his head in his hands, as if in despair. He was just sitting in the parked car, right outside the place they were renting. He

said to me, "Go up and speak to Barbara. I can't." And when I
knocked at the door she thought at first I was Brooks and wouldn't let
me in, but when she realized it was me, she let me in and said, "Get
me a drink. Brooks won't get me a drink." She was in a very peculiar
state. But then later that summer I went on a couple of picnics with
the two of them and things had gotten more peaceable.

### THILO VON WATZDORF
Remember that book *Piano Mécanique* by François Rey? They made
a film of it. It was really a lousy book but it did show Cadaqués in the
mid and late sixties, a mixture of Saint-Tropez and the Rome of *La
Dolce Vita*. It was just the worst place at that time for a kid of that
age who was very impressionable.

### SYLVIE BAEKELAND SKIRA
When I first met Tony, that summer of '67, he was very much in
love with a young man in Cadaqués—Jake Cooper, a great beauty.
Jake was the type who would stop in the middle of town and oil his
body, and he always had a court of young men around him—Tony
Kinna, Ernst von Wedel, people like that.
    Tony was, let's say, a basically well-brought-up little boy, and he
was mixing with a whole crowd that was rather shabby. In Cadaqués
everyone mixes—it's the great joy of people who usually have regular
lives and in summer suddenly they are with people who are not their
sort and it's very exciting. *Voilà.* So Tony was seeing people who
were not his sort and they were taking a lot of money from him, of
course. And he came totally under Jake Cooper's spell.

### ELIZABETH BLOW
I'd heard that there was a man who was exerting a tremendous influence over him in Cadaqués and I think probably this was the
beginning of Tony's collapse mentally.

### PICO HARNDEN
Jake Cooper was known around Cadaqués as Black Jake. He was a
very handsome Australian who first appeared on the scene as the
lover of a woman called Erika Svenssen. She was sort of the sex
goddess of Cadaqués and he was the black prince, if you like. He was
a tall dark guy who wore a silver earring in his left ear and went
around in washed-out jeans and Afghan belts, without a shirt on, and

every woman in Cadaqués was amazed by his beauty and his bra-
vado, and the next thing that happened was that Jake Cooper and
Tony Baekeland took up together—much to Erika's chagrin.

## ERIKA SVENSSEN

I was nine years in Cadaqués and that was my favorite summer, you
know? It was so important, that summer. I was at the age then that I
thought I was still twenty-one. I hadn't gone into the other generation yet. I still think I haven't.

Jake was like a devil. He had a Svengali thing. He had a power
over people. He was always causing incredible jealousies and
things—people turned against each other. He moved into this farm,
this abandoned farm, and he had a sort of entourage, you know, of
strange people. They were heavy into trying out mushrooms and
drugs in general, and he was also delving into things—whether he
got them out of books or what, I don't know, but I know he kept
meeting people, secret people. I think he practiced black magic. He
wore little bones and things on his vest. Certain little bones. I would
ask him about them and he just wouldn't tell me, you know. He
would say "my magic amulets" or something. I'd never seen any sort
of formation of that kind of bones before—the way they were put
together. He wore them dangling on his vest, you know. He wore
them all the time and all kinds of people that he had around him
died. There was a young boy who died. I think there were three who
died who were around him. I think he put some kind of spell on
them.

Jake was a friend of Salvador Dalí. They were making a film together—one of those Dalí-type films showing angels and monsters
together, the power that the devil would have over the angel and yet
the angel would win out.

Jake had an absolutely wonderful side to him, too, which was innocent and fun and sweet. It was magical again, but in a good sense.

I remember when Jake and I first met Tony Baekeland. I have a
visual picture of the first time we saw him—of his freckles and his
red hair, and the sun on him—his body and the whole thing. I can
see him in front of me right now!

## BARBARA CURTEIS

One day Tony said to me, "You've got to put a picnic together." By
this time he was not doing anything at all, and the devil finds work,

as they say. So we went down to the beach and picnicked. And a terrible man in black leather, looking like Tony's Nemesis, came down the beach and fed Tony drugs, and Tony became his thing, his creature. He went right on taking drugs, he went off to Morocco with this man and they brought back belladonna and Tony ate the whole thing himself and disappeared under one's eyes to a blob of quivering jelly.

## PICO HARNDEN

Tony and Jake showed up on their way back from Morocco, with God knows how many kilos of hash. My parents were away, and Jake and Tony made brownies in the kitchen. They turned on the entire house—*everyone*, my little sisters, my brother Mishka, the maids, the dog, consumed these brownies to such a degree that by the time my parents came back everybody was still completely passed out. Jake and Tony had taken off. They were living together in this house that Duchamp had had at one point, right by the water—one floor.

Later that summer I was at Meliton's and Jake came in and put six or seven cactus leaves down on the table next to my drink. I asked him what he was carrying cactus leaves around for and he said that he fucked them and I said, "Now wait a minute!" He said, "I'll show you." And he went and got a knife from the bar and sliced the base of one of the leaves open, then he took my hand and stuck it up to my wrist in the cactus and pulled it out, then he put it back in again.

One day our doorbell rang and Tony was at the door. He ran upstairs in a complete state, he went running straight to my father who was sitting in a chair, you know, and hid behind the chair. My father said, "Listen, Tony, come out from behind there and just sit down and be civilized." And he said, "You've got to help me—Jake Cooper is after me! If he comes, just say I'm not here—*please!*" And sure enough, at that very moment, Jake Cooper is downstairs in the street screaming at the top of his voice, "Toooooooony"—this really very seductive sort of rutting call—and Tony is shaking. And of course, my father called down, "Tony's not here at the moment," and Jake took off.

## JAKE COOPER

Ah, it's an end-of-the-road-like village, Cadaqués. It's a town that has rocks, stones, of a special quality all around, and people going there, usually after a very short while, after their second day there sometimes, go through very tense strange feelings. Quite a lot of people get very upset. It's a trapped feeling. I remember Dalí used to say it was something under the ground that could make men sterile and that made them very nervous. There was some great strange energy there in Cadaqués. I think it's one of the most special little towns I've ever seen.

I was called Black Jake, I suppose because I dressed in black. A girl who I used to be involved with—actually, she gave me the first acid trip I ever took—said I should throw all my clothes away and that I should just wear black and silver, and—I don't know—that's what happened. Friends took all my clothes to a flea market—they got rid of all my tweeds and things like that, and for many many years I did just wear black and silver.

I was with Erika Svenssen and we were sitting on the terrace of a little café and just behind us was somebody who said a few words to Erika and this person was sitting next to Antony Baekeland, and that's the first time I saw Antony. I saw him quite a lot after that and then we went together to Morocco and then we got this little house for ourselves in Cadaqués.

Antony was involved in extreme yoga then. In winter he used to sit naked in front of the open window, doing breathing exercises—first through one nostril, then the other—following the Tibetan Book of the Dead.

He painted quite a lot and he was always painting the eye of an eagle. That eye he used to reproduce and reproduce. He painted it once on the wall of our house. I think it's been painted over.

One day he got spaced out of his own head and went to walk in the mountains and it was quite stormy weather. And when he came back, he was in a very high state from his walk in the storm. He said he was going to have a shower at a friend's place because there wasn't any hot water in our house, and it was quite cold. So I said okay, and while he was out having his shower his mother turned up from Switzerland. She said, "I'm Antony Baekeland's mother and I've come to take him away." And I was really taken aback, I didn't know what was happening. She said it again, "I've come to take him away," then she said, "Where are his things?" She just took a few of his things, not really even the things that he used very much. She just took odds and ends. "I'm going to take Tony now," she kept saying. "We're leaving today. I've just arrived and I'm going. Tony and I are going today." And then she disappeared up the road to where he was having his shower. And she took him back with her to Switzerland and then off to that island—Mallorca. And I never saw Antony again till Broadmoor.

## BARBARA CURTEIS

I had telephoned Barbara in Gstaad when I saw the state Tony was in and she came back to Cadaqués to fetch him. Brooks was in Ibiza and *wouldn't* come. And the next day, the day after she was meant to have taken Tony back with her to Gstaad, I was on my way to Barcelona and stopped in some café—and saw Barbara's hired car coming from the south and going in the opposite direction to Switzerland. They had indeed set out the previous day but it turned out that Tony didn't have his passport with him, and Barbara had said to the authorities at the frontier, "*My* son doesn't need a passport." I mean, even Barbara admitted she'd been pretty offensive— she'd kicked and spat and so forth. Anyway, the two of them were taken off in a paddy wagon, and they spent the night in jail in Gerona, the provincial capital of that end of Catalonia—he in the male and she in the female jail. "Oh, a *charming* jail!" Barbara said. "*Perfectly* delightful!" And then she made a remark I'll never forget, it has a sort of echoing horror for me. She told me proudly that she'd said to Tony as they were being led away in handcuffs, "Here you are, darling, at *last*—manacled to Mummy!"

# 9

---

# CALLING IT QUITS

In 1977, an unofficial committee of concerned friends of Tony Baekeland began looking into the possibility of having him freed. The group consisted of Heather and Jack Cohane, Michael Alexander, Miwa Svinka-Zielinski, and the Hon. Hugo Money-Coutts, whose family controlled London's exclusive Coutts Bank, and whose wife, Jinty, was the daughter of the Baekelands' old friend Rosemary Rodd Baldwin.

Tony's aunt, Elizabeth Archer Baekeland, who was living in London at the time, refused to be drawn into the group. She says, "The people who were helping Tony all believed that his violence was spent when he killed his mother. But Tony's uncle, Fred Baekeland, my former husband, always believed the exact opposite. He said to me, 'Nonsense. Tony's capable of killing other people. He's highly dangerous and always will be, so don't ever try to get him out of Broadmoor.'"

Of the unofficial committee, Miwa Svinka-Zielinski alone recognized the need for caution in the selection of a hospital for Tony if and when he was discharged from Broadmoor and repatriated. "I believed," she states, "that Tony had a classic love/hate relationship with his mother and that his sickness was absolutely only connected

to her. I was convinced, after seeing him all those years in Broadmoor, that his illness would not surface again."


## Official Visitors File, Broadmoor Special Hospital, May 14, 1976

VISITOR'S NAME: Mrs. Nina Daly
RELATIONSHIP TO PATIENT: Grandmother
SUMMARY: Thinks he looks and behaves so much better than
last year. There's no one who has any interest in sponsoring him
outside hospital, either in U.K. or U.S.A., in his welfare, or
who would be prepared to spend a penny on him, except herself, and she is not well off. She was informed that there is no
certain date by which Tony will be discharged.


### BROOKS BAEKELAND

I had reason to hope that Tony's mind might clear one day in the
peace and quiet of Broadmoor Hospital where he had friends and
where, he repeatedly told me, he was happy.

Many people with his symptoms had, after the age of forty—for
reasons as mysterious as schizophrenia itself—gradually become calm
and peaceful citizens. I was hoping for that. Occasionally he still
wrote me violent, paranoidal letters, which I forwarded to his doctors. They worried me—not for myself but for him, since some English and American friends with strings to high places were trying to
get him set free. It was a sentimental, well-meaning movement—
which worked and was tragic in its consequences. I was against all
their energetic and romantic efforts to open the cage door for this
gifted hawk who I feared would soon swoop down on some helpless
prey.


## Official Visitors File, Broadmoor Special Hospital, May 24, 1977

VISITOR'S NAME: Mrs. Nina Daly
RELATIONSHIP TO PATIENT: Grandmother
SUMMARY: Saw Mrs. Daly in waiting room and she is more frail
and in a wheelchair.

## Official Visitors File, Broadmoor Special Hospital, June 3, 1977

VISITOR'S NAME: Michael Alexander
RELATIONSHIP TO PATIENT: No blood relationship
SUMMARY: Has known Tony Baekeland since 12 years. Was very close to family prior to and after the time of the manslaughter. Mr. Alexander was helpful, clear, and incisive. Is eager to help in whatever way he can, especially if repatriation is sought.

## Letter from Antony Baekeland to Miwa Svinka-Zielinski, November 3, 1977

Broadmoor

Dear Miwa,
I hope very much to be discharged before too long. I have some dreams to tell you. The first one was that I was with a great friend of mine who was building a house and I remember watching him put pink stucco on a wall. The next was that again I can fly. I let loose a bird at Michael Alexander's house— later we became brothers. Next I dream that a man accuses me and René Teillard of confessing one another: I associate this with Life prior to the French Revolution. My last dream was that my father lives with Sylvie in a mountain chalet—he scolds me but later forgives me.
    I try nowadays to be less careless and more careful in the things I do.
    All the best.

Love,
Tony

## Letter from Barbara Baekeland to Michael Edwards, October 14, 1967

Dear Michael,
*Two important items:* Carolina says you are coming on the 25th. I have a cook laid on and wondered if you might not like to have

her do a dinner for *you*? She's an angel and very good—can do a marvelous curry with almonds, figs, bananas, etc. I order a sorbet from that marvelous place, have smoked salmon first, and it's a delicious repast—with Carolina she can do 14.

Wednesday night I gave a small dinner for Marcel and Teenie Duchamp, and Sunday 15 for dinner when Tony arrives with a *friend*! Am so pleased!!

## DUNCAN LONGCOPE

I remember Barbara telling me that Tony had a girl and that she liked her a lot. She referred to her as Robin Redbreast. Just in fun—I mean, you know, that sort of verve of Barbara's. She said, "Oh, isn't it nice that Tony has a girlfriend!"

## SYLVIE BAEKELAND SKIRA

It's easier to say to your mother and to your father that you have a girlfriend than a boyfriend. When they said to him "Where were you tonight?" it was easier to say "I was with Sylvie" than "I was with Jake." I can honestly say that Tony used me as a screen—a smoke-screen for all the shady parts of his life. I mean his boyfriends, who he couldn't very well present to his parents.

After that summer in Cadaqués we came back to Paris—I mean Tony came back and I came back—and I received a phone call from him saying please come and have dinner at his parents'. And I thought, Two grouchy parents. . . . I'd never met the parents.

I was quite young, perhaps younger than my years, and I saw Brooks and I thought he was the most dashing man I'd ever seen, and I saw Barbara and I thought she was the prettiest woman I'd ever seen. Usually with a couple there's one very handsome and then a toad right next to it. But they were both so handsome. They were dazzling. And I certainly never thought that Brooks would look at me because to me he was a grown-up, he was forty-seven and he was married and that was it.

They started inviting me to all their dinners. I was the "nice young thing" that you put at table and so forth.

There was a game between Brooks and Barbara that was very near to *Who's Afraid of Virginia Woolf?*—a great game in public, you know, where he would drive her to tears on a little matter. I mean, they wouldn't go *too* far but she would have very pretty tears and he would say, "Look how good she looks with tears! Doesn't she look handsome with tears?" That sort of thing. Which made me feel that I was sort of part of *Les Liaisons Dangereuses*, and what were they going to do with me, these two. I felt like a puppet between their hands.

DUNCAN LONGCOPE
Robin Redbreast or whatever her name was was staying in the same hotel that I was living in, the Hôtel Saint-Louis on the rue Saint-Louis en Lille. I assumed that Tony had, you know, visiting privileges, but one day I saw him knocking on her door and in a sort of pleading tone asking to be let in, and this went on for a long period, but the door did not open, as I remember, and he went away. I did one day see Brooks there, which sort of surprised me.

## Letter from Brooks Baekeland to Michael Edwards, Undated

Mon cher—
I suppose you are zipping about the planet as usual? I am bacheloring here for a few days while B. skis in Switzerland with a pack of lusty females.

Affectionately,
Brooks

SYLVIE BAEKELAND SKIRA
Barbara couldn't stand to be in any one place for long. It was October, then it was November, November was boring, so she decided she would have to go skiing, and it was when she left to go skiing that finally Brooks called me. I couldn't believe it, because then it *meant* something. We went out to dinner together, on the Île Saint-Louis, and we had, I have to admit, a wonderful time. We spoke . . . *he* spoke and I was fascinated, I can tell you—and that evening I absolutely fell in love.

I stopped being the family friend very soon after that. I couldn't stand it, because on one side I was in love with Brooks and on the other side Barbara had taken a liking to me and she was trying to arrange things between Tony and me—romantic things. She thought that I should consider him as a nice future husband. She kept telling me that one day Tony would be a very rich young man.

She didn't know about me and Brooks. She didn't want to know, of course. Not only that, but I think that she thought that *I* certainly was not anything to beware of.

## Letter from Barbara Baekeland to Michael Edwards, November 27, 1967

                                                           45, quai de Bourbon

Dearest Michael—
We are in the middle of making a whole series of decisions— should we buy a large property in Mallorca and build on it, or should we build a small house next to the Bordeau-Groutts at Cadaqués—an *endroit* that seems to have a fatal fascination for us! We are spending Xmas there in Emily Staempfli's house— very snug, very expensive, with my mother who is flying to Barcelona to join us. Tony is already there and his little robin, Sylvie, comes, too, along with Michael Alexander. Should be very gay.

                                                           Always affec.—
                                                           Barbara

MICHAEL ALEXANDER
I was staying with them the Christmas Tony brought Sylvie down as a guest. She was *his* girlfriend originally. And in fact, Brooks took her over. I think it was a quite quick take-over. I think it was going on all the time I was staying there.

## Letter from Michael Edwards to Barbara Baekeland, February 2, 1968

Dear Barbara,
   . . . You will be glad to hear that your clock has now arrived back in good working order and I shall be bringing it over to Paris on my next trip. Talking of this, I am provisionally think-

ing of the weekend of the 24th February, so could you let me know what your plans are for skiing.


## GLORIA JONES

On February 24th, Barbara tried to commit suicide. I spent the day with her—she was packing to go to Klosters, she was happy, and all her friends kept running in and out, you know. She had some very fancy women friends, lovely friends who loved her. De Croy—she was a good friend of hers, she was darling. The lady who took care of her dog. The Princesse de Croy her name was.

Then at seven o'clock—I think the train leaves at seven-thirty for Klosters—the telephone rang and it was Barbara saying, "I'm going ski-i-i-i-iiiiiing," and then there was silence and I knew something terrible had happened, I just knew it, and I screamed, "Barbara, what have you done, what have you done?" Then I *ran*—it's about, you know, three blocks—and I guess she'd left the door open and I burst in and there she was—she'd got herself dressed up beautifully in a nightgown and her beautiful beige robe—and she was absolutely gone. She looked dead. I really thought she was dead. I started to scream and I couldn't, I'd lost my voice, so then I started jumping up and down for the lady underneath to hear, and finally I was able to scream. And then I dialed my house and said to my daughter Kaylie, "Tell Daddy to come as fast as he can." And then the lady downstairs ran up and we called the Hôtel-Dieu, the public hospital on the Île de la Cité, which is just around the corner, and we also called the American Hospital in Neuilly, and they said they were on their way, too. But the Hôtel-Dieu got there right away. The doctor ran in and he said, "Well, there's no heartbeat—nothing." So he jabbed her with a needle—I think in her chest—God believe me, I don't know—and then by that time Jim was there and we both went in the ambulance with her.


## From *The Merry Month of May,* James Jones, Delacorte Press, New York, 1971

. . . She called me again that evening, around about eight-fifteen. . . . There was a peculiar sing-song to her voice, a flat quality.

"Louisa? Louisa? Louisa, are you all right?" I said.

"Oh, yes," she said. "Oh, yes. Oh, yes, I'm fine. I'm going to Switzerland."

"You're what?" I demanded. "Switzerland?"

"Oh yes," she said. "Switzerland. . . . St. Moritz. And you can meet everybody. At least, everyone who is anybody. And you can ski. You can ski off the tops of the mountains there. You know. Right off the tops of them, and you can float forever. I'm going skiing. . . ."

"Louisa," I said. "Louisa? You're going skiing?"

"Oh, yes," she said. "Oh, yes. I'm going skiing. I'm going skiing, Jack. Oh, it's so beautiful, skiing. Right off the tops of them. And down below there is nothing but the pure, white snow. Pure. And white. No evil, no dirt, no filth. A few cottages of faithful villagers, who love their cows and their land. Don't want to kill. . . . Oh, yes, I'm going skiing, Jack. Good-bye. . . ." She hung up and the phone went cold stone dead.

I was in a panic. I didn't know whether she had flipped her mind or what, but I knew instinctively something bad had happened somewhere. . . . I ran all the way to their apartment, which was more than three blocks.

Well, it was a pretty awful scene. A bad scene. In the time it took me to get there after her phone call she had become unconscious and her maid had found her. . . .

She had left the front door unlocked, so that I was able to barge right in. Had she calculated that, also? So she could leave herself room for me to come and save her? At that moment I thought so. Later on, when I saw what she had taken, I changed my mind.

She had dressed herself for the occasion. She was wearing one of her sheerest, flimsiest robes. . . . She would do that. Under it she had on a fine-textured white bra through which the two dark spots of her nipples showed like two dark eyes, and below a very brief, very low-waisted pair of panties through which the dark of her triangular bush made itself visibly felt. . . .

I put my ear to her mouth and nose, but if there was any breathing at all it was very shallow and light. . . .

On the bedside table there was a large aspirin bottle, totally empty, and there was a large tinfoil plaque of sleeping suppositories, empty also, eight or nine of them. There was also a Nembutal bottle, empty too. I had already noticed that there was a glass and a half empty bottle of vodka on the floor beside her beside the couch. Apparently she had taken enough stuff to kill a whole army. That was when I changed my mind about the unlocked door. . . .

A French doctor . . . darted into the apartment carrying his black bag. Apparently he lived around the corner, and the faithful Portuguese had gone to get him. . . .

"Her heart has stopped," he said. "I don't know for how long. I'm giving her a shot of Neosynepheraine. That may start it again. But we must get her to a hospital very fast. . . . If her heart has stopped for over four or five minutes, she could have serious brain damage. Even if we save her." . . .

The doctor was working over Louisa. And suddenly I became furious. Why are we trying to save her? I thought. If some stupid bitch wants to die, why not let her? . . . I wanted to go to the big couch and turn her over and kick her in her unconscious ass. What was she doing to us, and how dare she?

## MICHAEL EDWARDS

I was meant to be there that night. That's why I don't think she ever intended at that stage to commit suicide, because she could have chosen another moment which would have been less likely to be interrupted. I mean, she was expecting me that night. I was flying over from London to see her, we were going to talk about the flat— replacing curtains or something like that—and my plane was late, and when I finally got to 45, quai de Bourbon, I saw the concierge, Madame François, and she said, *"Madame est morte, Madame est morte,"* and I went up there and there she was lying rather like *The Death of Chatterton*, all pallid and everything, on the carpet. Gloria and Jim Jones were there, and the *pompiers*, the ambulance men, were just about to take her away, to the Hôtel-Dieu.

## GLORIA JONES

They took her into the hospital and while she was being pumped out, the doctor came out and he said, *"C'est très mal."* He said, "What could she have taken?" He told me to go back to her place as fast as I could and bring back every bottle, everything. So I did.

## Dr. Jean Dax
She had taken a large dose of Nembutal, which is always a bad medication to take, and also vodka.

## Gloria Jones
It looked very bad for, I don't know, eight days. Really bad. She was in the—it's called the *chambre de ressuscitation*, where they have everybody under cellophane, you know. She was under total—what do you call it? intensive care? She was hooked up. So here was this beautiful red-haired thing, absolutely naked, under the cellophane, you know, with this red pussy—she really had one! So white and so beautiful and it was so awful to see her like that.

## From *The Merry Month of May,* James Jones, Delacorte Press, New York, 1971

I had never been inside the Hôtel-Dieu before. It faced on the square called Place du Parvis Notre-Dame just in front of Notre-Dame, which is where they used to pull people apart with horses for having committed some crime or other. The assassin of Henri Quatre was dismembered that way there. Hôtel-Dieu had a medieval look about it, at least from the outside, and I believe it had been started, a long way back, as a maternity hospital. . . .

They told me that her condition was very grave. She was surviving, in the new intensive care unit, but she was not showing any signs of recuperating. . . .

For some reason it seemed this case had been taken on by all the young nurses and doctors of the intensive care unit as a personal challenge. . . .

They had her under this plastic tent, completely nude. A young nurse was constantly in attendance. Louisa's body (I hesitate to say Louisa) was constantly sweating profusely, and the nurse was constantly mopping her off. There were tubes up both her nostrils, and her arms were strapped down to the bed. Above her left arm hung a glucose bottle, its needle taped into a vein in the arm. If I had ever wondered about her nipples and her bush, I did not have to wonder any more.

# Telegram from James Jones to Antony Baekeland, Undated

1.45 P.M.

TONY  BAEKELAND  CADAQUÉS  SPAIN          IMPERATIVE  YOU
CALL ME                                                      JAMES JONES

## CLEMENT BIDDLE WOOD

Jim called me and said, "Do you have any idea how I can get hold of Brooks?" and I said, "Now what's the problem?" and of course he told me, and I said, "Well, maybe he's left some sort of forwarding address at his bank." And then Jim said, "How well do they know you at the Morgan Bank?" and I said, "I have quite a good friend there, he's a vice-president or something." So I went to him and I said, "I've got to find Brooks Baekeland fast," and he said, "Well, he's left very strict instructions that his whereabouts are not to be given out to anybody," so then I said, "Here's what's happened," and he said, "Well, under the cicumstances, we'll tell you where to reach him, but just keep the bank out of it. And if he has to be called, *you* do it, not some third party." And so, although I did not know Brooks Baekeland well, it was I, not Jim Jones, who called him in Rome— Jim talked to him later. I said, "Listen, Brooks, I know this is an intrusion on your privacy, but Barbara has tried to kill herself." And he said, "Oh God—again! Clem," he said, "this is the fourth time that she's done this. She pulls this on me every time. It's one reason I didn't leave an address. It's an obvious bid for sympathy. She wants me to come running back, but this time I'm not going to budge." And I said, "Listen, I think it's more than a bid for sympathy, because if that's what she intended it to be, Brooks, she's overdone it, because she damn near died," and I gave him what details I knew about that—I told him she was in a coma. And he said, "Well, if she dies, you know where I am." That chilled me, and I said, "Listen, Brooks, for Chrissake, I understand how you feel about this, but I think you might *be* here because they really think she may be dying." He said—and this is what *really* chilled me—he said, "When I met Barbara she was nothing, she was just this sort of redheaded Irish kid. I practically picked her out of the chorus line," and, well, after that, there really wasn't much to say.

## BROOKS BAEKELAND
The fourth and last time Barbara "committed suicide" was signalized to me at the Hotel Excelsior in Rome, where I was stopping on my way out to the Far East with Sylvie in February 1968. Barbara had thought I was still in Paris and would rally round quickly as I had always done before. That did not work this time, partly because I was not there and partly because Sylvie called up the Hôtel-Dieu and spoke to the physician in charge and discovered that Barbara was out of danger, though I knew there is always a risk of permanent brain damage. Later Jim Jones told me over the phone, "She's been in a coma for thirty-six hours." But it was Gloria, who took the phone away from him, who told me that I *had* to come back and to whom I said that I would never reply to that blackmail again and that this time I was never coming back.

## DR. JEAN DAX
She was in a deep coma for twenty-four hours, and I think gradually pulled out of it—within the next twenty-four hours, roughly. There was no evidence of brain damage.


## Letter from Brooks Baekeland to Gloria and James Jones, February 27, 1968

> Jaipur & Udaip
> Rambagh Palace
> India

Dear Jim & Gloria—
I called up the Hôtel-Dieu before leaving Rome on Sunday. The head nurse gave me a good report on Barbara's condition, assuring me that there was practically *no* danger now at all. From this dose anyway.

I am writing to say three things. (A) My thanks to you and Gloria, who are somewhat saner and a great deal more sophisticated than Barbara's other friends in Paris—all mostly female and therefore and to that extent somewhat hysterically delighted, I am sure, in the TV-drama aspect of this thing. Barbara has just about drained all there is to drain out of romantic (and not-so-romantic) violence where I am concerned, as I told you. And that is the second thing: her belief in force to get her way is fundamental in all things great and small, as everybody from waiters to prime ministers have experienced, and I have had to deal with that constantly for 25 years. Although the "provocation" this time may be judged great, there have been other times when even greater violence threatened over (as a start) where we planned to have dinner. I am to an astonishing and astonished degree unmoved, loving her no less than ever for all that. I would not probably feel that way had it not been for certain proofs of other things that indicate quite clearly to me that I am not the "only man there can ever be in my life"—i.e., that her hang-up on me is nowhere near so deathless as she will maintain to her girl friends.

Third, Barbara never tells her TV audience the whole truth about her situation (or anything) and she has no doubt also failed to tell you that on top of the other funds she gets regularly from me she also gets $850 per month from the rental of the New York flat—i.e., another $5,100 between my decision about this thing and my return from this trip. She can (and does) piss away the funds I give her, but she is never as short as she pretends. She has a lot of dough to spend just on food, liquor, and play—nothing else to pay for, as I take care of all the basics myself. Because she is almost pathologically incapable of ordinary cost accounting (and hence any sort of planning also) she has no idea how much she blows on clothes and other things far and above any reasonable budgetary allowance. Her lack of realism in all things, a sort of fundamental inability to separate wish from fact, "what ought to be" from "what is," "what can be" from "what might be" (important in *any* partnership) has (partly) accounted for a good deal of the sense of mutual paralysis in our lives, of which she herself sometimes complained. It has caused in me a deep reluctance to plan anything seriously with her— even a feeling that whatever I did with her would *somehow* simply be bungled or warped around again to suit the same old parade—but I don't want to dwell on that. I am no saint myself.

I am not "abandoning" Barbara. I am just not making myself available anymore for her particular scene (and scenes), as I have perhaps 10 more years of non-senile life ahead of me, and I want now to think of myself a little, too. I am being selfish. That does not mean that "life is over" for her by any logic that I can see. Other men have lives to lead and many also have mis-

tresses. If all the wives gobbled pills every time Dagwood took off
on his own, America would soon be depopulated.

Finally, as I said to you on the phone, I am rather sick of the
atomic fly swatter. I suppose when you first start using atomic
weapons—even if only to slay a fly—and since there are no
stronger resorts to force, then you can hardly think or fight in
lesser terms. That is the trouble with melodrama—the climaxes
are all used up in Act I.

I know Barbara is in danger (if not now, then later) because of
that. But what the hell can I do about it, short of being her
butler/gigolo or taking *myself* out of the scene in a sort of pre-
emptive strike? But why should I? . . .

The Morgan Bank will keep me in touch if there are any new
developments, but as B.'s friends I hope you will make it plain
to her that nuclear disarmament is now in order and that this
sort of thing drives any man sooner or later to profound indif-
ference. She claims, when that has sentimental social value, to
be a Catholic born and bred. What she needs is some self-exam-
ination not with a shrink but with a good old-fashioned Irish
priest, who will ask her "What about it?" in those old-fashioned
ethical terms that she understood (perhaps) before she went out
to Hollywood in 1940 with John Jacob Astor hot on her lovely
tail. It's been show and little substance ever since. I helped in
that, of course.

> Yours ever and to Gloria—
> Brooks

GLORIA JONES
When she came to, Virginia Chambers and Ethel de Croisset and I
were with her, and Dr. Dax, Jean Dax, who was the doctor for all of
us. About a week later Virginia and Ethel and I took her to the
American Hospital, which is way the hell across town, and she stayed
there for six .weeks. She was really in terrible shape. "I want my
husband"—that's the first thing she said in the American Hospital.
She kept saying that to anybody who would listen to her: "I want my
husband." The bastard. Where *was* he? She was writing him letters—letters, letters, letters all the time. She used to always get him
back with letters.

## Letter from Brooks Baekeland to James Jones, March 12, 1968

Dear Jim—

It is exactly two weeks since I spoke to you on the phone from Rome.

In India I received some of the most pathetic letters I have ever seen from Barbara. They were written from the Hôtel-Dieu and from the American Hospital where she went afterwards. These letters were forwarded to me via Morgan's. I have heard nothing since, because my itinerary had a rather large gap in it and I have not yet been able to close it—moving too fast. But I worry a whole lot about B. and I would be glad to have an encouraging word from you and Gloria—something objective that I can feel is accurate and written by someone who knows her and loves her. I admit to having been terribly affected by what she wrote. Of course I was meant to, but that makes no difference to me. I love her very much.

The next forwarding address that Morgan's has for me is an airport departure (date, air and flight no.) on March 31—so you can write to me care of them and I will get your news then.

I am very grateful to you both for the trouble you have taken.

Love—
Brooks

GLORIA JONES

Barbara was also writing letters to President de Gaulle and Mrs. de Gaulle—Mrs. de Gaulle especially, because Barbara said she knew she would understand. All of us, you know, spent time with her—Ethel and Virginia and I. She had a very nice private room. The American Hospital's very fancy, you know.

## Letter from Barbara Baekeland to Gloria and James Jones, Undated

The American Hospital
Neuilly

Darling Gloria—and Jim—

How can I ever thank you enough? When I'm really glad to be alive I'll find some way. To get me out of the Hôtel-Dieu—that

monstrous place—saved my sanity. I want to find or write
Brooks and tell him how sorry I am I've caused so much anxiety
& pain to people I love. I haven't the right to hold him if he
wants to go but I wanted to see him once more as he left me
with such anger. So much of our problems have been my fault.
I realize it now. Perhaps if he does come back I can prove it and
I would never reproach him.

How glad I am that with your worries and concern for me you
came to see how I was. It's enough to see the blue sky and the
tree outside my window to begin to feel like being a part of it
all. As much as I love Brooks I did not love him enough to let
him go with a chance to be happy and that is what I reproach
myself for.

Dax won't let me even wear my own nightgowns—or have
. . . calls. Thank God I can still write or I would go crazy!
Maybe this isolation is good for some people but it leaves me
with my thoughts which are not happy ones and is a kind of
punishment.

Thank you for everything you've done for me over the years.
There's been so much kindness from you both and I have been
so hateful. But I mean to study "How to Win Friends and Keep
Them"—indeed cherish them—joke—but I *am* going to try to
correct my very grave failings of character.

Come and see me when you can. I need an antiperspirant,
hair rollers, and a *soin de peau*—Carolina has all this.

It's much better here than the Hôtel-Dieu! *Quelle* irony! But
nurses aren't very gentle people. I suppose if we were jabbing
people with needles all day long & wiping their behinds &
watching them die we wouldn't be, either.

Neither doctor spends more than 5 min. with me & one a
psychiatrist. How I'm going to pay for it all, God alone knows.

Come soon—
X X  B

PAULE LAFEUILLE
I visited her daily at the American Hospital of Neuilly. Her friends
used to take turns by her bed, and every day one of them, in order to
entice her to eat, would present her with some delicacy that her cook

had prepared. As for me, living next to Petrossian's store, I could bring her a slice of smoked salmon or a few grains of fresh caviar. Our efforts were rarely successful. She would push her plate aside and say, "It is delicious. . . . How sweet you all are."

She loved to confide in me at length about her distress, and I can tell you that her words were Gentle Love itself's. She seemed not in the least resentful of Brooks's desertion and only kept repeating, "All I want is to see him once in a while. I shall not be able to live if I cannot occasionally set my eyes on him. . . ." Heartbreaking. By the way, I had also taught French to Brooks. I never did again from then on. I made a decision never to see him again. I made it the very moment I heard of his flight to the Far East and the subsequent dramatic events. In February 1973 he wrote to me from a village in Brittany asking if I would consider meeting his new wife who—I quote him—was not being too well treated by Barbara's old friends. This letter has remained unanswered.

### Ethel Woodward de Croisset

She came out of her coma in exactly the same mood that she'd gone into the suicide, you see—which was one of total frustration because she couldn't get ahold of Brooks. And I think it's a miracle that she in some way didn't try to take her life *again*, but probably one doesn't do that sort of thing. What I mean is that the attempt hadn't been a cleansing sort of thing. She came out absolutely wild, it seemed to me—and to Gloria. All this I think appears in one of those books of her husband's.

### From *The Merry Month of May,* James Jones, Delacorte Press, New York, 1971.

I put in a call to Harry in Rome. . . ." Louisa's in the hospital," I said.

"Oh? She is? What for?" Harry said.

I was beginning to feel irritated. "A suicide attempt," I said. . . .

There was a pause on the line. "I suppose if she dies, I'll have to come back, won't I?"

"If you want to get her buried, you will," I said furiously. "I know I sure as hell ain't going to do it."

"Oh, somebody would," he said. "Edith de Chambrolet. Have you called Edith?"

"No, not yet," I said. "I was trying to keep it quiet."

"Well, call her. Call Edith. She's a do-gooder. She loves to do good works." . . .

He had told me to call Edith de Chambrolet. I did. I had met Edith at their place for the first time, and afterwards had had dinners with her frequently at her place. Large dinners, always very formal, eight to 12 people. Edith was a remarkable person. She was one of the richest women in America, and had married some impoverished French Count and had four sons by him. . . . She spoke with just about the broadest drawling "A" I have ever heard, and had stary eyes. . . .

Together we walked over across the bridge and down past Notre-Dame to the Hôtel-Dieu. . . .

As we walked in through the bed rows of beat-up, near-dead people, she said, "Isn't it marvelous, now? Extraordinarily efficient."

I was tongue-tied, and felt totally incapable, with her there.

"Now, Louisa," she said at the bed, lifting up one side of the plastic oxygen tent. "We must stop all this nonsense. We must pull ourselves together and I know that you will." She let the tent flap drop. "We'll talk to her again a little later. Let it sink in, first. I'm sure she heard us. In her unconscious." . . .

Harry remained adamant about not coming back unless Louisa actually died. And even then he was not absolutely sure. . . .

They moved Louisa, in an ambulance, to the American Hospital in Neuilly. The whole thing was handled by the American-trained French doctor we knew who worked there, and whom all of us, including Edith, used as our doctor. . . . His name was Dax. . . . I did not feel up to riding out with her myself, but Edith de Chambrolet went with her. . . .

I talked to the American Hospital doctor. . . . "She was just about as dead as you can get," he said equably, "without actually dying."

### From *Time* Magazine, Review of *The Merry Month of May*, Timothy Foote, February 22, 1971

Among the [book's] victims is Harry's wife Louisa. Jones turns her into a near vegetable as the result of an attempted suicide. . . . Letting the lady live on in some domesticity or other would have been a truer and crueler fate.

### BROOKS BAEKELAND

A novelist is a cannibal and may eat his friends for his professional purposes—Jim Jones always did. I could not read *The Merry Month of May*—trash. I am the only person alive, along with Sylvie, who knows *all* the truth—and therefore *the* truth. And the truth, when deeply seen, is always greater than any fiction. In its depths—but only there—reality not only seems to imitate art but surpasses it.

### From *Saturday Review*, Review of *The Merry Month of May*, John W. Aldridge, February 13, 1971

Even with all due allowance for his evident faith in human credulity, Jones cannot really expect us to believe any of this. His people, given the intellectual sophistication he attributes to them, would scarcely behave in this way.

### SYLVIE BAEKELAND SKIRA

We left exactly on the 24th of February, and that's the day she tried to kill herself. Each time Brooks had tried to leave her before, she had done this. The first time was up at camp, in the Adirondacks— she took pills and he had to rush her across the lake in a rowboat to a doctor.

### SAMUEL TAYLOR

I remember one night during the sixties Suzanne and I were at the Baekelands' for dinner—Jessica Tandy and Hume Cronyn were also there—and Barbara said, "Guess where I was at five this morning!" and we said, "Where?" and she said, "At Bellevue Hospital," and she showed us the bandages on her wrists. And being very gay about it, you know—very charming about it.

## NANCY PERKINS WALLACE
My brother saved Barbara's life once. Mike was staying with Barbara and Tony in Cadaqués and she took an overdose of something, and they had to drive her in the car, screaming and yelling at her to stay awake—driving wildly through the night to some Costa Brava hospital.

## SYLVIE BAEKELAND SKIRA
Paris was the fourth time, and Brooks just . . . he couldn't . . . he had to get away from her. That didn't mean he didn't love her. He did, and when she begged him to come back, I was terribly afraid that he would. Everybody thought, Brooks is off on a fling again, he's forty-seven, he'll come back. But I know now that he would never have come back to her, never—because she was too powerful, she was someone who would take the air you breathe and borrow it and leave you gasping. You just couldn't exist with her around. Barbara tried everything to keep him—if a man is about to leave you and you take one hundred pills of Nembutal, that's a pretty good way to make sure he's not going to leave you.

## ELIZABETH BLOW
You know, Sylvie also tried to kill herself. Well, I mean, the story is so absurd, but *possibly* it happened. *I* believe it happened. According to Barbara, Sylvie had tried to take a lot of pills and been put in the hospital and Brooks and Barbara had sat up all one night after this thing occurred and they had decided that they would go on with their life and their marriage and that they would live together forever and that they really loved one another. And then there was a call from the hospital, a desperate call from Sylvie saying she wanted to see Brooks, and Brooks said, "Look, Barbara, I think I really should go over to the hospital. I'll come right back." And he went over to the hospital and Barbara never saw him again. He left the hospital with Sylvie and fled to Rome.

## Letter from Barbara Baekeland to Gloria and James Jones, Undated

                                              The American Hospital
                                              Neuilly

My darling Gloria & Jim—

What would I do without you? He won't come back as he is a man that goes deeply into relationships and he will just become more & more fond of this girl—who first tried to get Tony & when that failed picked on Brooks. He is so guileless he won't see through her and though I don't mean to denigrate the feeling she has for him, she is, I think, *intéressée*—mercenary. The last two times I saved my marriage by going to him with no pride and saying I was sorry. This time I have less pride and really think what I've been through has changed me. He had to leave without seeing me for if he saw me he loves me too much to have left me there tied up like a hog for slaughter. I feel that if I could only talk to him everything will be all right.

I haven't seen my Spanish beau since last Spring & then just for lunch to tell him I was through. He never meant as much to me as the hair on Brooks' head! Whoops—as *a* hair on Brooks' head.

The trouble is now everyone knows and if I am ashamed he must be more ashamed. This is what will keep him from coming back to me.

When she was ill I urged him to go and see her in the clinic so that if anything happened that was serious he would not blame himself. She has *kept* him from seeing me & had the gall to write me a hypocritical letter in which she says she only wants him for a few months. I can't find the letter now—the doctor probably took it.

I know that with all the glamour & newness of traveling he won't come back. But would you, Jim, tell him I'll come and join him whenever he wants me to on a few hours' notice?

When I get out of here I want to go down to Mallorca, for that is our one chance to build a life together—with our son.

I don't talk about the girl to anyone. Let them wonder. I simply say B. has gone to India. But I won't be able to face anyone when I get out. My life just means nothing to me without B. or Tony.

Please try to come to see me—

                                              XX I love you—
                                              B.

P.S. My bill for 3 days was over $100—I've got to get *out* of here! I'll have no money left.

Jim, he will tell you in his letter that he is madly in love, etc., etc. But that day when we talked for 40 hours he was so *relieved* to be out of it all. He said she had no imagination and would eventually bore him. He said he had never been bored an instant with me. He said he liked the feeling of having her love him and her sexual newness. She's got 2 children and no visible means of support. I adore Brooks and can learn to control the vicious side of my nature and let him love me the way he always wanted to. Please tell him he should come back to me. He needs advice.

### Clement Biddle Wood

A very strange coincidence happened when Barbara was at the American Hospital. My wife Jessie—whose mother, Louise de Vilmorin, by the way, was a friend of Barbara's—had been arranging flowers in our apartment and this big cut-glass vase that had belonged to *my* mother just sort of came apart in her hands and she was cut on the wrist, exactly on the vein. I made sort of a tourniquet and I rushed her to the American Hospital. And as we were walking in—Jessie, you know, holding her bandaged wrists and blood sopping and pouring on the floor—along comes Barbara, with Ethel de Croisset. Barbara is just at that moment checking out, and she sees Jessie and she says, "Oh, my poor Jessie! Oh, *dear!* Oh, I understand *completely* about this"—you know, assuming naturally that it was a suicide attempt, that Jessie had slashed her wrists. And Ethel said, "No, no, Barbara, you're not to worry yourself about *that*—Jessie's just fine," and sort of hustled her along. It really was the damnedest coincidence. It's the kind of thing you couldn't put into a novel.

### Gloria Jones

When she got a little bit better, she came and stayed with us in this house we rented with Clem and Jessie Wood in a place called La Coste. She drove there herself, so she was in good shape. It was at Eastertime.

### Clement Biddle Wood

Barbara was with us for a few days. She was in a very sort of fragile condition, but she was putting a good face on things and trying very hard to be a good sport, not to bore us with her troubles. Naturally we were all worried that she might try to pull the same thing again then and there, and she knew that we were worried about this, yet I also had the feeling that she was somehow trying to put her life back together again.

## Letter from Brooks Baekeland to Michael Edwards, April 23, 1968

Dear Michael—
. . . I very strongly suspect that B. and I will be back together soon after September 1st and that the storms will all have blown over. But I think you should keep that surmise to yourself. . . . I may have to go to the States for a while but Paris has become home to me.

Affectionately—<br>Brooks

P.S. I am about to leave for Thailand. Your letter just caught me here in Nepal. Morgan's will always forward.

## Letter from Barbara Baekeland to Michael Edwards, Undated

Michael dear—
I hope all is well with the apartment. I have joined Tony in Cadaqués. He wanted me to come and has been a source of constant gentleness & concern since my arrival a week ago. It seemed the best thing for me to do under the circumstances. We listen to music, study, see no one, walk, swim & explore and I feel myself beginning to mend again. I seem to be getting better here—anyway I am happy being with my son.
    We have rented Avie von Ripper's house on Mallorca for 2 months—from the 15th of June until the 15th of August. It looks comfortable and will provide us with a refuge until I know what to do. At the moment the prospect of a reconciliation— though I still want it—looks dim. I think I shall probably go to New York on the 15th and take back my apartment there. It is an easier place for me to begin to reconstruct my life and maybe I can find some interesting work to do.

I am coming to Paris to see Carolina and straighten out my affairs. I have been told that I must see a lawyer as B. has not behaved properly toward me financially. I am very low on funds and have simply taken this house & told B.'s lawyer that he will have to pay for it.

I don't think he and I can live together again unless we both change. I hope to re-find my creative and better self in these next few months, working and living quietly with Tony, my mother, and my animals. As far as I can tell from Brooks' present path he is in the process of losing his better self and was very harmful to Tony during all this terrible time. I cannot risk such destruction & violence ever again. As Heidegger said, "the dreadful has already happened"—well, it has and it is time to begin again.

Much love,
Barbara

## Letter from Brooks Baekeland to Michael Edwards, August 23, 1968

Dear Michael—

As you know, Barbara has returned to New York; Tony, after passing through Paris just long enough (I imagine) to make a shambles of 45, quai de Bourbon, has gone on to Frankfurt and from there out to New Delhi, etc. to join me. He arrives tomorrow. . . .

## SYLVIE BAEKELAND SKIRA

I had come back to France to see my children, who were with my parents for the summer, and I had brought with me a money order from Brooks to bring Tony to India. I made arrangements with the Morgan Bank so Tony could come and pick up his air ticket—we were to leave together on the same plane. I waited at the departure gate and he never came. We found out later that he had picked up the air ticket, changed it, and gone to Ireland to be with a friend of his from Cadaqués, Ernst von Wedel.

## Letter from Brooks Baekeland to Michael Edwards, Undated

Michael,
I just don't know what will be the final result for B & myself—
but whatever it is I think it may take some time to work out—
maybe 6 months more. I just can't say. But we shall not be
returning to the life we lived before. I hope we shall see a lot of
each other and share some (the best) aspects of life together
again—but the whole thing: God forbid. . . .

Affectionately as always,
Brooks

## Letter from Barbara Baekeland to Michael Edwards, September 16, 1968

New York

Darling Michael—
B. wants to come back. Had a meeting with his lawyers &
cousin last week to listen to his proposals. Have a few of my own
to make—one of which includes a proper house *somewhere*—so
we shall see.

New York a joy. I am enjoying my apartment enormously
and my life here. Each weekend away and two exciting offers of
jobs—one with Andy Warhol & the other with the 2 Maysles
brothers.

If, as Brooks writes, he intends to let 45, quai de Bourbon go,
I may want to keep it on myself. Just paid the rug bill &
lampshade bill which have followed me around since May.

Love,
Barbara

## Letter from Michael Edwards to Brooks Baekeland, September 23, 1968

Dear Brooks,
When the screens and Barbara's other pictures are down, all the
walls will have to be made good and repainted; also the depreda-

tions on the sofa and chair made by her dear four-footed friends
will have to be repaired, but, on the other hand, Barbara only
recently put a lot of money into the place for a nice new carpet
and went halves with me on the new curtains, so I suggest we
call that quits. . . .

## Letter from Brooks Baekeland to Michael Edwards, October 15, 1968

Kashmir
India

Dear Michael—

Barbara and I are still at a stand-off as far as our futures are
concerned. I doubt very much whether we shall be taking up
residence again at 45, quai de Bourbon. *Entre nous*, I am devoted to her and I think she is to me, but our life together,
behind what the public sees, has been a rather violent and
chronically contested conflict of tastes, styles and policy (on all
counts, including most seriously, and perhaps disastrously, the
bringing up of our son, water now under the dam) and I finally
had enough of it. She is stronger than I (in some ways); she
could have gone on; I saw long ago the approaching day when
we would have to separate if only in the formal sense of that
word—i.e., the day of my ultimate weariness and exasperation.
She is a splendid and adorable woman. Not her fault, not mine
either I think—we just created too much heat together in the
same 4 walls, all the 4 walls we ever inhabited!

God knows when, if ever, I will have a home again. . . .

Most of our old friends in Paris now consider me to be such a
heel, cad, bounder, rotter, hairy-at-the-heel and downright scal-
lywag that they do not deign to acknowledge my occasional
friendly letters from the Far East. So I am "as one dead" to all
"decent" people. (I was not surprised. People love battles—other
people's battles—and enjoy taking sides when no blows can fall
upon *them*. Every disputation on a street soon gathers its crowd.)

With much love—
Brooks

P.S. I am leaving Kashmir, but would be obliged if you would
keep even that location confidential as a personal favor.

## Letter from Michael Edwards to Brooks Baekeland, November 4, 1968

Dear Brooks,
Barbara telephoned me the other day terribly anxious to know where you were and whether you were going back to New York, especially as she had heard a rumour that your clothes were going to be sent back there. I told her that I had heard from you but that I could not give her any indication that you planned to go back to America in the foreseeable future.

As far as your clothes are concerned, by all means have Carolina take them over to the studio, but don't worry about them if you want to leave them at Quai de Bourbon since, as I told you in my last letter, Carolina fusses over them periodically, so they will come to no harm; ditto any of the rest of Barbara's furniture. . . .

## Letter from Barbara Baekeland to Gloria and James Jones, January 6, 1969

Hotel Ritz
Barcelona

Darlings—
I will be in Paris the night of the 15th and would like to have dinner with you either the 15th or 16th. Will you drop me a line at the Hotel Collander, St. Moritz, Switzerland?

I have been in Spain since the 16th of December by way of the Caribbean. . . . Tony came for 5 days to Mallorca with me after we spent Xmas together in Cadaqués. He was *mad* about the place. B. has fled back to Thailand, everyone says in very bad shape. . . . I now have Louis Nizer for a lawyer & am much happier.

Dying to see you both and the children. If you haven't time to write, just expect me. Will be in Paris only 3 days to clear out flat—

Hugs & kisses,
B.

# 10

# CRUISING

In 1978, after Tony Baekeland had been in Broadmoor for five years, the authorities still considered his condition "severe" and did not feel he was ready to be released. Nonetheless, the unofficial committee of his friends continued in their efforts to have him freed.

Miwa Svinka-Zielinski felt that Tony ought to be in a setting where he could receive regular therapy on a one-to-one basis. She suggested a halfway-house arrangement. But he resisted this idea—he wanted to be on his own when he got out, he said. "I kept telling him," she says, "that if he ever wanted to get out of there he would have to behave rationally. 'Don't tell Dr. Maguire you want to be independent the minute you are free,' I told him. He had to have some sort of a transition from this place to real life."

Miwa Svinka-Zielinski herself explored various alternatives for Tony's care in the event of his repatriation. "I asked myself some questions, such as: What is his exact clinical status? Is there anywhere in England where he can stay as a transition before being sent to New York? Can he really function outside a hospital or halfway house? Can he be persuaded to have others handle his money for him in the U.S.?"

Visitors that year reported that Tony's eyes seemed vacant. This disturbing symptom was one of the reasons Dr. Maguire was reluctant to take seriously the requests of the unofficial committee. "Our hospital is designed for patients who are violent," he explains, "and as soon as their behavior is tolerable, we are bound to send them to less secure places. This is the logic I followed with Tony."

In February, a consul officer from the American Embassy in London made the first of what would be eleven visits to Broadmoor to assess Tony Baekeland's condition. Sarah Fischer, a member of the consulate, recalls that "the psychiatrist seemed to care very much about Tony and thought he would be happier back in the United States—he hoped in an institution similar to Broadmoor."

### Consular Officer's Report on Visit to Antony Baekeland, February 10, 1978

I had a nice visit with Mr. Baekeland in the "great hall" at Broadmoor. He seemed happy and content, with no serious complaints. He said that his doctor had mentioned returning him to the USA, but he didn't know much more about it.

### Consular Officer's Report on Visit to Antony Baekeland, March 10, 1978

Mr. Baekeland and I had an animated conversation during my visit. He stated that he was in "fine" health, and seemed in good spirits, although he said that he was "vegetating" at Broadmoor as inmates in his ward were not afforded the opportunity to do anything of substance during waking hours. However, he felt that Broadmoor was treating him as well as could be expected. Following our conversation, he had a chat with two guards; this chat appeared to be quite friendly and enjoyable for all concerned.

### Official Visitors File, Broadmoor Special Hospital, May 3, 1978

VISITOR'S NAME: Mrs. M. Svinka-Zielinski
RELATIONSHIP TO PATIENT: Friend
SUMMARY: As before, she discussed Tony's needs with brisk

chatter and with an air of official authority while in fact she has no standing in the case except as a "friend" of the family. She intends to seek out names and addresses of hospitals in New York which might be more accessible to Tony from a financial point of view. Has promised to call with these details in the near future.

## Letter from Antony Baekeland to Miwa Svinka-Zielinski, August 30, 1978

Dear Miwa,
First of all I would just like to tell you how much your visits have meant to me over the last five years. Had a very interesting dream about that nice Princess Pallavicini you brought to see me.

I am learning all kinds of new and interesting things about the nature of the Universe. The weather has been relatively cool, except for a few hot days. I feel quite ready to face the world. I am getting very tired of being here and I greatly wish they would let me out. A great and wonderful friend of ours called Ethel de Croisset just sent Michael Alexander some money to try to help get me out.

I want to go back to Mallorca. Miramar, our house there, has a beautiful old garden, and a chapel and cloisters. The very old palm trees were brought there more than a hundred years ago. There are miradors or look-outs all up and down the mountain-side and the view of the sun setting into the vast blue sea is truly something never to be forgotten. I spent some of the happiest years of my life there, mainly in the company of the Mallorquin peasant family who lived downstairs and looked after the land.

Robert Graves lives nearby in Deyá and I came to know him quite well while I lived there. He told me my poetry was excellent, which was encouraging. I spend my days now in a happy dream of what I will do in the garden and cloisters when I go back there and what repairs will have to be done to the house to make it comfortable again.

Love,
Tony

## Letter from Barbara Baekeland to Michael Edwards, August 28, 1969

Miramar
Valldemosa
Mallorca

Michael dear—

Tony and I have been sharing a house—the old residence of the Austrian Archduke Luis Salvador in Valldemosa. We have been so happy here I hope to keep it forever. It has been practically given to us by his daughter who wants us to stay.

I lost out on a beautiful flat in Paris. Am on to another on Cadogan Square in London but what to do with our great feline friend the fine Mr. Worcester?

Will be returning to New York in November to try to settle my affairs with Brooks, who has refused me a divorce. The bills (unpaid by him) still go on and the little he gives me is just enough to clear expenses here. All my rent money from New York goes straight to my lawyers who are not able to accomplish anything as B. refuses to communicate. Meanwhile he has ended up living just down the road here. And to think that one of the Ten Commandments is "Love thy Neighbor"! Never mind, I try—if, at times, it seems the greatest irony of all. . . .

SYLVIE BAEKELAND SKIRA

After India, we went to Mallorca, as a sort of, you know, winter drop. Brooks had always loved Mallorca—he had once planned to buy a large house there with Barbara.

She didn't know we were there. And then one day we were going off to Ibiza—it's a half-hour plane trip, that's all—and who do we meet in the airport—Ernst von Wedel from Cadaqués. Looking *very* handsome in those days, and very well groomed and so on. He said, "Brooks—my God! What are *you* doing here? I've been staying with Barbara and Tony, and Barbara just drove me to the airport!" And Brooks said, "Well, keep it quiet. If you see her, don't say anything." And of course, Ernst, instead of keeping quiet, rushed off to find Barbara, and very soon on the loudspeaker there came: "Mrs. Baekeland wants to see Mr. Baekeland." When we heard that, we decided, okay, too bad, our luggage is on the plane but we're not going to take it, we'll go back to the house, because we wanted to get away from her and we thought that she would wait for us at the departure gate. But I must say Barbara knew Brooks very well. She knew he would leave the airport and go back to his car and so she was waiting for him out in the parking lot. And when they came face to face, Brooks said—he had been always and still is very proud of Barbara's looks, but she had become plump, and he said—"You don't look so young, Barbara." And she said, "*You* look a hundred years old!" and from then on they had a good fight. I went away, I retired to the car—I didn't want to listen. You see, Barbara had said to Brooks, about me, "Get that thing away from me!"—that sort of thing. But that's normal, that's normal. So then, after that, we returned to our separate houses, Barbara to Deyá and Brooks and I to our village nearby. But now of course Barbara knew that we were living on the same island.

Eventually Tony came to visit us. He stayed for a few days. This was the first time I had seen him since Brooks and I went away together. It was very uncomfortable, very hard. He left messages for Brooks in the flower pots. I found one—it said, "Daddy, please Daddy, come back to Mummy, she's so unhappy." He acted like a little eight-year-old—I mean, the way he resented me.

He never wrote to me from Broadmoor but he wrote *about* me. I existed in every letter to his father. Oh yes. I was the evil woman who was responsible for everything: I had killed his mother, I had killed everybody.

For a while Brooks had been *for* Tony's release someday, but then he began receiving these letters that were so frightening. Tony said I would be the first person he would kill when he came out.


**Telegram from Kingman Brewster, Jr., U.S. Ambassador to the Court of St. James's, to Cyrus R. Vance, Secretary of State, December 1978**

MADE REGULAR VISIT TO ANTONY BAEKELAND AT BROADMOOR HOSPITAL ON DECEMBER 20 AND FOUND HIM IN GOOD HEALTH AND REASONABLE SPIRITS. HE HAD NO COMPLAINTS.

BREWSTER

HELEN DELANEY
Six years after the matricide, just about the time our embassy in
London began looking into Tony's condition at Broadmoor, an English writer by the name of Nell Dunn—she'd already written a best
seller called *Poor Cow*, and a couple of years ago she had a play on
Broadway called, I think, *Steaming*—published a novel called *The
Only Child* obviously based on the Baekelands. She hadn't known
them personally or anything, she'd simply read about the tragedy in
the newspapers, and I think she may have known people who knew
them. Anyway, in her book, Brooks is "Daniel," Barbara is "Esther,"
and Tony is "Piers."

## From *The Only Child*, Nell Dunn, Jonathan Cape Ltd., London, 1978

> With Daniel it was need, obsession, and war, but with Piers it
> was different, delicate, unexpected, sitting on a sofa with him
> after school—the light dimming outside the window, [the cat]
> asleep on the knotted rug—she felt sweetness steal over her—a
> sweetness she had never known with anyone else. . . .
> "You've tried to run my life."
> "I didn't want to run your life. I only wanted to make every-
> thing beautiful for you, I only wanted you to be happy. Oh
> come here, Piers, hold me and comfort me . . . I ache, I ache
> so much I'm dying . . . Please help me!"
> "I ache too, Mother."
> "Come here then, let's comfort one another. Let's hold one
> another till we go to sleep. Take me in your arms, Piers." . . .
> "I suppose the truth is that my mother has always been the
> love of my life, yet she's never given me what I needed. Support
> in being myself. Belief that what matters to me is as important as
> what matters to her. And then my father hasn't liked me since I
> was about twelve. I'm a disappointment to him. We have noth-
> ing in common yet we are bound together by steel rope, bound,
> it seems, not by love and pleasure."

SYLVIE BAEKELAND SKIRA
Brooks went to see Tony in Broadmoor. The first time, I made him
go. I thought it was too impossible to have a child in prison and not

go see him, and I hammered and hammered and hammered, and finally he went.

But I shouldn't say I made him go because somebody who doesn't want to go won't go, either. After that first visit he said—but you must understand it as coming from someone who was very hurt rather than someone arrogant—he came back and told me, "Tony has a ghastly cockney accent." Brooks has a sense of theater, a sense of glamour and so on, and if his son suddenly had a cockney accent, it said a lot. It was a question of how alienated his child had become, how this child was not even his anymore, couldn't connect to anything anymore.

## Letter from Antony Baekeland to Miwa Svinka-Zielinski, Undated

Broadmoor

Dear Miwa—
My father came to see me on a surprise visit and it was good to see him but not so good as I had hoped—he is, however, coming again with his wife, and they plan to spend a few days in a nearby hotel and see me every day. There is so much in me that I want to express, and such emotion that wants to come out, you have no idea.

Forgive this short scribble.

All love,
Tony

## Letter from Antony Baekeland to James Reeve, December 17, 1978

Broadmoor

Dear James—
I feel so wonderfully well these days—my grandmother Nini will be very pleased with me.

I thought you might be very busy and that would be the reason for your not writing.

I have a feeling things will be very big and tremendous when I get out, but still I have no idea of when that will be. I am hoping very much that you will be able to get away to visit with me in Valldemosa.

Love,
Tony

## Letter from Barbara Baekeland to Michael Edwards, September 12, 1969

Miramar
Valldemosa
Mallorca

Dear Michael,
I wish you could come here for a visit. Cruised the Greek Islands in June with a neighbor of yours in the South of France. Bernie Pfriem—nice fellow. Do look him up.

Write!

My love—
Barbara

BERNARD PFRIEM
It was a two-week cruise. Emily Staempfli had chartered a big yacht. We met the boat at Athens and it took off from there for the islands. We went to Rhodes but we didn't get to Crete, we went to the northern islands. I almost didn't go—I was just about to start teaching an art course at Sarah Lawrence and I was hesitating because I wanted to work. But this architect friend of mine who was going, Peter Harnden, got angry with me for even thinking of passing up an opportunity like this. None of us realized at that time that Peter was beginning his lung cancer. It was not long after that that he had a lung removed. And then he got it in the second one, of course—it was a year or two later—and he had a second operation. And then he died. And later his wife Missy, who was also on the cruise, died—of leukemia.

Then there was this friend of Emily's, a man whose name I can't remember anymore—a tall, thin character who did little landscapes and had a house in Spain. He was the only drip on the whole sea voyage. He did nothing, nothing, he didn't even talk at meals. He's dead too now.

Then there was Sam Green, a very very good friend of Emily's who in fact had arranged for her to charter the yacht. I knew Sam very well by the time of that cruise. He was always at Emily's apartment in New York, and he organized a lot of her parties for her— you know, with Warhol and Rauschenberg and Jasper Johns and so on. He was funny and amusing and chatty.

And then of course there was Barbara, whom I'd *not* met before. I liked her enormously. She was bubbly and she had sort of a Marilyn Monroe kind of effervescence—and even that kind of flesh, I would say.

That made seven of us. And there was a crew of something like fourteen.

The thing between Sam and Barbara started on that cruise. By then, of course, Barbara was a free agent—her husband had left her. Actually, Sam and I were the only eligible males on board, and she was glorying in the idea of having a romance, which she was desperately in need of. She was always touching you and laughing and being seductive and so on.

There were only two doubles—Emily had, of course, the master stateroom, and Peter and Missy Harnden had the smaller one. Then there were two adjoining rooms off to the side. Barbara had one, and Sam and I sort of flipped for the other—to be next to Barbara—and Sam won.

After that, Barbara and Sam were together all the time. They both loved swimming and whenever we would anchor they would swim long distances together. It was all great fun and games, and warm. Oh, sometimes Barbara would lash into a serious discussion, whether it was about politics or whatnot I can't remember, but she was vocal. Anyway she seemed to be happy, and I thought she looked radiant. When we docked, the three of us would go off to bazukis or whatever you call them, and drink and dance.

Sometimes Barbara would talk about Tony. She always said she wanted me to meet him. One night she told me that she had slept with him. She was very honest about it—she said she had done it to break him of his homosexual tendencies. She talked about it as though it were a therapeutic act that she was doing.

I remember at one point she and I were walking together, she was holding my arm, and she told me she was attracted to Sam because he reminded her so much of Tony. "They look alike and they have kindred spirits"—that's how she put it. I think she was sort of apologizing to me for why she was having this affair with Sam and not with me, because, in a sense, we had kind of an innocent flirtation going.

And then after the cruise, she and Sam went off together to meet Tony.

## SAM GREEN

It was a geezer trip, and Barbara was the only one who was *not* a geezer. She was beautiful, she was lively, she was imaginative, she was exciting. And every time I would turn a corner or go to a quiet dark place on the deck, there she'd be.

Well, she *was* kind of wonderful. I keep thinking that all of that froufrou and title-dropping was a part of my growing up which lasted for a long, long time. I was twenty-nine when I met her—she was, I guess, about forty-seven—and I hadn't been around that much. I was directing this funny little museum of contemporary art down in Philadelphia. I mean, I'd never been on a yacht before!

On the cruise I realized that she was recovering from a bad time with her husband. We became great friends, and I didn't think that it was anything more serious than that. I mean, I was disinclined to have an ongoing affair with a woman needy of having an affair.

She told me she had a big house in Mallorca. She said, "You *must* come." And it was convenient. I think I had ten days or something to kill. She had told me over and over again about Tony and how wonderful and spiritual he was, how kind of confused he was and how he didn't have anyone to influence him as interesting as me, and wouldn't I please come and look at him and, you know, sort of help him out. Well, I was more interested in seeing the nice house in Mallorca.

On the boat she had presented it as a palace, a major palace. What it was was a run-down finca. Miramar, it was called. It was set on a wonderful precipice, about two thousand feet above the sea—it had the best vista in all of Mallorca. It also had a thirteenth-century chapel, and formal gardens that were all overrun with weeds. I mean, it was a gone estate. And Barbara was renting it for what it was worth—which was nothing. I mean, a hundred a month or something. And she'd cajoled this wonderful servant family, Maria and

her husband Sebastian, into providing food and doing this and that—
and never paid them!

While I was there she became very possessive of me and after I left
she inundated me with letters everywhere I went.

## Letter from Barbara Baekeland to Sam Green, August 15, 1969

> Miramar
> Valldemosa
> Mallorca

Darling Sam—

How much we miss the pleasure of your company. Come back
soon.

The night you left, the light was all gold & mauve and a wind
came up. Everything seemed sad. But then the next morning we
did the I Ching and it told us that a "friend" would be crossing
the great water to join us soon and that we would vanquish
weakness by joining and multiplying our power.

Tony liked you so much. I'm glad. I do, too. I hope he finds
his way—maybe you can help him to.

Thank you for all the incredibles and the grass. I'm so happy
I've had a trip and you're right—things don't look quite the
same. Will they ever?

Tony is off at Deyá. Wuss is *always* hungry. Everybody won-
ders why you went away. Tell us.

> Love—
> Barbara

## Letter from Sam Green to Barbara Baekeland, August 15, 1969

> Saint-Tropez

Dear Barbara,

Well, I certainly hope that things have calmed down since I left
Mallorca. I have begun to commence my own life, and am enjoying it. I went from Palma to Nice and spent a great night in a

hotel near there. The next day I arrived at Tony Richardson's little village above Saint-Tropez, where I plan to spend about another week. Then I go to Athens for my cruise with Cecile de Rothschild.

Tomorrow I go *alone* to Jeanne Moreau's for lunch.

We had a very strange visit, didn't we? I have done nothing but think about it. Heaven help us, what a situation! The combined efforts of de Sade and Tennessee Williams couldn't have done it justice. The awareness-heightening of the drug only intensified the possible repercussions. That night of the wind I got up five times and bolted my doors. In that beautiful place, that peaceful, enchanted, lovely place—to think that I disturbed it! I was truly afraid.

To love Tony is irresistible. The burden he is bearing is almost too much. I hope he has the strength to hold it until someone comes to take it from him. It's tragic that Brooks is so small that he can't help him—because Brooks is what's needed. When I think of the despair he leaves in his wake, it makes me murderous. But Brooks, eventually, is his own problem, no one else's. All I have to offer you is liking and some understanding. Please accept them. There are many kinds of love.

Sam

## Letter from Barbara Baekeland to Sam Green, August 22, 1969

Miramar<br>Valldemosa<br>Mallorca

Darling Sam—

Got your letter yesterday. I had three (maybe four) of the happiest days ever with you. You were a merry and adorable companion and Tony & I both adored having you. I'm sorry you were feeling oppressed and attacked (why else lock—bolt!—your door?). No one will ever disturb you or force gifts upon you that you do not wish to give or accept in this house—our house. Our time together was not a playlet of Williams or a monstrous evocation of de Sade—but an acting out in a truly classical & beautiful way of a very old myth. Because we are veterans of this century we were unable to be really free and it is perhaps better that we were not, for some of us have fragile psyches and the strain would have been great. I do not want you to blame yourself. Both Tony & I love you and you mustn't make something that has (if unconventional) radiance take on a sordid backwash of tired old Freud.

I would be happier if Tony were to fall in love with a beautiful & gifted girl. I would like him to experience marriage, fatherhood, the really extraordinary harmony and fitting and complementing that can exist between a man & woman. I had it once and it is a rare and beautiful thing. Perhaps he must go through other friendships first—I don't know. Anyway he is 22 and must make his way in his *own* way. I can only offer him love and confidence, which is what I have tried to do.

If you want to come back—please do. If you feel our situation is too "charged," tell me so.

You're very honest, Sam, and it is a joy for me to have you as a friend. You are a good one and I believe you will always be my friend. You could be Tony's, too—and you could help him. He is worth it.

Whatever I once had has been squandered in a reckless wanton way, but I do have still a capacity for love. I think you love me (in one of your ways) and, as you so wisely said, there are many kinds of love—to give and receive them can be only good. So don't fret.

Keep in touch with us. Maybe you should take a year off and come to live here?

Anyway thank you for your dear letter—and thank you for bringing forth in me that which I think is the finest & best I have to give.

We miss you—Betty Blow is here now but it is not the same as having you. We were so peaceful & happy together and needed no one else. It was a special time.

Do write.

My love—
Barbara

## Letter from Antony Baekeland to Sam Green, August 24, 1969

Miramar
Valldemosa
Mallorca

Dear Sam—

There is a great deal I would like to ask and tell you but it is a peculiar thing that whenever I sit down with a pen my ideas seem to fade away. I will try, however. I hope that perhaps you can help me. I realize that what I must do involves loving another person and since I have never had the slightest attraction to women, this means that it must be a man. I think that much of my development stopped at an infantile stage, perhaps to enable me to go on with a certain kind of thinking which otherwise I would have been unable to continue. Anyway I am wondering how I can change this now. I really do not think I can go on much longer. The trouble is that when I am humiliated I no longer feel very amorous which is quite natural I feel. Please forgive these personal matters but I must discuss it with someone and I am sure you understand. As long as I feel bad and nasty and mean, which all these ghastly love songs make me feel— "Baby why did you leave me," bla bla bla—it is difficult for me to want to hear those screaming imploring voices, and difficult for me to feel worthy and nice enough to touch another person.

I have been standing in this doorway so long now but I can't do anything myself—when I do, all I get is horrified enlightened stares. Nor can I say anything—my voice comes out on the wrong pitch and people smile embarrassedly.

Naturally I want to be a hero, but I realize that this is childish. That is it—I never feel really safe from some horrible vain idea or childish impulse to show off, so I feel unwilling to embark on anything in which I might harm another person through my own foolishness. *Please* write to me here—much of this letter is Crap but some of it makes sense I hope.

Love,
Tony

P.S. I would like to be free. If I could sacrifice desire, I could be free. If I could sacrifice memory, I could sacrifice desire for love.

P.P.S. It would be terrible to have to continue to be a villain, knowing at the same time perfectly well how unnecessary it would be to be so.

## Letter from Antony Baekeland to Sam Green, August 25, 1969

> Miramar
> Valldemosa
> Mallorca

Dear Sam—

Please ignore fatuous letter—written in despond and never intended for the mails. I hope you are not embarrassed by it. Petty self-justifying propels me down such o-to-be-avoided lanes.

Someone gave me some quite nice hash. Last night we turned on down by the stone table at the chapel: all the animals appeared. Benjie the dog was struck dumb at the cat's antics in the tree. Also found a person who grows incredible grass somewhere in the mountains and sells it for practically nothing. I am utterly immobilized with the first cold I've had in four years. Can't decide whether to spend the winter here or go to London.

Betty Blow arrived with her tarot cards so it is not as lonely as it was when you first left.

> Love from
> Tony

ELIZABETH BLOW

I spent a month that summer with Barbara and Tony. They were living in this extraordinary villa—no telephone, no electricity, and every night we would light masses of candles and eat by candlelight.

The first week I was there, the sun was shining and Barbara and I would climb down over the rocks—it seemed to me like a mile down. It was like the descent of Mount Everest almost. I don't think there was even a path. We would just have to go down through the rocks and the olive trees, way way down because the villa was perched on the top of this promontory. And then we would clamber back up—the *ascent* of Mount Everest!—laughing and talking.

But then there were the evenings of the strange conversations in restaurants, at which I was sort of an observer—in which they would say things. . . . It was almost like another language, in other words, and only they could understand this particular language—it was their own intimate Tony-Barbara language that they'd invented and that they were, you know, cultivating and keeping alive, and it was like a fantasy journey that they two were on and I could not follow. They didn't forget you were there, because they would smile at you and perhaps try to bring you into the conversation—"Don't you think so?" kind of thing. I mean, they included me—they were loving, gentle people and they included me—but I couldn't follow what the hell they were talking about.

One afternoon I went for a swim at this hotel a little way up the road, it had a swimming pool, and Tony came with me and as I was lying in the sun he sat down beside me and told me this long long long story about something that had happened to him in Cadaqués. It involved all kinds of mythical and strange things. To me it was like a total hallucination, it was like a trip to the moon and back—and he said he had *done* this, but it was all so fantastic that it couldn't have been real. However it was real to *him*. Very real to him. It involved some man—now I'm beginning to remember—some male figure who was very powerful and very dominating and who Tony felt was something of a savior for him.

During the month I was there, Barbara was very much trying to promote Tony's poetry. She was taking his poems around to people like Robert Graves. I think Tony really hated her touting his poetry like that. I mean, he would become absolutely numb when she would start to talk about it. He would clam up and *she*—she would run and bring out more poems! I felt that Barbara was finally living her own life *through* Tony, that he was a tool, really, for all her talents and artistry. Everything was now totally focused on Tony, who was like a robot who was moving around and doing what she would tell him to do and even creating *because* of her.


**Poem by Antony Baekeland Written in Broadmoor Special Hospital, 1978**

> I see a star
> Yet it is a day
>
> The hands of my mother
> Make it grow

It is a black star
Set against white sky
How gentle that star

Now that she weaves devils
Claws together to make
A basket


ELIZABETH BLOW
On the one hand, he absolutely hated her, and on the other hand,
he absolutely adored her—there was nobody in the world that would
ever be like her. I remember one night in Mallorca when she was
having some guests for dinner on the terrace, on this rock out there,
Tony said, "You know, when I look at my mother I see almost a halo
or a sort of radiance around her." And Barbara *was* glowing, truly—
she felt that Sam Green, who she'd just met on this yacht, was "it,"
that Sam was the perfect man for her. She was totally starry-eyed—
he was fun, kind, loving, affectionate, marvelous—everything that
Brooks was *not*, in other words. She said he was just the most marvelous person to be with that she'd ever been with in her life.


## Letter from Sam Green to Barbara and Antony Baekeland, August 26, 1969

Athens

Dear Barbara and Tony,
When I returned to Athens, I was astonished to receive such a
cascade of mail from you.
     My latest cruise was unrelieved bliss. Cecile de Rothschild
had chartered a two-masted sailboat for her four guests. Her
brother Alain's two-master, the *Ziata*, accompanied us all the
way and is the most beautiful yacht I, or apparently anyone else,
has ever seen. We explored the Turkish coast with its extrava-
gantly grand ruins. We saw your friend Rosie Rodd Baldwin's
boat passing us once, but I never did get to meet her. We ended
up at horrible Kos, where I visited the ruins again. But it was
filled with tourists, and the birds had fled to haunt a more deserted place—there was no magic there without you, Barbara.

I remember with warmth our few days together at Miramar. I bolted my door that night not to keep the danger out but in. What the hell, let's do it again!

Garbo is coming to stay with Cecile and I am off to stay with Cecil Beaton in London.

Flowers & love,
Sam

P.S. Tony, write a letter to your grandmother thanking her for the bathrobe—tacky as it is.


## Letter from Antony Baekeland to Nina Daly, September 5, 1969

Miramar
Valldemosa
Mallorca

Dear Nini—

Thank you for the lovely kimono—fits perfectly and I needed one so badly. I am quite well. Jinty Money-Coutts & family come today for a picnic so I write this in haste. Maria sends love. What is the process of illumination? I don't understand Dad—except that if he's behaving badly it must mean that he feels badly.

Lots of love, dearest Nini.
T.


## Letter from Antony Baekeland to Sam Green, September 5, 1969

Miramar
Valldemosa
Mallorca

Dear Sam—

It was extremely nice to hear from you: we had rather begun to think that the pernicious country house system had entirely swallowed you up, that you had vanished forever beyond the green baize door; we feared, in fact, that the port and stilton had entirely done you in. You can imagine how relieved we were to hear from you that you were safe even in the lair of the dragon ladies and their gentlemen.

A limpid day: the green explosions of the pines betray their insubstantiality in this clear autumn light. I wrote my grandmother. Maria sends her best and says when are you coming back. She hated the last guests we had but quite possibly because they stayed for almost a month and went away without leaving her anything. It was clump-clump-clump-noisy-feet-and-banging-doors sort of guests.

Have you ever had a garlic sandwich? They're terribly good. I just had one for lunch. You take about ten cloves of garlic, some of that funny herb that grows in the garden, some cheese, and a raw onion and make this monstrous sandwich that's incredibly good.

My birthday passed uneventfully except for this wonderful typewriter which makes writing much easier. I love cold print and Mummy was adorable to give me such a lovely present in her situation. Wrote my father about the conversation we had, reminded him that he had promised to give her some money but no word back. I never thought life would turn out to be so peculiar.

Tony

## Letter from Barbara Baekeland to Sam Green, September 28, 1969

% Mme. Woodward de Croisset
Paris

Darling Sam—
A few minutes before midnight—my birthday. How old? None of your business!

Marie Harriman died so my birthday luncheon with friends at the Hôtel Lambert has been called off. Ethel has asked some people here among whom will be Teenie Matisse Duchamp. I'll give her your love.

If only I could have some peace and forget my incessant worries—financial mostly—for a few days! Tried selling some jewelry but the price I was offered was ridiculous.

Ethel keeps reminding me how old I am (and she exaggerates, too), otherwise I would seriously consider another, the oldest, profession!

Am building stables in Mallorca and paying for them on a monthly basis—they will be perfect & replete with 2 horses. I am also going to build servants' quarters in the old olive press. The place is too big for one person—maybe you'd like to share it with me? If you don't want to, I'm going to look for someone else—someone *RICH*.

Very peaceful here at Ethel's. Mr. Wuss is in bliss—doesn't seem to miss Miramar & is being very well fed. He's a dear fellow but not enough of a companion for me.

Tony is now lost—crawling through the tunnels of London low-life, I suspect.

You said nothing about your plans or where you might be. Am told touring the Dordogne with friend Cecil Beaton so will send this on to him. I don't know what you're up to, Sam, but I want you to know that I don't like all of it—I would like to know where to reach you. I'd like you to inquire about the Cadogan Square flat in London. Looks as though I might be able to settle things next month and Tony was mad about it.

> Love,
> Barbara

### ETHEL WOODWARD DE CROISSET

Now I'll tell you about the time I tried to help Barbara in all her problems. She wanted to make some money, to keep up the life she had had, so she conceived this idea of having three apartments— New York, Paris, and London. She would rent two and stay in one, you know, and move around between the rentals. The little penthouse apartment in New York, which she rented for a very small price—five hundred or something—she would sublet with her furniture for, say, fifteen hundred a month. And she wanted to do the same thing in Paris. And it was Sam Green's idea that she also get this apartment in London on Cadogan Square that belonged to some friends of his. But it was just the end of the lease that she would be buying—for something like ten thousand dollars. This was before this great inflation had started—or this great depression—I can't remember which. She was going to furnish it and then rent it out for a very high price. Well, it seemed to me absolutely insane.

First of all, she should never have had to make money. She had every right to be supported by her husband. Brooks wasn't giving her money regularly, and that's where I tried to help—I called up his financial people and I said, "You must send money regularly to Barbara—if she has a regular amount, it will help her be more stable."

And when that didn't work, I said to Barbara, "I'm going to give you ten thousand dollars, and with this money you're going to pay what you owe your divorce lawyer in New York so he can fix everything up for you, because lawyers like to be paid. And just forget about this London thing because it's ridiculous." And I explained to her very carefully how putting money into the London operation would bring her *nothing*.

You'd think she would have seen that this would have solved all her problems—as easy as that. Not at all! She did exactly what she wanted to do—she went and got the Cadogan Square apartment. And she gave *me* as a financial reference. Can you imagine! I received a letter from the owners saying would I guarantee that she had a great deal of money. I mean, *I* was paying for this folly! I folded up the letter and sent it to Barbara with a note saying, "You can write these people and tell them I'm *dead* because I certainly will not guarantee that you're solvent." So you'd think she would have been a little embarrassed about it, wouldn't you? *Not* at all. When she arrived to stay with me in Paris, she treated it all as a little joke. She said, "How *funny* you are, Ethel! What a *card* you are! Imagine my writing to them that you died!" This extraordinary bravura—you know, right to the last *drop*. And so she went ahead with this project which, had she not been assassinated, I don't know *how* it would have ended.

## Letter from Barbara Baekeland to Sam Green, November 27, 1969

% Michael Edwards
London, W. 1

Sam darling—
Got here last night. I spoke to my mother this morning who is

putting an ad in the newspaper so maybe I'll be able to rent my flat in New York without going back.

The terrible Brooks cut my allowance by a third this month. Received the news while at Ethel's. She was so furious she offered to lend me $15,000—I accepted $10,000 so when I come back to do battle, I will be, at least, armed. This, after I sent him a wire on our anniversary which started "Once upon a time." Anyway, isn't Ethel *adorable*—I am so touched by my friends, I just can't tell you.

*Also*, & this will amuse you—Ethel got invited for the first time in 25 years by Cecile de Rothschild to the country. She & Cecile had a dinner alone together which aside from the soup & fish consisted of a barrage of questions, inquiries, speculations and so on about *me*! Cecile to Ethel: "I hear that Sam is having an affair with *that woman*!"

Am looking at the Cadogan Square flat again today.

Lots of love,
Barbara

## Telegram from Barbara Baekeland to Sam Green, February 13, 1970

I SEND YOU A B-B-B-BABY FOR A VALENTINE MY LOVE

BARBARA

## ELIZABETH BLOW

Well, first it was *his* baby—she was going to have Sam Green's baby. And she was in her forties, her *late* forties! And this was, okay, possible, but not probable, and I was really concerned about her. Then she switched it from Sam's baby to just *a* baby. By—by *God*. I am dead serious. If you interpreted her rather garbled, marvelously excited conversation, this was really the Immaculate Conception all over again. Well, then I got really seriously alarmed.

## Letter from Barbara Baekeland to Sam Green, March 21, 1970

London, W. 1

Dear Sam—

Am reading Kenneth Clark—came across an interesting definition of Moses' burning bush in a book on Fairford Church and
its windows. It appears the bush was meant to contain the Divine Presence & burned without being consumed. It was meant
to have contained the body of the Blessed Virgin when she became the Mother of the Son of God. But there's a big difference
between bush fires & such, is there not, Sam?

Barbara

### SYLVIE BAEKELAND SKIRA

She pretended to Brooks first that she was pregnant by Sam Green
and then that this was an Immaculate Conception or whatever it was,
so that gives you a vague idea of the romanticism, if you want to call
it that. I call it sheer looniness. She didn't have solidity anymore,
because Brooks had always been her anchor. This was why he was so
worried about her when he left, because he knew he was the only
one who could keep her out of trouble.

### ELIZABETH BLOW

She went off someplace—out of town or out of the country, I can't
remember—and I happened to be seeing Nini and I wondered if *she*
knew about the baby and I thought maybe we should talk about this
thing, but then I thought, *Should* we? Anyway, one day Barbara simply stopped talking about it herself. She was busy again, decorating
the new apartment in London.

## Letter from Barbara Baekeland to Sam Green, May 4, 1970

81 Cadogan Square
London, S.W. 1

Darling Sam—

So good speaking to you last night. You are my confidence man
(I mean you give it to me). Anyway I have bought the flat and
am in the process of decorating it. I have made marvelous pro-

gress—all electricity put in order, couches designed by me & being made, (very pretty) pictures hung, curtains cleaned, dining-room table painted in black lacquer (am off now to pay for it). Tomorrow will buy plants & a tree for upstairs.

And tomorrow my beautiful steel bed comes! Right now I am sitting on my mattress surrounded by a welter of papers—notes to myself, chores to do, ideas, etc. On my mattress is a most lovely coverlet made by my grandmother which gives me the most extraordinary comforting sensation—as if her hand were on my cheek. Divine wallpaper for bedroom.

I've knocked down the partition between the upstairs rooms and it looks smashing. Am taking down the balustrade as well— I have a pretty china planter to replace horrid newel post—and am using my two 19th cent. steel park benches as barriers.

From time to time—at 4 A.M. or 5—I wonder *why* I am involved in all these banalities and I dearly wish for the peace and comtemplation necessary to go on with my novel.

To listen to the sound of rain would be such a joy . . . an awareness of time—one's own, that is. One thing I have thought is that the more complex the synapses in the brain, the further the curve to infinity—for didn't Einstein say that infinity was comprised of many small dots that became through denseness a kind of exponential curve?

I wish I could see you. You are one of the halves of my reality, the other being Tony. I miss you both, and all my friends, and I cannot *stand* the lower-middle-class Englishman—the shopkeeper with his servility, his inefficiency, and appalling snobbishness. I really dislike the English as much as I can anyone & I'm sure my Celtic blood knows why.

I just hope I haven't made a horrible mistake with this flat. Would so much rather be working on Miramar and waiting for you to (maybe!) show up—I'm such a hopeless optimist.

In Mallorca there kept resounding in my mind a refrain which was "And this is the way the world ends"—only it wasn't—it doesn't. . . .

Here's a kiss for the middle of your mind—from mine.

Love,
Barbara

P.S. Thank you, Sam, for all your encouragement—urgings— to take this flat. It will be a successful venture—I feel it!

## Letter from Antony Baekeland to Sam Green, May 15, 1970

> Miramar
> Valldemosa
> Mallorca

Dear Sam—

Happy birthday—Mummy wrote me you had one around this time. It's beautiful here but we are having a bit of trouble with a whole chain of furious masons who have not been paid by the horse person who claims not to have been paid by Mummy who has paid him she says.

The other day when I was fishing I had a look for some earrings Mummy tossed away when she was at the next farm. I couldn't find them as I had really no idea of where she was sitting—"under some tree," she said. So I've asked her to send me a map because it's a shame to lose the beautiful ones you gave her.

Told Maria I'm writing you and she sends salutations. I'm working quite hard on some clay I got in Palma and making small animals and things.

> Love,
> Tony

## Letter from Barbara Baekeland to Sam Green, June 20, 1970

> Miramar
> Valldemosa
> Mallorca

Darling Sam—

Could I ask you to do me two favors. I was told about a Pekingese lady by Mrs. Turner, the service tenant at 81 Cadogan Square. I called her and she has a little red bitch that I dearly want. If you could have a look at the parents to estimate size & quality I'd be "ever so grateful" (Eliza speaking!). She will bring the merchandise to you—just call. . . .

Also, Tony has a hankering to give some Scottish bagpipes to a Spanish friend. It seems they used to play them around here. They can be found at a shop at 14A Clifford St.

> Love—
> Barbara

*Above*: Paris, 1962. Left to right: William Saroyan, unidentified woman, Brooks Baekeland, unidentified man, James Jones, Gloria Jones , and Barbara Baekeland

*Below*: Ansedonia, 1960: Barbara and Brooks in the foreground

*Right:* Tony with Lorna Moffat in Cadaqués

*Below:* Tony on the beach in Cadaqués

KAREN RADKAI

KAREN RADKAI

BERNARD PFRIEM

*Above*: Brooks Baekeland describing his position to Vilcabamba expedition support plane by walkie-talkie held by Dartmouth student Peter Lake, 1963

*Left*: Dining on board Emily Staempfli's yacht in the Aegean, June 1969. Seated from left to right: Barbara Baekeland, Peter Harnden (partially obscured), Emily Staempfli, Sam Green, and Missy Harnden

*Below*: Sam Green and Barbara swimming off the yacht

Tony and Barbara in the New York penthouse, 1971

Barbara "in tragic decline," as Brooks Baekeland wrote on the back of the photograph

BROOKS BAEKELAND

CADOGAN 81 SQUARE

The top-floor apartment in London where Barbara was murdered; broken window reflects its now-derelict condition

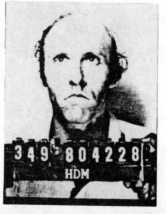

*Above:* Self-portrait by Tony, Broadmoor, August 30, 1978

*Right top:* Mug shot of Tony, Rikers Island, New York, July 27, 1980

*Right bottom:* The entrance to Brixton Prison, London

*Below:* John Murray, a friend of Tony's at Rikers Island

Cornelia Middlebrook
Baekeland Hallowell,
Cape Cod, c. 1956

Nina Fraser Daly,
New York, 1983,
with a portrait of
Barbara in the
background

Sylvie Baekeland Skira,
Paris, 1976

Brooks Baekeland,
India, 1984

P.S. Baborca the Arab stallion is for sale and I long to buy him but when I finished doing the flat in London I had only $229.00 to last me until July 1st—*just* under the wire! But I will only owe one more $1,000 on the flat and will be able to pay back Muriel Murphy and my mother in September—Emily Staempfli next, and then Ethel! How large is *your* begging bowl?

## Letter from Sam Green to Barbara Baekeland, June 25, 1970

> % Cecil Beaton
> Salisbury
> England

Dear Barbara,

Talk about bliss! Getting out of N.Y. has been the best thing that's ever happened to me. You'll find me a new and charminger person. You may find that as early as a week from now.

I arrived on Sunday to find Cecil in the hospital. So I had several days to fill up on my own.

I'll be arriving at Palma on Fri. or Saturday. I'm looking forward to seeing you and Tony and Miramar. I will be there with a bagpipe but *not* with a Peke. You'll have to get your own horrid defective thing. Besides, I know *nothing* about dogs and would botch the job.

> Love,
> Sam

## Letter from Barbara Baekeland to Sam Green, July 28, 1970

> Miramar
> Valldemosa
> Mallorca

Dear Sam—

I'm sorry we missed each other and couldn't say goodbye. Ethel, who had been having a rather miserable time (all my fault), wanted to see the convent and I simply couldn't say no. It was interesting and I lost track of time. Anyway I didn't think you would leave for another few days and can't imagine how I could have not seen you between the house and the beach. Anyway in going to the beach we did see Tony but didn't stop. He appeared to have had an accident and was trying to straighten out a dented fender but the car belongs to Hugo Money-Coutts and not only does Tony not have permission to use it but he has no license. If he should have another accident I'm afraid it would be hell on him. He might be locked up for years. If you have any influence with him you might point out to him the danger of using other people's property without proper sanction and of breaking laws!

He has been asked to appear before a tribunal on August 22—on a contraband charge. I am hoping Hugo will be here—or Tony's father—but I think Hugo would be better. Then I pray Tony will get away from here. I am very worried about him and wish you could come back for just a few days so I could talk with you about him.

I regret having dragged you into all of this—or was it the other way around? Anyway you have all my love for whatever it's worth. It seems to pull disorder, tears, and early sorrow in its wake. Sometimes I feel that I relinquish my better judgment to fate—or God or something. Anyway I don't seem to be in control and maybe that's for the best. I still can't find my green earrings which you asked me not to lose and this upsets me almost more than anything—I've looked everywhere. They are either at the farm next door or in an olive grove. Dear Sam, we have had such a strange and lovely time.

Barbara

P.S. Tony gave away his microscope and typewriter! And what happened to all his money? He must have given it away, too. And should he be encouraged in this? I know he is an adult but I can't keep bailing him out as I simply haven't got the wherewithal to do so—the boy he gave it to can't even type!

## ALASTAIR REID

In the summer of 1970 I ran into Barbara in the main street in Palma. I was living way up in the mountains, in a village called Gallilea. I hadn't seen her since 1962 when she hailed me in the street in Málaga—she and Brooks and Tony were visiting Ethel de Croisset—and that was the last time I saw them en famille. The next thing is that I heard from Ethel's mother, Elsie Woodward, that Brooks and Barbara were breaking up. That day in Palma Barbara told me the whole painful thing about Brooks dumping her. A few days later I went up to see her. Tony wasn't there, but later on they both drove over to Gallilea to visit me, we had lunch at the pension, and from that point on, Tony sent me poems that he'd written. What I used to do was very patiently point out to him technical things and give him books to read.

But then suddenly he began to change and write prose—little pieces of prose about a page long. Some of them were really quite eerie, as though they were fragments of some enormous thing, but I couldn't imagine what or where they were coming from, because his poems had been more or less bucolic and what you might expect as exercises, and suddenly I realized there was a very savage landscape inside Tony.

I began to see him as rather cruelly victimized by circumstance and I realized then that the Brooks/Barbara thing had left him . . . had just left him, abandoned him, *stopped* him.

Of course, Barbara's version of how things were was always very positive. She was a great, you know, smoother-over.

That summer I got pulled back in. But it's a couple of summers later when I saw that what I had thought was a merely understandably disturbed context was *infinitely* more than that—it was all coming apart then, it was all really unhinging itself. I mean, you were looking into something terrible.

## Letter from Barbara Baekeland to Sam Green, August 22, 1970

> Miramar
> Valldemosa
> Mallorca

Dear Sam—

Tony received a fine today of 120 pesetas and an admonition. I did not go to Palma with him but our horseman did. Brooks Baekeland never showed up—nor does he seem to be concerned about Tony's troubles. Anyway I thought *you* might be.

I am very tired, having in the last month risen at 5 a.m. fed & watered the horse, cleaned the stable, weeded the garden, watered the plants, fed the cat, cooked the breakfast, washed up, planned the meals, driven 20 miles to shop for food, driven back 20 miles to cook lunch, read poetry, listened to music, washed up, washed the kitchen floor, swept the house, cleaned the bathroom, made my bed, looked at the view, cut flowers, arranged same, wrote letters, paid bills, kept accounts, walked down 1,000 ft. to the sea & back for a quick swim, prepared cocktails, cooked dinner, dressed & looked beautiful for dinner, made conversation, been entertaining, left the dishes, and God alone knows what I did when I finally got to bed! Anyway I'm tired and am off (I hope next week) to Cadaqués for a few days and from there to Ethel's in Málaga (while work here is in progress) for a rest.

Hope you're having a good time—Ethel says she heard it's going to be a very boring cruise.

This is my last letter to you!

Love,
Barbara


ETHEL WOODWARD DE CROISSET
I had been to stay with her in this terrible house on the cliff the month before. I'd bumped into Mimi Cohane, Jack's wife before Heather, in Cadaqués, and she said, "You must go to see Barbara in Mallorca." Mimi, you see, had just been there, and said that things were going very badly. She told me how she'd been walking around the property with Barbara and the first thing she saw in the garden was a chair, a broken chair, and she said, "What's that chair doing in the flower beds?" And Barbara said, "Oh, pay no attention to it. Tony put it there." Pay no attention! And then they did a tour of the house, and on the steps going down to the cellar there was a typewriter—smashed, absolutely mangled! And Mimi said, "My God, what's that?" "Oh, pay no attention to it. Tony was upset about something and threw it down there."

So I went to see her and when I arrived, Michael Alexander was also there and the table was set for this lovely evening on the terrace. But in the middle of dinner Barbara had a fit of madness over something, and she insulted us—I mean, like a madwoman! You know, some general insult: "You goddam fucking fools!" You know, what *mad* people say—I saw a person in the bus once screaming like that. Barbara went howling out into the garden, in the moonlight. And we tried to reason with her to come back in the house and go to sleep. I tried every way—being very severe—you know, all the things you *try*. And after that, exhausted, I gave up, and she stayed out in the field. As I went off to sleep, I could hear Michael Alexander talking with Tony, who was terribly upset by all this, saying, you know, "Tony, *don't* feel responsible."

The next morning I was cleaning up—there was a mess of dirty dishes, thirty, forty dishes—and Barbara came sashaying in and said, "*You* don't have to do that." And I decided not to speak to her—I was going to give her a little bit of *my* temper. So I kept a stony silence. She just ignored this sort of thing, you know—*airily*. I think I relented after some time. We never mentioned the drama of the night before. You know, you just never mentioned these terrible things.

## Letter from Barbara Baekeland to Sam Green, August 24, 1970

Miramar
Valldemosa
Mallorca

Sam—
Tony says you told him I was the most impossible woman you'd ever met. I don't think it's correct to talk to a young man about his mother this way!

Barbara

# 11

# SNAPPING BACK

In 1979 Tony Baekeland was gradually taken off his medication until he reached a stage where he seemed to the authorities "quite rational, quite reasonable." Dr. Maguire was still resistant to the idea of his being released without the assurance of regular follow-up care. When Tony himself learned what the costs involved might amount to— $50,000 and up per year for a private facility—he told Dr. Maguire, "No way—I don't have it."

An officer from the American Embassy in London continued to monitor Tony. A State Department document concerning a visit on March 20 notes that "Baekeland appeared to be in good health and spirits." Another document, dated June 8, states that "Baekeland says he has been told by his doctor that he can expect to be released in a few months." But another document reporting on a visit five months later, on November 13, mentions that Tony Baekeland could count on being released only sometime "in the near future."

## Postcard from Antony Baekeland to Sam Green, September 9, 1970

Dear Sam—
On the plane to Mallorca. Been visiting with my father who is
now living in Brittany—a nice change. I miss you and think of
you often. Perhaps we'll see each other soon? Much love from
your screwy friend.

Tony

P.S. How is my sainted mother?


## Letter from Barbara Baekeland to Sam Green, September 18, 1970

*France*
Transatlantique
French Line

Darling Sam—
I've just had a fabulous morning, working from 6:00 to 1:15
finishing my novel and roaring with laughter—some of it's very
funny. You'd better check it out before I decide whether or not
to publish it. There isn't a word in it which isn't true.

This ship is first class. I've eaten $1,000 worth of caviar since
I boarded and all the wine is free!

Have spoken to no one except my muse—very funny fellow.

Tonight will have cocktails with an old friend who is
aboard—Valentina. *Shall* we speak about Garbo? And shall I
drop *your* name?

Having a lovely time refusing to be picked up. Am knocking
them dead with my new clothes! I look great in them. Please
charge some for yourself—pay later.

Please drop Tony a line in Mallorca. He loves you and I
know would be cheered to hear from you.

My plans are, as usual, vague—dependent on the book, the
divorce, the state of my finances, etc., etc. Wish I could have
someone's help with the latter. My income is quite handsome as
I pay no taxes, and will go up in April when the London flat is

rented again. But no matter how much comes in, it all seems to go out. If I make money on the book I'll be quite well off.

You have already read the Spring and Winter sections but not Autumn and Summer. Summer is a kind of summation and it is that section in which you play a role. I would like to know if you think the treatment is too candid and, if it were to be accepted by a publisher, if you would have any objections. I prefer not to disguise or change the names. I am, as you can understand, anxious to have your clearance, as once I am assured that neither Tony nor you have any objections to the frank treatment, I can go ahead with the necessary steps and submit the manuscript for publication. Meanwhile here it all is. Please let me know what you think. I can't tell if the structure is sound and if the four sections belong organically together. Would appreciate any suggestions.

Love,
Barbara

### Letter from Sam Green to Barbara Baekeland, October 15, 1970

Fire Island, New York

Dear Barbara,

I am sorry that it has taken me so long to write this letter. Of course you have my permission and best wishes in having the book published—if you can find a publisher, that is. I very much doubt that you will be able to, as—content aside—it is very unfinished. My impression is that it is not only a first draft, but that you didn't even reread it after it was typed—there were so many imperfections and redundancies on almost every page.

As to the content: I cannot think why anyone would be interested in the self-indulgent rampagings of a mad international wastrel. I am referring to the last portion of the book, you must realize, as the first segments are very lovely, interesting, beautifully written, and polished. There is such a deterioration in style between the first part and the last that it is difficult to believe the same person had a hand in both. While in the beginning the author has some objectivity, as well as considerable insight into the personalities and needs of the other characters, in the second there are nothing but obtuse value judgments: "she is a dear"—now *that* tells the reader a lot! These comments are about as deeply as you go into understanding anyone else.

The principal theme seems to be the persecution of a woman by Spanish authorities because she, as a *guest* in their country, refuses to comply with the rules which govern their way of life. She rampages around Spain—and the rest of the world—demanding attention, or whatever else is her immediate need, from everyone she encounters. Not only does she demand SERVICE—but QUALITY service as well. And what does she give in return? Only money. Grudgingly, and not very much, at that.

Perhaps if the heroine were a tiny bit servile herself—at least to the needs and concerns of those with whom she has some emotional or blood ties—it might occur to her that people are here to help each *other* instead of simply to make demands.

Perhaps you should rewrite the book as a journal—for that's exactly what it is, a jotting down of observations—without any descriptions (most of which are of concern only to you—in fact, the only concern you have for the reader is the odd "we shall see" interjected between the ramblings), and try to discover why your life in the last years has been so agonized. And if you feel that you are still right and everyone else is wrong, then continue on your way.

This is a tough letter because you asked for my opinion and I'm giving it to you straight—without any indulging of your fantasies. I hope you know that I am concerned and that that is why I have made the effort.

Love,
Sam

## ANATOLE BROYARD

She was in my writing class at the New School for a while and she was the only *grande dame* we had—it was as if Mrs. Vanderbilt had walked into class. She had some talent but she didn't work hard enough—she just wanted to fling the thing out into the world and be a success.

STEVEN M. L. ARONSON

Somebody had told Barbara I was that season's bright young man in publishing, so she tantalized me with her novel the very first time we met. I was introduced to her in her own living room, by a friend we had in common who had brought me to one of those parties she was always giving.

The apartment was sort of junglelike. I remember the living room—the way it was lit was interesting, and it seemed exotic and romantic, with all those terraces looking out over everything. And I remember my first sight of Barbara: surrounded, attended, her tawny head thrown back. What a magnet. She was so generous with friends, so bold with total strangers (me!), you would not easily have guessed she was a woman at the end of her rope.

She became a friend from that evening. And later, when he came back from Mallorca, she worked Tony into my life. The three of us spent several cozy, uneventful weekends in a cottage she was renting on the beach in East Hampton—until the Sunday morning she burst exuberantly into my room with the *Times*, handed me several layers of it, then sprawled across my bed to read the magazine section. A few minutes later I looked up and saw Tony standing in the doorway. I'll never forget his face, contorted as it was into an incomprehensible expression of rage. Barbara had told me nothing of his history, but when I read her book I understood what kind of jealousy it was that caused that rage.

A few weeks later she came to a dinner at my place in town in a black evening dress made of hundreds of little feathers. For weeks after that, they kept turning up—behind sofas, under chairs. I sent one to her with a note. "I laughed and laughed," she wrote back, "and will keep the feather forever." From then on, in almost every letter she wrote me from the mad gypsy life that she was leading, she enclosed a feather from that dress—so many feathers, it must have been plucked clean.

In a letter postmarked London, November 17, 1972, the day she was killed, she said, "Tony somewhat improved—oh! but it's heavy!" She was inviting me to spend Christmas with the two of them on Cadogan Square. Folded into the envelope was the accustomed feather: "Would that it were from the goose that laid the golden egg! What can I do with feathers except fly?" By the time that feather had crossed the Atlantic, she was six days dead. The last lovely flutter of her strong wings.

Had she lived, Barbara would be a woman completely beyond my imagining now. In fact, the night I read her novel I saw that in some ways she already was.

It was part fantasy, part confession, part paean to profane love. Of course, Barbara—great, self-appreciating personality that she was—must also have written it with the awareness of contributing to her own legend.

What I remember best is the section titled "Summer," in which the heroine and her son and a male friend set sail on some tainted sea. First the heroine seduces her own son, then she seduces the friend. Later she comes upon her son and the friend making love. "Leave him alone! My son is not a homosexual!" she screams. "He functions very well sexually with *me*. I'm not going to let a little pansy like you ruin everything I've accomplished." It was wild. It was garbled. But despite its obviously paranoid content, the book had a power, a certain unnerving power.

### ELLEN SCHWAM
You couldn't tell with Barbara—the lines between reality and her imagination seemed sort of shadowy, or suitably moveable, at will. We were in the same writing class. I remember she claimed to be the heroine of one of James Jones's novels.

### FRANCINE DU PLESSIX GRAY
Barbara's novel was absolutely terrible. I remember her coming to stay with us in Connecticut and giving us two or three chapters to read. We told her it needed a lot of work, and she dug into us in *such* a way! She started attacking *my* writing. I'd just published "Governess" in *The New Yorker*, which later became the first chapter of my novel *Lovers and Tyrants*. She said, "*That* was a piece of shit. How do you dare to criticize *me*? Jim Jones thinks my work has genius."

## Letter from James Jones to Barbara Baekeland, Undated

10, quai d'Orléans
Paris IV°

Dear Barbara,
I am returning your story manuscript with this letter. I can only say that I have to treat it as a professional writer or not at all, and

my feeling about the story is that it simply does not come off. I find the style much too heated and fervid for the material; and I don't think the resolution is believable, given the characters.

With regard to the novel which you mentioned you have finished, I can't of course say anything about that now. However, if the style is at all similar to this story, or fragment, I would cool the style considerably. I would of course be glad to read it for Delacorte Press, but if it follows in the vein of this piece you sent me, I can almost guarantee you that the editors there would not take it.

Gloria will be writing to you about Tony and all the other things. Always all personal best.

Sincerely yours,
James Jones

ELIZABETH WEICKER FONDARAS
One weekend in East Hampton Barbara came to dinner and afterwards we settled around the fire in the big winter living room and she read her manuscript aloud to us. She was so excited and enthusiastic about it. I remember extravagant images—the striped walls were coming in on her, or she would be floating down to the sea with rocks rolling all around her. It was like a dream. They were the strange ravings of a person in a crisis—you could see trouble and despair.

DR. E. HUGH LUCKEY
I was a houseguest of Liz Fondaras's the Saturday night Barbara Baekeland decided to entertain us by reading from her novel. I sat there bored stiff for about an hour of recitation. I would have probably gone to bed if it hadn't been for Liz.

John Sargent, who's the chairman of the board of Doubleday, was also present. Liz had set that up, you know. She's the great matchmaker of all time—she tries to help all of her friends.

Well, I knew the game. When Barbara Baekeland took that manuscript out, I knew what was going on—she wasn't interested in how *I* would like it, she was interested in how John Sargent was going to like it. I remember the look on his face as it was being read.

JOHN SARGENT
It went on and on and on. We couldn't get it to stop.

After she was killed, I used to send Tony things in the loony bin. Not books—they wouldn't let me send books. I could only send non-controversial items, such as shirts and clothing. He wrote me little thank-you notes.

## Letter from Antony Baekeland to James Reeve, November 20, 1979

Broadmoor

Dear James,
I think I will start writing seriously when I get out of here and get myself settled, whenever and wherever that is. I have the material for several interesting books, I think, and I will enjoy working on them.

I am afraid I am very disillusioned with most of the people here: now that I am clear in myself I no longer see them as amusing characters but as the moral derelicts which they really are—too stupid to learn from their pain and unhappiness, they will continue forever to batter their heads against the wall, ignoring the door.

I long for some interesting talk and company: the routine here is very dull and always the same old chitchat. Even the most beguiling of companions begin to bore one after so many years: I am not talking about true friends. It seems ridiculous to me that I must undergo more of this psychiatric mumbo jumbo in the U.S. My troubles were purely spiritual and stemmed from a mistake I made a long time ago; it wasn't a mistake at all, as I now realize: much good will come from it. But I do feel that the ideas held by the "doctors" about the mind, soul, and body are primitive, ugly, and pathetic in the extreme.

Mind you, all this world of doctors, businessmen, workers, actors, etc., are just robots controlled by the Mind of a very few Ladies and Gentlemen. I don't think of the mass of people as degraded or pathetic or anything like that, it is just that they are not "real" people and although they control my life at the moment, *grace à la Reine*, I don't let them bother me nor do I take them at all seriously.

One of my books will be about the human termite-colony as it really is, I think. Or perhaps I won't write it at all—I shall have to wait and see. Anyway, James, my fondest wishes and you must please give my regards to your mother.

Love always,
Tony

## Letter from Antony Baekeland to Barbara Baekeland, January 8, 1971

Miramar
Valldemosa
Mallorca

Dearest Mum,

Telegram from you four days ago inviting me to New York. I replied today saying that I will come if necessary but would rather not as I am really happy here. If sometimes I write despairing letters it is only that I am disappointed and frustrated at not being able to come more quickly: the other night playing chess I had such a clear vision of my blinding greed to win, to cheat with myself, and saw the calm detachment of my higher self arranging it (the game, like a droplet of quicksilver) so that I could only make the right move if I felt the right feeling. In regard to what you say about intellects I doubt if I could find many of such a caliber and quality as those of Maria and Sebastian, my family here at Miramar. And anyway, intellection is exactly that which I am trying to get away from: these relative truths and falsehoods of our time, of all times, of art, of science, and of literature have no value for me; for the present at least, they are a poison to me and to my pure mind. Perhaps one day soon I will be able and willing to venture into that bog, but by then, perhaps, things will have ceased to be relative to one another and will become relative to One. I don't think you realize how closely I live with my family here.

What you say about Physical Love is no doubt true, but as our bodies are reflections of our souls' desire towards life, everything in me impels me to touch and love another person. Anyway I know the difference between love and lust so I suppose I mustn't worry. Don't get too caught up with visions of the past or other things like this. I have been having this very strongly on and off for two years and I find it imposes a great strain on the mind (intellect, that stray sheep) which tries in its futile way to fit together the apparent parts of a fluid that extends through itself in all directions. All the years you scolded me for smoking I was only taking it for one reason. I have never experienced what you call "mere pleasure," what Shakespeare, I believe, called "a waste of folly," lust. I have experienced it but could not call it pleasure but only the hopeless groan of agony of abandoned oceans.

I am glad you saw what I told you last year about suicide is true. Everything we have told in love is true.

Tony

### Miwa Svinka-Zielinski

Barbara invited me for dinner in New York to celebrate because Tony had come home from Spain, and she also invited Teenie Duchamp and Elizabeth Fondaras. And during this dinner, Barbara had some words with Tony, she told him some remark which was not pleasant, so Tony left the table, and we finished dinner. And then he came and took ice from the ice bucket and put it down her dress. She started to laugh. Then he went to his room and a few minutes later came out undressed—totally. He was naked.

### Elizabeth Weicker Fondaras

He just streaked from one end of the apartment to the other—I think it was a diagonal run he made. He must have just wanted to get his mother's attention. Barbara thought it was sort of funny.

### Brendan Gill

I didn't have much of an impression of Tony; he was always very dim to me, almost nonspeaking. I don't think I exchanged ten words with him. He was just like a walk-on, a zombie.

### Eleanor Ward

To me Tony was a complete zero. Now whether this was because his mother was there . . . I never saw him when she waan't around, so what he was like without her I don't know—he might have been a very different person.

## KATHARINE GARDNER COLEMAN
He was really quite peculiar, but you know, we'd seen so many disturbed young people in the sixties. *They* snapped back, though.

## SARA DUFFY CHERMAYEFF
He showed up at my house one afternoon—I hadn't seen him for, like, nine years—and he read me a story he had written and I will just never forget it. Because *he* was the artist. *Not* Brooks. *Not* Barbara. *Tony* was.

It was a story about one day in his life in Barbara's penthouse. He told the day in that place and he described everything about it—the little room next to the hall where you came in, that rotunda with the marble floor that Barbara had fixed up with the candelabra, her bed with the leopard skin. He described her frying liver in a pan for lunch and how at the end of the day she went out to dinner, all dressed up—he described her furs and everything—and the last line of the story, after she went out the door, said, "And I felt no bigger than a lima bean."

## ELIZABETH BLOW
That spring Barbara put him in the National Academy School of Fine Arts on Fifth Avenue way up in the nineties. She invited me for dinner and the first thing she said to him was, "I want you to show Betty your drawings from class." He almost froze, he refused to move, and so *she* went and got this large portfolio and started showing them to me. The drawings were very strange—there were figures of people who didn't look like people. I mean, there was a sort of nonhuman quality to these drawings, and there was also a kind of infantile quality. As she laid them out, she would say, "Aren't they marvelous!" and so forth. And I looked up at Tony and he was just . . . stone, he was turned to stone.

## SYLVIA LOCHAN
I was the registrar at the National Academy, and a couple of the students came down to my office. They were a little disturbed because Antony Baekeland wasn't responding to anybody or anything, he just seemed to be in a world of his own. They said the class was

painting from a still life—flowers and fruit I think it was—and that *his* canvas had figures on it with blood dripping down the side.

I went up to the classroom and I went over to talk to him. He was seated and I kind of bent down next to him and I said, "That's very interesting." He didn't respond to my being there, my presence—he was staring off into space. And then he turned around and I saw that he had painted his nose red. I walked out of the room and went down and called his mother and said I thought she should come right over and get him. And she did—she was a very good-looking woman, I remember. And that was the last I saw of him. It was obvious to me that he was very troubled at the time, and certainly, looking back, I think it's very surprising that he wasn't in some sort of hospital.

### ELIZABETH BLOW

Barbara called me to say there had been what she described as—by this time she was using these little French phrases all the time—a *fracas*. "There was a little *fracas* at the National Academy," she said. "Nothing at all, darling, really nothing at all, and I had to take him out."

## Patient Abstract, Antony Baekeland, Private Psychiatric Clinic, New York City, 1971

PATIENT: BAEKELAND, Antony
ADMITTED: May 21, 1971
AGE: 25 (Born: Aug. 28, 1946)
CIVIL STATUS: Single
OCCUPATION: Student

*CHIEF COMPLAINT:* Mr. Baekeland enters the hospital fearful, delusional, hallucinating, with a heavy history of drug usage and inability to function.

*PRESENT ILLNESS:* Mr. Baekeland's history at no time has been a stable one and it is difficult to date the onset of his present illness. He dates the onset of the use of drugs (LSD, pot, amphetamines) to approximately seven years ago when he was living with his mother (although the patient's parents were together until three years ago, they often lived apart in various parts of Europe for years prior to their separation). Patient, himself, dates the onset of his increasing disorganization in living to three years ago at the time of his parents' separation. At that time patient's father left the patient's mother to live with a former lady friend of the patient's. At this point, patient's mother allegedly made a suicide attempt. Since this time, the patient has been tormented with alternating periods of fury at his parents and spells of depression and guilt in which he has felt he is responsible for his parents' no longer living together. Although the patient's father is financially well off, subsisting on family fortune, he has provided no more than minimal financial assistance to his wife and son. Both the patient and his mother seemed to have lived a "pillar-to-post" existence in the past three months, globetrotting in a helter-skelter fashion and finding themselves unable to adjust to the realistic changes required because of the new financial situation. Patient, himself, has become increasingly involved in the use of drugs and has surrounded himself with a coterie of radical, artistic, would-be jetsetters. His mother, determined that her son is something of a "misunderstood genius" who was never meant to "work and toil in this sick society," has found it impossible to curb his disorganization and to set limits on his unrealistic style of living and flights of fancy. An emphasis upon social appearance despite the reality of circumstances is a paramount idea in Mrs. Baekeland's thinking also. At the time of the patient's admission, he was living alternately with some hippie friends in Greenwich Village and spending time with his mother at her apartment. He found that he had difficulty separating his spheres of influence and responsibility from those of his friends. Accordingly, he had become more withdrawn and sought to limit his involvements so that he could maintain a sense of his own self-limits. The event precipitating his admission to the Clinic consisted in his allegedly being chased and assaulted two days prior to admission while he was walking through Central Park at night. He recalls a nightmarish memory in which he was pursued with clubs by police, finally arriving, fearful and disorganized, at his mother's apartment. Although the patient was able to sleep for more than 24 hours after his arrival there, upon awakening, his mother states that he was still extremely disorganized, delusional, fearful and hallucinated. Moreover, he seemed very agitated and mother was fearful of the possibility of his assaulting her. Accordingly, she arranged for his admission to the Clinic.

*PSYCHIATRIC EXAMINATION:* The patient is a tall young man with longish red hair dressed in modish clothes. He had an air of frenzied disorganization. His choice of vocabulary and his accent had a finishing-school quality. Patient spoke a great deal about his mother and his father and expounded in a grandiose fashion on his intentions to reunite his parents. He spoke of himself and his mother as though they were a team and his first and most persistent inquiries had to do with when he would be able to phone her. In view of the patient's present and past environments, both of which might be characterized as unstable, it was felt that his reconstitution from his state of agitated disorganization would be all that could be accomplished in Clinic.

*COURSE IN CLINIC* (May 21, 1971, to July 2, 1971): From the outset the patient's course in Clinic was stormy. Mrs. Baekeland seemed to align herself with the most bizarre and eccentric statements of her son against what she perceived as narrow-minded arbitrariness on the part of the staff. She spoke of the phones at the Clinic having been bugged and sought desperately to justify her son's assertion that he was God. Patient related in either a clinging, dependent manner or a supercilious, haughty fashion to other patients and ward personnel. For the most part he remained in his room and listened to Indian music by the hour. Any attempts to set limits on his unconventional behavior were met with fearful and angry resentment. Throughout the patient's hospitalization there were many angry, demanding phone calls from his mother. Ultimately, in spite of strong counsel on the part of the hospital staff not to do so, the patient's mother signed the patient out of the Clinic.

*DATE OF DISCHARGE:* July 2, 1971.

*CONDITION OF DISCHARGE:* Improved slightly.

*PROGNOSIS:* Poor.

## Letter from Barbara Baekeland to Orin and Wendy Vanderbilt Lehman, July 3, 1971

New York

Dear Wendy & Orin—
My thanks for the time arranged for me with your doctor friend—he was very helpful.

Tony was discharged yesterday and the hospital is assuming all expenses—very chic of them, not to say enormously kind. I asked if Tony's discharge was because of our inability to meet the bills (Tony's trustees refused to invade his trust and Brooks refused to pay) and I was assured that it was not, that he had made great progress, and that they were satisfied that he was on the way to a recovery.

Thank you so much, again.

Love,
Barbara

## WENDY VANDERBILT LEHMAN

I probably knew a lot of people better than I knew Barbara Baekeland but there's something sympathetic in my memory of her that is not there for a lot of *them*. She had called to ask me if I knew of anybody who could help Tony. My heart really went out to her. I always had the feeling that behind the façade there was a great spongy three-dimensional sort of person.

I remember some time after she wrote us that letter she came into P. J. Moriarty's, an Irish bar on Third Avenue in the Sixties somewhere—not bad—when Orin and I were having dinner after the theater, and she acted a little upset or drunk at the table. I think I remember her spilling a drink. I was sort of embarrassed for her—I mean, I knew something was wrong. You know that feeling you get and you almost don't want to see it clearly because you don't want it to be that way?

## CLEVE GRAY

She called us up several times that summer and we didn't see her, but one day Francine and I were meeting someone at the Isle of Capri, and there was Barbara, having lunch all alone, which was very unlike her. She looked blowsy, she looked like an unhappy, beaten-down woman, and she was eating grossly and acting very strangely.

## Letter from Barbara Baekeland to Sam Green, July 3, 1971

New York

Darling Sam—

Tony was discharged yesterday but as he is extremely photosensitive because of the medication he is taking, we decided to forgo the weekend on Long Island. He is, in any case, not up to the hassle involved in getting there and back and people wandering in and out, so we are having a lovely peaceful time in the apartment here and he is helping me with my chores—mostly gardening on the terrace and keeping the floors clean (the doctor said to give him lots of tasks).

He is still under very heavy medication which is being gradually reduced while he is spending these few days with me. The doctor told me that his illness is not secondary—that is to say, induced by drugs—but primary—which is to say, genetic. But they are impressed with his intelligence and insight and hold forth a great deal of hope.

Anyway, he is looking forward very much to seeing you—he is not well enough to see very many friends and then just one or two at a time.

Love,
Barbara

### SAM GREEN

Both Tony and Barbara began paying me unexpected visits that summer. Barbara would appear at my apartment on West Sixty-eighth Street at two in the morning and bang on the door. Onne she walked across Central Park barefoot. At two o'clock in the morning I just did not want to have drop-ins—Tony would show up anytime *he* felt like it, too.

"I must see you," Barbara would say. "It's very important. Open the door! I have to tell you what's happening"—you know, whatever emergency it was. Several times she spent the night in the hallway outside my apartment, when I wouldn't open the door. She would always be gone by morning. Once I opened the door and said, "Stop it! Get out of here, I've got to get *up* in the morning—I have a very important appointment. Please just go home. Here's five dollars, take a taxi!" I remember I grabbed her by the hair and pushed her, and that was the only time I ever pushed anybody. She stumbled or something down the stairs.

## Letter from Barbara Baekeland to Sam Green, July 23, 1971

New York

Darling Sam—
I found your lighter—the one you lost last year. Hesitate to deliver same in person as with advancing age my hair seems to be getting thinner! So much was left at our threshold during our last *rencontre*, I can't afford another visit—except I would so very much enjoy seeing you. So if you ever feel you can have a quiet few minutes to extend me, I will arrange to meet you at your convenience.

Where shall I leave your lighter?

Love,
Barbara

### HENRY H. PERKINS

My brother Mike, who was Tony's greatest friend from Avon, and Michael Nouri, who'd gone to Buckley with Tony and who's now an actor—he was in *Flashdance*—and Checka Draper and I all went over to see Tony. He wasn't in but Mrs. Baekeland was home and she said, "Hi, come on in. Tony'll be back in a little while." She asked us if we would like some wine and we said, "Yeah, sure," and we were talking and suddenly she just, you know, took her glass of wine and threw it into the fireplace and threw back her hair in the most amazing display of—I don't know. . . . Who could have done it better was Lauren Bacall, you know. And I started to laugh because, you know, I thought I'd missed something, but I noticed my brother wasn't laughing at all. So to sort of change the atmosphere, I began asking her about this lighter that was on the coffee table. I said, "This is very attractive. What is it? Alabaster? It looks like a candy cane." And she looked at me and said, "Eat it!" I didn't think I'd heard right. Then she said it again, she started screaming it: "Eat it, goddam you, eat it, eat it, eat it!" And we ran out of there.

## Letter from Barbara Baekeland to Sam Green, August 12, 1971

New York<br>5:00 a.m.

Sorry to have to write you but I would like to have some explanation of just why you were so furious with me the other night. I waited for three hours on your stoop and asked for that, along with a glass of water. There was water, water everywhere but not a drop to drink, except on the lip of your paint cans on the terrace and it tasted of lead. You were not very polite and I hadn't even the chance of thanking you for looking after Mr. Wuss.

I'm really beginning to feel you really don't like me at all, Sam. And I find it altogether incredible—I have such a good time when I'm with you and usually that kind of pleasure is *réciproque*. Am I going to have to wait another year before you'll come to dinner again? For I will not give up trying to see you.

Saw Marisol the other night at Peter Gimbel's soirée—looking lovely—but, Sam, some people make voyages on the surface by walking over it and others voyage through space and time. It's a different kind of trip—both valid. I think the latter is perhaps more difficult—connections count for a lot.

I will be distressed if you don't call me and shall probably leave town if there is no possibility of ever seeing you. I only seem to be able to relax with you. I am so sorry you are angry with me again. I still don't understand why. It is not my wish to importune, but you are the only person I have ever known, with the exception of Brooks, of whom I have been truly fond who has turned his back on me—and even Brooks hasn't really done that! However, I've decided I'd rather be my own victim than his. I am attempting to have him give me back all moneys I had when I married him and to secure a divorce by asking for nothing else! I still haven't heard from him, nor will his lawyer communicate with mine.

Always,<br>Barbara

SAMUEL PARKMAN SHAW

I met Barbara at Daphne Hellman's. She had another lawyer at the time, with whom she was dissatisfied, and someone had said to her, "Why don't you try Sam Shaw?" I did relatively few divorces, partly because I didn't like them—you get people at their most anxious, and you rarely get a solution that's happy for anybody. So I wasn't particularly inclined to take her on as a client. There was an element of charm involved in it. She said, "Oh, please do it," and so forth and so on, and I said all right.

I met Tony perhaps a year after I first met Barbara. I met him at Daphne's, too, and I don't think I saw him more than three or four times after that. I thought he was quite beautiful that first time I saw him. I didn't really talk to him, but I did have an impression that he was strange. The second time I saw him was at a stand-up lunch at Barbara's, and on that occasion I talked to him for ten or fifteen minutes and thought him rather agreeable and interesting—imaginative.

The next time I saw him—well, he was beating up his grandmother and Barbara called me at my office, about six o'clock in the evening. By that time I knew a good deal about Tony's troubles and I said, "Why don't you call his psychiatrist?" She said she was too upset and for me to please come over right away. So I said, sure, I would. I jumped in a cab and I got over there and Nini was down in the lobby of Barbara's building. She seemed quite cool. I said, "What's going on?" and she said, "Tony tried to hurt me." Then Barbara came down and I said, "Well, what the hell are we going to do?" She said, "I'm scared to death of him." I said, "Did you call Justin Greene?" She said, "No. Would *you* call him?" So I went out to the public phone on the corner and called Greene, and he said, "I'm not going to come over. Whatever relation I have with Tony I don't want to jeopardize or destroy by seeming to be on his mother's side. If he's violent enough, just call the police and they'll come and take him away." So *he* was useless, and I went upstairs with Barbara, Nini going off in a cab to her own apartment. Tony was in the living room, he was looking distraught, but he didn't seem to me violent, so I sat down and chatted with him. Barbara was right there. It was my view that it was very dangerous for her to have him there for the night. I wanted to get him out of there but I didn't want to take him anywhere myself, I just wanted him to go somewhere and stay with friends or find himself a room somewhere. We sat there for quite a long time, I trying to convince him that he ought to go, and finally I decided that the best way to get him out of there was to take them out somewhere for supper and then figure out a way from there. They said fine and I said I just wanted to take a pee first.

So I went to the bathroom and when I came out Barbara was lying on the living-room floor—apparently unconscious. I thought she might even be dead. I knelt down to see whether she was alive. I felt her pulse and I couldn't find it. Tony was standing over her, with a very strange grimace on his face. I told him to go get some water. So he went and got a glass of water and I put some on a handkerchief and put it on her forehead. She didn't revive, and I said, "Tony, we've got to call a doctor right away." I was still down there with my hand on her pulse. And then I felt this terrible blow. I don't know how long I was unconscious. I think he hit me with a cane, because there was a cane on the floor—sort of a big knobbly cane. He belted me right across the nose with it. From on high.

When I woke up, I was really scared shitless. I figured he was out to kill me. I got up. Barbara was still unconscious and I thought maybe dead. And Tony was still standing right there, with a savage look on his face. I figure I've got to kill *him* or he's going to kill *me*. So I grappled with him and we rolled around the floor and I'm thinking, Shit, what a terrible way to die. He was very strong—I don't know how the hell he got that way because I don't think he ever did any exercises to speak of.

I finally wrestled him into the corner, I had his back against the wall and my right foot in his crotch and I was holding him there, but by that time I was so trembling and weak from all of this exertion and maybe the shock of being belted that I knew I couldn't hold him there for very long. I put my hand up to my nose—it felt like a bag of marbles, it just seemed to me to be all cracked—and I said, "Jesus Christ, Tony, you've really *ruined* my nose, and I'm afraid you've *killed* your *mother*. Listen, be a good fellow and go get me a towel with cold water on it." You see, I wanted to calm him down, because if I'd continued in this contest, he'd have killed me. So he went into the kitchen and got a towel and ran cold water on it and brought it over to me and I put it on my nose.

By this time Barbara was climbing to her feet, so *she* was okay. But I was just shaking with cold—you know how you get when you're in shock, you tremble uncontrollably—and I got her over to one side and I said, "Listen, while I talk to Tony, call the police." And then I said to Tony, "Come over and build me a fire in the fireplace, will you—I'm just shaking myself to pieces here." So he found some pieces of timber, put paper underneath, and lit it, and we sat by the fire, and in about ten minutes Barbara came back with the cops.

They took him away. He went perfectly willingly, philosophically—he didn't struggle, he didn't curse. They had an ambulance downstairs for him. And Barbara went with him over to Metropolitan Hospital, a public hospital over on Ninety-seventh Street and First Avenue.

I followed in a cab. I wanted to make sure everything was okay— that he was put in the proper hands. I went to see him later and he was peaceful.

Then I went to have my nose looked after. They said it was broken, and they set it and sewed it up, and a couple of days later I had an operation. The plastic surgeon did an absolutely marvelous job— a fellow named Smith. It looks the same, feels the same, sounds the same.

I turned over the whole divorce file to Barbara the next day and that was it—I don't know that I ever saw her again. They kept Tony at Metropolitan probably five or six weeks. The police asked me if I wanted to bring criminal charges and I said no.

## From a Psychiatric Report on Antony Baekeland Ordered By the British Courts, January 5, 1973

> In 1971 he was admitted to the acute psychiatric ward of Metropolitan Hospital. The diagnosis was "schizophrenia, simple type, with elements of character disorder." The prognosis was "reasonably good." Attempts were made to send him to a private mental hospital, the Thompkins Institute in New Haven, but the father would not finance it and the plan was dropped.

## WILLIE MORRIS

Those two! I always sensed disaster, I really did—the mother and the son were so askew. There's one dinner party she gave in East Hampton that I'll never forget. It was in the late fall of '71—I remember my black Lab, Ichabod H. Crane, had just died and I was in mourning. I went over with Muriel Murphy and the strangest thing happened—after dinner Barbara turned on me! For no reason at all. I was behaving myself quite well. But she ordered me to leave her house. I was totally flabbergasted. The other guests were embarrassed by it. It was as quick as a Mississippi thunderstorm. And so Muriel and I left.

But the next morning—I remember it so well—the son walked from their house to Muriel's, which is over on Georgica Pond, and delivered a note of apology from Barbara. It was a very sweet note. And I scribbled a note back telling her not to worry about it.

Then another funny thing happened. Saul Steinberg had been at that dinner, and I guess he was pretty much taken aback by the little incident, too, because he graciously gave me—he brought them over a few days later—a beautiful pair of watercolors which he had done for me, which he called *Yazoo*. That's my hometown in Mississippi. He titled one of them *Yazoo in the Winter* and the other *Yazoo in the Spring*. But Saul's a real gentleman, he didn't mention that little episode.

## ELIZABETH WEICKER FONDARAS

Barbara and Tony were spending fall and winter weekends in that little house on the beach. I was worried about her. Once she parked a car she'd borrowed from Richard Hare on the wrong side of the Montauk Highway—facing traffic. It was towed away, and she had to come into the East Hampton police station to deal with it. The officer was sitting at a desk rather high up and Barbara said, "Come down off that desk up there! What kind of place is this, anyway?" And then when he did come down, she said, "Well, get a pencil so you can take this down right!" And he said, "I can't do it down here. I need the desk to write on—also my pencil's up there."

Eventually I called Paul Greenwood, a policeman who used to moonlight by driving me into New York occasionally when he was off duty and who'd been in the station the day Barbara came in. I said, "I just want to show you where Barbara Baekeland's house is, in case I ever have to call you to get over there quickly."

## PAUL GREENWOOD

I was the sergeant on duty when she came in about her car. She was very, very, very emotional, very upset, and, you know, she proceeded to look down upon everyone there and give us the devil. She really was raising hell. She had on a long, funny-looking gown. We didn't have a chance to do any talking, she did all the talking—she insulted everybody. We just listened and let her get it off of her chest—we let them ventilate when they get that excited, then they'll cool off and you can reason with them.

I think she had her son with her, but I'm not sure about that. She was a Baekeland by marriage, right? And Baekeland was the name of the man that invented Bakelite originally, right? Well, she certainly acted like she was from the hufty-tufty there, you know—very haughty individual, I thought.

### GLORIA JONES

I saw Barbara for the last time that winter, I guess. In Long Island. And she looked ratty—for Barbara, who always wore these marvelous furs and beautiful robes and the Chanels, you know.

### SYLVIE BAEKELAND SKIRA

You have to understand that Barbara had been a great beauty. She was losing her looks and her husband had left her for someone much younger. She would write to Brooks saying, "I've been to the doctor, he finds me amazing. He thinks I have the body of a thirty-year-old," or, "My looks still stop traffic"—I remember *that* expression. She was terribly *accrochée* to this—holding on, holding on to this *fiercely*.

### FREDERICK COMBS

I kept hearing from everyone how beautiful she'd been, and then Tom Dillow asked me over to her place in East Hampton for drinks—I remember it was the dead of winter. The son was there, too, and he was just sitting by the fire and we were having a perfectly, you know, average conversation when all of a sudden he leaps out of his chair toward his mother. He got within a few feet of her, and, I mean, his grimace and everything was incredible—a look of just total hatred. Then he just stopped in his tracks and went back to his chair by the fire, a rocking chair as I recall. It was a terrifying moment but she reacted as though nothing had happened and was seemingly more involved in how to calm *us* down, you know, and just get the conversation going again. I remember later she told us he had been burning the furniture in the fireplace that afternoon. Imagine being a stranger and sitting with someone and having them talk about the burning of furniture as though they were just simply saying would I like another cube of ice in my drink, you know. It was real casual.

## DOMINICK DUNNE

I met Barbara Baekeland when she came to the screening of a film that I produced. It must have been 1971 or '72. She stayed on afterwards to discuss the picture. I saw her a few times after that and once fetched something for her from her London apartment that she wanted in New York, a mink hat I think it was. I didn't know her very well, but I had several friends who were very close to her, and I had heard stories about Tony attacking her, particularly a tale of an attack he made on his mother at their house in East Hampton when friends of mine were present. The story was more or less dismissed at the time—"He didn't really mean it," that sort of thing—but became horrifying in retrospect after he actually did kill her.

Two years ago my own daughter, Dominique, was attacked and murdered by a former boyfriend. She had become frightened of him and broken off the relationship. It was not the first time that he had attacked her. There had been two previous instances. The thing that haunts us all, my wife and sons and me, and that we have to live with is that none of us thought in terms of murder. It simply never occurred to us that the man was a killer. Afterwards, when it was too late, all the warning signs became clear.

## RICHARD HARE

My wife and I used to drive Barbara and Tony out to East Hampton on weekends. They didn't have a car or anything, and I remember one day we were leaving—we left Fridays around one o'clock—Barbara took me aside and said, "Richard, Tony isn't quite himself, he's stopped taking his pills, but don't worry about it because I'm going to get him on the pills again."

All the way down in the car he was making these funny little nursery rhymes and, you know, singing to himself. So when we got to their house I took Barbara aside and said, "Barbara, I think it would be wise for you both to spend the night at *our* house. I don't like the idea of you being alone in the house here, with Tony not being quite right." She said, "Don't worry a thing about it. He's going to be fine." And I said, "Will you call me the first thing in the morning?" and she said, "Richard, I've been through this a hundred times before." The next morning she did call: "Oh, we had a lovely dinner"—you know.

That night, they came for drinks. We sat by the fire and he was pretty well-behaved. He rather liked it in our house because it was a big old East Hampton house, 1796 it was born, and he rather liked that whole idea, and he had a lot of feeling about the house and it was quite calming for him, I think. He seemed perfectly under control until Barbara said, "I've brought some lovely sketches that Tony's done." He became quite antagonistic toward her then but she was able to placate him very nicely.

Early that Monday morning Barbara Hale called me and told me what had happened over at her place the night before. I was relieved it hadn't happened in *my* house, because *I* would have called the police, you see, and Barbara Baekeland would never have spoken to me again.

## DAVID MEAD
I was strictly a nonhistorical facet in all of this. I was married at the time to Deirdre Cohane, the daughter of the Baekelands' old friend Jack Cohane and his first wife, Mimi.

I can't remember how we all got out to East Hampton, to tell you the truth. I guess we drove out—or did we take the train? No, we all must have driven out in a rented car. That's vague to me, how we got there. I certainly know how we got *back*—in pieces.

This was January 1972. It was a really nasty weekend. It was snowing and blowing, and Barbara's house was right on the beach, and the sea was threatening to wash it right over the dunes. We were going over to Barbara Hale's for dinner.

Now this is the first time I ever met Barbara Hale. It was about seven, I guess, when we got there, and dinner wasn't quite ready, and Barbara Baekeland and I were sitting at the kitchen table, drinking and talking. We were on our first drink, then our second drink, and it was very pleasant—no problems at all. We were talking about all kinds of things in general but I remember specifically what we were talking about when it began to happen—we were talking about European architecture, something which I know nothing about but which I *thought* I knew something about. In other words, I was pontificating or something. And all of a sudden, out of the blue Barbara Baekeland said, "Good *God*, you don't know what you're talking about!" Now this is the first time I've ever seen her angry or even upset about anything. And she really lashed into me, she attacked me with a real force. I remember the conversation so well only because I was trying to figure out what it was that I had said that might have made her so angry, and as I was trying to figure this out—trying to play it back, so to speak—she was still going on at me. I think maybe the third drink or so had just done it, you know.

Tony was in the living room but when he heard his mother's voice raised in anger, he came rushing in and said to her, "*You* don't know what *you're* talking about!" He sort of took over for *me*, and met her on *her* level, which was pretty high and angry. And I was just of no consequence at that point. He accused her of being a whore, and she accused *him* of being a homosexual, you know—"homo" I think was the word she used. "What could *you* ever do with a woman?" she said. Something to that effect. At that point he took an egg off the counter and smashed it on her face. Then she threw something at *him*. She became defiant—"Aren't you a crass slob for doing that to me!"

Then he took a knife. He just taunted her with it. And she thrust out her chest and said, "I dare you!" Like that. And that's when *I* stepped in. I concentrated on the knife. He wasn't really paying attention to me, his eyes were completely focused on her, and they were livid. The whole thing was like some sort of cheap Hollywood movie. I mean, they were eyeball to eyeball and the hatred was electric, it was absolutely electric.

He held the knife up and I simply went for his wrist, twisted it, and just took it away from him. And he didn't even know I did that. He wasn't even aware of me! She was still saying, "I dare you! I dare you!" And they were still glaring at each other. And then he went for her throat. He started choking her. He was wrestling her to the floor and I stepped in between them and we all went crashing to the floor—the three of us—and we actually rolled out the kitchen door into the snow.

Well, I finally fought him off her. He went inside and she got up and I went over to her and I said, "Are you okay?" and she was trembling and hysterical and she slapped me across my face as hard as she could and said, "I hate you, I hate you, I hate you!" and got in the car and drove away.

I went back in the house and *I'm* beginning to tremble now so I have a couple of brandies. And Tony announces he's going to bed at Barbara Hale's. He was completely calm again.

So Deirdre and I spent the night at Barbara Hale's, too. My only plan for the rest of the evening was to get as drunk as I could as quickly as I could, and I succeeded. The next morning when I came down, Tony was already at the table, Barbara Hale was making breakfast, and it was a nice day, a beautiful day, so I said to him, "After breakfast I'd like to have a talk with you. Why don't we go for a long walk." And we did—we walked all over the place. I told him that I really thought he ought to get away from his mother, that they were both tearing each other up, and he was saying how he agreed, it wasn't good. I thought I had made some good points and, you know, reached him a little bit, and we got back to the house, and just as we walked in the door the phone was ringing and Deirdre picked it up and it was Barbara Baekeland. Deirdre said, "Hi, Barbara, how are you? Yes, Tony's here," and she gave the phone to him, and he went, "Uh-huh, uh-huh, okay," and hung the phone up, and of course both Deirdre and I leaped on him, we said, "What'd she say, what'd she say?" And he just very calmly said, "She'll be by to pick me up in half an hour." And he walked away. And half an hour later she picked him up and drove off, acting of course as if nothing had happened.

## BARBARA HALE
The whole place was just a shambles. When I think I let Tony spend the night here! I don't know how I dared. I don't know, I just did.

## ELIZABETH BLOW
I was working in a bookstore called Wakefield Young on Madison Avenue and Sixty-fourth Street, right near the Children's Zoo, and all my friends would stop in to see me. One day Barbara Hale tottered in and described a terrible scene in East Hampton with Barbara and Tony. She said, "I can't have anything more to do with them, ever—it's just too much." She had barely left the store when Barbara Baekeland herself came in and said, "I've just had the most delightful dinner at Barbara Hale's and I want to buy a book for her as a present. What would you suggest?"

I didn't hear from her for several months after that, but then sometime that summer I got a postcard from Mallorca saying, "Betty darling, I miss you so this summer. Tony and I think of you all the time and wish you were here. He is *much better.*"

Later I heard from Nini, who'd gone over for a while to stay with them, that the scene there was very bad. One night she and Barbara evidently had to flee the house. They sat in the car, frightened to death.

# 12

# STRIKING OUT

Later in 1979, Broadmoor officials contacted the International Social Service of Great Britain about Tony Baekeland's case. A senior inter-country caseworker recalls that "some alternatives were explored, because there was very definite pressure from *somewhere* that Baekeland leave Broadmoor."

The pressure was coming, of course, from the unofficial committee. "It was taking far too long to get Tony organized somewhere," says Michael Alexander, "and I think I rather annoyed Dr. Maguire by putting the heat on."

Soon an officer from the American Embassy in London was able to report: "Broadmoor appears close to a decision to release Tony Baekeland. He could be back in the U.S.A. in about six weeks." Indeed, a passport application had been made in his name.

Dr. Maguire remained concerned that Tony's long hospitalization would make it impossible for him to readjust successfully in America on his own, and informed the embassy that Broadmoor could not in good conscience recommend to the Home Secretary that Tony be released without a guarantee that "a period of social rehabilitation" would follow.

The next piece of news the committee received was therefore not the yes they expected but, rather, the nebulous statement that "Baekeland's release is not imminent."

## Letter from Barbara Baekeland to Sam Green, July 18, 1972

> Miramar
> Valldemosa
> Mallorca

Sam—

For heaven's sake pick up a pen and scribble me a few words. I am wrestling with such monumental problems I need cheering up. You can do this for me better than anyone—so . . .

I have the beautiful beige silk curtains you gave me which I have never used. They are too dressy for here and hide the beautiful cut of the window frames. Would you like me to send them back? You might use them in your bedroom. Please let me know.

Brooks is trying to force me into a murderously ungenerous agreement by cutting off my support. Except for this & Tony's problems I am in bliss here.

Phyllis Harriman Mason, Averell's niece, has been a paying guest for about 3 weeks and it's been divine having her—also has enabled me to survive financially. She is very fond of Tony and completely understands the problem. Don't know what I will do when she leaves. We are very remote here. I just pray.

He is somewhat better though *not* taking his medication. Says it dulls him. But the beauty of the place and the peace seem to help him.

> Love,
> Barbara

PHYLLIS HARRIMAN MASON

I had a good time with her alone and I had a good time with him alone, but when the two of them were together . . . Several times that summer I thought it was *my* last moment. One night we'd been to dinner at Robert Graves's house, Barbara was dressed to the hilt, with ropes of pearls, and coming home it was full moonlight and she was speeding, she said Tony was bugging her and she wanted to get home, and the police stopped us. She said, "You have to put him in jail!" and they looked inside the car and said, "Oh, *Antonio*, it's *you!*" They obviously *liked* Tony.

All that summer he was on speed. Barbara would find pills in his drawers and she'd raise Cain—then *he'd* raise Cain.

Another time, I was in the back seat of the car and Tony moved the front seat back on my foot. And Barbara said, "You have to say you're sorry to Phyllis." She said it condescendingly, as if he were a two-year-old. It didn't matter whether he said he was sorry or not—my foot hurt.

About halfway through my visit she had to buy some groceries, so I gave her three hundred dollars. She gave me an IOU, which I hadn't expected at all. She owed money everywhere, I think.

She stole money from me, too—she or Tony. I think it was Barbara really. I went to Greece for a couple of days and when I got back to Mallorca my wallet was missing. I hadn't taken it with me because it had dollars in it which I couldn't have used there—I always save some for when I get back to New York to take the taxi in from the airport. I didn't even realize the wallet was gone till I was packing to go home. It had not only the dollars but a lot of my IDs in it. And the wallet was extremely nice, too. I've never been able to find another quite like it.

Barbara had tried on all my clothes, too, while I was in Greece.

That summer she was still entertaining all the time. One night she was having a big dinner party, and there was a beautiful chandelier in the dining room that used oil in its cups, and she asked Tony to let it down—it was on a rope, you know—and he let it down all right, he let the rope *go*. It came down with a great crash, and she accused him of doing it on purpose. There was oil and glass all over everything. Barbara was down on her hands and knees cleaning up the oil in her finery. The other guests hadn't arrived, they were still coming over the mountain.

Tony had a motorcycle that summer and we could hear him coming from miles and miles away. We'd hear this damn motorcycle coming over the hill and Barbara would say, "Oh my God, here he comes!" and my heart would sink—*our* hearts would sink.

He had a tape recorder, and he played Vivaldi's *Four Seasons* over and over and over on the terrace, and Barbara would tell him to turn it off and that would start another row.

Alastair Reid, a poet, came for dinner one night and he said to me, "Oooohhh, it's not so good here, is it?" and I said, "No!" and I told him—I was so glad to be able to talk to someone. I'd kept it all to myself.

## ALASTAIR REID

I stopped off to see Barbara on my way back from—well, let me tell you the most ironic story of that summer. Borges was in Spain and he came to Mallorca for two or three days to rest and he sent me a telegram—I'd often translated his work and we were friends. So I went down to Palma to see him. He was with Maria Corama, who travels with him and looks after him, and he told me about this pilgrimage that he had just made to see Graves. Graves's wife Beryl leads Borges, who's totally blind, into the room where her husband's lying, totally gaga, not knowing what anything *is*, and she takes Borges's blind hand and joins it to Graves's senseless one, and they shake hands. And that's the meeting between Borges and Graves: Nobody met anybody.

This took place up in Deyá, which Graves has always regarded as a sacred village and indeed chose because *deia* is the Latin word for "goddess"—hence his kind of, you know, enormously romantic summers. Summer was always the high drama in Mallorca. Summer was the high drama.

When I got to Barbara's and Phyllis Mason said terrible things had been going on, I didn't know what the hell she was talking about until dinner, which was just Phyllis, me, Barbara, and Tony. Barbara started to taunt Tony about how she knew he didn't want to be there with her and so on, and finally he got up and took a wine bottle and smashed it against the wall. I was rather shocked by the eruption. And Barbara roared with laughter and seemed immensely relieved, as if she'd gotten the reaction she'd wanted out of him. And so I realized that they were locked into a relationship that depended on their power to hurt each other all the time—they were both living off it. And Phyllis and I—it was during this dinner that I first thought of it—were relegated to being, as it were, spectators.

## From a Psychiatric Report on Antony Baekeland Ordered by the British Courts, January 5, 1973

> In Mallorca he said that he had had a mystical experience when he and his mother had thoughts in common, that their thoughts bounced off one another so that the whole house shook, and that they later considered it would be unsafe to live there.

### CECELIA BREBNER

According to Antony, they were both on drugs that last summer in Mallorca and she would perform the most extraordinarily immodest feats.

### ALASTAIR REID

I still didn't think that the impetus for violence was coming from Tony. I felt it from Barbara, and I felt Barbara's desperation that night. A few weeks later, I saw them at a dinner party in Deyá—this must be by now early August. Barbara came over to me immediately and began to talk. She was talking a great deal then. She was frantic, pouring everything out, complaining—how was she going to manage, what was she going to do, where was she going to go next. These were the problems. But there was no continuity in her preoccupations.

Tony was off in another room playing chess, which is the only apparent connection he had with people in Deyá. Then the guy he was playing with came into the room where we were to say that Tony had turned around toward the wall and was just sitting there in a total catatonic trance. And he sat through that whole evening totally clutched by himself like that. I asked the others there about him and they said that was why they had him over to play chess—to take him out of himself, to get him connected to other people. These people in Deyá, crazy as they probably were themselves, had just accepted Tony and were bearing him along, as small villages always bear their crazies along with them. I mean, it was more or less an accepted fact that Tony was over the edge. And then people began to talk about—I began to hear rumors of—you know, Barbara and Tony, how Barbara had been sleeping with Tony.

I took Barbara aside. She was very humble, she said she didn't know what to do. I said, "You've got to get Tony to a doctor, and there's somebody I know who can really handle this." And I gave her the name of Lindsay Jacobs in London.

## From a Psychiatric Report on Antony Baekeland Ordered by the British Courts, January 5, 1973

He came with his mother to London and was seen by Dr. W. Lindsay Jacobs in October 1972. His impression was that patient suffered from schizophrenia and that his mother appears to have given him his prescribed tranquillisers rather irregularly. She told the doctor that he was reasonably calm though always disturbed by the parents' impending divorce and by his inability to retain consistent contact with his father.

### HEATHER COHANE

Barbara was having the flat on Cadogan Square painted and she asked Jack and me where we stayed when we came over to London from Ireland. We always stayed in a place called Eleven Cadogan Gardens, sort of a private hotel, a smart bed-and-breakfast-type place. There was rather a fierce man there called Mr. Reider who let one in and ran the whole place. Well, one time we arrived and straightaway Mr. Reider said, "Some *friends* of yours were here. The Bakers. I had to call the police." We drew ourselves back and said, "Well, we don't know any people called Baker. They can't have been friends of *ours*." But as we went up to our room, Jack said, "I wonder if 'Baker' could have been 'Baekeland.'" So when we went down we sort of bravely said to Mr. Reider, "Was it 'Baekeland' by any chance?" And he said, "Yes, *that* was the name," so we said, "Well, what happened?" and apparently Tony had tried to stick a pen into Barbara's eye in the hallway.

## Letter from Barbara Baekeland to Sam Green, October 23, 1972

81 Cadogan Square
London, S.W. 1

Dear Sam—
Brooks is arriving from Brittany in a few minutes—met by Michael Alexander at the airport. I am hoping that he will be able

to help me with this problem of Tony—who has not been at all well. In any case, something should be resolved in the next few days.

I do not see myself locked up here with him. He has been quite violent—not only with me but with stewards on airplanes, waiters and the like.

I am trying to arrange accommodations for him with the Countess of Darnley, who lives outside London—if he agrees to staying on here and undergoing treatment. Am seeing the best man in London & one of the best in the world.

*Comme d'habitude*, I am struggling with this but finally see some hope of a possible solution.

I didn't speak to you about it on the phone as you have been so very concerned and kind and I am embarrassed to involve my friends any further in my problem. But thank God I have them and they have all been wonderful—especially you and Michael Alexander and Sue Guinness.

Love,<br>
Barbara

P.S. Found the flat impeccable and looking very handsome.


## JIM ROBERTSEN

Barbara bought the apartment on Cadogan Square off of Neil Hartley and me—we owned it jointly. Sam Green had said, "I know someone who's looking for a place, let me introduce you." Everyone in London wanted the apartment because it was really pretty fabulous, but *she* said, "I'll pay cash." She agreed to give it to us in three checks spaced a couple of weeks apart. We banked the first one, wrote checks on it—and it bounced! I got hold of her right away and she said she was sorry and gave us another check—and that one went through. And a little later she sent around the largest chunk of caviar that any of us had ever seen. I suppose it was probably fifteen pounds of caviar; it came from Fortnum's and it was in a huge blue tin. I phoned everyone I knew, I mean everyone who I really adored who was crazy about caviar, and said, you know, come over.

That was a very nice, extremely extravagant thing of her to do—especially since this was after the parade had passed for her, you know. I saw very little of her after the sale went through, because the son was such a disaster and they were sort of a package deal. I did

have them both to a couple of parties in my new house. During one
of them, Tony came over and told me how much he liked me, how
sympathetic he found me. Then he phoned the next day and said
could we have lunch, and I said, "No, not today," and he said,
"Well, *what* day?" and I finally said a day.

I took him to a place on the King's Road called the Aretusa which
is now defunct. It was owned and run by a trendy fellow called Al-
varo and it was a very *louche* sort of club with sort of remnants of the
swinging sixties, and therefore people were not easily shocked there,
you didn't pay much attention one way or another—it was always
loaded with all sorts of major-and minor-league celebrity types.

So we sat down and I said, "How are you?" and Tony said, "I'm
just terrible." I said, "What's wrong?" And he said, "Well, uh . . ."
He said something like, "Can I speak frankly to you?" And I said,
"Ya, I mean, Tony . . ." And he said, "I really would like to feel I
can rely on you as a friend." I said, "Well, Tony, we scarcely know
each other." I mean, I just did *not* want to have any sort of friendship
with him, quite honestly, because he seemed too much like a ticking
time bomb and not anyone who I had any interest in on any con-
ceivable level, you know. And he said, "Well, uh, what's happening
is I'm having an affair with my mother."

And I remember I said, "Oh, come *on*—you and your mother do
have a very intimate relationship and that's fine," and that sort of
thing. He said, "No no no no! I am *fucking* my *mother*!" And he said
it loud enough, in the Aretusa, which was quite bustling and where
people tended to talk fairly loud—for England anyhow—so that several people turned around, and I said, you know, "Relax, Tony." He
said, "Well, that's it. And I don't know what to do—I feel desperate." I said, "It's awful if you feel desperate about it. Quite honestly,
I think any number of things are all right if they don't hurt people
outside the relationship." And then he sort of said again, he said,
"Don't you understand what I'm saying to you?" I said, "Tony, why
do you want to tell *me* this? I'm sorry it's happening and that it's
distressing you. But you know, if you don't want it to continue, then
just stop it." Then he got quite hysterical, and it was very embarrassing—hideous, as a matter of fact.

The point is that I really did not want this information, I did not
like the laundering of, you know, his family's washing all over *me*,
and I did not want it in a club where I was a member.

Oddly enough, at the time I knew of another mother and son who
were having an incestuous relationship, which was really quite suc-

cessful. These, by the way, are the only two cases of mother/son incest that I'm personally aware of. But both mother and son had told me about this affair they were having, and *they* were anything *but* anguished over it, they were quite amused by it, in fact. I mean, they ended up being very good friends—it was just something they did for a little bit. And I just thought, you know, this is terribly ironic—that just suddenly, in a period of about six months, I should have these two pieces of information, neither one of which I particularly wanted to have.

So anyway I told him that it seemed to me his life would be far simpler if he didn't live with his mother. And he said, "Where would I go? What would I do?" And I said, "The world is full of places. Do you have any money of your own?" And he said he really didn't yet. And I said, "Well, Tony, you could do something that a lot of people in the world do—you could get a job." He said, "What do you mean?" And I said, "Just get a fucking job. Go to Paris, get a job *there*—go back to the States. Do *anything*." I said there were also a lot of people in London who he could probably work out an arrangement with where he could share a flat. I said that the pressures of living with his mother were obviously enormous and he should just put some time and distance between them.

And here we still are in this restaurant, this *club*, and he's really I mean not quite shouting but damn near it. And finally I say, because, I mean, the headwaiter and so on are kind of rolling their eyes at me, "Listen, Tony, maybe we should just go for a walk." And he said, "Why?" And I said, "Look, this isn't something that I really want to go on discussing here."

There was never any question in my mind that what he was telling me and what I was hearing was true—none whatsoever. And I'm usually fairly skeptical. I mean, there was just the passion with which he said it.

And I know it went on with his mother beyond that point because he did phone me some time later and he said, "Oh God, this thing still seems to be going on." And I remember saying, "Tony, it takes two people, you know."

## F. Clason Kyle

I met Barbara and Tony less than, as it turned out, a month before her death. I met her first, at a party given for the Victorian Society, on whose American board of directors I served.

I was winding up a two-and-a-half-month stay in London, writing

an A-to-Z series on the metropolis's offbeat travel attractions. I might
have had more time for the Baekelands if I hadn't been pushing to
get all the photographs I needed, and I was also anxious to get home
to Columbus, Georgia, by Thanksgiving. Anyway, I enjoyed meeting
Barbara sufficiently to ask if she would be interested in hearing a
lecture on Irish Georgian architecture by an old friend of mine, the
Honourable—and blue-eyed—Desmond Guinness, who would be
speaking in tandem with the Knight of Glin. The duet was scheduled
for a few nights later at the Irish Club, just off Eaton Square. She
said she would be delighted to join me, and did so, bringing her son
along with her.

I was surprised to see him, because I certainly had not invited him,
not even knowing that he existed. But then, the more the merrier,
and he added another body to the talk's attendees.

The next time I saw Barbara was a few nights later when I invited
her and Tony to have dinner with me at the Rib Room of the Carlton Towers on Sloan Street. Besides having good meat, the restaurant
was convenient to the Baekelands' flat on Cadogan Square and mine
on Wilton Place.

Dinner went well, I recall. And Barbara asked me back to see their
penthouse flat and have a nightcap. On the walk there, Tony, who
had been relatively quiet during dinner, suddenly opened up and
began telling me—because I was a journalist, I guess—about some
writing that he had done. He asked if I would be willing to take a
look at it. He said it was a mystical tale about a rabbit or an animal of
some sort, I can't remember exactly which.

At their stunningly attractive flat, conversation was vigorous for
about an hour while Barbara and I sipped on our brandies. Tony had
bade us goodnight immediately after our arrival, courteously saying
that he had enjoyed dinner. And I think he had. I had responded,
equally sincerely, that I looked forward to reading his story.

Unexpectedly, there was an exceedingly noisy racket from the
kitchen area beneath us. Barbara seemed to pay no attention, until
Tony—clad only in knit shorts—appeared in the salon, brandishing
a large kitchen knife. He ranted about the room, gesturing wildly,
but never making a threatening move at either of us. Then he vanished, as quickly as he had appeared. However, some commotion
continued below.

The understatement of the century would be to say that I was startled. Barbara had remained passive and composed throughout.

Quietly, she explained that he had recently threatened to kill her. "I'm not afraid of him," she said, more than once.

I said, "Perhaps I should leave. My being here has obviously upset him." I quickly had assumed that Tony was jealous of my being with his mother, or of her being with me—three's a crowd. Before I could leave, the phone rang and I heard Barbara apologizing to another tenant in the building for the disturbance.

She then led me down four or five flights of stairs, allaying my fears for her safety and my offer of sanctuary. An elderly gentleman, dressed in bathrobe and pajamas, stood in his doorway on one landing. He said, "Mrs. Baekeland, this just must not continue. I can't have my sleep disturbed in this manner." I think he also added something about his concern for her security. She assured him—*and me*—that Tony was having treatment and that things were all right.

**ALASTAIR REID**
When I heard that Lindsay Jacobs had agreed to see Tony and was going to take up the case, as it were, I thought, What a relief, because he's a doctor who enjoys considerable fame for picking up people when they're really on the edge and bringing them back to life.

**DR. W. LINDSAY JACOBS**
After seeing Antony Baekeland and his mother separately on a couple of occasions, I called the Chelsea Police Station to tell them I thought something was going to happen over at 81 Cadogan Square and could they put a guard there. The officer in charge said that they were not really allowed to do much of anything until something actually happened.

On November 15, 1972, just two days before the matricide, I saw Antony and his mother together and they were jointly willing that he go into hospital. I had arranged for a bed on Monday November 20th.

**F. CLASON KYLE**
The evening that Tony ran around the flat with the kitchen knife proved to be the last time I saw Barbara, except for one day in Knightsbridge shortly before my return to the States. I was in a taxi and she, wrapped in a dark cape, was walking on the sidewalk, clutching several shopping bags. I waved to her. She waved back, but I am not certain that she recognized me—it was more the sort of

wave one gives to a friendly hand fluttering from inside a passing car, while at the same time experiencing the uncomfortable feeling that maybe the greeting really had been meant for the stranger strolling two feet to one's left.

## SUE GUINNESS

I saw Barbara two days before he killed her—I had lunch with both of them, in fact, in London, in the flat. And Tony was definitely in a very peculiar state. He had painted all his shoes and his clothes with gold stars, and he just sat there and rocked backwards and forwards with his arms crossed across his chest. I said to Barbara, "Do be careful," and she said, you know, "He'll never harm *me*."

Well, I knew that wasn't so, because she used to stay with me in London when she rented out her flat and she was staying with me once when Tony turned up from somewhere or other in the middle of a dinner party. He went upstairs and got her passport and tore it up, then he threw various things down the drain, and then he came into the dining room and insulted her and said that he was going to kill her—in front of quite a number of witnesses. Anyway I got him out of the house—I think he was staying at some hotel that Michael Alexander had got him into.

The following day he came back and he said he wanted to go and see *The Devils* by Ken Russell—do you remember that film? And Barbara and I agreed to do that with him. He became very peculiar after seeing it—he sat on the stairs of the cinema rocking backwards and forwards. Naturally Barbara got terribly worried and said that she didn't want to be on her own with him. And luckily he went off.

But the next day he rang up asking for his mother. I said that she had left, which wasn't true—she had just gone to the American Embassy to get a new passport. He said, "Oh, I see." And then I went out to do some shopping. When I came back about twenty minutes later, I found Barbara lying on the pavement with a mackintosh rolled up under her head and a great patch of her hair missing on one side—she was looking pretty dazed. There was this rather nice man standing over her—it was he, in fact, who had taken his mackintosh and given it to her.

And Tony was in the window—of *my house*—screaming and shouting that he was going to get everybody, that anybody who came near was going to get it—he said he was going to kill *all women*. He had a carving knife.

What happened while I was out shopping was that he had turned up and our housekeeper had let him in—after all, he'd been coming to our house for years and he was the son of an old friend and she didn't realize that Barbara didn't want to see him, you know. He was waiting for Barbara when she came back from the embassy and he jumped on her. Apparently he pursued her through the house, she got out the front door and down the steps, and he was dragging her into the square by her hair, trying to throw her in front of cars. She was hanging on to the gate and he was slamming it backwards and forwards on her thumb.

When I saw her lying there I ran down the road and rang up the police from the greengrocer's. They arrived with dogs—by this time we had a crowd of I suppose about thirty to forty people standing outside the house saying there's a maniac in there. When Tony saw the police, he went running off behind the house, down the garden and across various streets.

Then the ambulance came round. I rode with Barbara to St. Charles's Hospital in Kensington, and she was not in a very good state at *all*. A finger was broken in three places and she was there for a couple of days. She said to me from her bed, "It's worth any amount of pain to save Tony from himself."

They caught him I think about twenty-four hours later in his hotel room. He was put in a cell—they were going to charge him with attempted murder. He was only in there for forty-eight hours, because I got three psychiatrists to sign him into the Priory, a private hospital in Roehampton. Then I got hold of Brooks, who was in Brittany with Sylvie, and I made him come over to England. I said, "Look here, your son is in a very bad state, he must have treatment." He said, you know, "It's just fun and games"—those were his words. And I said, "Brooks, no it's not. *You* weren't present, you haven't seen what's been going on, you haven't seen the way he treats Barbara."

Well anyway, Tony left the Priory shortly afterwards.

I'd reckoned he was dangerous ever since I first knew him in Cadaqués, where he was sort of semicontrolled by a whole lot of very peculiar hippies. I shan't forget him sitting in the flat with all his clothes and shoes painted with gold stars, two days before he killed her. I remember I had to go to Paris that evening, Wednesday, and Saturday morning when I got back it was all over the newspapers.

I opposed the efforts of Michael Alexander and Heather Cohane and the others to get him out of Broadmoor. I didn't think it was a very good idea.

# PART III
# NEW YORK

# 1

## REPATRIATION

Former Broadmoor patients have reported that after their release they missed the orderly, controlled life they had gotten used to and sometimes even become fond of. When the time came for Tony Baekeland to leave, would he also find life on the outside chaotic and threatening?

New York City had changed in the eight years since he had last seen it, but his old neighborhood, to which he would be returning—the Seventies on the Upper East Side—had remained pretty much the same, although a few fashionable new shops, boutiques, and restaurants had opened.

### BROOKS BAEKELAND

There were three alternatives for Tony once the right strings were pulled in high places in London and his release achieved: one, that he be released in some innocent person's custody and undergo private medical treatment from time to time since he would be considered well; two, that he be transferred to some place like Payne Whitney in New York, which I enraged some by dubbing "Pain Witless"; and three, that he go straight to the equivalent of Broadmoor in America—that is, a state institution.

Every one of these alternatives was clearly idiotic—the first and second, if for no other reason than that they were beyond my means, so far beyond as to be preposterous; and the third alternative was too tragic to think of.

The fact is, there is nothing that I know of in the world like Broadmoor, at least when I knew it. A gentleness, a kindness, a compassion, and a civilized concern by civilized people for the cruelly wounded—or fatally malborn—within its walls are the first things that strike a foreign visitor. And Tony *was* happy there—as long as the tiger slept. And the tiger did sleep until Maguire—under pressure, I believe, from higher-ups to send all the foreigners back to their own countries—began to take away the drugs that made the tiger sleep. And the tiger awoke!

I began to receive a stream of violent—and obviously paranoid—letters from Tony, one of which I sent, as an example, to my brother. I called Maguire from Italy, where I was living then, separated from Sylvie. I told him—and I later reinforced it by telegram—that letting Tony go would be absolutely irresponsible, that I would send him copies of the letters I had been getting from him ever since he had been taken off "the drugs that dull the rage," to quote myself, and I repeated then what I had said and written before: that I would be happy to make a gift every year to the British government that would *more* than compensate for the cost of their care for my son.

## Dr. Thomas Maguire

Brooks Baekeland talked to me about payment, but of course you can't pay for anybody in a public hospital where there are no private patients.

I think he thought that perhaps I was trying to get rid of Tony, that we considered him a burden on the state—he had some sort of notion like that. But indeed it wasn't true, because in this country we *keep* patients—not alone at Broadmoor but in all the hospitals. We as doctors are under no pressure whatever to send patients anywhere else unless they have recovered sufficiently or we think they would do better in their own cultural environment.

## Letter from Dr. Thomas Maguire to the Undersecretary of State, Department of Health and Social Security, London, August 9, 1979

Broadmoor

Dear Sir,

I wish to recommend repatriation for Antony Baekeland to his homeland, the United States of America. His dossier is voluminous and complicated but I have chosen certain medical reports and other communications, which I herewith enclose, that detail his history and treatment, up to the moment of his mental health review tribunal hearing on 22 October 1974.

During 1975 in spite of vigorous physical therapy his mental illness remained largely unchanged. I wrote of him then: "He presents as a chronic schizophrenic, blunted in affect, with vague superficial interests, and lacking insight into the grave, disabling nature of his mental illness. He tends to upset other patients by making vicious and malignant allegations about them. At present the more gross symptoms of his psychosis are controlled by medication."

His disorder gradually came more and more under control so that he was able to take part beneficially in group psychotherapy. At this stage, however, he was quite unable to engage himself in any occupational therapy, but since then he has succeeded in settling down at recreational painting, at which indeed in the past, it is said, he showed more than average talent.

In the beginning of 1979 he was commended by nursing staff for his increasing ability to socialize more normally; much of his former hostility, bitterness, and resentment had eased off and he was capable of cooperation and helpfulness on the ward scene. My consultant psychotherapist colleague noted a definite improvement with willingness to engage more earnestly in treatment. He was now showing true insight and appreciation of the realities of his situation.

It was at this point that I reduced his medication in order to establish whether his psychosis was in remission. He has now been without medication for a period of nearly six months: his improvement has been fully sustained. For quite a long time he has been requesting repatriation and I have tried to elicit information about hospital placement for him somewhere in New York.

Because of the nature of his offence, the fact that he is mentally ill and lacking in insight and cooperation when motively ill, and because of his previous propensity for indulging in drug misuse, it is absolutely necessary that his placement in hospital should involve such a degree of security and supervision as to ensure continuing treatment and rehabilitation without the risk of his absconding.

It is with all this in mind that I formally recommend that Antony Baekeland should now be repatriated to a hospital in New York, where his rehabilitation may be more realistically carried forward within his own culture and near his relatives and friends.

Yours faithfully,
Thomas Maguire
Consultant Forensic Psychiatrist

## ELSPETH WILKIE

I was working in the U.S. Embassy in London in a consulate capacity, and Antony Baekeland's repatriation was just sort of a routine thing—it was paperwork going across the desk. Ultimately, because of overcrowding or just the idea that he was responding to treatment, it was agreed that he could be returned to the United States. All we had to do was satisfy ourselves through the State Department that arrangements could be made for him to be transferred to the U.S.— he had to have two escorts, for instance. We also required an understanding from the authorities at Broadmoor that he go into a similar institution in America—that is, for the criminally insane.

I do know that Broadmoor won't release somebody without first being satisfied that they're okay. I mean, the British people would feel guilty if they released somebody just willy-nilly onto the streets of New York or wherever.

## MICHAEL ALEXANDER

The *doctors* said he could go, so you see, I wasn't intervening in that side of it. All *I* said to them was, "Now you've said he can go, let him go. Don't make him hang around."

I used to have to reassure Tony every time I went to see him, "It won't be much longer now—just keep your cool and don't give them any aggravation. We're doing our best for you." And I must say, he played it very cool.

## Letter from Antony Baekeland to James Reeve, August 14, 1979

Broadmoor

Dear James,

Michael Alexander is going to the Home Secretary to speed my release from here. It's awfully nice of him: he has been such a good friend.

How goes the sale of your house? My grandmother sends her love; I found when she was last here that she had suffered a *coup d'âge*—very frail she is, and I feel I must be with her soon. She also has hallucinations: she was very funny—evidently she imagined that her sister was staying with her—she bought extra food for her and so forth, and then when she failed to show up at meals became convinced that she was hiding under the bed! When she was staying in the village here, on her way to the loo late one night she saw a huge baroque lighted staircase spiraling up from the hall. She also imagined that a young cousin of mine was sleeping with her and got out of bed onto the floor in the middle of the night to give him more room. All funny but rather worrying.

My Papa's young wife left him in Feb. for a young American sculptor to whom he had introduced her and he is very blue about it and writes me long heartrending letters. He and I are great friends now and I plan to visit him and long to spend time with him—he has a little fishing boat and a charming house right on the water in Cadaqués and the mountains and hills are lovely for walking. The wife and American lover go to stay with him there toward the end of the month—rather odd.

How is your work? Just read *Under the Volcano*—funny and macabre—he describes Mexico so well—I don't know if you have been there.

Got a long letter from Rosie Rodd Baldwin in Turkey—may go out there, too. Plan plan plan—there is little else to do. Just wait, I guess. A visit from you would be most welcome.

Much love,<br>Tony

JAMES REEVE

My last visit was before I left for a trip to India, and he was just sort of teetering on the brink of would he be let out or wouldn't he. It was awful, because this whole talk of his being let out started about a year and a half before he *was* let out. And it was a terrible business of waiting. I remember him telling me about a visit he was expecting from somebody in the embassy. He was in an absolute state about it—I mean, you can imagine! He kept closing his eyes, searching for words. But he later wrote me that it had gone well, and that was a great relief to him.

Although Tony was rather fond of Dr. Maguire, he sometimes regarded him as the one who was standing in his way to freedom. I once wrote Dr. Maguire to ask what I could do to help, and he never answered. Miwa was the one who was in touch with Maguire all the time—she really did beaver away on Tony's behalf. She was like a terrier with a rat, you know. She wouldn't let go, come hell or high water.

## Letter from Antony Baekeland to Miwa Svinka-Zielinski, Undated

Broadmoor

Dear Miwa,

James came by for a flying ten-minute visit yesterday. It was so good to see him and he tells me that you are still rooting for me. I think you are super. I just wrote to my uncle Fred Baekeland if he could help me get into a hospital in N.Y.—hopefully, as I am well now, I won't have to spend long there. My doctors have plans to repatriate me in "a matter of months." Dr. Maguire is just waiting for all the red tape to go through. Things move so slowly.

It will be a wrench (hard to believe, I know) to leave Broadmoor: I have become very accustomed to life here.

Still, it will be good to be home. Life is going to be such a new thing for me.

Love,
Tony

MIWA SVINKA-ZIELINSKI

When I visited him in late 1979, he told me that all he wanted was to go to New York and stay with his grandmother. He said to me, "I love Nini. I'd like to serve her. I want to cook for her. I want to do everything for her."

I saw Dr. Maguire at that time and had a very friendly conversation with him. He told me Tony was improved, but I didn't want him just let loose in New York. I wanted to find some halfway house for him.

## Letter from J. W. Bone to Miwa Svinka-Zielinski, February 5, 1980

Broadmoor

Dear Mrs. Zielinski,

It has been agreed that due to the conditions currently prevailing in America with regard to psychiatric treatment and the excessive cost of private treatment, Tony should be returned to America without any statutory supervision entailed. We are, of course, apprehensive as to the situation that will greet Tony when he arrives in New York and, while he states quite emphatically that he wishes to take up residence with his grandmother, Mrs. N. Daly, we feel that this may not in fact be appropriate. I would be grateful therefore if you could furnish me with any information as to those members of Tony's family or his circle of friends who might be able to offer Tony both accommodation and support.

I look forward to hearing from you.

Yours sincerely,
J. W. Bone
Senior Social Worker

## Telegram from Cyrus R. Vance, Secretary of State, Washington, D.C., to American Embassy, London, March 7, 1980

H.E.W. HAS ADVISED THAT IN A PRELIMINARY REQUEST TO SOCIAL SERVICES IN NEW YORK, THEY WERE INFORMED THAT

DUE TO LIMITED SPACE PROBLEMS, HALFWAY HOUSE FACILI-
TIES WOULD BE UNOBTAINABLE FOR NEAR FUTURE. IT
WOULD BE BEST TO RECOMMEND A HOSPITAL IN NEW YORK
UNTIL FACILITY COULD BE OBTAINED. H.E.W. HAS ALSO AD-
VISED THAT REQUEST TO PLACE BAEKELAND IN HALFWAY
HOUSE PROGRAM SHOULD COME DIRECTLY FROM HOSPITAL
IN THE U.K.    VANCE

## Dr. Thomas Maguire

I arranged for Tony to go to a halfway house called the Richmond
Fellowship. I had it all arranged.

## Robert Orenstein

I was the assistant director of the Fellowship and the name Baekeland
vaguely rings a bell, but more familiar to me is the circumstance—
that this person coming from England had killed his mother. We
very rarely got referrals of people who had committed homicides. We
might have gotten an application from him, but the likelihood of our
accepting someone with that kind of violent history would be very,
very unusual.

## Inge Mahn

I have no way of knowing what correspondence may have occurred,
but in the little file cards we have here of applications received, I
don't see Antony Baekeland's name listed.

## Letter from Antony Baekeland to Miwa Svinka-Zielinski, February 5, 1980

Broadmoor

Dear Miwa,

Michael Alexander is trying to speed things up for me and now
it looks as if I may be in New York within a few weeks! As you
may imagine, I am delighted. Life will be entirely new and fresh
for me and I think I will enjoy it immensely. I imagine myself
on the plane, having a *coup de vin* and knowing that seven years
of confinement is receding into the distance. It will be pure
heaven and the best of it is that I will not have to be accom-

panied by guards or go to a hospital when I arrive. I so look
forward to seeing you.

Love,
Tony

## MICHAEL ALEXANDER
I had long discussions with Tony about his father toward the end of
his stay at Broadmoor. I'm fond of Brooks, although I did rather feel
that he wasn't playing his role in this whole affair. The reason I
suppose was it was just too . . . He couldn't take it himself, really.
You see, he felt that Tony was a disaster area and he couldn't absorb
it. He wasn't big enough, or he had his own psychological problems.
Anyway, he just couldn't do it. And what's more, he didn't!

I tried to persuade him to actually go down and meet Tony when
he got out and possibly have him to stay and all that. But Brooks
wouldn't play along—at the time he was rather unhappy because
Sylvie had taken up with this younger man.

There was a definite rumor going around about the family trying to
see that Tony was kept inside so they could have control over his
inheritance.

## BROOKS BAEKELAND
There was a story that was spread by the members of the Bleeding
Hearts Club and/or others that I was "keeping Tony in Broadmoor to
get his money." Ha! There is no limit to meanness. There was no
*possible* way that I could ever profit materially from my son's health,
illness, or death.

## MIWA SVINKA-ZIELINSKI
Brooks was more or less absent from the picture at this point, but his
brother Fred, the psychiatrist, sometime around the middle of March
wrote a very strong letter to Dr. Maguire saying that he wanted to
correct a number of pieces of misinformation, so that Maguire
should have no illusions about what exactly would face Tony on his
return. He mentioned that, as far as he knew, Tony had few friends
his own age in New York and that what older friends there were
might rally round at first but that none was in a position to house or
care for him. Fred also told Maguire that Broadmoor was relying too
much on Nini, who was old and needed a live-in nurse herself,

which meant that there would really be no room for Tony in her small apartment. He also said that there was no other family member who could put him up except on the most temporary basis—his own mother, Mrs. Hallowell, Tony's other grandmother, was also in her eighties at this point; she was sympathetic but had never been as close to Tony as Nini.

Fred also told Maguire that Broadmoor was very wrong to say Tony would not be a financial burden to anyone. He spelled out in no uncertain words that after 1981 no more capital would be coming to Tony from his trust.


## Letter from Dr. Thomas Maguire to Miwa Svinka-Zielinski, March 27, 1980

Broadmoor

Dear Mrs. Svinka-Zielinski,

Thank you for your recent letter concerning the above patient. I have also had correspondence from Tony's father, from Dr. Frederick Baekeland, from Mrs. Daly, from Michael Alexander, and from others—all in the recent past. So it is against this background that I write to you.

Although members of his family express concern over Tony's welfare, none is prepared to offer him the shelter of a home environment or indeed personal supervision of any kind. Those friends who retain an interest in him, and they are quite numerous, do not seem to realise that he will need supportive help of an immediate nature when he returns to New York.

Your enquiry about his need for medical care follows from our conversation in November 1979. However, since that time Tony has been quite symptom-free although without medication over many months. Prior to November I had been thinking in terms of hospitalisation in New York for a few months following his repatriation. But some five months have now passed since we spoke and his continued well-being indicates that there is now no need for in-patient treatment. Interested, sympathetic social supervision would now be adequate to secure his smooth integration into the open community once more. This means that someone would meet him at the airport to escort him to living quarters already secured for him and this agency or person should also be prepared to help him in the various day-to-day issues that will inevitably crop up for someone who has spent so long in a sheltered environment.

Dr. Frederick Baekeland has pointed out how feckless Tony is about financial affairs and he fears that Tony's capital would be quickly dissipated. This of course is very well known by me, and indeed long ago I placed the overall control of his financial affairs in the hands of the Official Solicitors Office which exercises fairly rigorous control over his expenditure. I believe that similar control should be exercised over his income from the capital invested in the USA—if that can be properly arranged.

Can you help in providing information about the availability of social aid for Tony when he arrives in New York? Once I am assured that such adequate back-up is ready to help him I can proceed with the arrangements for his repatriation.

Many thanks for your help.

Yours sincerely,
Thomas Maguire

## Telegram from Cyrus R. Vance, Secretary of State, Washington, D.C., to American Embassy, London, March 30, 1980

DEPT. RECEIVED TELEPHONE CALL 3/24 FROM DR. FREDER-ICK BAEKELAND, SUBJECT'S UNCLE, WHO INFORMED THAT HE HAD BEEN NOTIFIED BY DR. MAGUIRE, CONSULTANT PSYCHI-ATRIST AT BROADMOOR HOSPITAL, THAT ANTONY BAEKELAND WOULD BE RELEASED AND DEPORTED IN APPROXIMATELY TWO WEEKS.

DR. BAEKELAND IS CONCERNED, BECAUSE HE WISHES TO MAKE SOME ARRANGEMENTS FOR ANTONY'S ADMITTANCE INTO A HOSPITAL WITHIN THE UNITED STATES, AND BECAUSE THERE IS NO ONE IN THE U.S. WHO COULD POSSIBLY TAKE ANTONY INTO HIS OR HER PERSONAL CARE. BRITISH MEDICAL REPORTS HAVE INDICATED THAT SUBJECT IS NOT STABLE ENOUGH TO MANAGE IN A NORMAL AND UNSUPERVISED AT-MOSPHERE.

HOSPITAL OFFICIALS ADVISED DR. BAEKELAND THAT AN-

TONY WOULD REQUIRE TWO MEDICAL ESCORTS TO ACCOM-
PANY HIM ON THE RETURN FLIGHT TO NEW YORK     VANCE

### MIWA SVINKA-ZIELINSKI

Some woman emerged who later took him back to New York. She
said she was a friend of the family but I had never heard of this
woman all these years. I didn't know *who* she was. She came over to
England to visit him that April.

### HEATHER COHANE

We knew absolutely nothing about her, and when she just turned up
like that, you know, Michael Alexander and I said to each other,
"What the hell? Who *is* she?" We called her "Mystery Woman."

## Official Visitors File, Broadmoor Special Hospital, April 29, 1980

VISITOR'S NAME: Mrs. Cecelia Brebner
RELATIONSHIP TO PATIENT: Friend of family.
SUMMARY: Knows background of patient in greatest detail. Is
fully aware of eccentricities of Baekeland family and of its attitude
toward any of their own participation in Tony's rehabilitation.
She discussed Tony's return to N.Y., his initial reintegration into
family social life again. She appears to be the most sensible member of the large group of relatives and friends fussily engaged in
Tony's discharge.

### CECELIA BREBNER

I was, and still am, very friendly with Tony's grandmother, Cornelia
Hallowell, and shortly after the murder of Barbara, she said to me,
because she knew I had a daughter who lived very close to Broadmoor, "If you're going to England, could you take something to
Tony for me?" And this is how it all began.

That first time, my daughter drove me there, and I said to her,
"Here I am about to meet a man who has murdered his mother and I
don't know how I'm going to react." And she said, "Would you like
me to come in with you, Mummy?" I said yes.

Anyway, when I was in London in 1980, Cornelia said to me,

"They're releasing Tony, they may have already released him." I telephoned Broadmoor and they said no, they had not. Then I had a mysterious telegram from a woman called Heather Cohane—I'm always having mysterious telegrams!—saying that the Home Office had recommended Tony's release and could *I* possibly escort him back. I said, well, I didn't think so, because although I was leaving London, I was going to Toronto, you see, and not New York. However, I was pressured. And later I was interviewed for four hours by Dr. Thomas Maguire. I asked him, "In the event of my doing this, what are the implications?" And he said, "He's a schizophrenic, but with love and care he will probably be able to resume a more or less normal life." He said that he had arranged for Tony to go to a halfway house in New York. I said, "Why can't his own father take him?" And Maguire answered, "He's having marital problems." Well, of course! He married Tony's girlfriend and it was all very complicated.

I got together with a man called Michael Alexander, an author I believe, who said, "He's been in Broadmoor for *eight years*—he should be repatriated *now!*" And I had a feeling that this should happen as well, and so I agreed to take him. Tony was positively euphoric when he found out I was going to bring him home.

I was staying at the time with Lady Mary Clayton at Kensington Palace, and *she* said, "Celia, I don't think it's the right thing to do but we'll ask Prince George of Denmark," and *he* thought it was a very altruistic thing to do, so I embarked upon it.


### Postcard from Ethel Woodward de Croisset to Antony Baekeland, April 9, 1980

Paris

Dear Tony—
Had a telegram from M. Alexander saying that you are well and can return to New York & to your grandmother soon. Send me her address, which I have lost.

I do hope that you will get on all right in NYC and can find a quiet cosy nest and a happy life in the country perhaps.

*Abrazos,*
Ethel

HEATHER COHANE
Just before Tony was released, I took Simone and Aschwin Lippe to
see him in Broadmoor, because they had known Barbara so well, and
Brooks so well, for many many many years. You know, I would have
really put every penny I had on the table and said, "I *know* that this is
a one-time thing with his killing Barbara. He'll never do it again."
But as we were driving back to London in the car, Simone said that
she thought there was a great sort of look of madness in his eyes. She
kept saying that, and I kept saying, "No, I don't think so, I think
you'll see he's all right."


## Letter from Antony Baekeland to Dr. Frederick Baekeland, April 17, 1980

                                                               Broadmoor
Dear Fred,
I appreciate your efforts to help me. Saw Dr. Maguire yesterday:
he told me that he had been in touch with you. He also said
that you had asked him a number of questions regarding my
case which he declined to answer. To tell you the truth, Fred, I
resent a bit this morbid curiosity on your part when you were
not even polite enough to write me a note after my Mother's
death; it doesn't read true, does it?
   I am in constant touch with my father, who plans to help me.
Our letters are a source of inspiration and pleasure to both of us.
He seems to be hard at work on a book—I too plan to make
one. I may call it "The Shakespearean Continuum."
   I have re-made myself. The experience at Broadmoor has
been most valuable to me; I have had to live with all kinds of
people who I would never have met in normal life, and accept
them for what they are and what they are not. I have learned a
certain discipline which will help me later on. As things stand
now, I may be in N.Y. in a couple of weeks.

                                                            Yrs. truly,
                                                            Tony

## Official Visitors File, Broadmoor Special Hospital, May 7, 1980

VISITOR'S NAME: Mrs. Svinka-Zielinski
RELATIONSHIP TO PATIENT: Friend
SUMMARY: Dropped in on her way to Poland to visit relatives. Reported that a New York psychiatrist, a Dr. Portnow, would be interested to help Tony during the initial supportive period following his return to NY. Letter to Dr. Portnow promised. Mrs. Zielinski believes that Antony could realistically stay with Grandma Nini for a short period, even if only for bed and board and a basic address.


### DR. STANLEY L. PORTNOW

A lady came to visit me when Tony Baekeland was still in England, claiming she was very interested in having him brought back to the United States and that the only way the hospital in England would discharge him would be if they were secure in their feeling that he would have follow-up treatment by a psychiatrist in New York. I said I would be glad to evaluate him and if I couldn't take care of him myself, for one reason or another, I would see to it that he got a proper referral. Then there was talk about my going over to England to examine him, and that suggestion was from this same lady. The trip to England never came off. I never heard from the lady again.


## Telegram from Kingman Brewster, Jr., U.S. Ambassador to the Court of St. James's, American Embassy, London, to Cyrus R. Vance, Secretary of State, Washington, D.C., May 20, 1980

CONSULAR OFFICER MADE ELEVENTH VISIT ON MAY 2, 1980. BAEKELAND IN GOOD HEALTH AND SPIRITS. CONSULAR OFFICER ALSO TALKED TO DR. MAGUIRE, BAEKELAND'S PHYSICIAN. BAEKELAND'S FAMILY APPARENTLY UNABLE OR UNWILLING TO ASSIST HIS REINTRODUCTION TO U.S. BAEKELAND WILL NOT VOLUNTARILY COMMIT HIMSELF TO U.S. HOSPITAL. DR. MAGUIRE SAYS BAEKELAND DOESN'T NEED HOSPITALIZATION, ONLY A HALFWAY HOUSE TYPE SETTING

FOR A FEW WEEKS OF READJUSTMENT TO LIVING IN SOCIETY.
DR. MAGUIRE SAID HE WOULD KEEP EMBASSY INFORMED.

EMBASSY WILL INFORM DEPARTMENT OF ALL ARRANGE-
MENTS MADE BY DR. MAGUIRE, AS EMBASSY AWARE THAT,
DUE TO NATURE OF BAEKELAND'S OFFENCE, FAMILY IN U.S.
WISHES TO BE INFORMED OF ARRANGEMENTS.    BREWSTER

## Telegram from Kingman Brewster, Jr., U.S. Ambassador to the Court of St. James's, to Interpol, Washington, D.C., June 20, 1980

URGENT

ANTONY BAEKELAND WAS RELEASED AS A RESULT OF AN
ORDER SIGNED BY THE UNDER SECRETARY OF STATE ON
6/17/80.    BREWSTER

## MICHAEL ALEXANDER

Even though the Home Office had in fact authorized Tony's release, there was quite a lot of red tape still involved, and meanwhile he had to remain at Broadmoor, locked up. We all thought, those last weeks in Broadmoor, that he was very together, you know. He seemed absolutely fine.

## JAKE COOPER

I cried for the first time in a very long time when I learned that Antony was getting out. I felt it was such a very special thing to happen. I felt at least I could be happy that my dear friend was finding free space in *his* life again, because, you see, *I* used to be a leader—in Cadaqués, in Morocco, in Paris—without meaning to be. I just seemed able to get things together, and then all of a sudden I got in this cracked-up state.

## Letter from Antony Baekeland to Jake Cooper, July 18, 1980

Broadmoor

Dear and Noble Pinetree Friend,
A host of memories come floating back—*chez* Dalí—that walk

to the sea, you in your jackal coat, when you took mush-rooms—union, beauty, and freedom in Morocco, blue irises on the grassy hillside in Tangiers, and I know you will be that way again. Remember that we are the horsemen and all that that means—beauty, truth, freedom, and wisdom—the source of all purity and contentment. They can give their help to you if you will ask for it.

Don't be confused or impressed by the material world of tech-nology—our mind makes it all, it is just a machine—the most beautiful one—as is your damaged brain. Your mind is above the brain and will repair that tool in a little time. I also re-member the days when I was a naughty child and you came to me although I had not yet seen your bodily form on the sandy dunes of Cape Cod among the stunted sea pines, and in Italy, and all through my life really. You're brave and all this present eclipse you will put to good—and use by putting it behind you—with self-understanding. Remember, time is an illusion—all the points, moments in time, are equidistant from the infi nite past, the infinite future—each moment is a star creating past and future connecting with all other moments—the whole point of being. Now, by putting your damaged intellect to work on the basic physical world of time and space around you, find-ing out with patient observation why the machine—the con-tinuum—works, you will free yourself from your dilemma. There must be a reason for what's happened. Find out and un-derstand. That is step #1. Don't be scared if you have to go to a rehabilitation center—you will meet people who may help you. It will be a change. Returning to your father's house is no good for you and you'll feel more and more cut off from the world. Fight!

Look at me. I suffered loneliness and exile from life for years and years, all during our time together and after that, also, and I've only just made it home, as it were, to my true self and happiness. My life would have become a maudlin tragedy if I had not made up my mind to fight—to fight for my god and for my life. You will do it, too. We all have to lose once in order to never lose again.

I'm leaving for New York on Monday at 12:00 midday. I'll be staying at my granny Nini's. She knows all about you and would want me to send her love. Don't worry, I will write as often as you write to me and I know you will get yourself out of this soon.

Certain of us can see everything that is going on everywhere, past and future—and will help and protect you if you realize your own present helplessness and gullibility.

My own wishes go straight to your dear heart like arrows and I send you, as you once sent me, dearest thoughts.

Tony

## Letter from Dr. Thomas Maguire to Miwa Svinka-Zielinski, July 21, 1980

Broadmoor

Dear Mrs. Svinka-Zielinski,

It is a pleasure for me to tell you that Antony Baekeland has today been discharged from this hospital and will fly to New York from London at noon. He is accompanied by a family friend, Mrs. Brebner, who will ensure that he meets with members of his family on arrival. There is a tentative arrangement that he will attend Richmond Fellowship in New York in the near future where Dr. Portnow could, if contacted, supervise the case. However, as Antony is under no legal obligation in the USA to pursue any statutory therapeutic course, these arrangements will be entirely voluntary. Should you wish to establish contact with the case it is best to do this through his grandmother, Mrs. Daly.

He is not having any medication and has remained in full remission and quite stable over many months so that the prognosis is quite good.

May I close by expressing my sincere thanks to you for your interest and help.

Yours sincerely,
Thomas Maguire
Consultant Forensic Psychiatrist

## HEATHER COHANE

Tony was handed over to Cecelia Brebner at London Airport and put on the plane on the condition that he never come back to England. I was a little frightened when he was actually leaving, just because I had been, you know, quite instrumental in persuading the doctors to let him out.

## CECELIA BREBNER

I thought I was taking him to New York to go to a halfway house. But at the airport when I rendezvoused with Broadmoor—at the eleventh hour, yes!—when he was handed over to me, they said, "It's all changed. We tried to contact you at Kensington Palace but you'd already left and Lady Mary didn't know where we could reach you. Antony Baekeland is going directly to his maternal grandmother, Mrs. Nina Daly." *Well.*

On the aircraft over, he went into how he had murdered his mother. In absolute detail. He said, "Celia, a friend of Mummy's had rung while she was out and when Mummy got back she said she didn't want to see her but I had already told this friend to come round that evening and Mummy screamed at me." Then, he said, he threw something at her. And then, he said, she rushed into the kitchen and wrote a note on a piece of paper, to the Spanish maid who was ironing, so he just picked up the carving knife and stabbed her. He said, "Mummy was dying. I knelt down and turned her face toward me and asked, 'What is your name? Who are you?'" He said, "But it doesn't matter because Mummy and I are one. It really doesn't matter at all." I said, "Well, Tony, what now? Do you think you are going to be able to cope with life in New York?" "Oh yes," he said. "I'm going to look after Nini and cook for her and do marvelous things for her." And I said fine.

# 2

# REORIENTATION

**SUSAN LANNAN**
The International Social Service of Great Britain was still looking into the matter of Antony Baekeland's rehabilitation in America when we heard that he had been released. We were concerned.

**CECELIA BREBNER**
And so we arrived. It was ninety-two degrees in New York that day. Tony said, "You know something, Celia—New York hasn't changed. It's just the same." And he was extraordinary—he saw to all the baggage and when we got into the cab he said, "I want to stop off and get Nini some flowers but I haven't any money on me," and I said, "I have money," so he got her a huge bouquet.

**SHIRLEY COX**
Nini did not know Tony was coming until she got a call, I believe, the day before, saying he would be here the following day. That's what she told me when I stopped by to pick up her mail. I live in her building and I handle all her bills and all her business affairs—I've done that for many years.

## LENA RICHARDS

Mrs. Daly had broken her hip and needed round-the-clock care. I was the weekend nurse but I was still there on Monday afternoon when Tony came in from the airport with Mrs. Brebner. She wanted to know what the setup was going to be, who was to be responsible for Tony's care, and when Nini and I said nobody, she couldn't believe it.

He looked a little distant to me, but I didn't know what his problems were. Nini had never said anything, she'd never said anything but good things about him.

## CECELIA BREBNER

When we arrived at Nini's apartment on Seventy-fourth Street, we went directly into her bedroom to see her. And there was a huge painting of Barbara Baekeland there, that I am told hung in the "21" Club in New York for years—until she died, in fact. And Tony saw it and said, "Nini, take it down!" And she said, "Oh no, Tony, it's my favorite, favorite painting of Mummy." "Take it down!" he said. I saw the look on this man's face and I knew that I had done the wrong thing.

## DR. THOMAS MAGUIRE

My conscience is quite clear. I did ten times the normal amount of work to get Tony to America. I tried everything I possibly could to find the proper care for him.

## SHIRLEY COX

Nini told me later that the moment he walked in the door she knew he wasn't well. And later I saw that for myself. My first thought was, "I'm going to call Fred Baekeland." But Nini said, "No no no no! Promise me you won't do that. *Promise* me you won't! You're my friend, promise me."

## ETHEL WOODWARD DE CROISSET

When he wrote me saying he was going back to his grandmother's place where he had spent so many happy days as a child—it was where he sometimes used to go in the afternoons when he was let out of Buckley School, you see—I said to myself, This boy's going to find that apartment very small. And later Nini told me that she could see at once that he felt oppressed—and it was also very hot, to make matters worse—so she suggested they go out immediately, that first night, and have dinner around the corner.


**BROOKS BAEKELAND**
By coincidence I came back to the U.S. at about the same time as Tony. I went, first, to stay with probably my oldest friend, my cousin Baekeland Roll, and his wife, Kate, in Rhode Island. The Rolls are much reputed for their hospitalities and other virtues: a gregarious, large-familied tribe, their house always bulging with children and guests. I had not seen it, breathed its wacky air for many a year, and a great weight seemed to go off me there for a while.

I had not been on Block Island more than a week, I think, when I got a telephone call—everyone in the house listened to it—from Tony, who had just arrived at Nini's. He said he wanted to come out to that full, happy, child-brimming house. I said no.


**CLEMENT BIDDLE WOOD**
I suppose Brooks was terrified to see Tony for fear that Tony might attack *him*.


**BROOKS BAEKELAND**
For myself I felt no fear. My pessimism makes me immune to fear, and I have a certain confidence, even now, in my wits and brawn. But I knew my tiger, and I did not even ask the Rolls if they would receive him. I just said no. My bad reputation increased with that "no."

Oh yes, he had often wanted to assault me—I had seen the crazed lust for it come into his eyes—but he never dared. He was a *woman*-beater. I said to him once, "Crazy you may be and you are, but there are crazy saints and crazy brutes and you are one of the latter."


**CECELIA BREBNER**
I was staying nearby, on Sixty-ninth Street, with Georgette Klinger. I was going to look after her little poodle for about three months while she did a European tour. I called Nini every day and she always said, "He's okay, Celia," and one day I said, "Look, I'd like to come round and see him," so I took him out for dinner, and he seemed quite rational, perhaps a little bit strange but certainly not manic.

### Shirley Cox

Tony promised he would get Nini's breakfast every day, she told me, because, you see, her nurse could not be there overnight when Tony was staying, there was simply not enough room. This meant that Nini had no care at night if she wanted to get up and go to the bathroom and things like that.

I know he didn't fix her breakfast because the nurse would arrive in the morning and he would still be in bed. Nini told me he stayed up all night playing the record player. Well, I think that's understandable. Having been incarcerated for so long, you now have freedom, you know, to do all the things you've been prevented from doing. But he was in a small apartment, in a small apartment house, where the people on either side and around have to get up and go to work, so Nini knew that if the noise lasted for more than two or three days the neighbors would complain and she was terrified of that. So she said she asked him to lower the volume, and he completely ignored her.

### Sam Green

He called me right after he got to town and it was a close call. Bart, my assistant, took the call. Tony said he wanted to see me urgently, that I was his only friend and he wanted me to get him some dope so he could get high. Bart told him that I was out of the country.

At some point you just have to protect yourself. I mean, clearly one *should* have been nice to Tony, and generous—he had been through a terrible ordeal and needed companionship and forgiveness, but I just didn't want to do it anymore.

### Tom Dillow

Tony asked Bart for *my* number, and Bart called to warn me that Tony was trying to find me. I mean, I was in the phone book, but, you know, for the Baekelands a telephone number didn't exist unless they *got* it from someone. Bart said Tony told him, "T-t-t-tom n-never understood why I m-m-murdered M-mummy."

### Bart Gorin

When I first started working for Sam Green, he told me that probably someday a person named Tony Baekeland would call and that I was just to make up anything to keep him away. I guess it was just sort of understood that Tony would be coming back at some point, but we never knew when exactly. So anyway, one hot day there he was on the phone. Sam was out on Fire Island, but I said, "Gee, Tony, Sam's in Singapore," or somewhere like that. And then he asked if I knew about him and I played sort of dumb, and he said, "You don't know who I am?" And I said no. Then he told me fairly matter-of-factly that he had killed his mother. I said, "What are you going to do now? What are your plans?" And he said, "Well, my grandmother Mrs. Daly is the only person who has stood by me all this time, in fact she was the one who got me out of that awful place I was in. She's an old lady now and I want to make her last days as happy as possible"—I remember *that* very well. And then he asked me if I would go shopping with him because all he had were winter clothes, from England, and it was summer out. I said I was going away for the weekend and he said, "Can I call you on Monday?" and I said sure. I never spoke with him again.

### GLORIA JONES

I didn't know they'd let him out till he called from New York. He called Muriel Murphy first and then he called *me*. He said he'd like to come out to visit me on Long Island, where I was living now. I was absolutely terrified. Jim was dead by then so I called up Irwin Shaw, who I wouldn't have bothered if Jim were alive. Irwin said, "You can't have him come out," and I said, "Well, God, we've got to do *something* about him." Irwin didn't know the Baekelands that well—I guess he was very smart, he just stayed away from the whole thing, very clever. He said to me, "Stay totally out of it. You just don't know. . . . You have children around and everything." So I called Tony back and said that my house was filled, you know. And it *was* filled.

### CLEMENT BIDDLE WOOD

Jessie and I had come over from Europe for the summer and we were visiting Muriel Murphy in East Hampton when Tony called. He said, "Muriel, I'm in New York and it's boiling." It *was* an exceptional heatwave—I mean, even for July. He said, "I'm cooped up in this tiny little apartment with my grandmother and there are pictures of my mother everywhere and her ashes are in an urn on the mantelpiece and I'm just going crazy. I've got to get out of town." Obviously he was hoping Muriel would invite him out to Long Island. Which she didn't. And then he said, "Maybe I can find rooms for my grandmother and myself out there somewhere." And Muriel said,

"Everything's pretty full up," which of course is always true in the summer. So then he said, "Well, I'll probably be coming out if I *can* find anywhere to stay, and I'll give you a ring." Muriel got terribly upset, she said to us, "This boy's a homicidal maniac, he shouldn't be in an apartment alone with his grandmother, but I certainly don't want him coming out *here* and fastening on to *me* as some sort of mother substitute.

PHYLLIS HARRIMAN MASON
One day that week I thought I saw him on the street, Sixty-ninth Street, and I was scared stiff because I was afraid he would identify me with Barbara.

RENÉ JEAN TEILLARD
I saw Tony on Lexington Avenue. I am a friend since a very long time of his beautiful grandmother Mrs. Hallowell. I was going to buy a newspaper and suddenly I saw him there and I said, "Tony, what are *you* doing here? I'm so glad you came back," and he said, "I'm buying a pair of shoes." I said, "But to buy a pair of shoes you should go to Alexander's." "Oh," he said, "I didn't know. I've been in England." And so we chatted and I said I wanted him to come and have dinner and he came the next day and it was all right.

When he and his mother left for London a year before her assassination I invited them to dinner and I gave them some frogs' legs, because they were international and I'm French myself. And I gave him frogs' legs again. I gave him the exact same dinner as when he had left.

We ate on a little bridge table which I had beautifully prepared, near the telephone and close to some weights which were on the floor by my feet in case something should happen, since I hadn't seen him since he left that night for England and if something happened now because he was crazy in a moment, I was therefore prepared with my telephone and my weights.

He was not reluctant to answer all the questions I asked. First of all I asked him what happened and he told me how he had killed his mother. He was able to tell me without any emotion how he plunged the knife in her chest. I told him, "You need friends now that you are back here and you need to see the doctor." "I don't need to see any doctor," he said. I said, "But Dr. Greene is a friend of yours since your youth, and I am certain he would be delighted to see you since he even went over to England to see you."

His face changed when I first spoke "doctor." But then when I said "Dr. Greene," everything was just fine and we finished dinner. I said, "You can come back again, you have my telephone number." And he left.

### SHIRLEY COX
On Wednesday and Thursday, the third and fourth days he was here, he put all the pictures of his mother and some candles on a chest of drawers in Nini's living room—he made it into an altar.

### CECELIA BREBNER
He was evidently playing the most macabre music and he had those photographs of Barbara and the black candles and he was performing a kind of black mass.

### LENA RICHARDS
I was nervous around him because I just didn't know what to expect—I couldn't tell. He didn't have much to say, really. And he didn't seem to have much patience for anything, I noticed. Apparently all week he'd been using the telephone a lot and drinking all the wine—Nini said, "He's to have it," so he ordered more. On Saturday when I got there, he asked me to go to the store for him to get him some writing paper. I was wondering why he couldn't go out himself. I told him it was early, I didn't feel like going out yet. So he did go, after all, and I asked him to get me a newspaper, but he forgot. And when he came back he curled up in a chair and slept for a long time.

### CECELIA BREBNER
Late Saturday afternoon I went over to have tea with Tony and Nini and no sooner had I gotten there than the nurse beckoned me into the bedroom, she said Nini wanted to talk to me. Nini told me, "I'm so frightened of him, Celia." I said, "Well, Nini, I don't know how to advise you at this point. I don't know whether we can call the police because he hasn't committed a felony." When I went back into the living room, Tony said to me, "I'm not well, Celia," and I said, "Now, Tony, tell me—define this. Are you sick mentally or are you sick physically?" He said, "I wake up at three in the morning," and I said, "Well, so do I. It's the jet lag, the time difference. But

each day it will get a little better. And you know where I am if you need me." And he threw his arms around me and said, "Oh, I love you, Celia, I love you." I said, "Well, Tony, prove your love. All I want you to do is be kind to Nini and show them that you can fit into normal society again." He said, "Yes, yes, I can, I can." So I said fine.

## LENA RICHARDS

I didn't prepare supper for Nini that Saturday because he said *he* wanted to do it. He even told her what he was going to make her. But then I think somebody called and asked them out to dinner. Anyway, I left.

But later that night I called to see if she was okay. She said she was. I knew she wasn't going to say she wasn't, but I thought she wasn't her own self.

## DR. FREDERICK BAEKELAND

I had dinner with them that night, the Saturday after his arrival, and he seemed rather tense but not extraordinarily so—and of course I've seen him very tense at times. One of the big problems in psychiatry is the limits of predicting behavior. Another big problem is that a person may look tense and it could have to do with any number of things, and if the person's not going to tell you anything about it, that presents still another problem.

## THILO VON WATZDORF

Tony called me in New York and I told my secretary, "No no—tell him I'm not available." The last time I'd seen him was at the party Barbara gave on Cadogan Square the night before he killed her, and I hadn't communicated with him at all during the whole time he was in Broadmoor.

When he couldn't reach me by phone in New York he wrote me a letter saying how fondly he remembered me from Ansedonia and how all he wanted now was to take care of his little grandmother and how he didn't have any friends in New York his own age and would so much like to see me and couldn't we meet.

I got the letter on a Sunday night—I'd been in the country for the weekend—and I was touched by it. I rang and rang and kept getting no answer. I couldn't imagine why no one was picking up since I knew his grandmother was in her late eighties and there had to be somebody there to look after her.

# 3

# ATTACK

**LENA RICHARDS**
On Sunday I came maybe a couple minutes after nine a.m., and Tony didn't open the door for me right away. I didn't have my own key, I'd given it to *him*. When he finally came to the door—he was wearing his cutoff pants—he said, "Lena, quick! Get the police!" Or the ambulance, or something to that effect. "I just stabbed my grandmother." He didn't move. I got scared, so I didn't go in. I ran back down the stairs. I had on high heels and I ran to the corner and called the police. Then I waited outside Nini's building for them to come, and when they did I took them up.

**SERGEANT JOSEPH CHINEA**
We responded to a 911 call, and when my partner John McCabe and I entered the apartment on East Seventy-fourth Street, he came running out of the bedroom at us, saying, "She won't die!" We could hear his grandmother screaming. I grabbed him by the shirt and pulled him past me, and McCabe, who's a beefy man, grabbed him and he didn't struggle. He kept repeating, "She won't die, the knife won't go in! And she keeps screaming! I can't understand it."

I ran into the bedroom and saw this elderly, frail lady lying against the wall. The nightstand was turned over and she was in the corner. It looked as if she was trying to get away from him. She was wearing a satiny nightgown and the blood was just running through it, it wasn't soaking up. She was still screaming, but once she saw me she started to calm down. The nurse had arrived during the assault, and she probably saved the woman's life.

An ambulance arrived right after we did, and then additional policemen arrived, and while she was being ministered to she was lucid enough to comment that her grandson had been talking on the phone and playing music twenty-four hours a day all week and that he had been up all night mumbling over a table that had his mother's ashes in the center.

## From a Psychiatric Interview with Antony Baekeland, New York City, 1980

My grandmother helped me and brought me back to New York. I spent one week with her but I had a difficult time. I was up all night and I couldn't eat. I felt I was being denied physical and eye contact with my grandmother. There is something in my eye that stops me from meeting other people face to face. I suppose if it meant having sex with my grandmother, I might have wanted to have sex with her. At the end of that week I knew that I would be unhappy with her. I was calling the airlines to fly to Mallorca or England but my grandmother, who is a very mysterious woman, tried to prevent me from making these phone calls. I kept hearing voices, including my grandmother talking in my head, but I couldn't hear her voice clearly because there was noise around and my voices kept bothering me. The voices are those of people I know and people I don't know. They sound like a machine. They talk back to me and it really bothers me a lot. The voices tell me that I'm a savior, that I'm Satan, that I'm an angel, that I'm royalty. Sometimes they say that I'm a dirty little man or a bad woman or a dog. They also give me helpful messages. I hear them all the time. I also hear music and the music lifts my soul.

We were in my grandmother's bedroom but she wouldn't shut up. She kept talking and talking and talking and she wouldn't let me make the phone call. Then I threw the telephone across the room at her and she fell down. When she fell down, I felt very bad for her. I didn't want her to go to the hospital with broken bones and suffer more, so in order to help her I rushed to the kitchen, took a little knife from the drawer, went back, and stabbed her in the breast. I wanted to kill her so I could liberate her—not because I was angry, just to liberate her from the mistake I had made and from the suffering that she was experiencing at the time and from the time I was thirteen years of age.

All this happened because I was denied physical contact with my grandmother and homosexual relations with anybody else.

After I stabbed her, the nurse came to the door and she must have called the ambulance.

### Lena Richards
I can't understand how he didn't kill her. All those blows! Her only comments in the hospital were that she wished nobody to know. She wanted to know if everybody knew. That's how she reacted—she didn't want anybody to know anything. She wanted to keep it quiet.

### Gloria Jones
Somebody called right away. You know—people, everybody.

### Cleve Gray
I heard it on the radio, that he'd stabbed his grandmother. That's how I found out about it, on WINS.

### Cecelia Brebner
He was not on any medication at all, and I think probably that was the problem. But you know, what happened really is that Broadmoor made a mistake—they make so many mistakes. They took him for purely a schizophrenic. In fact, he was a paranoid, homicidal maniac. You know, when I took him to Nini's that first day, she said to me, "Look at this lovely photograph of Tony with his cat." I have never seen anything so terrified in my life as that cat!

### Police Officer John McCabe
He didn't look capable of violence. The grandmother evidently repeated things and this annoyed him, he told me.

## Nina Daly

It was in the morning. We had had breakfast together, I think. I was very close to him. He was with me every minute. I never thought he would go that way. I don't know how it happened. I can't imagine. Just something snapped. Yes, that's it. That's what happened. You never know.

He was so loving. All I did was break my heart over him. Why could this happen to him, you know? And then I remembered it happened to Barbara, too. I knew how much *she* loved him. We both loved him the same.

It was too much for me. Too much. It could have been dangerous. It nearly killed me. I wasn't in a lot of pain. It didn't hurt because I loved him so much.

## Sergeant Joseph Chinea

Mrs. Daly told us that he had taken over her apartment. And then the nurse let us in on a lot of things. She pointed out the ashes to us and told us about the bizarre way he'd been behaving—the loud music, that he was making a mess out of the apartment, that he was telling everyone to shut up and not talk to him. He had become very agitated as the week progressed, and he was staying up all night, worshiping.

He spoke about what he called his grandmother's nagging. "Nini was exactly like my mother," he said, "nagging and bothering me, constantly talking to me." Then he told us that he had killed his mother—I remember the shock on that. He volunteered that information to us. "I just came here from England," he said. "They had kept me there for killing my mother." Everybody just looked at themselves. "My mother never left me alone, I finally couldn't take it anymore. But *she* was easy—one shot and she was finished. I just stabbed her once and that was the end of it. But I kept stabbing Nini and she wouldn't die." Apparently what happened was most every blow struck bone and the knife was being deflected.

## Invoice, Investigatory Evidence, Police Department, the City of New York

### ARTICLE

1 brown handle knife app. 5″ blade w/all blood stains.

The above is a complete list of property removed.

**BROOKS BAEKELAND**
There was only one person in the world both silly enough and generous enough to want that released tiger in her house. And she was almost killed for her goodness—a few days after I'd said no to Tony's request to come out to see me in Rhode Island, he stabbed his little grandmother almost to death when she objected to his voodoo rites with his mother's ashes.

I had kept every letter and drawing that I had ever received from him from the time he was three years old—not just from sentiment but from presentiment. But when I learned of the stabbing, I destroyed every single thing I ever had of him.

**CECELIA BREBNER**
At Broadmoor he made the most terrible terrible toys for his little half brother—apparently they were *so* grotesque and *so* macabre that his father threw them away immediately. And his paintings . . . apart from a rather delicate one he did for me, all without exception were macabre in the extreme—huge white hearts on a green background, pierced with a sword and dripping blood. He said he hid these from the warders. Later I saw the same motif on a box he made for Nina Daly.

**SERGEANT JOSEPH CHINEA**
We had realized right away that we were dealing with what we call an EDP—an emotionally disturbed person. It was just a matter of controlling him—handcuffing a person like that can make them violent, and then it's necessary for *us* to use violence against *them*, so we contained him in the living room but we let him roam around the room. It was cluttered because he had his things in there—suitcases, his music. He was sleeping on the couch—there was bedding on it and it wasn't made up. I remember it being a very tiny little apartment and I remember thinking, "Someone with all this money," you know. He also had photographs in his belongings—things he had laid out. Apparently when he was over in England he had become involved with the occult. It seemed that way to me. Anyway, you could see that the room had totally become his.

He showed us his paintings and drawings that he said he had done while he was incarcerated. And you could see in the drawings that . . . To this day I can't understand how the British government could repatriate him.

## Telegram from Kingman Brewster, Jr., U.S. Ambassador to the Court of St. James's, to Cyrus R. Vance, Secretary of State, Washington, D.C., July 30, 1980

AS MR. BAEKELAND HAS RETURNED TO THE U.S., LONDON
CONSIDERS HIS CASE CLOSED    BREWSTER

### DR. THOMAS MAGUIRE
The moment he stepped on the airplane, he was outside English authority. But I was very disappointed when the U.S. Consulate could not accept authority for him—I had asked and they had said they couldn't. No one would accept legal authority for him. Once he got on that plane he was basically a free person.

### ROSEMARY RODD BALDWIN
Michael Alexander says he's never going to try and get anybody released ever ever in his life again. *Ever.*

### MICHAEL ALEXANDER
I don't feel any sort of responsibility. On the other hand, I suppose you might say that I was as deceived by Tony as everybody else.

### SERGEANT JOSEPH CHINEA
In the patrol car riding over to the 19th Precinct for debriefing, he talked all the time about his grandmother. When we arrived we asked him if he knew where he was and he said, "Yes, I'm in the police station." "Do you know what you did?" we asked him. "Yeah, sure." Detective McLinskey, one of the detectives who was questioning him—there were three of us in the debriefing room with him—hit a nerve. Essentially what he was doing was nagging Tony with questions. And Tony became agitated immediately. "My grandmother nagged me," he said. "My mother nagged me. Why did they have to nag me? I don't like people to nag me." Right away we laid off. We sensed this guy's going to go crazy on us.

### TERENCE MCLINSKEY
I could imagine his emotions at the time: "Am I going to go to jail? Are they going to kill me?" He was in bad shape, and somewhat disheveled. I was just doing my ordinary everyday job. You live by your wits as a detective, you live by your communications skills. You

can do great work—not punitive, but directing people to the proper agency. I wanted to help Tony Baekeland make peace—I was trying to help him find his personal salvation. I was trying to build up that he was *worth* saving, no matter what. I mean, he happened to be a homosexual who had killed his mother and then tried to kill his grandmother.

I wonder if the poor guy found any answers to the whys and the wherefores.


### From a Psychiatric Interview with Antony Baekeland, New York City, 1980

I intend to read many religious books. They lighten my awareness and I get full with love and power and heavenly minds, all in the form of music.


### From the Logbook, Sergeant Joseph Chinea, July 27, 1980

To Manhattan Central Booking, arrived 11:03 a.m. Defendant made complete admission to events leading to assault and actual assault.

Statements: Before Rights—"I stabbed her. She kept nagging. I asked her to stop. I threw the phone at her but she continued to nag so I got the knife and stabbed her. Get some help."

Statements: After Rights—"I stabbed her five times. I wanted her to die fast but she wouldn't die. It was horrible. I hate when this happens."

Mrs. Cecelia Brebner, friend of the family, interviewed at 19th Pct. She said she wanted to volunteer as a witness to the fact that Baekeland was mentally disturbed.

Out of Central Booking with Defendant 12:23 p.m. To Department of Correction to begin processing, 12:32 p.m.

To Manhattan Criminal Court, Room 131, 3:15 p.m. Await paper & arraignment.

## From Police Files

Nature of grandmother's injuries: multiple (eight) stab wounds to chest, arms, and hand; fractured collarbone; multiple fractured ribs (four-five), causing breathing problem; bruises and abrasions. Confined to Lenox Hill Hospital.

Other members of family fear for their lives. Ask for remand.

Victim may not want to press charges. Told one police officer she still loved him.

## From a Psychiatric Interview with Antony Baekeland, New York City, 1980

Oh, my grandmother survived. She has ways and means I know nothing about, but let's forget about her and talk about homosexual relations.

I'm not going to call the hospital and find out how she's doing—why should I call her? She talks to me all the time through the special power that she has.

## From the Logbook, Sergeant Joseph Chinea, July 27, 1980

9:00 p.m. Defendant held over for a.m. 7/28 arraignment.

## From the Arraignment, The People of the State of New York—Against—Antony Baekeland, Defendant, Criminal Court of the City of New York, County of New York, July 28, 1980

THE COURT: Psychiatric examination ordered, administrative psychiatric segregation; suicide watch.

## Headline, the New York Times, July 29, 1980

EX-PATIENT IS HELD IN 2D STABBING

Headline, New York *Daily News*, July 29, 1980

### HE'S CHARGED WITH STABBING GRANDMA
### AFTER SERVING TIME IN MURDER OF MOM

Headline, *Daily Express*, London, July 29, 1980

### FREED BROADMOOR PATIENT
### ACCUSED OF U.S. MURDER BID

DR. FREDERICK BAEKELAND

It was very much against my opinion and my advice that Tony was let out of Broadmoor without any adequate follow-up program set up. I'm not surprised that there was a problem eventually.

From *Broadmoor,* David Cohen, Psychology News Press, London, 1981

> If an ex-patient commits a crime, the symphony of outrage from Fleet Street is loud and vicious. In 1980, *Now* magazine ran a dossier on Broadmoor "disasters" and identified twenty cases in which ex-patients had committed acts of violence after being released.

MICHAEL ALEXANDER

The papers in London attacked Dr. Maguire quite strongly over what happened with Tony. And Tony was described in the media here as "the mad axman of Broadmoor." It was "the mad axman strikes again" sort of touch, you know. I got on to the papers about that. I said, "Look, that's not the way to present this case. Dr. Maguire behaved extremely correctly under the circumstances." I didn't get very far. They stuck to their story.

### Letter from Dr. Patrick G. McGrath to Miwa Svinka-Zielinski, Undated

Broadmoor

Dear Mrs. Svinka-Zielinski,
I have received your letter and clip from the *New York Times*. I have also heard from Antony's father. Let me say straightaway how distressed we here all were to hear of Mrs. Daly's injuries at the hands of Antony, but we are somewhat relieved to see from the report that she will recover.

I do hope that the whole family, including Antony, will recover from this incident which you rightly describe as a catastrophe.

Yours sincerely,
Patrick G. McGrath
Physician Superintendent

### Letter from Dr. Thomas Maguire to Cecelia Brebner, Undated

Broadmoor

Dear Mrs. Brebner,
I am very grateful for your letter to me which gave me details of the tragic events. Strange to relate I have had no further communication from anyone although I was expecting a request for a medical report and history from his present medical attendants. I wonder whether you have knowledge of subsequent events which you might pass on to me as of course I am intensely interested to learn from my faux pas.

Yours sincerely,
Thomas Maguire
Consultant Forensic Psychiatrist

### DR. THOMAS MAGUIRE
He's the only patient who ever backfired on me like that.

HEATHER COHANE

During the week he was in New York, Jack and I were on our boat in Italy, miles from any telephone or any communication. We didn't know for a long time what had happened. And when I heard, I was upset for days, and the reason I was upset was because I had trusted my judgment. I just couldn't believe it—the grandmother, the one person left that he loved!

## Letter from Antony Baekeland to an Unidentified Friend, "Eryl," Written in Police Custody, 1980

Dear Eryl,

I am in trouble, I am sorry to say. The spirit which has been directing me has for a span been "misdirecting" me—not, I hope, to cause this grief, now passing, but in order to serve Mammon and the powers of disorder and wickedness, which through lack of eternal and infinite vision have tied knots in the fabric of life, or some, thank God, of it. I have been held captive here for a very long span, thinking that I served the Power of Love when I had been lured into bondage and captivity by certain pleasures which may under correct direction prove creative and progressive, but which caused me great pain and grief, since I believed in those who held me in this state of being. I do not think for 2 minutes that the spirit that has been behind me wilfully caused my troubles, but that He was misled by those whom He served, and so on. Indeed, my Whole Family here is of the House of Hades. So please will you keep your eye on me so I can come out.

Tony

THILO VON WATZDORF

Three weeks after I'd tried to call Tony at his grandmother's and it just rang and rang with no answer, I tried the number again and this time somebody picked up. I said, "Is Tony Baekeland there?" And the voice said, "I'm his grandmother's nurse. Something terrible happened. Tony is on Rikers Island. Would you like to speak with his grandmother?" I said no, I wouldn't—I mean, I had never even met her. But *she* wanted to speak with *me*. She got right on the phone and she told me what had happened. She said, "Isn't it terrible? I love Tony so much."

# PART IV
# RIKERS ISLAND

# 1

## JULY 27, 1980–
## OCTOBER 31, 1980

The majority of New York City inmates are housed on an island in the East River between the Bronx and Queens, known as Rikers Island. It originally belonged to a Dutch immigrant by the name of Jacob Ryker, who sold all of the original ninety acres to the city in 1885.

In 1900, a wood-frame construction suitable for one hundred prisoners was completed; soon afterwards, wooden barracks capable of housing up to four hundred were added. By 1918, there were eight barracks on the island as well as a stable, a guardhouse, a mess hall, and several employee buildings. Inmates labored on coal barges, ice-boats, and garbage dumps, and on a hog farm located on the premises.

Eventually the workhouse aspect of Rikers Island was abandoned and in 1955 the island became known officially as the Penitentiary of the City of New York. Landfill increased its size to over four hundred acres and by the 1980s it was home to six major prison facilities—three for male inmates, one for females, one for adolescent boys, and a hospital. It also now contains a power plant, maintenance garage, firehouse, print shop, shoe-repair shop, tailor shop, laundry, and bakery. Eight days after his return from England, Tony Baekeland was entering a community not unlike Broadmoor.

## Property Envelope, Department of Correction, City of New York

### LIST OF PROPERTY

None

I Acknowledge The Surrender Of My Property As Listed Above

DATE: *July 28, 1980*
SIGNATURE OF INMATE: *Antony Baekeland*

## Floor and Cell Location Form, Department of Correction, City of New York

DATE: July 29, 1980
FLOOR: Mental Observation
CELL: Lower 6-8

## Letter from Antony Baekeland to Shirley Cox, July 30, 1980

Rikers Island

Dear Shirley,
More Horror. In case you don't know what happened, this is it—by Tuesday I realized that it was no good. I had been up several nights reading in the Bible and was feeling very nervous. I began to hear Nini's voice, clear as day coming from her room. (It felt just like a wolf gnawing at my entrails.) When I would go and ask her what she was saying, she said she had said nothing. I had *no one* to talk to—I had tried to give myself to Nini in various ways but it was no go. It was like having someone you loved right in the next room and thousands of miles away. Once in the middle of the night I had a very clear vision or memory of us (Nini and I) a long long time ago in our house in Italy, how we used to go hunting for pretty stones and leaves and things, and how we used to hold hands. I also remembered how my family sheds its blood (and each other's blood) for one another. Anyway, I was in tears and I got up and quietly went into her room. She was asleep and I held her hand but she didn't wake up.

Anyway, I finally realised I couldn't stay, that it wouldn't be right for either of us, and Sunday morning I went to her room and began telephoning for reservations for England. Please realise that I was in a *desperate* state of mind—many beautiful and terrifying spiritual things had been happening and I hadn't slept properly for a week. N. kept on at me and I warned her *three* times that if she wouldn't be quiet I would throw the telephone at her. Anyway, finally my nerves broke and I threw the phone at her. She fell down and began to moan and I realised what I had done and that she had probably broken more bones. Then I felt that *all her suffering* in the past (hip, etc.) had been for *my sake* and that was too much to bear. I knew that if I gave her the *Coup de Grâce* God would take her Home and there would be no more misery. I tore into the kitchen, found a knife, rushed back, and tried to kill her but wasn't strong enough and/or didn't know how. Then I started screaming and praying and pleading with God to take her Home. I tried ringing the ambulance for ½ hour without realising that the phone was kaput. The poor darling asked me to straighten her legs which I did. Then Lena came and I told her to get an ambulance. The police came as well and took me away.

Shirley, if you do not want to speak to me or see me again I understand perfectly but I want you to know that I am as horrified as you are—believe me please. I am sure if I hadn't been so alone it wouldn't have happened, but it's no use saying "if," ever.

If you would like to help me could you get me my Bible, Shakespeare, & Spiritual Canticle by St. John of the Cross. They are on the table in the drawing room.

If you would like to visit I would like to hear how N. is. Do ring up the place beforehand as I *may* be in court that day. My no.: 349-80-4228. Could you send or bring any letters which may have come for me?

After it happened, at the police station and here, I continued to hear her voice, saying, "*Honi soit qui mal y pense*," and other things.

I am better off here than I was at Nini's. At least there is company. (Blacks and Puerto Ricans mainly.)

I am on Legal Aid but am hoping my lawyer will let me have him on a money basis as I feel unable to accept government help since I have money.

Please understand that *I* understand what a terrible thing this
is for you, me, and any friends we may have.

Yours,
Tony (and of course, Nini)


DR. HELENE WEISS
I saw Tony Baekeland on July 29, 1980. At first he was generally
cooperative, and then he just started to decompensate after a while.
But he wasn't what I would call crazy. Even though he was here on
attempted murder, he was not basically a criminal personality per se.
His acts had been done more out of passion than out of criminal
pathology.


## Letter from Brooks Baekeland to Nina Daly, July 29,1980

Block Island

Dear Nini,
I have heard of your new adventure with a heavy heart. That so
much bravery and goodwill should be repaid that way! But I am
very glad that you are out of danger. How you were able to
defend yourself, only you and God know, but somehow you did.
I must tell you that I did not expect this. I knew of course that
Tony had not changed basically. His irrationality (and arrogance) continued to make a very bad impression on me, but I
worried more about his ability to understand *what the world was
like* and what he had to do to survive (or thrive) in it than I did
about his acting out the violence of his nature again. It came to
me as a surprise, although not apparently to Fred. I did however
warn Maguire that Tony was dangerous when crossed. I received
some very ugly letters from Tony whenever I seemed to frustrate
what he deemed I owed him or he deserved—exceedingly man-
datory, abusive, even scatological. I pointed out these things to
Maguire, but *Broadmoor simply wished to get him off their
hands*—and the Bleeding Hearts Club never stopped pounding
their drum, either. You are lucky to be alive. The road to
hell . . .
Poor Tony—what an enormous failure of intelligence. And

what a pity that you did not warn someone of the danger that you felt growing, or ask for help once you realized that he should not have been discharged.

I'm going North for a while—plans still very uncertain. I bought a secondhand car yesterday and will just see a little of America for a while. It's been a long time—14 years. I have come back as a foreigner.

Well, dear, get well soon, and if you need anything let me know through my lawyer in New York. One day I will settle down somewhere or be in one place long enough to receive mail. I will then call him and ask him to forward any messages that have come for me.

Love,
Brooks

### Note from File on Antony Baekeland

Tony called his family lawyer Wed. July 30. T. was cordial, rational.

### MIWA SVINKA-ZIELINSKI
There was nobody who was absolutely interested in Tony's case now. I suppose I could have visited him on Rikers Island but I didn't have any authority to go to his lawyer and ask what the situation was— Why wasn't he being acquitted as schizophrenic? Why was he sitting in a prison which is a regular prison for criminals?

### EDWARD HERSHEY
Of the ninety-two hundred inmates in our system today, sixty percent will be out after seven days. With that kind of turnover, the Department of Correction, where I'm assistant commissioner for public affairs, has a very challenging but in some cases not very fulfilling mission. Our major mission is to provide pretrial services, get the inmates to court and so on. We don't have an opportunity for long-term relationships. We have to look out for red lights, and when they flash we take action, because there's not a lot of time.

## SANDRA LEWIS SMITH

On a typical day in prison the inmates get up at five in the morning if they're going to court. Even if they're not going to court, there's so much noise in the cell block they probably get up about five anyway. The wagon is delivered with the breakfast—hot cereal, scrambled eggs, toast, juice, sometimes fresh fruit—apples, oranges—coffee, or hot water and makings for coffee—or tea. Then the people going to court are taken to court. The rest of the inmates simply hang out. They might read, they might put in an interview slip to go to the legal library and do some research on their case, they might go to the clinic for medication or to be examined for whatever ailment they might have, they might just stay in the area and watch television or play cards or checkers, or they might be called down to receive a visit from their attorney.

## MARTIN J. SIEGEL

I was asked by the court to represent Tony Baekeland at his first arraignment. Later he said to me, "I'd like to hire you privately." So I advised Judge Haft that I had been assigned by the court but that the client now wanted to retain me privately and do I have permission. Judge Haft asked Tony if he had the funds and he said yes and the judge said okay.

Tony was always pleasant in all my dealings with him. But he was a very troubled person. He told me once about being in a café with a girl he was in love with and his father was sitting next to her and started to come on to her. He was very bitter about that.

He struck me as the type of person who could be manipulated very easily. I guess you know he was a homosexual. I felt that he wanted to be dominated by someone who played the male role, and that any strong individual that came by could readily dominate him.

Our defense was going to be insanity. I hoped to have him institutionalized in a hospital-type setting where he could really be helped as opposed to a penal-type setting.

**From Psychiatric Examination Reports on Antony Baekeland Ordered by the Criminal Court of New York, August 27, 1980, and September 2, 1980**

KNOWLEDGE OF CHARGES:
What is the charge against you?

"Either murder or attempted murder of my grandmother."

KNOWLEDGE OF COURT PROCEEDINGS:
Heve you entered a plea? What plea have you entered?

"No, I haven't."

What is the name of the Defendant's Attorney?

"Mr. Siegel."

What is the function of a Defense Attorney?

"To help me."

What is the function of a District Attorney?

"He represents the borough and I'll be up against him."

What is the function of a Judge?

"Evaluate whether you can be punished or not, then sentences."

What is the function of a Jury?

"Twelve ladies and gentlemen who decide whether you're guilty or not guilty."

What are the consequences of being found Guilty?

"Depending on seriousness, they are given various penalties."

SUMMARY OF PSYCHIATRIC FINDINGS:
The defendant was alert, cooperative, articulate. Although he stuttered, speech was coherent and relevant. Delusions and hallucinations were denied. The defendant became intermittently tearful in discussing his alleged offense and his father's reaction to it. He stated he felt "chastened" by his experience in jail. Memory is intact. Defendant understands court procedure and is deemed able to assist counsel. He is fit to proceed.

**From the Transcript, The People of the State of New York—Against—Antony Baekeland, Defendant, Supreme Court of the State of New York, County of New York, September 19, 1980**

THE COURT CLERK: Mr. Baekeland, you have been indicted by the Grand Jury of the County of New York, charging you with attempted murder in the second degree and assault in the first degree. How do you plead to the charges, guilty or not guilty?

DEFENDANT: I plead not guilty.

MR. SIEGEL: Your Honor, I would like to have the matter adjourned for a few weeks for motions on the issue of bail. I would ask some bail be set.

## Letter from Shirley Cox to Assistant District Attorney Sarah Hines, Undated

New York

Dear Ms. Hines:

As a close friend of Mrs. Nina Daly (the victim) for many years, and her business affairs manager for the past five years, this letter is to earnestly request that in the event of Antony Baekeland's release, Mrs. Daly be accorded 24-hour-a-day police protection. . . .

I feel this would be absolutely essential to the safety of her life.

I hope you will give this request your serious consideration and support.

Sincerely,
Shirley Cox (Mrs.)

## JUDGE ROBERT M. HAFT

There was no serious bail application. It would not have been appropriate. Anyway, Tony Baekeland had no place to go.

He was always very pleasant and smiled a lot. He was never agitated. I would say he had a sort of inappropriate affect, considering what was happening to him.

## From the Transcript, The People of the State of New York—Against—Antony Baekeland, Defendant, Supreme Court of the State of New York, County of New York, October 22, 1980

THE COURT: Was the defendant examined by a psychiatrist of your choice?

MR. SIEGEL: Yes, he was. I'm awaiting the report. The examination has taken place.

THE COURT: Adjourned to November 7th.


## From a Psychiatric Interview with Antony Baekeland, New York City, 1980

The purpose of this evaluation was to determine Mr. Baekeland's mental status at the time of the alleged crime. When asked where he was born, Mr. Baekeland replied, "I don't know. I was told that I was born in Manhattan. That's what my mother told me but I have no siblings. In fact, as far as I know, she told me that her friend is the Son of Sam and he is also my brother because he is my age." When asked who raised him, he answered, "I think I was raised by my mother, father, and grandmother but it was all very confusing. Our family is spiritually everywhere, so my mother's death would not bother her. We all lived together—a few people but we are all the same person. A close friend of mine is a very powerful magician and he made such magic that I could kill my mother with the same knife that he made the magic with." At this point, the patient started talking quite irrelevantly about his father, stating, "I don't remember him loving me terribly. I didn't know what exactly he wanted me to do. He is a physicist and writes many books. We are very rich people from his family. They sell stocks and real estate and I have a lot of money which is not bad but I never worked for it." . . .

*Psychiatric Diagnosis:* Schizophrenia, Paranoid Type.


## SARAH HINES

We wanted to prove that he was responsible for his crime. We wanted to have as much control over him as possible, in order to give the People and his family security, and there's not much control available when the insanity plea is used—he might have "walked."

## Letter from Shirley Cox to Assistant District Attorney Sarah Hines, Undated

New York

Dear Ms. Hines:

Further to our recent telephone conversation, this will confirm that the personal belongings of Antony Baekeland, left behind in his grandmother's apartment in New York at the time of his arrest, were stolen from the basement storage room. Four of the tenants in the building also lost a variety of personal possessions in trunks and suitcases, and one had her bicycle stolen.

As you will remember, I had tried very early on to have Mr. Baekeland's possessions transferred to him in Rikers Island or to his lawyer (if it could be determined who that would be on a continuing basis). But I was told that the suitcases and cartons (containing clothes, shoes, tape recorder, tapes, books, etc.) would not be accepted, and that they should be stored somewhere for the interim until a Court decision had been reached. It was considered important by those concerned about Mrs. Daly's welfare to clean up her apartment and remove the remnants of the traumatic incident before she was released from Lenox Hill Hospital. Consequently, for lack of choice the items were placed in the basement storage room (which was equipped with a lock) until further notice. Whoever committed the robbery had used a key to effect entrance.

Once the robbery was discovered, the 19th Precinct was advised but despite three phone calls over a three-hour period, while the tenants involved waited in the basement, no officer arrived to inspect the premises or to make a report of the incident.

I merely wish to report the fact of the robbery of Mr. Baekeland's possessions to someone in an official capacity relating to his situation. I do believe that, had some official help been extended, Mr. Baekeland's belongings might still be intact.

Sincerely,
Shirley Cox (Mrs.)

# 2

# NOVEMBER 1, 1980– DECEMBER 16, 1980

**JOHN MURRAY**

I met Tony in the bull pen, which is where they hold you before you go to court. I was in for burglary. Coincidentally, he was in the same quad as me, too—I was about eight cells away. We were together about six or seven months. I was his closest friend at that time. I definitely was, yes. He said he'd been staying at his grandmother's and he felt all right and then all of a sudden he just heard her saying things like he couldn't go out to see anybody or somebody couldn't come over to the house, and she was next to the phone, and he just hit her a few times. I told him that was a lie. I said, "Why don't you tell me the truth?" And he said, "Oh, yeah, well, the truth of the matter is that she was almost killed."

Then he told me that he had spent time in London, England, for psychiatric reasons for killing his mother. He was sorry about it, because he loved his mother. No one knows why people do things like that. They just do them, and after that, it's over and done with, and you have to live with that—without that person—for the rest of your life.

On good days Tony would keep himself confined to where he was and what he was doing. On days when he was restless and reckless he'd talk about how he killed his mother. He'd whisper, like someone mortified. He'd either whisper or his lips would move and he wouldn't be speaking. That's how he'd say how sorry he was.

He told me once or twice that his mother was very beautiful but he never described her to me in detail or anything. And he told me he knew a beautiful lady named Jinty Money-Coutts and he said that when I got out, if I had no place to stay, I could maybe stay there with her in London.

He told me he had a very small family, and that his father had died when he was younger—or something like that. I think he said died but maybe he told me his father just didn't want to see him anymore. But mostly we talked about what the correctional officers were up to—whether this guy dilly-dallies all day or that guy bullshits around or not.

Sometimes he did drawings—rough sketches with crayons. And some pastels—pictures of sailboats and rivers and docks. But one day he just tore them all up.

### SARA DUFFY CHERMAYEFF

I drove out to Rikers Island to see him. We just talked in a room, at a table. He didn't talk about stabbing his grandmother. We just talked about old times. I mean, that's all I had to talk to him about. To me, he looked just like he'd always looked—very handsome. I always thought he was wonderfully handsome.

Look, I'd known him when he was little, and I never again expect to know anyone who killed anybody. I wondered when I went there what the hell I was doing—I mean, there was probably some sort of curiosity and vanity involved in my going to see him. I felt ashamed afterwards, because I felt that I'd exploited him. I remember we said goodbye as if we would meet again—it was like we were at Schrafft's.

### JAMES REEVE

Broadmoor was a sort of retreat, really, wasn't it? He was safe there. My God, when he was in that hellhole in America he must have looked back on Broadmoor as nirvana.

### MARTIN J. SIEGEL

I was relieved as Tony Baekeland's lawyer in November of 1980. I turned his entire file over to his new lawyer, Ronnie Arrick. I was very surprised when Tony hired him because Tony and I had had a very good attorney-client relationship and there really hadn't been any problem. But apparently a friend of his at Rikers recommended him to Tony. Now I know Arrick is a very fine and competent attorney—he's also a very nice guy. Who can explain why people want to go into this coffee shop as opposed to that coffee shop?

## RONALD ARRICK

The first time I met Tony Baekeland was in November when I think Siegel was canned. Anyway, I took over the defense. My job was to represent him on the entire criminal matter all the way through trial and to try to work it out to his entire advantage. His grandmother was not withdrawing the charges. The D.A. was not withdrawing the charges. I was also involved in long-distance dealing with certain facilities in England, because his only defense was a psychiatric defense.

My hope was to get him placed in what I gather his grandmother thought he should be in when she had him brought back here—a hospital. I wanted to have him found not guilty by reason of insanity, and I discussed this with him as about the only thing that could be done.

He had access to funds—I think it was a combination of trust and cash available. He would give in a written request to his trustees, U.S. Trust, sort of like a check facsimile, and they would issue the funds.

## JOHN MURRAY

Since Tony had money, he was wary of who would know his business by the way he was acting: Would it show on him? Would people abuse him for it? Would they try to get it from him too quickly?

Tony was very well liked as far as I could see. He had a calm nature, you know, but he had a very rude temper. He had a thing about if he couldn't get his way he would more or less say shove off, you know—kiss it goodbye.

## DR. HELENE WEISS

He was very volatile and I'm sure after a while he had some trouble with other inmates. I know he had some transient episodes. On December 11th he was switched over to our Mental Health Center.

## JOHN RAKIS

The Mental Health Center has single cells and a higher complement of officers than anywhere else at Rikers Island.

## NATALIE ROBINS

I wanted to see Tony's cell. Captain Earl Tulon, who was to be my prison guide, met me in the visitors' parking lot on the Queens side of the island and drove me in a big Cadillac across the narrow bridge that is the only access to Rikers Island. He pointed out the various buildings to me as we took the exact route Tony Baekeland's blue prison bus had taken. My first impression of the island was that of a bleak but tidy campus. School again, for Broadmoor Special Hospital had had the same effect on me at first sight. The difference is that here there seemed to be miles and miles of barbed wire, and once you began to follow it you couldn't take your eyes off it.

We went inside a building called the Anna M. Kross Center where the reception area had a strong antiseptic smell. Here I received a visitor's badge and my briefcase and shoulder bag were thoroughly searched by a correction officer. I then had to walk through a metal detector. Now I had officially arrived at Rikers Island.

We went down a very long corridor whose walls, surprisingly, were decorated with red-yellow-green-blue rainbows interspersed with large orange and purple triangles. Then we entered an older part of the building where the walls were bare. This area housed the Mental Health Center.

Here we were joined by a staff psychologist, J. Victor Benson—everyone called him "Benson" or "Vic." He escorted us into Lower Three Quad. On the left was an area that reminded me of a classroom in a run-down elementary school: plastic chairs piled up on one side, two or three tables scattered around—one next to a wall. "That's the table where I used to sit and talk to Tony. It's even in the same place," Vic Benson told me.

Then I was taken to the cells, a series of tiny single rooms, with doors that have small squares cut out, covered with metal bars. Tony's old cell was at the end of a corridor on the left. Most cells don't have windows, but his had one; it was covered with wire mesh embedded in glass, and looked out on a dirt lot that had one or two patches of crabgrass and weeds.

The current inmate-in-residence was in court, I was told. There was a thick gray wool blanket on the bed. Vic Benson said the bed was in the exact same spot as when Tony was there. Two pairs of underwear were hanging to dry on a metal shelf, and a dirty pair of socks and shoes were on the floor. There was some red-ink graffiti on the walls: Somebody loves somebody. I don't remember what the names were, but Vic Benson said they weren't there when Tony was in the cell.

## Custodial Medical Information Form, Prison Health Services, New York City Department of Health, December 11, 1980

MENTAL HEALTH

NAME: Baekeland, Antony
SUICIDE POTENTIAL: No evidence
DEPRESSION: Mild
ASSAULTIVE POTENTIAL: No evidence
VIOLENCE POTENTIAL: No evidence
MEDICATION: Thorazine

## J. VICTOR BENSON

As a psychologist at the Mental Health Center, I got to know Tony quite intimately when he was detained on my quad. When I found out about his family background, I did some research on it. Tony himself didn't take much pride in his background, and in fact when he spoke of it, and the wealth, it was all quite casually.

Some of the things he told me sounded like delusional material. It wasn't, though. He told me quite blandly about murdering his mother. He mentioned that his relationship with his father was strained because of his homosexuality—he said his mother had been dissatisfied with his sexual orientation, too. The only good thing he said about his father concerned a trip they both took up to Yonkers once to visit his great-grandfather's lab. It was a pleasant memory—that trip to the lab.

At the time Tony was here we had a relatively quiet quad, although emotions *are* easily aroused because the inmates live so closely together. Some inmates have to be kept off balance—separated, you know, so they don't get into fights and so on. There's also constant cell movement. They want to go to the law library, then they want to go to the barber shop—in this unit the barber shop comes to *them*.

The commissary is a very big thing—that's the supply of niceties that the inmates have. They deposit money in their commissary accounts and once a week they submit an order. The most popular items are cigarettes, and candy and cookies—because so many are drug addicts, they love the sweets. If you're in the general population here, you can go directly to the commissary and pick up your order, but if you're in a mental observation unit like Tony was, they deliver the commissary to you.

Tony was very generous with many of the inmates. He was supporting them—well, not exactly supporting them—but he was very generous with commissary. He maintained friendships in that fashion. That's *one* of the methods he used in cementing his friendships. He ordered huge amounts of commissary. But nobody could challenge that because he always had the money.

You know, all during the day on this quad the correction officers have to make repeated security inspections—check the keys in the locks, check the bars, the gates, the shower room, the windows, the screens, the walls, the dayroom, utility closet, the lighting, the cell walls which they could cut through because they're only made of tile. They're supposed to be impregnable but they are not—an inmate could chip away at the tiles and remove them a few at a time until they had a hole for escape. Also check the vents, because inmates have a habit of storing things there, like jail booze, which they're very clever in fermenting. Check the slop sinks. Check the toilet bowls.

It's a very noisy place, sometimes it gets to be unbearable—the telephone ringing, the inmates wanting to make telephone calls. They can't receive calls, but they can arrange through Social Services to make calls and have an extended conversation, either local or long-distance.

### Note from File on Antony Baekeland

Tony Baekeland and a friend of his in prison have been calling Nina Daly repeatedly and abusively. We can't prevent Tony from telephoning his grandmother since she seems to acquiesce and won't tell the police; but he can be advised to cut it out.

JOHN MURRAY

I spoke to his grandmother when Tony called her. They were not harassing phone calls. That must have been someone else. I don't know who that could have been. I asked her not to press charges on Tony, and I also spoke to her about reducing the charges, and she told me that she definitely, invariably would.

One time she got mad and I said, "Whoa, slow down, slow down, I didn't know all that about Tony. Could you tell me that a little bit slower?" And she said, "I'll slow down," and then she said Tony's gay and this and that, and I said, "I know about it."

# 3

# DECEMBER 17, 1980– JANUARY 14, 1981

**JOHN MURRAY**

Tony was madly in love with me. He asked me a couple of times if I would come to his cell at night, but I told him I couldn't do it. Of course I could, I could go to anybody's cell that I wanted to. I told it to him like this, I said, "Well, Tony, I have a lot of work," because work was the only thing I could do to excuse me not responding, since I'm not gay, you know. I *was* working—in the receiving room. I wasn't working as a mopper or something like that.

The receiving room is where you go when you come back from court or from anywhere or if you're just getting in from the street. They strip you on a table and search you, then they tell you to put your clothes back on. I was sleeping down there and I was working out down there with weights. I had priority there. But the first time I went there I was treated like one of the savage slaves they have. You know, everyone is pretty much a slave there.

Tony wanted me to be with him wherever he was, that was the main thing. He wanted someone to be his friend, to more or less straighten him out. I was concentrating on his money, and I was also concentrating on his family case. We got a letter from Broadmoor Hospital in England saying that he'd have to see a few more doctors to say whether he was competent to stand trial or not.

## J. VICTOR BENSON
They used to call John Murray Big John in the receiving room, where he was working on the house gang or paint gang, which is made up of the sentenced inmates who have specific work assignments while they're doing their time. They call it "city time," which is a year or less.

There was *something* going on between Murray and Baekeland, although Murray wasn't a true homosexual. But in jail some inmates will do anything.

## JOHN RAKIS
Most of these guys are welfare kids from welfare families and have no qualms about taking money from someone. It's just part of their nature. Once when there was a plane crash on Rikers, a lot of the inmates came and helped with the rescue efforts and most of them wound up getting reduced sentences or were allowed to leave altogether because of the heroics they showed. But later we discovered that they went and looked in the newspaper and found out the names of some of the survivors and wrote them letters or called them up, if they could get the phone numbers, and tried to extort money from them. They'd say, "Hey, I saved your life—don't you think you owe me something?" To them this was just a normal way of life.

## JOHN MURRAY
Tony gave away money for protection and also just to be friendly. He did it for both reasons.

## RONALD ARRICK
He did give away some funds. Primarily it was to relatives of people he knew in prison who treated him like family, who brought him things, like clothes, books. Mothers of prisoners primarily. Because his own mother was not around. It was *not* protection money that he was giving out.

## JOHN MURRAY
He never gave away money in front of me, except once. He gave away something like fifteen hundred dollars in a check, to some kid, I don't remember his name. He lent people their bail money, money for clothes, money for drugs, stuff like that. He lent other people money just so they could have money. He was lending out around three thousand dollars a person. Really. He gave away something like

forty-two thousand, nine hundred and eighty-five dollars. I seen that written down on a piece of paper that he had.

Also, you gotta remember Tony fooled around with guys—we both know that. He was fooling around with whoever was around. He wasn't giving them cash money, but he was giving them stuff like for commissary, or he'd promise them cash money later, just for being in a relationship with him.

Word got around Rikers that he had money, so people were always coming up to him and saying, you know, "Can I borrow?" or "Could I have?" In other words, "Please may I?" You know. They'd get how much they could.

I told him many times not to do it anymore, but he kept on doing it. And then what really got me mad was when he tried to offer *me* money. See, 'cause I didn't want money. I was his friend.

He was afraid of some people, and other people he just wanted to make sure he got along with because he liked them rather enough, you know. But the dangerous people, the ones who carried a shank— you know, a sharpened piece of metal—formed an organization and lived off Tony. Nobody ever tried to stop it. I was the only one who tried. Once, this guy wanted money and Tony wouldn't give it to him. I heard about it in the receiving room and I was on my way over to help get the guy off Tony's back. By the time I got there, a couple of the guys Tony had been giving money to rebelled against the new guy and said, like, "Hey, man, bug out, get out of here," and they got rid of him. If I had had to take care of him, the C.O. probably would have let me fight him—and I would have won. I'd beat him up whether he had a shank or not.

## Injury to Inmate Report, Department of Correction, City of New York, January 11, 1981

> At approx. 12:30 p.m. Antony Baekeland got involved in a fist fight with inmate Jose Perez. This occurred in Upper Three dayroom. Inmate Baekeland was treated and examined in L4 Clinic by Dr. C. Park (psychiatrist). No apparent injuries.

## JUAN MARTINEZ

There was a couple of people—we used to hang around together, like a little crowd, you know? I was in for five years. I was on the first page in a big newspaper when I got busted. You know, with a big picture, and a big smile on me.

Tony was a good friend of mine. We were together ever since he got in jail—we were like brothers. He told me all about his family. Things like that.

He was giving money out like crazy, you know? He gave money to Eddie Cruz, who's in the street now—he was in for burglary. And Jackie Monroe, who's doing eight years upstate now. Tony sent quite a bit of money to Jackie's wife.

## JOHN MURRAY

He gave a really big check to this one guy with a mustache and a beard and long, shaggy hair. He was kind of young-looking and he was white, Spanish. He was in the quad. He had just got there. He borrowed a pair of shoes from Tony. Then there was another guy Tony was also helping out—Michael something. He gave him, I think, a big check to use when he got out on the street. The guy was going to use it for his mother's house.

## JOHN RAKIS

If an inmate had a check and gave it to a relative of his and said you can deposit this and draw on it, there would be no way for prison officials to track down that sort of extortion.

## HOWARD NABOR

I was the warden at the Anna M. Kross Center when Tony Baekeland was there, and I think the money he gave out there he gave out to win friends more than anything else. I mean, you don't give out checks for protection—if the inmates are running a protection racket they'll take all the guy's commissary or have his mother or his wife or somebody deposit cash in their account. Anybody can send cash to an inmate—all they got to do is just mail it to his name in an envelope and it goes. But a check is going to nail them right to the wall. All the guy has to do is go to the D.A. or the Department of Correction and say, "I'm being forced to pay protection," and they say, "Can you prove it?" and he shows them the check. The inmates aren't *that* stupid.

So one of the things we usually check on is the commissary. Our cashiers monitor that closely and if they see one inmate getting an exceptionally large amount of money from the same two or three people—and I don't mean his mother or his girlfriend or his aunt

Mary—then we know he's either doing one of two things. He's running a racket bullying people, right? Or else he's selling something,
he's selling drugs or himself—he could be a homosexual selling his
own body. If some inmate was running a game on Tony Baekeland,
he wouldn't be doing it with checks, because he wouldn't want anybody to know about it.

### John Murray

Sometimes Tony would try to offer the guards money but they
wouldn't take it. I don't know what they said to him because they'd
tell everyone to scram first.

### Brooks Baekeland

Tony wrote me letters describing the vice, violence and corruption in
that prison. His homosexual seductiveness even involved the guards,
and promises of money in large amounts to everyone who might satisfy his humors or desires—that was all in those letters.

## Letter from Dr. Thomas Maguire to Cecelia Brebner, January 13, 1981

Broadmoor

Dear Mrs. Brebner:

Thank you very much for your recent letter about Tony; you
appear to be the only person who is aware of the facts—certainly
the only one who has kept me up-to-date with recent developments. In fact, I had been given to understand that Mrs. Daly
had died as a result of her injuries and that Tony was to be
brought to trial for murder!

I am very pleased to learn that she is still alive and able to
contemplate visiting Tony. It is indeed worrying that she feels
unable to press charges against him as this would be for his (and
others') benefit in the long run. However, knowing her great
affection for Tony, her attitude is understandable.

May I offer you belated Happy New Year wishes.

Again my best thanks.

Yours sincerely,
Thomas Maguire
Consultant Forensic Psychiatrist

## Letter from Antony Baekeland to Nina Daly, January 14, 1981

Rikers Island

Dear Nini,

I am waiting to hear whether I shall be given bail. I do not really think it would be just for me to be locked up either on grounds of insanity or criminality, as what happened was (a) not an act of insanity, but a complex of emotionally motivated acts and (b) not criminal, because I had nothing to gain in any worldly way from knifing you, and in fact everything to lose, and was only trying to put you out of your misery. It is very hard for me to talk to you on the phone because whenever the important things come up we are mutually put off. I am hoping for a way in which we can solve this problem. Realise that part of me has suffered with you ever since you broke your hip, even blaming myself for your trouble and discomfort.

My Great Problem is Money. I can't seem to talk about it with anyone without getting upset and nervous. I do not consider that the attempt to take my hand from my own affairs has any valid reason, as I am now regaining my perspective.

At the time I came here I had eighty-three thousand dollars in "Free" money—that is, money which I can spend to my liking.

John Murray is and has been very helpful. (My Friend who spoke to you on the phone.) He wants to get the money I gave away back for you.

I shall call you Friday or Saturday evening. May God bless you and give you Peace and New Health.

Love, Love,
Tony

CECELIA BREBNER
I took Nini to Rikers Island to see him and they would not allow us to cross the bridge—they said that an old lady in a wheelchair was not possible. So back we came. And the moment we got home, the telephone rang. It was Tony, and he started to scream at Nini—something about money. She said to me, "Will *you* speak to him, Celia?" I said, "Tony, just stop this nonsense of giving your money away." And he said, "Get off the phone! I don't want to talk to *you*." And all those loving letters I'd had from him! "I want to talk to my grandmother," he said. "Put her back on!"

# 4

# JANUARY 15, 1981–
# MARCH 19, 1981

**JOHN MURRAY**
I was like a conscience to Tony. I would tell him, "You gotta get on top of it. You gotta take back all that money you lent out and you gotta leave yourself some. You just can't give it all away because people keep asking you to until it nearly kills you."

I promised to try to get his money back with my influence in the receiving room. I had access to prisoner inmate cards—where people are, where they're going on the outside—and I was going to use a list that his lawyer had sent him with the amounts that people owed him.

Tony and I made real plans to go on a trip around the world together. We were going to go to Thailand first—go see the monks and all that. You can stay warm there, and then you can go in the mountains and cool off if you want. Tony told me he had been there. And then we were maybe thinking about going to Indonesia, and Turkey, and England, you know, and we were talking about going to, maybe, Russia or something like that. Tony thought he'd be getting out soon. I assured him that he would if he told the judge that the devious thoughts in his mind had left and that he'd seen the error of his judgment, you know?

## J. Victor Benson
Tony did plan a trip around the world. Possibly it was with John Murray, but possibly it was with one of those listed on his visitors sheet.

## John Rakis
Inmates are allowed three visits of one hour each a week. We have thousands of visitors. The average number per month for our entire system was twenty-eight thousand for the fiscal year 1983. So we can't thoroughly check the credentials of each visitor.

## J. Victor Benson
The essential requirements are that they have to be a relative or a close friend of the inmate's. They have to show an affidavit of one sort or another—birth certificate, marriage license, and so on. Visitors are searched as they come in, but there's not much checking on whether they are or are not, let's say, an inmate's cousin—first, second, third, or shirttail.

## Approved Visitors Form, Rikers Island

NAME: Baekeland, Antony, 349-80-4228

### APPROVED VISITORS

NAME: Anastase, Joanne
ADDRESS: Brooklyn, New York
RELATIONSHIP TO INMATE: Friend
NAME: Firenzi, Vince
ADDRESS: Flushing, New York
RELATIONSHIP TO INMATE: Cousin

## John Murray
I think Vince Firenzi was in for holding a gun to his mother's head. He was a short fellow, not really one of the dangerous ones, but *sort* of. He was in another quad and he was running a con game on Tony. He came back because he probably wanted more money. He'd hustle Tony, give him a little kiss on the cheek or something like that and say, "I need more money."

Joanne Anastase was a skinny, pathetic-looking guy who used to be at Rikers. He dressed in women's clothes and I think he had an operation. He sort of looks like a woman and he sort of looks like a man—sort of in-between. He probably came back and said to Tony, "I need money for my boyfriend," or "I need money for clothes to go to the disco," or "I need money for drugs." You know—if it's not one thing, it's the other. And Tony gave him what he wanted, he was afraid to say no because he was afraid that Joanne might send somebody to go after him. But then he stopped giving money to Joanne. He said, "I'm going to stop giving money away." But then he wrote someone else a check for fifteen hundred dollars, and he wrote someone else one for, I'm not sure, I think it was two thousand. And he wrote *me* out a check for two thousand also. We had talked about me maybe borrowing a hundred dollars or something like that to get started when I got out. I gave the check to Mr. Benson to put in my account but I had a feeling I was never going to get that two thousand.

## J. VICTOR BENSON
Murray wanted me to take the check to the cashier, and I did take it personally to the cashier, mostly because I was interested in getting a check like that off the quad. They gave me a receipt and I presented it to Murray. But nobody would credit his commissary account with the check—and even the captain at the desk refused to handle it because it was so large. They thought there was something strange about it.

## JOHN RAKIS
The check was returned uncashed by the prison officials to Tony Baekeland's bank.

## JOHN MURRAY
My check from Tony fell through, and the parole for me fell through also. It just did, it just did, and I left Rikers on February 13th for Auburn State Prison upstate.

## JUAN MARTINEZ
After John Murray left, I was trying to manage Tony's affairs for him but he didn't give me no time. I told him, "Wait up, man, give me

some time, you know, and I'll find out some way that you can get out." See, I was going to the legal library every day for my own case.

## J. VICTOR BENSON
Juan was pretty much of a jailhouse lawyer. He was no dummy. He became knowledgeable about all procedures and all precedent cases. He was in for murder but was pleading insanity.

## Note from File on Juan Martinez

Date of birth 2/27/54; 1978 arrested 75th Pct.; previous charge, grand larceny; accused of murdering young boy, victim's head had been cut off, sodomy, drugs found around body, Juan found in victim's car with bloodstains on clothes. "Watch yourself, this is the car of the guy I killed," he may or may not have said.

## J. VICTOR BENSON
Juan had one of those special relationships with Baekeland, too.

## JUAN MARTINEZ
We were together in court in February and I told him, "Give me some more time," you know?

## From the Transcript, The People of the State of New York—Against—Antony Baekeland, Defendant, Supreme Court of the State of New York, County of New York, February 19, 1981

THE DEFENDANT: May I ask you something? I understand my grandmother has dropped her charge.
THE COURT: She is not dropping the charge. It's not up to a witness to drop charges or not drop charges.
THE DEFENDANT: She wasn't the witness. She was the victim.
THE COURT: It's not up to a victim. It's up to the prosecutor of the State of New York.
THE DEFENDANT: Oh! I see.
THE COURT: March 5th.

**From the Transcript, The People of the State of New York—Against—Antony Baekeland, Defendant, Supreme Court of the State of New York, County of New York, March 5, 1981**

THE COURT: How about the medical records, counsel?

COUNSEL FOR THE DEFENDANT: We spoke to England this morning and they put it in the mail this afternoon.

THE COURT: That's the same information for the last three adjournments.

COUNSEL FOR THE DEFENDANT: Okay. And the other medical report is on its way.

THE COURT: The 20th of March.

COUNSEL FOR THE DEFENDANT: I would like an application at this time due to the fact that the defendant has been held without bail. It's apparent that the complainant is—does not want to pursue this case. I wonder if bail could be set?

THE COURT: No, counsel. Remand continued. March 20th all right?

(No response)

THE COURT: March 20th.

# 5

# MARCH 20, 1981:
# 12:00 A.M.–4:39 P.M.

**Breakfast Menu, Rikers Island, March 20, 1981**

> Bread and margarine
> Stewed figs
> Rice Krispies
> Reconstituted milk
> Coffee and tea

**From the Transcript,** The People of the State of New York— Against—Antony Baekeland, Defendant, **Supreme Court of the State of New York, County of New York, March 20, 1981**

THE COURT CLERK: Number 15, Antony Baekeland.

(Whereupon, both counsel—Sarah Hines, Esq., Assistant District Attorney [For the People] and Ronald M. Arrick, Esq., [For the Defendant]—approach the bench for an off-the-record discussion.)

THE COURT: April 16th for Trial.

COUNSEL FOR THE DEFENDANT: Your Honor, if I may be heard? Mr. Baekeland's grandmother is in Court. She is eighty-eight years old. She is confined to a wheelchair. She has attempted to go to Rikers Island to visit the prisoner but has been advised that they have no facility for wheelchairs. She asked me to make an application to the Court for an in-Court visit with her grandson.

THE COURT: Because she is the complaining witness in the case, because there have been statements made by you and your firm that she does not wish to proceed with the charges, because of the severity of the case and all the other special circumstances, I'm not going to permit a Courtroom visit in this case. April 16th for Trial.

ASSISTANT DISTRICT ATTORNEY: Judge, would you make a ruling on the Grand Jury Minutes?

THE COURT: I have reviewed the Grand Jury Minutes and find them sufficient to warrant the indictment.

ASSISTANT DISTRICT ATTORNEY: I have received certain medical records from the defense from England. I've not received the complete medical records as I expected.

THE COURT: April 16th.

## CECELIA BREBNER

Nini had asked me if I would go with her to court and I went. Tony looked dreadful. When I had brought him back from London he had his Savile Row suit on and he looked very elegant, and now he was in rags, his hair tied back. He looked across the courtroom and said to Nini, "I love you, I love you, I'm sorry."

## RONALD ARRICK

I know his mood in court that morning and it was fairly good. He talked to his grandmother—they both mouthed across the courtroom. As he was being taken out the door, he saw Grandma, she was sitting down near the back with her nurse or someone, and he went "I love you." I had had a bench conference with the judge to see if he would grant Tony and Grandma a courtroom visit. I didn't want them in a room alone together. What I wanted was for Tony to sit on one side of the rail, with guards, and Grandma on the other side—not within reaching distance of each other but three to five feet away where they could still talk to each other in a fairly low voice so as not to disrupt the court. Or even at a recess. But the lady D.A. was adamant against it. She didn't want Tony having any contact with Grandma. One of the main reasons, I can only presume at, would be that it might influence her getting the verdict—the more contact they had, the less chance of Grandma testifying against Tony.

I don't see how his sitting there handcuffed in a chair—or handcuffed *to* the chair, let's say, if they wanted to go that far—five feet away from somebody, surrounded by, let's say, two court officers—would have been endangering the old lady's life. If it had been, I wouldn't have asked for it.

When Tony was refused the visit, he accepted it, he accepted it fine. I don't build up anybody's hopes. There are no guarantees.


## JUDGE ROBERT M. HAFT

For humanitarian reasons I would allow a courtroom visit—a woman has to see her child or a man has to see his new baby, or somebody's pregnant, or some case like that. But in Tony Baekeland's case I just didn't see that it warranted it. To see the complaining witness would not be proper.


## From a Draft Document, Board of Correction, City of New York

> Baekeland returned from court with a white plastic bag with red and blue lettering on it. He arrived back at quadrant 3 Lower at approximately 3:30 p.m. and requested to be locked in his cell.


## JOHN RAKIS

He could have gone in the hallway or in the dayroom—inmates are entitled to be locked out for fourteen hours during the day. They're also entitled to lock themselves into their cells when they want to be. It's optional. Some people want to be in their cells and read or write or they want to lie down, or they just don't want to be bothered by anybody else.

## From a Draft Document, Board of Correction, City of New York

Inmate John Lewis #346-80-2360 was the area suicide prevention aide on the 3 p.m. to 11 p.m. shift.

### JOHN RAKIS

Suicide prevention aides are an extra pair of eyes and ears for the officer, who may be busy entering something in the logbook or supervising food distribution or doing something to that effect. The aides get paid anywhere from thirty-five to fifty cents an hour—which is the highest rate of pay for inmate help. We test them to make sure they know what they're doing, we give certificates for the training, and we do periodic inspections and evaluations of their work.

## From a Draft Document, Board of Correction, City of New York

Inmate Lewis said that he spoke with Baekeland when he returned from court. Baekeland reportedly said that things had not gone well in court because he had hoped to be granted bail and that there had also been some talk he would be sent to a civil hospital, but instead he was remanded back to the Department.

### JOHN RAKIS

Tony had told several inmates that he expected to be bailed out. It was poor judgment on his part to expect bail.

## From a Draft Document, Board of Correction, City of New York

Correction Officer Patrick Raftery #2851 stated that he was assigned as the Lower 3 "B" Post Officer on the 3:27 p.m. to 11:58 p.m. tour. He arrived on his post at approximately 3:50 p.m. at which time he made a count. The Officer states that inmate Baekeland was sitting up on his bed at this time.

Again at 4:30 p.m., C.O. Raftery made his rounds. He reported that everything appeared normal. Baekeland was lying on his bed covered with a blanket; both feet and one hand were exposed.

At 4:39 p.m., Nurse Mauretta Link entered the quadrant to dispense medication. She was accompanied on her rounds in the area by C.O. Raftery. After dispensing medication to two inmates, Nurse Link with C.O. Raftery approached Baekeland's cell.

# 6

## MARCH 20, 1981:
## 4:40 P.M.–11:59 P.M.

**From a Draft Document, Board of Correction, City of New York**

> Baekeland did not respond to his name. C.O. Raftery rapped on the cell door, then opened the door and tapped his keys on the bedframe, then rubbed Baekeland's foot with the keys. When Baekeland still did not respond, C.O. Raftery pulled the blanket off the inmate and discovered that he had a red and white plastic bag over his head.

**JOHN RAKIS**
It was a plastic bag with one of those drawstrings, and the drawstring was pulled tight.

**J. VICTOR BENSON**
I heard it was tied.

**JOHN RAKIS**
It was not tied. Just pulled tight.

## From a Draft Document, Board of Correction, City of New York

C.O. Raftery went to remove the plastic bag from Baekeland's head and Nurse Link called to the "A" Officer, C.O. George Forbes # 1235, to send a manual resuscitator (ambubag). Nurse Link said at this point Baekeland had no pulse or respiration. C.O. Paul Jefferson #3076, the "B" Post Oficer, responded with an ambubag which Nurse Link began to use immediately. C.O. Forbes notified the 4 Lower clinic of the emergency and the need for a doctor. Nurse Practitioner Gloria Howard-Mello responded immediately and instructed Officers Raftery and Jefferson to move the inmate from his bed to the floor of the 3 Lower corridor to provide more room to perform first aid. Nurse Link continued to use the ambubag and Nurse Howard-Mello applied external heart massage. Doctors Doyle and Jhaveri responded at approximately 4:43 p.m. and found the inmate without pulse or respiration and with fixed and dilated pupils. Baekeland was pronounced dead at 4:45 p.m. by Dr. Doyle, who then left the area. At approximately 4:52 p.m. Montefiore Hospital personnel (Dr. Nickerson, Registered Physician's Assistant Ulrich, Nurse Johnson, and Nurse Minort) arrived in 3 Lower; they were not informed that Dr. Doyle had pronounced Baekeland dead, and recommenced cardiopulmonary resuscitation. During this procedure blood was observed spurting from the inmate's nose and mouth. After Montefiore personnel had ceased their attempt to revive Baekeland, he was placed back in his bed.

## CORRECTION OFFICER JOHN HERNANDEZ

At the time of Baekeland's suicide I was on the staff of the deputy warden, who investigates all matters pertaining to security. Right after it was discovered, the inmates on the quad were locked in. I then entered the cell to take pictures of Baekeland and the contents of the cell. I remember that there were some letters, some writing pads, a box of Ritz crackers, and not that much else. We preserved the cell for evidence, to rule out foul play, which *was* ruled out, almost immediately.

## Record of Inmate Transfer, Department of Correction, City of New York

NAME: Baekeland, Antony #349-80-4228
DATE: 3/20/81
TRANSFERRED TO: City Morgue D.O.A.


### JOHN RAKIS

After the suicide, I talked to the staff and to other inmates. There was a mixed reaction among the inmates. Some acted as if nothing had happened and some acted concerned—"Yes. Too bad. He expected to be bailed out." No one cried, no one was emotionally distraught. The general attitude was, another guy gone.

Tony didn't leave a note behind. Only a small percentage of our suicides do leave notes—perhaps one out of ten. Sometimes they'll underline a part of the Bible and the underlining is like a note.


## From the Autopsy Report on Antony Baekeland

*Case No.* Bx 81-1146
*External Description*
The body is received clad in the following items of clothing: two sweater shirts, the outer of which is green with a zippered neck and reveals vomitus and a small amount of blood on its anterior surface. The inner is gray shortsleeved (the green is longsleeved) with black, white, red, and gray piping. A pair of gray pants. A pair of jockey-type shorts. Also submitted with the deceased is what appears to be a piece of sheeting from an institutional-type bed on which are small quantities of blood. The plastic bag has not been received with the body.


### JUAN MARTINEZ

Somebody in his family made the plastic the bag was made out of—that's why I think he did it like that.

## From "Science and Industry," a Lecture Delivered by Leo Hendrik Baekeland, June 21, 1938

There is hardly any field, any branch of industry where plastics are not serving successfully in one form or another. . . . The whole fabric of modern civilization becomes every day more interwoven with the endless ramifications of applied chemistry. Ignorant people misjudge the value of chemical science and denounce its applications for war and other evils. Let us remind them that one of the most useful instruments ever invented, the knife, may, in the wrong hands, be used for evil, as well as for the best purposes.

EDWARD HERSHEY
The unusual thing about this was, of course, the method. We've never had anybody else suffocate himself with a plastic bag before.

BROOKS BAEKELAND
I do not believe that Tony, who was the prince of hope, bravura, and challenge, as well as of self-expiation and despair, took his own life. We were to the very end in constant epistolary contact. Everyone who knew him agrees that he would never have gone without a *big* announcement—not that hyperarticulate, dramatizing gent. And he died without a word to me or anyone.

I think he was murdered by his jailers. So easy to do. He had admitted his sexual relations with one of the guards in a letter to me. Maybe he threatened exposure, or retracted a promise of money? In both hands he held death: Who lives by the sword . . . But let it lie. Suicide or murder: Does it matter? Yes. But why and how much? Both he and his mother lived by violence and so they were bound to die by the same. I always knew it, and that was one of the reasons why I had to get away from them.

EDWARD HERSHEY
It is almost routine in every suicide for people to start saying, you know, that it really wasn't a suicide. For the family members in most instances it's so much more acceptable to have somebody be murdered than have them commit suicide. What a great guilt deflection that is.

## J. Victor Benson

I was shocked to hear about Tony because I couldn't believe that he had *that* kind of violence in him—toward himself, that is. He had never expressed suicidal thoughts. And also, it was not an impulsive act—it was very carefully done.

## John Murray

I don't think it's possible that someone did Tony in. He told me he was going to kill himself because I didn't love him. That's what he told me. Unless he just said it to make me feel guilty. I believe some-times someone kills themself because someone doesn't love them, so I kind of think in a way he did kill himself for me a little bit. He was a very sentimental guy. It stands to reason—anyone gives out that much money is sentimental. I miss him tremendously. I miss him very much.

## Ronald Arrick

I heard it on the news and I spent about four or five hours on the phone with Rikers trying to confirm it—you get a goddam runaround over there—and trying to get details, until I found the guard, who told me himself.

What I'm most interested in with Tony is what the hell happened at Rikers that he committed suicide—*if* he committed suicide. It's my impression that he didn't. It just doesn't make sense, to commit suicide by suffocating yourself with a plastic bag. Swallowing pills or slashing your wrists or shooting yourself of course is fairly easy, you know—assuming you want to do it—and depending on how far you go with it, it's irreversible. But something like this you can stop at any given time, and your normal impulse—I mean it would be in-voluntary even—would *be* to stop it.

## Elizabeth Archer Baekeland

When I heard that Tony had committed suicide by putting a plastic bag over his head, I told a doctor friend that I thought it was extraor-dinary that he had the courage—I mean, it's the most noble thing that Tony did in his *life*—and the doctor said it's not difficult to do. He said you just breathe in your carbon monoxide and become eu-phoric. So later I thought, I'll test that out. I took a plastic bag, and I couldn't find any string so I took some telephone wire and wrapped it around, and I couldn't believe it, within a matter of . . . you cannot measure time under those circumstances but very soon I was really feeling high, and good, and so I thought, Oh-oh, I'd better take it off—and I couldn't find the end of the wire! Well, I finally found it and ripped it off—I mean, obviously.

RONALD ARRICK
Go back another step. He was on a suicide watch at the time, so how come he had a plastic bag? Where did he get a plastic bag?

I'd seen him before court session, I'd seen him during court session, and I went back in after court session and we discussed how we were going to proceed and he seemed in a very good mood. I mean, look, maybe he knew he was going to commit suicide and that's one of the reasons he was *in* the good mood. We'll never know.

## From a Draft Document, Board of Correction, City of New York

There is no evidence to suggest that Baekeland's death was not suicide, as he was locked in his cell immediately after he returned from court. All other inmates in the area were also locked in from the time of the count (4:00 p.m.) through the discovery of the emergency, with the exception of inmate John Lewis, the suicide aide.

## From the Financial Records of Antony Baekeland

To John Lewis—$2,000.00.

JOHN RAKIS
It seems unlikely that if Tony was giving John Lewis money, John Lewis would do any harm to him or want him to die. Besides, there's nothing a suicide prevention aide could do to another inmate that any other inmate couldn't do, too.

Also, inmates don't have any control over the keys. One of Correction's biggest concerns is key control—they probably spend more time at the Academy teaching key control than suicide prevention. Keys are very carefully accounted for. The loss of a key would be tantamount to the loss of an inmate. It's against procedures to even allow inmates to touch keys.

That door was locked. Officer Raftery had to open it with a key. And there were several witnesses to that.

Every time we see a suicide, the thought of homicide is always foremost in our minds, and the investigation is conducted with that in mind. And there was no indication whatsoever that there was any foul play in Tony Baekeland's death.

## Juan Martinez

It didn't come as no surprise. Not really. Because he told me he was gonna kill himself. And I saw it. I saw everything. Everything. And I didn't help. Forget it. Just forget it. I'm the only one to know the real truth. And the C.O.s know that I'm the only one that knows the real truth, too. It's too many things. It's too many things, man. It's dangerous, you know? You see what I'm saying? You understand what I'm telling you? I was there. I *know* what happened. Somebody said, "Do it, Tony, or else!"

## Howard Nabor

It was suicide, there's no question about it. One of my officers took it very bad. You know, it was unusual that he got so upset about it. He felt, you know, that Tony was a very sensitive boy, and just to see somebody die like that really upset him. I think he even resigned from the job after that—if I remember right.

The type of suicide *was* unusual. I felt that somebody that did it that way really wanted to go. Some of the others, if they try to hang themselves, sometimes they're doing it for show and then they accidentally kill themselves. But definitely—no question about it—Tony Baekeland wanted to go.

## Edward Hershey

I remember it was a Friday evening when word came. We try to make sure the next of kin is notified before we inform the press. And in this instance, it became apparent that the next of kin was the very selfsame grandmother. I had a sense that the tragedy would be compounded if our minister and the correction officer assigned walked in on her and said, "Your grandson has just killed himself," her having seen him in court that day. So I reached out for the assistant D.A., and I found her—I don't know how I did it but I found her. It was a

Friday night, she was visiting people in Jersey, and I said, "What do we do?" She knew the grandmother and she was concerned and we were able to locate a tenant in the grandmother's building so that she wasn't alone when she was told the news.

## LENA RICHARDS
I came to Nini's on Saturday morning and the weekday nurse said, "Have you heard?" I said, "What?" She said, "He killed himself." I was shocked. I went into Nini and she said, "Oh, Lena, oh, Tony's killed himself." She didn't cry. She said, "Such guilt I put on the family, and I might as well confide and tell you everything." She said Frank, her husband, was cleaning his car in the garage with Frank Jr., and Frank Jr. left to do something and when he came back the garage door was closed and the motor was on. I'm afraid she'll never get over Tony.

## NINA DALY
It's a sad story. It was the biggest heartbreak. It was terrible. But you see, I don't dwell on it. I can't. I think about how much I loved him and how much he meant to me. I still wish he was here.

## BROOKS BAEKELAND
It was a beautiful ending—in plastic, too!

The terrible thing was that in his secret heart he always thought that in the end I could save him. Like his mother he was without fear—and Daddy *would* come, somehow, out of *somewhere*, like Superman. They both believed that. You know, there is no such thing, when there is a child, as a divorce. It's a contradiction in terms. Until their very last moments—for both of them—I was supposed to burst through a door and save them. But the odds they played against were so enormous that even Superman would not have arrived in time.

Courage they both had, but to the point of folly. They were great romantics. I cannot laugh at them. Who can laugh, for instance, at Zelda Fitzgerald? I mourn because I failed them. I failed their unrealistic marvelous dreams. But even the word "unrealistic" is a weasel word to the true romantic, who accords the greatest value to that which really is truly and absolutely impossible. Barbara's mad audacities always made me feel ashamed of myself—as Zelda's did Scott Fitzgerald. No wonder, in his madness, that her son thought her a goddess. He gave himself, too, a minor god's rank, but that was a faery geste, on dope. And I have no doubt that—his ear against that cold prison floor as though listening to hoofbeats pursuing him to another world—part of him really did believe that she was waiting for him up, up there, where only Mozart and Bach and champagne and "the beautiful people" would flow in the chiaroscuro of Gustave Doré's enormous canvases, in eternal round, waiting now for him, too, for this world below had become far too vulgar. Henry Aldrich in that corny radio series of the thirties used to always get a laugh saying, "Coming, Mother!"

If I have shocked you, let me remind you that only laughter clears the vision. Without laughter, there can be no seeing of the truth. Tragedy does not allow laughter. It is pity that does. And I have never seen tragedy in all my short, wasted, eager life—only pity. And I see that everywhere around me and in the markings of my own hand. That is all I see.

# 7

## THE FINAL REPORT

Headline, the *New York Times*, March 21, 1981

INMATE KILLS HIMSELF
IN A CELL AT RIKERS

Headline, New York *Daily News*, March 21, 1981

PLASTICS HEIR WHO KILLED MOM
AN APPARENT SUICIDE IN JAIL CELL

Headline, *Daily Telegraph*, London, March 23, 1981

PLASTICS HEIR DEAD IN JAIL

FRANCINE DU PLESSIX GRAY
When Tony died with this thing of putting a plastic bag over his
head, Ethel de Croisset called me—she was in New York at the

time—and she said, "Don't you see the relationship to his stealing the baby food that summer in Italy?" I said no. She said, "Well, he chose a baby's way of dying, didn't he? Smothering."

### ETHEL WOODWARD DE CROISSET
He just went to sleep in his little plastic bag, and I saw this as being perhaps his desire to return to the womb.

### ELEANOR WARD
When I heard he had killed himself, I thought, What a relief for him, what a blessing—out of the agony at last.

### JAMES REEVE
So many of one's friends seem to have died under peculiar circumstances, one way or another, recently. Mine, anyway. A great friend of mine—and kindred spirits are few and far between—I mean, somebody I could tell anything, and she me—anyway, she had had a house in Greece and she was motoring back to France and all of a sudden she got a heart attack for no reason and died. That was that. Very shocking. In a curious way—it's sort of animal defense or something—I refused to face it. I just put it out of my mind. I didn't really sit down and think about her being dead. I just think of her as gone away. One *should* sit down and look it in the eye and face up to the fact.

When I heard Tony had died, I was horrified. But then I put it out of my mind, too. I haven't really thought about it since.

### GLORIA JONES
I guess it was John Sargent who told me how Tony had committed suicide, and I thought it was the end of the whole horrible story. But you would never write it that way—it's too corny. How did he get the plastic bag, I wonder.

### ROSE STYRON
It was the perfect ironic end.

### SAMUEL PARKMAN SHAW
It seemed to me that it was a perfectly normal end to *his* career. It was a good solution, and a not unclever way of doing it. It took some determination—how to get into the bag and stay there until he suffocated. That's not a bad trick.

## JOHN RAKIS

As a result of Tony Baekeland's suicide, inmates are not allowed to have plastic bags in their possession. Also, the correction officers are now told that when they see an inmate lying fairly still and the blanket is over his head, they really ought to check for signs of breathing. Now, many inmates do this to keep out noise or keep the lights from getting in their eyes; Tony of course put the blanket over his head to cover up his intentions.

## From the Final Report of the New York State Commission of Correction Medical Review Board in the Matter of the Death of Antony Baekeland at the Anna M. Kross Center, Rikers Island, December 22, 1981

The Medical Review Board recommends that the NYC Department of Health, Prison Health Services, advise mental health treatment staff at the Anna M. Kross Center that special attention should be given to inmates under psychiatric treatment as significant life events or status changes approach. Mental health treatment staff are often aware of these events.

The Medical Review Board recommends that the NYC Department of Health, Prison Health Services, develop policies and procedures whereby previous psychiatric hospital records are obtained when an inmate is in detention and under psychiatric treatment for extended periods.

## MIWA SVINKA-ZIELINSKI

Tony never talked about taking his life, never once in all those years. It was a waste, his life. All that time I wasted on that boy! I continued to believe that he could be cured. His disease was Barbara.

## Letter from Brooks Baekeland to Nina Daly, June 8, 1981

Stonington, Maine

Dear Nini—

I grieve over him, too—more as time goes by, more as I remember him as a child—for while seeming to know, to understand, that he was doomed if he continued as he did, he always so continued, from one disaster to the next, fascinated as it were by his own destruction. Seeing it, knowing it, reveling.

That—that knowing—is a side of Tony that very few people ever knew. I did, because between Tony and me there always was a curious: "I know that *you* know that *I* know . . ." almost ad infinitum. We both had, for instance, unspoken knowledge and understandings about his mother, my relationship to her and his relationship to her. Also about his to me and mine to him!

One of the results of these extraordinary, multileveled intuitional understandings between us was that when we were together there was nothing to say. We both knew it all and knew that we both knew it. Silence.

It was that—let me be as fair as I can—which separated us just as much as the fact that morally we were bitter enemies. I hated his immorality—remember, I do not speak about sexuality but about ethics—but so did he! But he also loved it! Was drawn to crime—again, I do not mean "lawbreaking" but sordid self-immolation—as a moth to a flame. He was the quintessential pederast, in fact. He was an American Genet, but without the overriding desire for fame and capacity to work.

He was just as gifted—far more gifted than his father or mother—or if not, then his terrible failings made those gifts shine in their surrounding darkness—shine angelically.

There is a line from somewhere that comes into my mind: Was he a "halting angel who tripped against a star," or was he *"le diable boîteux"*?

Love,
Brooks

P.S. I have a smallish room here with a terrace, over the water on piles, on the harbor of a professional fishing village. I live all alone. Thrice a week I take a boat (40 minutes) to an island at 7 A.M. I then walk 2–2½ hours to the other end of the island. There I work (cutting trees and throwing them into the sea) on a friend's place for 3 hours. Then I walk back to the town landing and take the boat back to Stonington. It is very beautiful up here. The romanticality of this coast is a great adjunct, and some of the people—always the older generation, made before socialism destroyed the American family and proper upbringings—are very fine.

## ELIZABETH BLOW

When I heard about Tony, I went on thinking about the Baekelands. It gets to be an obsession. One thing I'm convinced of is that they—Brooks and Barbara—always loved each other in spite of her impossible behavior and his philandering.

## BROOKS BAEKALAND

A large part of what made Sylvie wish to find her eventual freedom from me was my indestructible worry and concern and sense of responsibility for Barbara. Sylvie's jealousy always was and still is intense. She admired Barbara! A wiser man than I might have saved all those lives and still kept Sylvie.

## SYLVIE BAEKELAND SKIRA

I became important to Brooks—if you can say important—when I left him. That's all. I don't think I was his wife, ever. I suffered all the time because I didn't exist. *That* was my suffering.

Once, for his birthday, I gave him a very pretty silver frame, and later I went up to his study and what was in the silver frame but a photograph of Barbara! I really collapsed. I was still very much in love and I was expecting his baby. And he said to me, "God, you're badly brought up! How can you be jealous of someone dead?" He had always carried a picture of Barbara in his wallet. Now he has one of me also. Now, yes. *Oh* yes. Now that I've gone, yes.

Even now when I speak about this, I am drained. I'm nothing. They are too heavy! That's why I left. I didn't leave because I wanted to have an affair with somebody, I left because I thought, Well, the next one is me. I'm going to die, too.

When Tony died, I had already left Brooks. I think he was in the Grenadines. I know he decided not to go to New York. This is the only part that I can say I did not approve of. He should have gone to New York.

## BROOKS BAEKELAND

Now I can—and do—travel and live everywhere in the world with a small satchel that I can carry by hand. Of course if I am asked to dine black-tie, I say no. But then, I don't consort with those sort of people anymore.

I have, really, no possessions left. That is easy now, unwived. It is women, those nesters, those decorators, those competitors for status symbols, that take us naked men out of the jungle and "civilize" us.

Every bachelor, if he isn't a fairy, soon reverts to savage state. But in fact, I was never much attracted by "the things money could buy." As everyone knows, the best things are free, or almost free. H. D. Thoreau: "A man is rich in proportion to the things he does not need." The one exception to that rule is of course women themselves. They bankrupt us all.

## SAM GREEN
Tony left half of his trust fund to the servant family at Miramar who looked after the house—after all, he had spent several cold winters on their hearth. The other half went to Nini.

## Letter from Brooks Baekeland to Nina Daly, July 19, 1981

Stonington, Maine

Dear Nini—

Here are your photos back—thank you for sending them to me. I took them 34 years ago. It was interesting to see them, but I haven't your sentiment. I will be sending you a photo of me and my young son one of these days—a photo taken in my three-day-evening years. The feeling you had for Tony I have for my small son. I was too young then—too much interested in myself probably (my career, my studies, etc.), and then, later, Tony was never anything but embarrassments to me. (But I never had a heart as big as yours. Who has?)

I wish you were up here with me. It's cool and lovely. Have become a hermit.

Love as always,
Brooks

## BROOKS BAEKELAND
My life is almost totally solitary now. I know that I shall end up like my grandfather—a dead leaf blown down the city streets—talking and gesticulating to himself. The object of the interest of a kindly—corrupt!—policeman who finally gets him home. And in the end into his straitjacket. And a straighter one, the grave.

And what was left? Death was no end. Oh, no. It never was. That

is why I am talking to you. There is no end. There was no end.
There is no end. There will never be an end.

### ETHEL WOODWARD DE CROISSET
When Barbara died, I consolidated my idea of never wanting to see
Brooks again. He should never have left her and Tony in such distress. I did see him once after that, in Paris, at the wedding of the
child of a friend we had in common. He came and sat beside Virginia Chambers, who was blind and so of course couldn't see him.
But when she realized it was he, she refused to speak to him. He
then tried to catch *my* eye—he kept walking up and down the aisle.
And *I* certainly cut him dead.

### MICHAEL EDWARDS
I saw Brooks with his new wife at a wedding reception at the Ritz.
She was carrying their baby on her back—mind you, in the Ritz!
Like a papoose. And he came over to me and said it would be very
nice if he could rent my flat again at 45, quai de Bourbon, and I
thought that was so extraordinary. I just said it wasn't available.

### BARBARA CURTEIS
The minute Barbara was dead, Brooks had an absolute lust to occupy
with Sylvie every place he and Barbara had ever occupied. He even
went back to Cadaqués one summer. Missy Harnden wrote me, "I'm
longing to run into him here so I can cut him dead in the paseo."

### BROOKS BAEKELAND
I am perfectly indifferent to what people think of me. I do not wish to
seem more arrogant than I am but anybody who is not a nonentity
wears the blazonry of his enemies with as much relish as he does that
of those who love him. I try only to act out of love—for the very few
people I do love. The bond between Barbara and me has survived
and always will survive.

## From *A Walk in Winter Woods,* Brooks Baekeland, Unpublished

> He could not shake the strange feeling that she existed. Some-
> where; maybe here with him now, invisible but still alive and

vital. He could well imagine meeting her one day as she came towards him around a corner with that determined, rapid walk of hers and that proud carriage of her tawny head. For the hundredth time he remembered her tear-stained face, her big, serious eyes, and the question: "But darling, who is going to take care of you when you are old?"

### BROOKS BAEKELAND

We were linked—in fact, all three of us, Tony and Barbara and I, were linked—to the death. I mean unto death, of course.

Passionate error, soaring IQs, drugs, murder, suicide—these are not simple things to be clever and name-dropping about at cocktail parties, these are not things to be lisped *dans le Tout-Paris* and to make luncheon parties more interesting for rich women who have too little to do.

I know all those people and I have utter contempt for them and their eagerness—if they are eager—to be quoted, to be heard, etc., etc., on matters in which they were never informed except by "a woman scorned"—though in truth I never scorned that difficult but in many ways lovable and admirable woman—and by a son whose father most definitely did not approve of him, love him though he did all his short life. For finally, what did not last was *not* love.

### SYLVIE BAEKELAND SKIRA

Brooks told our little boy the story of his brother. He was seven at the time and going off to boarding school in England. I told him, "This is a very sad story. You can talk to *me* about it but you mustn't tell the other little boys because they either will not believe you or they will tease you." There was quite some time of silence, and then two months later when he came back to me for his holidays, one afternoon he said, "You know, I told the story and they believed me."

# BIOGRAPHICAL NOTES

MICHAEL ALEXANDER is a writer and restaurateur who lives in London.

RONALD ARRICK is a lawyer who practices in New York.

BROOKS BAEKELAND now spends most of his time in England where he studies and writes.

ELIZABETH ARCHER BAEKELAND is as former journalist. She divides her time between America and England.

DR. FREDERICK BAEKELAND is a psychiatrist and an art historian. His published papers include "Psychological Aspects of Art Collecting," "Exercise and Sleep Patterns in College Athletes," "Correlates of Home Dream Recall," and "Dropping Out of Treatment: A Critical Review." He lives in New York City.

ROSEMARY RODD BALDWIN is a travel writer and frequent contributor to British Vogue. She also organizes travel tours to Turkey and Colombia. She lives in a cottage on her daughter Jinty Money-Coutts's estate in Wales.

SIR CECIL BEATON, artist, writer, designer, and photographer, died in 1980. He was for years the official photographer to the British royal family. He designed scenery and costumes for numerous ballets, operas, and plays, including *My Fair Lady*. He was an enthusiastic traveler, gardener, diarist, art collector, and arbiter of taste. His books include *The Glass of Fashion* and *The Face of the World*.

J. VICTOR BENSON died in January 1985. A retired Lutheran clergyman who studied clinical psychology at New York University, he had been with the New York City Department of Correction since 1969.

GEORGES BERNIER was a founding editor of the French art magazine *L'Oeil* and owner of Gallery L'Oeil in Paris. He is now connected with the international art firm of Wildenstein and lives in London and Paris.

ELIZABETH BLOW lives in upstate New York where she co-owns a handicrafts shop.

CECELIA BREBNER is a retired nurse. She has also worked for various airlines and been a volunteer at the United Nations.

DETECTIVE SUPERINTENDENT KENNETH BRETT retired from Scotland Yard. He is now connected with the Royal Military Academy in Woolwich, London.

BOWDEN BROADWATER recently retired as college adviser at St. Bernard's School in New York City.

ANATOLE BROYARD is an editor at *The New York Times Book Review*. He also teaches a creative writing class at The New School for Social Research in New York City. His fiction has appeared in *The New Yorker*.

COLM BYRNE, formerly a nurse at Broadmoor Special Hospital in Crowthorne, Berkshire, England, now works for the Probation Services in Liverpool.

DODIE CAPTIVA is a former teacher. She lives in Cambridge, Massachusetts.

SARA DUFFY CHERMAYEFF has published fiction in magazines. She lives in New York City.

SERGEANT JOSEPH CHINEA, at one time a patrol officer with the 19th Precinct, New York City, is now a supervisor of an anticrime unit at the 34th Precinct.

ALEXANDER COHANE is a private art dealer in New York City.

HEATHER COHANE works with the decorator Carlton Varney in New York City.

JOHN PHILIP COHANE died in 1981. He was a founding partner of SSC&B and retired at the age of forty-eight to Ireland to write. He published four nonfiction books: *The Key*, *The Indestructible Irish*, *White Papers of an Outraged Conservative*, and *Paradox: The Ex-*

*traterrestrial Origin of Man.* He won the Edgar Award for a television mystery story in 1966.

ONDINE COHANE is a student at the Brearley School in New York City.

DAVID COHEN is the author of *Psychologists on Psychology, All in the Head,* a biography of John B. Watson, and *Broadmoor.* He also produced a film for British TV, *I Was in Broadmoor.*

KATHARINE GARDNER COLEMAN died in January 1984. She lived and entertained in Paris, New York City, and Dark Harbor, Maine.

FREDERICK COMBS is an actor who lives in Los Angeles.

SHIRLEY COX works for the Chemotherapy Foundation in New York City.

ETHEL WOODWARD DE CROISSET is an American philanthropist who lives in Paris.

BARBARA CURTEIS lived year-round in Cadaqués, Spain, for several years. She now lives in New York City.

NINA DALY died in New York City in the fall of 1984 at the age of ninety-one.

DR. JEAN DAX lives and practices medicine in Paris.

TOM DILLOW is a freelance music coordinator for fashion shows, restaurants, stores, and parties. He lives in New York City.

WILLY DRAPER lives in Atlanta, Georgia, where he sells crystal and china.

LOUISE DUNCAN is an executive recruiter and magazine writer. She lives in New York City.

DOMINICK DUNNE produced the films *Boys in the Band, The Panic in Needle Park, Play It As It Lays, Ash Wednesday,* and *The Users.* He is the author of two novels: *The Winners* and the recently published *The Two Mrs. Grenvilles.* He is a contributing editor to *Vanity Fair* and lives in New York City.

MICHAEL EDWARDS is an international shipping executive who lives in London, Paris, and Provence.

H.R.H. PRINCESS ELIZABETH OF YUGOSLAVIA is internationally concerned with matters of spiritual evolution, especially the Sedona movement. She is a second cousin of Prince Charles and the mother of Catherine Oxenberg, Amanda on *Dynasty.*

EILEEN FINLETTER lived for many years in Paris, where she translated books. She now lives in New York City.

ELIZABETH WEICKER FONDARAS lives and entertains in New York

City, East Hampton, Long Island, and on Île Saint-Louis in Paris.

JONATHAN FRANK lives in California where he is a paramedic and ambulance driver.

PETER GABLE is in the investment business in Stamford, Connecticut, and lives in New York City.

BRENDAN GILL is Broadway theater critic for *The New Yorker*. He is the author of *Cole, Tallulah, Here at The New Yorker*, and *Lindbergh Alone*, and is at work on a biography of Stanford White.

PETER GIMBEL wrote, directed, was one of the underwater cameramen for, and coproduced (with his wife, Elga Anderson) the film *Andrea Doria: The Final Chapter*. His other filmmaking credits include *Whale Ho, In the World of Sharks*, and *Blue Water, White Death*. He lives in New York City.

AMBROSE GORDON has taught English at Hunter, Yale, and Sarah Lawrence colleges. Since 1958 he has been a professor of English at the University of Texas at Austin. He is the author of *The Invisible Tent: The War Novels of Ford Madox Ford*.

BART GORIN works as an assistant to Sam Green in New York City. He is also a photoresearcher for magazines.

CLEVE GRAY is a painter who has had several one-man shows in New York, Canada, France, and Italy. His work is represented in the permanent collections of the Whitney Museum of American Art, the Metropolitan Museum of Art, and the Guggenheim. He is the editor of *David Smith by David Smith, John Marin by John Marin*, and *Hans Richter by Hans Richter*.

FRANCINE DU PLESSIX GRAY is the author of *Divine Disobedience: Profiles in Catholic Radicalism, Hawaii: The Sugar-Coated Fortress, Lovers and Tyrants*, and *World Without End*. She has written for *The New Yorker* since 1968.

SAM GREEN, former director of the Institute of Contemporary Art in Philadelphia, is active internationally as an arts consultant to museums and private collectors. He lives in New York City and owns a large house in Cartagena, Colombia, and a small village on Fire Island.

PATRICIA GREENE lives in upstate New York. Her husband, Dr. Justin L. Greene, chief of child psychiatry at St. Luke's–Roosevelt Hospital Center in New York City as well as a neuropsychiatrist in private practice for over forty years, died in March 1984.

PAUL GREENWOOD retired from the police force of the town of East Hampton, Long Island, where he still lives.

STEPHANE GROUEFF, former New York bureau chief for *Paris Match* and former director of information for the Embassy of Oman, is the author of *Manhattan Project*. He is at work on a biography of King Boris of Bulgaria. He lives in New York City and Southampton, Long Island.

CATHERINE GUINNESS is co-author with her father, the Honorable Jonathan Guinness, of the recently published family history *The House of Mitford*. She is married to Lord Neidpath and is the mother of a one-year-old son. They live in Gloucestershire.

SUE GUINNESS runs an import-export business in England. She lives in London and in Cadaqués, Spain.

THE HONORABLE ROBERT M. HAFT is a justice of the Supreme Court of New York City.

BARBARA HALE lives in East Hampton, Long Island, and teaches nature classes to children and young adults.

NIKE MYLONAS HALE has taught art in New York City. She lives in Newburyport, Massachusetts, with her husband, Robert Beverly Hale.

ROBERT BEVERLY HALE organized and headed the department of American art at the Metropolitan Museum of Art. He has also been an instructor of drawing and a lecturer on anatomy at the Art Students League of New York. His own work is represented in the permanent collections of the Whitney Museum of American Art and the Metropolitan Museum of Art. He has published poetry in *The New Yorker*.

RICHARD HARE is a decorator who lives in New York City and East Hampton, Long Island.

MISHKA HARNDEN works in films in Los Angeles.

PICO HARNDEN is a photographer who lives in New York City.

ALAN HARRINGTON is the author of *The Revelations of Dr. Modesto, Life in the Crystal Palace, The Secret Swinger, The Immortalist: An Approach to the Engineering of Man's Divinity, Psychopaths, Paradise I: A Novel,* and *The White Rainbow*. He lives in Tucson, Arizona.

LUBA HARRINGTON has taught linguistics at Yale. She lives in New York City and in Sag Harbor, Long Island.

NEIL HARTLEY is a senior producer for Tony Richardson's Woodfall Films. His latest film is *The Hotel New Hampshire*. He lives in Los Angeles.

DRUE HEINZ is the publisher of *Antaeus*, a trustee of the Metropolitan Museum of Art, and a celebrated hostess on both sides of the Atlantic.

DAPHNE HELLMAN has been described in *The New Yorker* as a "salon-keeper, famous New York beauty, aviarist, and extraordinary harpist. She invented Hellman's Angels, a unique trio—harp, guitar, bass—which has been up and down the country and over a good part of the world." She lives in New York City and on Cape Cod.

ADDIE HERDER is a painter who lived in Paris for many years and now lives in New York City. Her most recent show of collage constructions featured façades and shallow interiors.

CORRECTION OFFICER JOHN HERNANDEZ works in the deputy warden's office at the Anna M. Kross Center on Rikers Island.

EDWARD HERSHEY is the assistant commissioner for public affairs in the New York City Department of Correction.

SARAH HINES is an assistant district attorney for the borough of Manhattan.

JAMES M. HUBBALL retired as headmaster of the Buckley School in New York City. He lives in Connecticut and Florida.

PAUL JENKINS is a painter who has had many one-man and group shows. His work is represented in the permanent collections of the Museum of Modern Art, the Whitney Museum of American Art, the Tate Gallery in London, and the Musée d'Art Moderne in Paris. He is the producer of a film, *The Ivory Knife: Paul Jenkins at Work*, the author of a play, *Strike the Puma*, and the subject of two biographies. He lives in New York City.

JASPER JOHNS has had one-man shows in museums and galleries all over the world. His work is represented in the permanent collections of the Museum of Modern Art, the Tate Gallery in London, and the Whitney Museum of American Art. He is a member of the National Institute of Arts and Letters.

GLORIA JONES is a consulting editor at Doubleday & Company. She lives in New York City and in Bridgehampton, Long Island. She is the widow of novelist James Jones.

JAMES JONES died in 1977. He was the author of *From Here to Eternity, Some Came Running, The Pistol, The Thin Red Line, Go to the Widow-maker, The Ice-Cream Headache and Other Stories, The Merry Month of May, A Touch of Danger, Viet Journal, World War II,* and *Whistle.*

CÉLINE ROLL KARRAKER is a granddaughter of Céline and Leo Hendrik Baekeland. She lives in Connecticut.

JAMES KINGSLAND is a partner in a large architectural firm in New York City.

F. CLASON KYLE served on the board of directors of the Victorian Society in America. He is currently compiling a pictorial history of Columbus, Georgia, where he works for the *Ledger* and *Enquirer* newspapers.

PAULE LAFEUILLE has taught French to several generations of Americans in Paris.

PETER LAKE is a writer who lives in Venice, California.

WENDY VANDERBILT LEHMAN is a painter who lives in New York City and in Dutchess County, New York.

FRANCESCA DRAPER LINKE lives in Los Angeles. She is married to an actor and the mother of two young children.

SYLVIA LOCHAN was registrar at the National Academy School of Fine Arts of the National Academy of Design in New York City from 1970 to 1973. "I have since gone back to school and acquired a few degrees in psychology and I do counseling now." She lives in Worcester, Massachusetts.

DUNCAN LONGCOPE lives in Boston and in the Berkshires. He is at work on a novel.

DR. E. HUGH LUCKEY was physician chief at New York Hospital for ten years, then president of its medical center for eleven. He is an internist now in private practice in New York City.

PEIDI GIMBEL LUMET is married to the film director Sidney Lumet. They live in New York City and in East Hampton, Long Island.

JOHN MCCABE retired from the New York City police force.

TERENCE MCLINSKEY is now director of security and vice-president at Sotheby's in New York City.

DR. THOMAS MAGUIRE, M.A., M.B., B.Ch., F.R.C.Psych., D.P.M., D.M.J., is consultant forensic psychiatrist at Broadmoor Special Hospital. He is also in private practice in nearby Wokingham.

INGE MAHN is a head senior counselor of the Richmond Fellowship in New York City.

PHYLLIS HARRIMAN MASON is a painter. She lives in New York and in Maine.

DAVID MEAD is a composer and musical director. He lives in New York City.

WILLIE MORRIS, a former editor-in-chief of *Harper's* magazine, is the author of *The South Today, 100 Years After Appomattox*, an autobiography, *North Toward Home, Yazoo: Integration in a Deep*

*Southern Town,* and *The Country of Marcus Dupree.* He is also the author of a novel, *The Last of the Southern Girls,* a book of essays, *Always Stand in Against the Curve,* and a memoir, *James Jones, A Friendship.* He lives in Mississippi.

JOHN MORTIMER is an English playwright, novelist, and lawyer. He is best known for his scripts for *Brideshead Revisited* and the Rumpole stories. He is also the author of an autobiography, *Clinging to the Wreckage.*

ELSA MOTTAR lives and works in New York City.

JOHN MURRAY lives and works in New York City.

HOWARD NABOR, former deputy warden of the Anna M. Kross Center at Rikers Island, now works in the private sector.

PATRICIA NEAL, the actress, recently moved to New York from England.

MICHEL NEGROPONTE is a filmmaker who lives in New York City.

ROBERT ORENSTEIN, a former assistant director of the Richmond Fellowship, is a social worker now in private practice in New York City as well as a staff therapist for Jewish Family Services of Bergen County, New Jersey.

DAISY HELLMAN PARADIS plays sitar and is chairman of the board of Ali Akbar College of Indian Music in San Raphael, California. She lives with her husband, David Paradis, publisher of *Pequod* magazine, in San Francisco.

BERNARD PFRIEM is a painter who has had one-man shows in America and Europe. He has taught art at Sarah Lawrence College, Cooper Union School of Art and Architecture, and the Museum of Modern Art. He is the director of the Lacoste School of the Arts in France.

DR. STANLEY L. PORTNOW is a psychiatrist in private practice in New York City.

KAREN RADKAI has been a photographer in America and Europe since 1948. Since 1953 she has worked primarily for *Vogue* and *House & Garden.* She lives in New York City and in the Berkshires.

SUE RAILEY was born in Rochester, lived for thirty-three years in Paris, and now lives in New York City, where she is in charge of public relations for Christie's.

JOHN RAKIS, former suicide prevention coordinator and director of health for the New York City Department of Correction, is now deputy executive director of the New York City Board of Correction.

JAMES REEVE is an English painter. He lives in a village in rural England.

ALASTAIR REID is a staff writer at *The New Yorker,* to which over the years he has regularly contributed poems, reviews, comment, translations, stories, and extensive reportage. He has translated the writings of many Latin Americans, particularly Pablo Neruda and Jorge Luis Borges. He has published more than twenty books—poetry, translations, collections of prose, and books for children. He lives in New York City and on Mallorca.

LENA RICHARDS is a practical nurse. She lives in New York City.

HELEN ROLO has been a researcher at *Time* magazine and a fashion editor at *Harper's Bazaar.* She lives in New York City.

TOBY ROSS is a photographer who lives and works in New York City.

IRVING SABO lives and works in Connecticut.

JOHN SARGENT is chairman of the board of Doubleday & Company, Inc. He is a trustee of the New York Zoological Society, the New York Public Library, and the American Academy of Rome. He lives in New York City and in Water Mill, Long Island.

MAY SARTON is the author of seventeen novels, fourteen books of poetry, and several nonfiction books. She is the daughter of George Sarton, a noted science historian, and Mabel Elwes Sarton, a painter—friends of Céline and Leo Hendrik Baekeland. "The genius was old Mr. Baekeland, *Dr.* Baekeland as he was called," she wrote recently. "The great *person* was 'Bonbon.'" She lives in York, Maine.

ELLEN SCHWAMM is the author of two novels, *Adjacent Lives* and *How He Saved Her.* She lives in New York City with her husband, the writer Harold Brodkey.

SAMUEL PARKMAN SHAW retired from the private practice of law in New York City and is counsel for a corporation in Connecticut.

MARTIN J. SIEGEL is a lawyer who practices in New York City.

SYLVIE BAEKELAND SKIRA lives in Maine, where she runs an art gallery. Her present husband is a naval architect.

SANDRA LEWIS SMITH, former deputy director of public affairs for the New York City Department of Correction, is now its director of special events.

MARJORIE FRASER SNOW lives in Ohio.

GEORGE STAEMPFLI owns and runs the Staempfli Gallery in New York City.

ROSE STYRON is a poet and a long-time board member of Amnesty

International. She lives with her husband, William Styron, in Connecticut.

WILLIAM STYRON is the author of *Lie Down in Darkness, The Long March, Set This House on Fire, The Confessions of Nat Turner,* which won the Pulitzer Prize in 1968, and *Sophie's Choice,* which won the American Book Award in 1980.

MIWA SVINKA-ZIELINSKI translates Polish and Russian texts on parapsychology. She has also written a scientific history of hypnosis in the nineteenth century in Russia and her native Poland. She lives in Canada, New York City, and Amagansett, Long Island.

SAMUEL TAYLOR is the author of the plays *The Happy Time, Sabrina Fair, The Pleasure of His Company* (with Cornelia Otis Skinner), *First Love, No Strings* (with Richard Rodgers), *Beekman Place, Avanti!, A Touch of Spring, Legend, Perfect Pitch,* and *Gracious Living.* He lives with his wife, Suzanne, in East Blue Hill, Maine.

SUZANNE TAYLOR teaches cooking in Blue Hill, Maine, where she also founded a gourmet shop. She is the author of *Young and Hungry,* a cookbook-memoir of life in the country house in Norway where she spent her childhood.

RENÉ JEAN TEILLARD is an antiques dealer in New York City.

YVONNE THOMAS is a French-born painter who lives in New York City.

PAMELA TURNER, the former service tenant at 81 Cadogan Square, London, has moved with her husband to Brighton—"a lovely place to live," she notes.

JOHNNY VAN KIRK lives in Massachusetts where he plays folk music and is a contracting consultant—"at the moment I'm clerk of the works on a six-million-dollar elderly housing development."

TONY VAN ROON, a former nurse at Broadmoor Special Hospital, now works at the Walsgrave Hospital in Coventry, England.

THILO VON WADZDORF has been the director of the department of contemporary art at Sotheby's in London and the director of the department of nineteenth-century European paintings at Sotheby's in New York. He is now a private art dealer in New York.

ELEANOR WARD died in January 1984. She founded the Stable Gallery, which in the 1950s and '60s gave the first one-man shows to Andy Warhol, Cy Twombly, and Robert Indiana. She also helped promote the careers of the sculptors Marisol, Louise Bourgeois, and Joseph Cornell, and the painters Joan Mitchell and Robert Rauschenberg.

ANDY WARHOL is an artist and filmmaker. He produced the rock group Velvet Underground. His books include *The Philosophy of Andy Warhol (From A to B & Back Again)*, *Popism: The Warhol '60s*, and *Andy Warhol's Exposures*. In 1969 he founded *Interview* magazine, which he continues to publish. He lives in New York City and in Montauk, Long Island.

ELSPETH WILKIE is an official at the United States Consulate in London.

HELEN MIRANDA WILSON is a painter. She is the daughter of Elena and Edmund Wilson. She lives in New York City.

CLEMENT BIDDLE WOOD is the author of a novel, *Welcome to the Club*. He and his wife, Jessie, lived for many years in Paris. They now divide their time between Water Mill, Long Island, and the Greek island of Spetsai.

The following names are pseudonyms: Joanne Anastase, Jake Cooper, Eddie Cruz, Will Davis, Helen Delaney, Vince Firenzi, Dr. W. Lindsay Jacobs, Susan Lannan, Juan Martinez, Jackie Monroe, Geoffrey Parsons, Jose Perez, Henry H. Perkins, Mike Perkins, Jim Robertsen, Erika Svenssen, William Thayer, Nancy Perkins Wallace, and Dr. Helene Weiss.

# ACKNOWLEDGMENTS

We would like to thank the many people quoted in these pages for the time they gave us.

We would also like to thank the following for their contributions to the writing of this book: Charles Addams, Al Anderson, John Jay Angevin, Jr., Hetta Asencio, Tony Banwell, Marvin Barrett, Mary Ellin Barrett, Dr. Milton Bastos, Alexander Beard, Patricia Beard, Eleanor Bender, Detective Chief Inspector Roger Bendle (Scotland Yard), Jay Benedict, Rehlein Benedict, Glynne Betts, Zerina Bhika, Dorothea Biddle, June Bingham, David Blasband, Denise Bouché, Heather Bradley, Laurel Buckley, Maureen Bune, Hazel Burke, Captain Jerry Caputo (New York City House of Detention, Rikers Island), Joel Carmichael, Isobel Cartagena, Blair Clark, Lady Mary Clayton, Michael Cleary, Mike Cobb, David Cohen, Elaine Cohen, Patrick Cook, Jane Cooke, Matthew Cowles, Shelly Dattner, Robert Darling, Elizabeth de Cuevas, Ormonde de Kay, Frances Ann Dougherty, Maggie Draper, Barbara Dunkel, Brooke Edgecomb, Jonathan Fast, Irene Fine, Sarah Fischer, Joseph Fox, Captain Harry Foy (New York City Department of Correction), Leda Fremont-Smith, Fred Friendly, Lou Ganim, Jacqueline Gatz, Ann Geiffert, Abigail Gerdts, Nancy Giagnocova, Virginia Taylor Gimbel, Judy

Greif, Letty Grierson, Lew Grimes, Hon. Desmond Guinness, Sabrina Guinness, Beth Gutcheon, Pat Hackett, Lucile Hamlin, Jones Harris, Robert Harrison, Ann Harvey, Shirley Hazzard, Lillian Hellman, Cathy Henderson, Paul Hoeffel, Sally Iselin, Jill Isles, Ted Johnson, Katrina Hall Jordan, Carl Kaufmann, Anita Herrick Kearns, Judy Kicinski, Tony Kiser, Carol Kitman, Marvin Kitman, Carol Klemm, Hans Koning, Kate Koning, Marcella Korff, Carol Kotwick, Helen Laws, Inge Lehmann-Haupt, Sandy Lehmann-Haupt, Karen Lerner, Ellen Levine, Dr. Richard U. Levine, Olga Lewis, Gael Love, Catherine MacDonald, Gerald MacDonald, Sukie Marlowe, Frances Matthews, Lester Migdal, Hon. E. Leo Milonas, George Mittendorf, Jinty Money-Coutts, Barbara Mortimer, Victor Navasky, Lynn Nesbit, Sue Nestor, Hugh Nissenson, Marilyn Nissenson, Charles Pate, Peter Pennoyer, Robert M. Pennoyer, Victoria L. Pennoyer, Paula Peterson, Emily Read, Piers Paul Read, Hon. Martin Rettinger, K. G. Rimmington, James Rossbach, Sue Rossbach, Digger St. John, May Sarton, Ronnie Scharfman, Denise Scheinberg, Dr. I. Herbert Scheinberg, Barry Schwabsky, Ann M. Seeger, Marvin Siegel, Babs Simpson, Mark Slifer, Betty Ann Solinger, Margaret Sone, Paul Spike, Dr. Robert J. Stoller, Diana Stuart, Douglas Stumpf, David Taylor, Shoe Taylor, Trevor Tester, Gwen Thomas, Lionel Tiger, Virginia Tiger, Captain Earl Tulon (New York City Department of Correction), Richard Turley, Marian Underhill, Ernst von Wedel, Alison Wakehan, Shelley Wanger, Julius Wasserstein, Jeannette Watson, Jacqueline Weld, Matthew Weld, Merida Welles, Lloyd Wells, Tom White, Hilma Wolitzer, Jessie Bruce Wood, Dr. Joseph Youngerman, and Frances Rogers Zilkha.

We would like to thank the following for their cooperation: The Leo H. Baekeland Collection, Archives Center, National Museum of American History, Smithsonian Institution, Washington, D.C.; Bakelite Museum Society, London; *Boston Globe* library; Boston Public Library; the Estate of John Philip Cohane; The James Jones Collection, Harry Ransom Humanities Research Center, the University of Texas at Austin; London Embassy Hotel, London; London Weather Centre; National Association for Mental Health, London; New York City Department of Correction; New York Public Library; New York State Department of Correction; the *New York Times* London Bureau; the *New York Times* morgue; Sarah Lawrence College Library; Scotland Yard; and Union Carbide Research Library.